3 9094 00861 6136

D1207381

Century
VAGABOND
BOOKS
of TRAVEL

JUNGLE PATHS
AND INCA RUINS

"Far away and
long ago" Hudson

Devils' Island

BY THE SAME AUTHOR

TO LHASA IN DISGUISE

MODERN JAPAN

INTRODUCTION TO MAHAYAMA
BUDDHISM

MANUAL OF BUDDHIST PHI-
LOSOPHY

An Indian "cradle"

JUNGLE PATHS
AND INCA RUINS

BY

WILLIAM MONTGOMERY McGOVERN
D.Phil. (Oxon.), F.R.G.S.

ASSISTANT CURATOR OF SOUTH AMERICAN ETHNOLOGY, FIELD
MUSEUM OF NATURAL HISTORY, MEMBER OF THE BOARD OF
ORIENTAL STUDIES, UNIVERSITY OF LONDON

ILLUSTRATED WITH
PHOTOGRAPHS

THE CENTURY CO.
New York & London

Copyright, 1927, by
The Century Co.

360

PRINTED IN U. S. A.

918
m17j

DEDICATED TO

STANLEY FIELD, Esq.

*As a slight token of appreciation for the interest he has taken
in the results of my expedition*

6573

CONTENTS

CONTENTS

LIST OF ILLUSTRATIONS

Jungle Paths and Inca Ruins

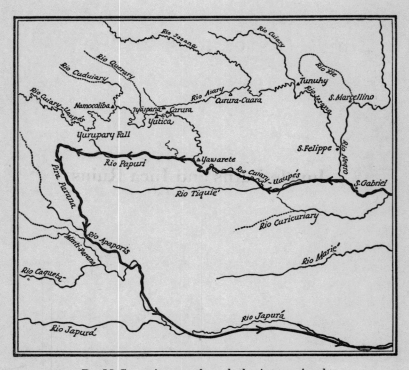

Dr. McGovern's route through the Amazon jungle

Jungle Paths and Inca Ruins

CHAPTER I

THE BEGINNING OF THE EXPEDITION

THERE is always a touch of romance about the Unknown, and in my journey through South America I was to see and study the Unknown both of the Present and of the Past.

The Amazon basin represents the Unknown of the Present. Now that Africa has been opened up, and both of the poles have been discovered, there remain few places in the world as untouched and unexplored as the vast stretches of territory watered by the Amazon, the largest of all rivers. The main stream and its principal tributaries have indeed been charted, but there are still hundreds of important by-streams—by-streams which, in Europe, would be considered huge rivers— the position and source of which are unknown. Above all, only very small portions of the immense expanses of jungle, lying between the various rivers of the Amazon system, have ever been visited by an explorer.

There are still hundreds of thousands of square miles of virgin forests through which no white man has ever penetrated, forests in which dwell many curious and unknown species of animal life.

In the border-lands there is still more or less perpetual warfare between pioneers of European blood and Indian tribes attempting to preserve their independence and their undisputed hold over the jungle. Further in the heart of the forest there are many other tribes to whom not even pioneers or rubber men have come as yet, and who know of the white man only through wild rumors which spread through the jungle.

The table-lands of the Andes which rise to the west of the Amazon basin represent the Unknown of the Past. On the desolate plains of these table-lands lie many unexplored ruins of ancient days. There are the remnants of mighty buildings reminiscent of the magic culture of the Incas. Of some of these we know the history and the meaning, but there are many more concerning which even tradition is silent. Other ruins, even more strange, bear record of magnificent civilizations which had disappeared and been forgotten even in the days of long, long ago, when the Inca emperors ruled over their great empire.

There are many things still to be discovered concerning the nature and the origin of the Inca culture. Of the pre-Inca civilizations we know almost nothing at all. It is only within the last few years that their existence has been suspected; and until further excavation has been done, we shall have no further knowledge of when these civilizations sprang into being, how long they flourished, and why they disappeared. A whole new chapter of human history awaits the explorer and the archæologist in this region.

It was to explore a large section of the northwest Amazon basin, and to study some of the ancient ruins of Peru, that I undertook my adventure. But like many other of life's happenings, this journey was largely the result of chance. After having spent several years in various wanderings and expeditions in other parts of the world, I was attempting to settle down and lead a humdrum and more or less respectable existence in London, when an old college friend, Viscount Hastings, looked me up and announced that he was planning an Amazon-Andes expedition. He asked me to be the co-leader of the new undertaking. To this I eventually agreed. We were busy making final preparations for departure when urgent family matters suddenly forced Lord Hastings to remain in England; consequently I was left with the sole burden of the expedition on my shoulders.

There is always much hectic rushing about just before an expedition starts, no matter how long it has been in preparation; in this case there was perfect pandemonium. At the last moment, the "Ufa" decided to lend me one of their best camera men, in order that I might obtain a permanent record of the new territory through which I was to pass; and as this man had never before been outside Europe it was necessary to initiate him into the mysteries of exploring and to purchase for him his kit. Like most other people who set out for the wilds for the first time, he had bought far too much—in his case fifteen boxes full of all imaginable paraphernalia, from patent foot-warmers to collapsible bedsteads—and it was first of all necessary to persuade him to abandon these and to limit his outfit to what would go into a small trunk.

It had been agreed that Lord Hastings was to look after the collection of zoölogical specimens, while I continued with my anthropological work, but with Hastings's withdrawal I had now to learn to prepare skins myself; consequently the day before our departure I spent in the South Kensington Museum listening to all sorts of weighty scientific instructions from the experts there, not one third of which could I understand. I was then set to skin half a dozen rats by way of practice. By the time I had finished with them, they looked like representatives of a new and hitherto unsuspected species; but I felt that at least a start had been made, and that I could perfect my taxidermic art by catching and skinning the rats on the ship going out.

In the meantime my telephone had been kept busy by a hundred people sending all sorts of confused but important messages. From one of these messages I learned that the Brazilian government had just prohibited the importation or carrying of fire-arms, because of a recent revolution, so that with my rifle and shotgun for use in the jungles I was likely to be arrested as a gun-runner. But it was too late to mend matters, and as his Excellency Senhor Oliveira, the Brazilian ambassador in London, had been kind enough to provide me with letters of introduction, I hoped that I should be able to smooth things out.

Eventually, on May 12, 1925, accompanied only by Mannling, my camera man, I set out from Liverpool on board the Booth liner *Hildebrand,* which was to take me a certain distance up the main stream of the Amazon. It is remarkable that a modern and luxuriously appointed steamer should connect the traveler directly with one of the most romantic and least explored portions of the world, so that pleasure-seeking tourists are now able to journey at ease more than a thousand miles up the river to the very borders of the Great Unknown. Even a band was on board to function for our entertainment; though as luck would have it, its members were new to the sea, and the qualms of the ocean made themselves occasionally felt in the music.

The countries of the New World have some very interesting immigration laws. In order to visit the United States one is probed to great depths regarding one's political and moral beliefs. In order to enter Brazil—and Brazil is the gateway of the Amazon— one must have two letters asserting that one is a highly proper and respectable person; also one must be possessed of a vaccination certificate. With considerable difficulty I had secured letters vouching for my propriety and respectability, but in order to obtain the vaccination certificate I had had to be vaccinated, and the doctor who had conducted this operation was so determined to see that the job was done properly that he gave me a double dose. This began to "take" doubly as soon as I got on board the steamer. I was therefore forced to keep to my cabin for several days with an arm so swollen that I began to dream about amputation.

Hardly had I begun to improve when we arrived in Portugal. It was only fitting that on the voyage to the Amazon we should make the acquaintance of this little country. It vividly recalled to our minds the days of Portugal's grandeur when she shared with Spain the mastery of the seas, the days when little barks set out from Lisbon to traverse the unknown waters, and succeeded in circumnavigating the globe for the first time. Those were the days when the whole of the unknown world was divided equally between the two Iberian kingdoms. And it was Portugal that founded the colony of Brazil which was to embrace the greater part of the huge region drained by the Amazon River.

We stayed for a few days in Oporto and in Lisbon. I was particularly impressed by Lisbon, which certainly has one of the most beautiful harbors in the world. As the effects of the vaccination were still heavily upon me,

I decided to see all the more out-of-the-way places through the eyes of my camera man, and to tick off in the guide as "seen" everything that he told me was interesting, including Cintra, the Versailles of Portugal, and the marvelous mausoleum of the dead kings. But to me the most interesting things, and these I saw personally, were the Manoeline style of architecture—and the faces of the people.

Under the reign of King Manoel (in the seventeenth century) Portugal developed a strikingly original, and though over-elaborate, yet a very beautiful style of building. Something of a combination of Baroque and Gothic. Considering the distinction of this style and its popularity in Portugal, it is rather remarkable that the ordinary treatises on architecture so completely ignore it.

But, in the long run, people are more interesting than buildings, and it was the interesting nature of the Portuguese faces that particularly caught my eye as I roamed aimlessly through the streets. Since the downfall of the older version of the Aryan race theory, according to which all the European peoples were grouped into a single race, the anthropologists have attempted to establish three main racial types in Europe, the Nordic, the Alpine, and the Mediterranean. The last, with its dark hair and eyes and long face and head, is supposed to be most purely represented in the Spanish Peninsula. Considering this fact, it is remarkable that one sees so many blonds or half-blonds, with at least blue eyes and fair skins, in the streets of Portuguese cities. Negroid features are also extremely common; but a large number of the townsmen looked more like American octoroons than a mixture of negro and Mediterranean races.

It was only after leaving Portugal that the pas-

sengers began to know one another; and there were
types for every taste. There were first of all the "excur-
sionists" who were bent on securing a six weeks' dose
of the Romance of the Amazon. Most of these, for some
curious reason, were from the North Country of England and not a few from Scotland—as one could see
from the bad business the beggars did. Even the sea-
gulls must have noticed the predominance of Scotsmen,
and they gave up following the ship two days before
schedule time.

Others were going out to the Amazon region to
spend their lives there, in some little settlement perched
at a jumping-off place for the Unknown. There
was the distinguished figure of Suarez, the mysterious
uncrowned king of a vast area of the Bolivian Amazon,[1]
who owned, virtually as slaves, thousands of Indians,
who worked for him the rubber-trees of his immense
estate. He was one of the small group of men who own
property in the Amazon, largely unmapped, but as
large as a European kingdom.

There were two or three old hands at the game,
English merchants who had lived abroad for years.
How alike in type they are, whether China, India, or
the Amazon be the field of their activity! For some reason they do not seem to flourish in the dominions. They
must have a "native"—and dark—background for their
temperament to wax forth into full bloom. A curious
type, but good-humored, and one which has accomplished great things.

Americans, curiously enough, were absent. It is surprising that these globe-trotters *par excellence* have not

[1] In accordance with local custom, the word "Amazon" is used to indicate the whole region watered by the main Amazon River and its many
tributaries.

discovered the Amazon as a field for touristing. Certainly no place could afford more charm. But there were representatives of all the "fancy nationalities"—French, German, Italian, as well as all variations of Spanish and Portuguese stock, both from the mother and daughter countries. The poor purser had a good deal of difficulty in arranging cabin-mates. An Alsatian named Klein, who got on board at Lisbon, was on the strength of his German name given a cabin with a young Prussian, but it turned out that Monsieur Klein was violently pro-French, and a pitched battle ensued; the combatants had to be separated by force and then given cabins on different sides of the ship.

A very dapper Italian traveled first-class while his wife was stowed away with the third-class passengers. By special favor the spouse was allowed to visit her husband. He, of course, never dreamed of demeaning himself by going into the steerage.

The first port of call after Lisbon was at the enchanted islands of Madeira, a cluster of verdure-covered mountain-peaks which pierce the surface of the ocean, springing up as if miraculously from the bowels of the deep. To me Madeira seemed like a modern Garden of Eden, so luxuriant was it, with the most beautiful flowers I had ever seen. The steep, narrow, winding streets of the harbor town of Funchal were paved with tiny smooth cobblestones, over which carts with sleds instead of wheels were pulled by oxen.

There are many who believe that these islands are the last remnants of the supposed continent of Atlantis which spread over a vast area now occupied by the sea. To the student of human history it is more interesting to learn that the islands, and most of the other islands in the Atlantic, were uninhabited until they were discovered by the Portuguese. There are very few places indeed, suitable for human habitation, which have not been inhabited by some race of man from time immemorial. Even far outlying islands like Hawaii had been discovered and settled by human beings long before the arrival of the white man. The Atlantic islands alone seem to have lain outside of the ancient economy.

After leaving Madeira we were well within the tropics, and a few days later we scraped over the equator. By a queer little quip of fortune, a cool breeze sprang up that same evening, and the ladies had to send downstairs for their wraps. Although in the equatorial regions of the Atlantic there is nothing like the chilly arctic or rather antarctic current which sweeps up the west coast of South America, yet it was surprising how little we were troubled by oppressive heat. Never did the thermometer register more than ninety degrees. On a voyage out to India it is taken for granted that one sleeps on deck after passing the Suez Canal even though one is washed downstairs by the deck scrubbers at dawn; but here on the Atlantic, although directly under the equator, we continued to sleep serenely in our cabins, and not infrequently with blankets over us.

Good old Aristotle laid down the dogma that the torrid zone was not only uninhabitable but also impassable because of its excessive heat. Along with other Aristotelian dicta, this one was adopted by the wise men of the succeeding ages. It is rather extraordinary, however, that more than a century after the discovery of America, and long after Pizarro had led his men south of the equator, one of the grounds for the trial of poor Sir Walter Raleigh on the charge of skepticism and atheism was his denial of the Aristotelian doctrine of the impassability of the torrid zone.

When we were still more than a hundred miles out at sea, and long before we came in sight of land, the water began to assume a vague brownish tinge—a sign of the tribute which the Amazon, the mightiest of rivers, pays to the ocean into which it flows.

The next day we caught our first glimpse of the continent of South America. It was the pilot station of Salinas, and as the pilot who was to take us up to Pará, "the Gateway of the Amazon," came on board, we made our first acquaintance with the United States of Brazil.

Brazil differs very noticeably from all the other South American countries. This is no doubt due to the difference in its cultural background, for while with the other countries it was Spain, with Brazil it was Portugal which played the part of the mother-land, and the cultural cleavage has left a very strong impress upon the erstwhile colonies.

From one point of view Brazil has perhaps not quite so much historical romance surrounding it as the countries to the west of it—such as Colombia, the New Granada of earlier days, which was the Spanish Main to the old-time English swashbucklers and buccaneers, who intercepted many a galleon loaded with gold, sent from the harbor of Cartagena, and destined for the court of Spain. Nor perhaps can Brazil bathe in that glamour which belongs to Peru, hallowed by the traditions of the ancient Inca Empire, adorned with untold riches, and ruled over by the Children of the Sun—an empire overthrown by the most romantic figure in history, Pizarro, the swineherd, aided by a mere handful of soldiers.

No, Brazil has not this romance, but it has a romance of its own. In many ways it is the most royal of all the countries of South America, and an air of courtly circles still pervades it. While Spain was performing her mighty deeds to the north and west, Portugal directed her activities to that part of the newly discovered continent which lay nearest her. Various expeditions which set sail from Lisbon between 1500 and 1530 brought Brazil under the suzerainty of the Portuguese crown.

The new land was parceled out among a number of the grandees of the court, who became little kings in their own way, and who sent out needy and adventurous courtiers to settle their new domains. The aristocratic tradition was thus established, although in time the governor-general of the whole country appointed by the king succeeded in centralizing all authority in his own hands. It was not long before the colony of Brazil became the chief jewel in the crown of Portugal.

Brazil was destined to have an even closer acquaintance with kings and emperors. During the Napoleonic conquests, when Portugal was invaded by the French, the whole of the Portuguese royal family fled to America; and even after the invaders had been expelled from the mother-country, the court remained in the New World, Rio de Janeiro became the capital of Portugal as well as of Brazil, and Brazil itself was declared to be no longer a colony but an integral part of the United Kingdom of Brazil, Portugal, and the Algarves. Thus for the first and only time in history a European country was ruled from the shores of the New World.

The luster was indeed short-lived. In 1820 King João was forced to return to Lisbon; but two years later the king's son, who had been left in charge of the Portuguese possessions in the New World, declared Brazil to be an independent empire with himself as its ruler; and for nearly seventy years Brazil was graced with an imperial court with its cohorts of dukes and marquises. It was not until 1889 that a short and bloodless revolution extinguished the light of imperial romance in the New World, and Brazil joined the ranks of plain plebeian republics.

The pseudo-grandeur of an imperial court has departed from Brazil, but the real grandeur of immensity remains to her. Brazil is more than a country; it is half a continent, for it contains within its bosom very nearly half of the whole of South America. In size it is exceeded only by the British Empire, the United States of America, and the old Russian and Chinese empires. Amazonas, the largest of the twenty federal States into which Brazil is divided, is larger than France, Germany, Spain, Italy, and Belgium combined; even Sergipe, the smallest of the States, is larger than Denmark.

With a variety of climate ranging from the tropical to the temperate, Brazil possesses almost every type of country. It contains dense jungle, wide open plains, and high mountain plateaus, with land suitable for farming, for timber, and for grazing, to say nothing of vast hidden stores of mineral wealth. There can be no doubt that Brazil is destined to be one of the great countries of the future.

CHAPTER II

THE GATEWAY TO THE AMAZON

GUIDED by our pilot we slowly steamed up the river until we arrived at the city with the imposing name of Santa Maria de Belem de Grão Pará—known to the tourist and the foreigner merely as Pará, though in reality this is the name of the State and not of the city.

Pará is the gateway to the Amazon, the port of the greatest river system in the world, although, with a certain humorous inconsistency, the city, strictly speaking, does not lie on the Amazon River at all, but on the Rio Pará, which forms no true part of the Amazon system. The mouth of the real Amazon River lies nearly a hundred miles further to the north; but the great river, upon which ocean-going steamers can voyage for more than two thousand miles, has so shallow a mouth that only small fishing-boats can sail through it.[1] The Rio Pará, which is deep enough for all purposes, though an independent river, is yet connected with the Amazon by a number of deep narrow channels. By passing

[1] So I was told by several competent navigators. In the huge mouth, which is some two hundred miles wide, there are probably certain channels which are deep enough to allow the passage of larger vessels, but these channels change so frequently, and are so little known or charted, that they are still useless for practical purposes.

through these channels, the ocean liners, which are turned back by the shoals at the mouth of the Amazon, can get into the deep water beyond.

Pará lies at the side, or servants', entrance to the great river; but as it is the only effective gateway, the city is already of great importance, and this importance is bound to grow as the Amazon region is more and more opened up.

Shortly after our arrival, the brother of the governor of the State of Pará came down to the ship to welcome me, and to invite me in his brother's name to visit the Government Palace. Unfortunately I found that here customs were followed which originated in lands far away from the equator, so that, following instructions, I donned a morning-coat, a silk hat, and a high collar, and sallied forth to the fray, though I must confess that I carried the collar in my hand and only put it on when just outside the palace.

To make matters worse, his Excellency insisted upon carrying on a long conversation in French—always a collar-wilting experience with me at the best of times. His Excellency was very affable, however, and gave me all manner of good advice as to how I might best conduct my new expedition.

Brazil, when it became a republic, based its constitution very largely upon that of the United States of the North. Among other things it adopted the federal idea, whereby each of the twenty constituent States is self-governing as regards all domestic matters, and is subject to the central government at Rio only as regards matters of national importance. Each State has its own congress, and elects its own governor; but unlike most of the State governors of the United States, many of the Brazilian governors belong to the diplo-

matic class, think in terms of Paris, and talk a French
of fair quality.

All over South America I was to find this inherit-
ance of the French tradition. Poor flashy Louis XIV,
who was too much bound up by local intrigues to be
willing to back up his exploring captains in their attempts to capture a large part of the colonial world,
has still, for this colonial world—and particularly for
South America—an extraordinary romance.

His Excellency the Governor himself showed me
over the palace, a very interesting building in the old
part of the town dating from colonial times. It was particularly remarkable for its inlaid floors and furniture
made of Amazonian wood. I have no doubt that in years
to come some of the precious wood from the surrounding forests will be exported to all parts of the world, for
certainly nothing can equal its finish when "dressed."

Subsequently I was handed over to the governor's
brother once more, in order to see the sights of the city.
These included the old cathedral, built more than three
hundred years ago, and which, with its severe simplicity,
is, in my opinion, one of the finest in the world; also the
ruins of the old fort where the Portuguese first landed
and took possession of the surrounding country at the
beginning of the colonial régime. But even more interesting to me were the Zoölogical Gardens, where
were gathered together specimens of many of the mysterious dwellers of the Amazonian jungles—egrets,
macaws, parrakeets, coatis, tapirs, and fierce prowling
jaguars.

Here, too, in the principal park one could get an
insight into the real nature of the hinterland jungles,
for the park is a remnant of the old jungle, which was
left untouched when the space all around it was cleared

to make room for the growing city. To me the charm of Pará lay in the fact that it gave a foretaste of what we were to experience in our own battles with the unexplored jungles of the far-away interior.

Kind as my august guide was, it was rather a relief when I was able to relapse into my unofficial capacity, in which, after doffing the garb of ceremony, I loafed in one of the cafés until I managed to scrape the acquaintance of a rather shabby little English clerk, who proceeded to initiate me into the unofficial side of Pará. With him I wandered through the narrow crowded streets to the market-place by the side of the quay, where were gathered queer little craft from up the river, with sails of every color.

All around were wild, babbling, gesticulating specimens of humanity, haggling over strange fish which are to be found only in the Amazon, or over queer outlandish fruits grown in some Indian village only a few miles away in the interior. On other stalls were displayed the skins of huge anaconda snakes, and the hides and teeth of Amazonian crocodiles. It was a scene more picturesque than ever an Eastern port could have presented.

I was especially struck by the exotic beauty of the women, both of high and low degree. They combined the haughty languor of the Portuguese, the soft lines of the negro, with a touch of the sweet melancholy of the Indian. The race was far more mixed than even in the erstwhile Spanish possessions. To have unraveled its genealogies would have puzzled the College of Heralds; but the dominant note, even in the very highest classes, was the negro.

To the Brazilian there is no such thing as race; there is only nationality. To the Brazilian an Englishman is an Englishman, and he makes no distinction between a

highfalutin Nordic and a Barbado negro. Within the
boundaries of Brazil a man is a despised savage so long
as he wears no trousers and goes around with a blowpipe; but as soon as shirt, trousers, and the Portuguese
language have been adopted, he becomes not a civilized
aborigine, but a Brazilian. After all, color is only skin-
deep, and who cares about Mendelian laws?

Strangely enough in this clime even the Anglo-
Saxon becomes affected by the local attitude. Even my
young guide was having a native romance. For months
after coming to Brazil he had paid but casual attention
to the Portuguese language. On one of his trading trips
far up the river, however, he had seen a dusky maiden
who had won his heart. In order to pay the lady
proper courtship, he had applied himself to linguistic
studies, and he was now a fluent linguist—and engaged!

A tropical romance truly, worthy of the pen of a
Loti; but when I, not being a Loti, asked for irrelevant
details concerning the lady's race, the only answer was
that she was a—Brazilian, and I was unable to discover
whether white, black, or brown predominated in her
genealogy. But in other ways, when suitably stimulated
by the local beer, my new-found friend turned out to be
a mine of information.

It was from him I learned of the great struggle
which Pará had had to keep its head above water. In
1910, at the time of the great rubber boom, Pará was
for its size one of the richest places in the world. Champagne, opera companies, and prima donnas, not entirely
averse to attentions and to Paris gowns, were plentiful.
Then almost overnight rubber became a drug on the
market. From about $2.50 a pound it fell to eighteen
cents; opera companies came no more, and champagne-
glasses remained unfilled. Palatial houses, half built,

were never finished. The State, largely as a luxury, was building a huge penitentiary, but with the return to poverty, crime and taxes decreased, and the uncompleted penitentiary is now a rival ruin to the old Portuguese fort.

In a way this depression seems to have had a useful effect. In the old days rubber monopolized public attention, and no attempt was made to develop the other resources of the Amazon basin, but in the last few years of tribulation attempts have been made to instil into the natives of the surrounding districts the principles of industry and agriculture. Sometimes, to be sure, these attempts have led to rather woeful results. Parcels of land were doled out to natives for agrarian exploitation. One such native came to see the governor a year later to announce that nothing would grow on his allotment, neither rice, coffee, potatoes, nor even beans. The governor, surprised at this, asked the man under what conditions he had sown the seeds. "Sown the seeds?" said the native. "I didn't think that was necessary." In a land such as the Amazon, where things grow so luxuriantly, such a statement on the part of the Indian is quite credible, for here one shoves a walking-stick into the ground and it blossoms forth into a tree.

Seemingly as a reward for industry under such adverse circumstances, just as I came to Pará, Fate deigned to smile once more upon the Amazon region by sending up the price of rubber, and I found that local merchants were once more dreaming of days when champagne would flow like water.

Much of the trade of Pará lies in the hands of aliens, chiefly English and Germans. Americans I found but slightly represented, in contrast to the huge American concerns in most Spanish-American republics. Unlike these countries, in another respect, Pará and the whole Amazon region has very few "tropical tramps," Anglo-Saxon youngsters full of the wanderlust who drift from one job to another. All the clerks were "contract men" who had been specially engaged at home. The young man who drifts out to Pará looking for a job has a fine chance of knowing what famine rations are.

One of the most interesting of the local Englishmen was the chaplain whose parish is the whole of the Amazon district, Porto Velho, one of his stations, being more than two thousand miles away. Among the Anglo-Saxons the Amazonian climate does not make for religiosity, so that though the padre is a favorite guest at all dinners, his congregation consists largely of coal-black ladies and gentlemen from the Barbados, who are very strictly Church of England.

The padre, however, has made himself distinguished as a collector of butterflies and moths and has secured quasi-immortality by having his name given to a member of a new species which he has discovered. A few miles outside the town he has erected an electric lantern, whose light shines far into the jungle, and many a rare moth with its eternal passion for a flame has been lured from its haunts in the forests only to fall into the padre's hands.

In common with all true bug-hunters, the padre finds his collecting zeal all-absorbing. I even heard it whispered that once when he was reading the burial service over an open grave, he saw a particularly rare species of butterfly, which he managed very dexterously to get hold of while continuing verbally to consign dust to dust, and ashes to ashes.

Two days later we left the Gateway City behind us and continued up the Pará River in order to make our

way through to the Amazon. For many hours the great
island of Marajo lay to the north of us. This island,
almost a little continent in itself, blocks the Pará from
the real Amazon River. It is quite typical of conditions
in the Amazon basin that whereas the coast of Marajo
Island has long been opened up to exploitation, with
thousands of cattle grazing up its meadows, there are
still large portions of the interior completely unexplored. Not long ago some pottery was dug up on
Marajo which indicated that a high civilization must
have existed there in the long-forgotten past. The style
of the pottery is so peculiar that cultural anthropologists have been unable to link it up with any of the other
ancient American cultures.

The whole Amazon region is a mixture of the known
and the unknown. The main stream has been charted
and recharted; explorers and pioneers have forced their
way up most of the tributaries; prosperous communities
are found along the banks of the river, hundreds and
even thousands of miles from its mouth; and yet in
most cases almost within a stone's throw from these
settlements lies jungle which is completely unexplored.

That same night we came to the entrance of the
Narrows. There we anchored until daybreak, for in
spite of pilots and charts, no ship dare pass through
these tiny channels in the dark. The next morning we
proceeded to grope our way through. The Narrows, it
will be remembered, consist of a number of natural but
canal-like channels which link up the Pará River with
the Amazon. Most of these channels are so shallow that
they can only be used by flat-bottomed river boats, but
one or two are suitable even for great ocean-going liners,
such as the one on which we were traveling. But deep
or shallow, all these passages are exceedingly narrow,

and several times the trees of the surrounding forests almost brushed our ship on either side. It seemed as if the jungle had closed in and was trying to throttle us, and that we were winding, twisting, pushing forward, seeking an escape.

By nightfall we had wormed our way out of the Narrows and at long last were floating on the main stream of the Amazon River. Our first glimpse of it when the glory of the setting sun had been caught by masses of clouds, and reflected in the dark yellow water which surged past us, was so beautiful that it seemed like the realization of dreams.

It is strange that this, the largest river of the world, should have been called the River of the Amazons, the women warriors of ancient fable. The reason for the name is still uncertain, though it is probably due to some of the romantic tales told by its discoverer. Although Portuguese navigators entered the estuary of the Amazon in 1500, they thought they were in some inland sea and gave it the name of Mar Dulce, the sea of fresh water; and the real discovery took place forty years or so later.

Gonzalo Pizarro, the brother of the great adventurer who subdued the empire of the Incas, followed his more famous brother to Peru, and was eager to vie with him in deeds of exploration and conquest. Hearing the wild tales of El Dorado, the Golden Kingdom, which was supposed to lie on the other side of the Andes, he assembled a body of adventurers and set out on a journey of exploration, starting out from a point in Ecuador. But once the mountains had been crossed and the lowlands reached, Pizarro found, instead of golden kingdoms, only dense jungles, swamps, and slinking hostile tribes. Strange fevers and hunger overtook his little party, and it was soon reduced to a state of desperation.

On the banks of a river, the Rio Napo, a crude boat was constructed and intrusted to a few men headed by Orellana with orders to sail down the river and secure food for the whole party. Weeks passed, and as the boat did not return Pizarro and his remaining men were forced to fight their way back to the Andes. But Orellana was not lost. The swift current of the Napo prevented his return to the main party, and he was carried down-stream to the point where the Napo joins the waters of the upper Amazon, and then down the main stream until the Atlantic Ocean was eventually reached.

Alone with his little band, without maps or any knowledge of the country, never knowing what the next day would bring forth during the whole course of the two-thousand-mile journey, Orellana had an adventure well worthy of record. Many a strange tale he had to tell when he arrived at the court of Spain. Some of his tales were true, others the creation of pure fancy; others again were based upon error or misunderstanding.

Among the stories which belong to the last category were those which told of frequent attacks by women warriors with long fair hair and pale bronzed skins. The Spanish explorer probably mistook for women the male warriors of the Yagua tribe, who to this day dress in capes and skirts of grass and wear their hair long. The apocryphal story of the women warriors persisted for nearly two centuries (it is not entirely dead yet), and it is for this reason that the great river received its curious name.

But to come back to my own less heroic journey of exploration. For the next several days we continued our voyage up the main stream. On either side of us was the dense low-lying forest, the river-banks being an unbroken wall of trees. It was very seldom, however, that we could see both of the real banks of the river at the same time, because of a constant succession of islands which break the stream up into a number of channels, many of which are scarcely broader than those of the so-called Narrows.

We had come at the end of the rainy season, but the river was still extraordinarily high. The Amazon lies so close to the equator that there is scarcely any perceptible difference between summer and winter, so that the seasons are reckoned by the rise and fall of the water. But in no other river is there such a difference between high and low water. The difference varies from place to place, but throughout most of the lower Amazon basin the river is nearly always between fifty and sixty feet higher during the wet season than it is during the dry.

As we passed close by the banks, with the jungle right under our noses, we could see what a great difference the high water makes. Throughout a great portion of the Amazon basin the land is very flat and low, so that when the river rises it overflows its banks for many hundreds of miles on either side. So immense is the volume of water carried by the Amazon that the extent of country which is inundated every year is greater than the areas of Spain, Portugal, and France combined. No wonder that the natives call the Amazon the Ocean River!

As we peered at the banks, the jungle which covered them seemed more than ever impenetrable, by reason of the water which covered the roots and crept far up the trunks of the trees. And how thick and entangled this jungle was! Every foot of ground was occupied by trees, and the little space left between the tree-trunks was covered with bushes, creepers, and clinging vines. One had only to gaze at the density of the jungle to realize why it was that the inner fastnesses of the Amazon region had remained so long unexplored.

The mystery of the jungle seemed inviolable. The forests teemed with life, but though from time to time strange sounds came out of it, only very seldom could we see anything of the wild creatures that lived there. A monkey or two was seen swinging in the boughs of the trees, but quickly disappeared. It was only at sunset that we saw birds, macaws and parrots chiefly, hovering over the trees seeking their perch for the night. From time to time we could hear a jaguar shrieking in the distance, but never could we catch sight of this, the most formidable dweller of the forests.

Very occasionally we passed by tiny settlements, three or four huts, perched for the most part right on the water's edge, as if the jungle had baffled inland settlement. Several of these huts were built on long wooden poles to protect them from the rise of the waters, which, even so, lapped against the floors, and had made of each hut a tiny island. The huts were inhabited by quaint folk, constituting a veritable cocktail of races. The Indian element predominated, but an Indian element duly baptized and clothed. Nowhere along the main stream does one see anything of primeval Indian life. This has been driven back into the vast stretches of jungle which lie between the rivers, or to the banks of the unexplored tributaries.

Two days after entering the Amazon we could see on our right a series of hills, a contrast to the otherwise continuous low-lying swamps that lay around us. These hills, known as Serra Jutahy, are probably connected geologically with the mountain ranges of the Guianas, far away to the north; consequently they formed once part of the old Guiana continent.

It is generally supposed that the Amazon which is to-day called the Ocean River was in times long past really an ocean, or in any case an extensive, even though shallow, sea, separating three continents. Of these one was formed by the countries of the Andes to the west, another by the highlands of southern and central Brazil, and the third by the highlands of the Guianas.

When the Amazon was really a sea it was cut off from the Pacific by the mountains of the Andean continent, but was connected with the Atlantic by three channels represented to-day by the basins of the Orinoco, the Rio de la Plata, and the Amazon proper. These three rivers were therefore originally part of the same great sea, and even at the present time there is intercommunication between the three river systems, the Amazon being connected with the Orinoco by means of the Rio Negro and the Cassiquiare, and with the La Plata by means of the Paraná.[1] It is therefore possible for a small boat to sail up the Orinoco and emerge eventually at the mouth of the La Plata.

The great inland sea has gradually silted up, giving rise to the low-lying Amazonian jungles. At the same time changes have taken place in the three ancient continents, which have now been welded into one. The land to the west, the region of the Andes, has gradually risen; while in the two former continents to the east, an exactly opposite process has taken place. The Brazil and

[1] For the connection between the Orinoco and the Amazon, see Dr. Hamilton Rice's papers in the "Journal of the Royal Geographical Society"; for the intercommunication of the Amazon and La Plata, see introduction to Joyce's "South American Archæology."

Guiana highlands seem to be remnants of mountain country older and formerly far more imposing than the Andes, which has now been reduced to insignificance by the wear and tear of ages. This state of affairs corresponds very closely to that which is found in North America, where the mountains that lie to the east are older and lower than the great Rocky Mountains in the west, though they are supposed to have once been higher.

After leaving these hills behind us we caught a brief glimpse of two settlements, larger and more important than most of those we had seen. The first of these, Santarem, lay near the junction of the Amazon with the Tapajos, one of the most important southern tributaries. It is only natural that the larger settlements should have grown up at the meeting points of rivers. Santarem was not particularly imposing, but there was a touch of romance about it, the romance of a lost cause. When, after the Civil War in the United States, the old Southern chivalry was ruined, and the courtly traditions of its slave-owning aristocracy was destroyed, several of the defeated Southern gentlemen, unwilling to bow their heads to Yankee rule, came and settled in this far-away corner of the Amazon.

Their task was not an easy one. Years of toil were needed, and obstacles innumerable presented themselves. Some of the settlers returned to North America broken in body and in spirit, but others held on and achieved success. The old generation is rapidly passing away; many of its members have already died—far from the land which they loved and for which they fought. But there are sons and grandsons to carry on their ideas and their ideals, and in many a hut there are still to be seen the Stars and Bars of a dream that was never realized. Not infrequently underneath an aged and time-worn flag are written the words of a modern and alien poet:

> Lord God of Hosts, be with us yet,
> Lest we forget, lest we forget.

Obidos, the second settlement, was of interest for quite different reasons. It is here that the Amazon narrows down to a single channel, unobstructed by islands. Because of the strategic position, the Brazilian government has erected here a fortress to guard the Amazon from naval attack. This fortress, five hundred miles from the mouth of the river, is the sole defense of the Amazon region from foreign invasion. Another notable fact is that the effects of the ocean tides are felt up to this point, a remarkable proof of the lowness and levelness of the lower Amazon basin.

Shortly after leaving Obidos, in the dead of night, we had a little excitement, caused by the fact that a native fishing-boat tried too late to cross our bows and was immediately swamped. But the crew were all picked up, and without more ado we steamed steadily on. Although we had now come hundreds of miles up-stream, the river showed no signs of growing narrower. It was as vast and as majestic as ever. There were still on either side of us huge stretches of inundated and unbroken jungle.

Moonlight nights and the magic of the Amazon did not fail to have their effect upon our fellow-passengers. It was less than three weeks since we had left England, but we were now able to rejoice over two couples who had met for the first time on board ship, and who now announced themselves engaged (and high time too! snorted Mrs. Grundy). One was a youngish couple, of which the man was going up to distant Iquitos to make his fortune. The other was more truly romantic, for the man was a retired colonel of sixty, and his blushing bride to be was a siren of at least forty-five summers.

But all of us, even those who were not fortunate enough to become engaged, mellowed under the glamour of our surroundings. One thinks of the Amazon in terms of heat, fevers, and mosquitoes. Later on I was destined to have more than my fair share of these, but as long as we remained on the great ocean liner we traveled in luxury and at ease. We had all of the charm and none of the unpleasantness of a voyage in tropical waters.

At last we came to a parting of the ways—the point where the Negro River divides from the Amazon. The Negro is the most important of the tributaries which enter the Amazon from the north. In fact, so important is this tributary that the Brazilians only give the name "Amazon" to the main river after its junction with this stream, terming the higher waters of the Amazon the Solimões.

The junction of the two rivers presents a beautiful spectacle. The Amazon is a muddy brown, while the waters of the Negro, as its name implies, although exceedingly pure and clear, are of so dark a hue as to appear almost black. The beautiful waters of the Negro are swallowed up by the main river, but the point of junction is as clearly marked as a plumb-line. For some extraordinary reason fish are exceedingly plentiful at this point, and they come so close to the surface of the water that huge shoals of them could be seen from the deck of the ship.

Equally noticeable were the Amazonian dolphins, which seemed to find pleasure in racing just along the cleavage line of the waters. The presence of the dolphins was another reminder of the sea-like nature of the Amazon, for with the exception of one species, which inhabits the Ganges, these curious animals are only to be found in the great oceans. There are three distinct types of dolphins found in the Amazon. None of them is ever speared by the fishermen, as catching them is supposed to bring bad luck; one species is regarded by the fishermen as the demon of the waters.

CHAPTER III

MANÁOS, THE PEARL OF THE JUNGLE

DEPARTING from the main stream, we proceeded up the black waters of the Negro for an hour and at last came in sight of our immediate goal, the city of Manáos, where Mannling, my camera man, and I were to disembark and make final preparations for our journey into the interior.

Brazilians love to call Manáos the jewel lost in the wilderness. It is the capital of the enormous State of Amazonas, which contains within its ample bosom the greater part of the whole Amazon area. To the simple dwellers in the interior, Manáos is the capital of the world. Its very name takes us back to the legends of old. Manáos was named after the tribe of Indians called, Manao or Manoa, who formerly inhabited its site, but Manoa was also the name of the capital of the fabled country of El Dorado, which was supposed to exist in the Amazon, and for which so many explorers of old sacrificed their lives. The stories tell us that this old Manoa was a great city full of palaces, built of stones riveted with silver, and tiled with plates of gold.

Under the tranquil light shed by modern geographical research the legend of El Dorado has died away. But in view of the great potentialities of Amazonas, it may be that in the future the modern Manáos may

rival the dream city of the past. In its present aspect
Manáos does not remind one of dreams or of legends.
It is startlingly modern and progressive. One has only
to walk a half a mile beyond the city to be caught in the
primeval jungle, unmapped and unexplored; no one in
the city knows what lies in the forest twenty miles away.
But Manáos wishes to forget the mystery of her surroundings and the charm of her tropical setting. She
prefers to be a little Paris.

The city is full of flamboyant modern buildings.
Motor-cars rush through its crowded streets. The "city
lost in the jungle" is provided with telephones and electric light. Instead of brooding over the mystery of the
forest primeval, its inhabitants spend their evenings
witnessing the latest exploits of Doug and Mary. There
are far fewer negroes, far fewer types dressed in outlandish fashion, than in Pará. The citizens are for the
most part either "Brazilian" (i.e., Portuguese) or an
admixture of Brazilian with the aborigines. But even the
"mixtures" have borrowed the clothes, the habits, the
ideas, and the language of Portugal. The women are
dressed in the latest Paris gowns, and are painted and
powdered in approved Paris fashion. The average man
is far more fashionably dressed than in England, and
if the Oxford trousers have made little inroad, at least
more than one of the young men of Manáos has learned
the use of rouge and lip-stick.

It was difficult for me to believe that I was in the
capital of a State two thirds of which are unexplored, a
State containing thousands of wild naked savages. Some
of these savages sweep down in the jungle to within
forty miles of Manáos, but were one to appear in the
streets of the city, he would attract almost as much
attention as in London.

I had even to remind myself that I was in the tropics, for though the temperature was decidedly warm (an average of about eighty-six degrees Fahrenheit), it refused to be equatorial. All the good school-books tell us that a damp heat is more unbearable than a dry heat; but although Manáos lies within three degrees of the equator, and its air reeks with the moisture soaked up from the rivers and swamps, the heat I experienced was nothing compared with the heat of India or Africa. The very moisture of the air seems to act as a screen against the sun's rays, and though sun-helmets are unknown, there is no recorded case of sunstroke.

Many of the men I saw wore, indeed, straw hats, but there were an equal number content with ordinary felt hats, and dark clothes seemed to be as common as ducks or drills.

No, at first sight there was nothing of romance about Manáos, except the romance which attends the building of a modern city in the heart of the unexplored jungle, but I was soon to find many examples of the quaint and unexpected. Hovering over the town were thousands of urubus or Amazonian vultures, which no one was allowed to shoot, as they were the universal scavengers and street-cleaners, forming the only substitute for a municipal sanitary department. The gardens of the private houses were crowded with other strange birds which have their habitat only in the Amazon basin: egrets with their marvelously delicate feathers, duckbills, curious snipe with claws in the bend of their wings, and raucous-voiced parrots which swore strange oaths at all passers-by.

Above all there was the bullying, blustering *jaribu,* or Amazonian heron, which not only lorded it over all the other birds, but tried to bulldoze any stray human

who invaded his precinct. I saw one *jaribu* left in charge
of an infant, and a very useful nurse he was, for not only
did he keep all larger intruders away, but he soon gobbled up any mosquito or other insect which came too
near the sleeping child.

Even among the people of Manáos I was to find a
romantic attitude toward life which was not a little
startling. On disembarking we went to the one hotel
in the city (needless to say it was called the Grand
Hotel), but the extreme dirtiness of the room into which
I was shown made me ask very mildly that things be
cleaned up a bit. The proprietor immediately flared out
and, declaring that he had been insulted, refused to
allow me or Mannling to stay in the hotel at all. At
first it seemed that we should have to sleep in the streets
that night, as the only other possible habitation, a pension, was already overcrowded. But at last I persuaded
the proprietress of the pension to allow us to share an
outroom with two of her servants until better quarters
could be provided.

Donna Amalia, the proprietress, is worthy of a book
all to herself. Hailing originally from somewhere in
the Balkan hinterland, she has seen much of life in many
aspects and in many lands. She has forgotten her
mother-tongue, whatever that may have been, but has
picked up a smattering of twenty others to take its place.
She has acquired and shed husbands, as she has acquired
and shed languages, casually and carelessly. Her present spouse, a retired Brazilian sea-captain, has been
meaning to marry her officially for years, but Donna
Amalia has forgotten whether her divorce from her previous husband was ever completed; so she prefers to
remain as she is. She and the captain have entered upon

the evening of life, and it is probable that they will go on as they are until the end.

Though Donna Amalia's position was, certainly at the time I was in Manáos, a trifle ambiguous, she was everywhere respected and admired. She had a tongue that could sting like a hornet, but a heart of gold, and being childless had adopted two or three starving waifs and strays. It was whispered that in ancient days she had conducted establishments of a looser kind, but her present pension was a bulwark of respectability. While we were there one of the maids thought of running away with an already much married man, but after Donna Amalia had given her underling an hour's sound advice, to say nothing of a black eye, the girl decided to continue her life of dull respectability.

The guests were almost as interesting as the lady of the house. Among them were some of the highest State officials, including the chief of police, a mighty man in this part of the world, and the federal interventor, or military governor, of Amazonas, who preferred to use his palace merely as an office and to trust himself to Donna Amalia's care and cooking.

Being possessed of several letters of introduction, I presented myself to his Excellency, and we were soon on very friendly terms. He was kind enough to render my little party many services in the days which followed. The presence of the interventor, a sort of military dictator, in place of the usual State governor, was an aftermath of a revolution through which Manáos had passed during the preceding year. Even in the wilds of the jungle the South American likes to keep up his revolutions and other frolics.

For a number of years the State of Amazonas had been dominated by a rather corrupt and inefficient, but

powerful, political machine. When quite independently
a revolution broke out in the extreme south of Brazil,
which occupied all the attentions of the central government, the good citizens of Manáos thought it would
be a fine time to have a political holiday. They stormed
the barracks, put the garrison to flight, and imprisoned
the governor; then their new leaders proceeded to dole
out the offices of state among themselves.

The revolution was a gentlemanly affair. There
was more flag-waving and speech-making than bloodshed, and every one seemed content. But things took a
different turn when the federal government, in spite of
its distractions elsewhere, managed to send two gun-
boats up the river. The federal boats recaptured the
"impregnable" fortress of Obidos, which the revolutionaries in their turn had seized, and eventually trained
their guns on the city of Manáos itself.

Most of the citizens, having had their fair share of
fun, promptly derevolutionized themselves, and hid
away their rifles for use on some more auspicious occasion. The leaders, thus deserted, were soon captured and
imprisoned. But the federal government wisely decided
not to reinstate the old governor, but to appoint, instead,
a federal interventor to rule over the State until things
should have "normalized" themselves. The old governor fled to Europe, and as he had not paid any salaries
for some time before his deposition, he took with him
a tidy sum which he spent later in Paris.

The interventor was a man of very different type
from the governor who had preceded him. Although
stern and strict, he was scrupulously honest, and I found
that the administration of the whole State of Amazonas
was rapidly being reorganized on a much sounder basis

than, according to all reports, had hitherto been the case.

Manáos served as our headquarters for about a month, as it took some time to get my outfit together, and I wished to acclimatize myself as far as possible before starting out for the Unknown. During this time I had occasion to see a good deal of various aspects of Brazilian life. I was interested to see how strong was the line of demarcation between the "Brazilians" (even those of pure Portuguese descent) and the Portuguese who within the last few years have come over to the New World. The difference between the two types is somewhat the same as between the English and the Americans, but—with extraordinary contrariness— the Brazilian is the counterpart of the Englishman, and the Portuguese of the American.

This distinction holds good even as regards language. The Brazilian speaks a more suave, more polished, and a longer-winded form of Portuguese than does his cousin from Portugal, who is blunter, snappier, and more to the point. The Brazilian is more lackadaisical, more given to little details of politeness. He regards himself as more cultured. The Portuguese is more direct and businesslike. He is a harder worker, though (and here the parallel between England and America no longer holds good) he is generally dirtier than the Brazilian, who for the most part is scrupulously clean.

As Manáos is the chief city and capital of the State of Amazonas, most of the exports and imports of the whole Amazon basin pass through its portals. But I was surprised to see how little personal contact the edu- cated man in Manáos has with the interior. The Manáos merchant buys the goods which are brought down the river by the half-breed pioneers, and exports them to Europe, but he seldom or never dares to go into the interior himself. To him the upper reaches of the river are full of all the terror of the Unknown, strange diseases, wild savages, and the horrors of the jungle. Hence my attempts to secure an educated young Brazilian who would go with me through the unexplored territory proved fruitless.

But at least I was able to see something of the wealth which passes through the city on its way from the jungle to the outer world. As yet very few of the valuable products of the forests have been exploited. Many of them are still scarcely known to the outside world. Among the few things which are already exported in large quantities are rubber, balata, Brazil-nuts, ivory-nuts, and piassava.

Rubber, as is well known, is indigenous to the Amazon basin and was for long confined to this region. Only within the last few decades have the seeds been taken from their home and planted in the Far East. In quality the Amazonian rubber still ranks higher than any other. The usefulness of balata has only been discovered within the last few years. Like rubber, balata is tapped from trees, but it has a different consistency, and resembles a cross between rubber, leather, and flexible wood.

The Brazil-nut is also an indigenous product of the Amazon. Enormous quantities of it are gathered during the wet season (from December to June—rubber can be collected only during the dry season) and shipped abroad; for the Brazilian seems to think that Brazil-nuts are fit only for pigs—and for foreigners. The ivory-nut is one of the anomalies of nature. It is similar in size and shape to the chestnut, and during its green stage can be, and frequently is, eaten; but when it reaches maturity it is almost as hard as ivory, and can only be cut by special machines. From these nuts are manufactured some of the best buttons in use.

Piassava, a type of brush, is also in great demand for export, as it is made into first-class ropes and brooms, but, as might be expected, the Manáos house-wife prefers to buy cheap brooms imported from America.

It was while I was in Manáos that I was introduced to guarana, the favorite drink of the Amazon region. The guarana berry is found only near the little settle-ment of Maués, lower down the river. The export of the seeds is strictly prohibited by law. The berries are ground down into powder, from which the guarana in-fusion is made. In most cases it is taken with soda-water, and resembles a pinkish ginger-ale, or the Amer-ican Coca-Cola. But guarana contains not only tannin, the essence of tea, and caffeine, the essence of coffee, but has a special guaranine essence of its own. The drink is not only extremely stimulating and refreshing, but very palatable as well, and I was surprised that no en-terprising capitalist had attempted to put it on the world market.

While our outfit was gradually being assembled, I managed from time to time to slip away from Manáos and make several short excursions by motor-boat to various places in the neighborhood. On one of these excursions I was afforded interesting proof of how little known the Amazon region really is. Quite by accident I came upon a tributary of considerable size a few miles down the main stream which is not marked on any of the existing maps. There are numerous huge back-waters and lakes on both sides of the main river, joined up with the main river by one or more narrow channels. We made our way up several of these lakes, and flowing into one of them (situated near the island of Eva) we came across a large stream, with water even darker than that of the Rio Negro, and which, judging from its breadth, must be hundreds of miles long.

We followed this river up-stream for several miles. At one place we came upon a number of curiously carved and painted stones, and near-by the vestiges of an old native settlement of very considerable dimensions showing traces of advanced culture, but of the people who had left these traces of their handiwork there was no sign. They had no doubt made their way many miles further up the river, or else had been overtaken by some sudden calamity and annihilated. Even tradition relates nothing about them.

It was on the banks of this river that I saw large outcroppings of coal, which proved of very good quality though leaving a good deal of ash. The discovery of coal was very curious, and proved that at some early period the great inland sea of former times must have been cut off at this point from the Atlantic Ocean by a huge jungle-bearing shoal, of which the decaying trees have in this way been preserved to us. No doubt the gradual upheaval of the land in other parts of the Amazon basin caused the dammed-up water to break through once more to the sea.

It was on another of these little expeditions that I got my first taste of Amazonian fishing. In another of the lakes lying to the north of the main river, but in this case several miles up-stream, near the little settlement of Manacapuru, I found a veritable anglers' paradise. Although a poor fisherman at the best of times, I managed in seventeen minutes by my watch to catch twenty-eight fish, with an ordinary hook and line.

In this same lake are found in great numbers three

of the most interesting species of the dwellers in the Amazonian waters, and I was able to see how the native fishermen set about catching them. One of the "fish" in question was the manatee, or sea-cow, really a river mammal, which averages about six feet in length, with huge flappers and a snout, reminding one very strongly of its bovine namesake. On account of its peculiar coloring, it is almost invisible in the water, and in addition it is possessed of very acute senses of sight, smell, and hearing, so that it is a very difficult animal to catch. I found that even the natives were only able to secure one by stampeding it into a large trap placed near the entrance of one of the side streams.

Equally interesting was the *pirarucú,* the largest of all the Amazonian fishes. Several of the specimens I saw caught weighed more than three hundred pounds. The catching of each such fish caused a good deal of excitement. Hook and line were out of the question. An expert fisherman stood in the prow of the canoe holding a spear, attached to a rope in his hand. When at last a *pirarucú* was seen in the clear waters below, he let fly with his spear, and the huge fish was fairly caught in the back. But the animal was by no means done for. He bolted away across the lake with such an impetus that the whole boat to which the other end of the rope was tied was carried along for half a mile at what seemed to be lightning speed. Then the great fish turned and twisted and made huge circles, carrying the boat along with him, until at the end of half an hour he was exhausted and could gradually be drawn in and his struggles ended by a terrific blow on the head from an iron bar.

I was especially impressed, however, by the savage little *piranha* fish, known as the cannibal of the waters, because with his sharp little teeth he tears everything to pieces. We threw the carcass of a sheep into the lake, and it disappeared entirely in two and a half minutes under the savage attack of the *piranhas*. Even the skeleton was not safe from their teeth. It was obvious that swimming in such waters is more than an idle pastime, and two of the fishermen who accompanied us showed me the results of *piranha* bites. One of the men had lost a toe and the other a finger. Unfortunately these little fish usually swarm together in large numbers, and unless their victim is able to get out of the water quickly he is torn to pieces in a few moments. These *piranha* fish even bit through the copper wire to which I had attached the hook, so that it took some time before I could catch a specimen. At last, however, I learned the trick of pulling in the line as soon as there was a bite, so that the fish did not have time to snap through it. I was in fact fortunate enough to secure specimens of an entirely new species of this curious little creature.

The *piranhas* were not the only dangers lurking in the waters. At various parts of the river, and more particularly in the lakes, we saw enormous numbers of crocodiles. In many cases these reptiles rose up to the surface of the water as we approached in order to peer at our boat. At Manacapuru I counted more than a hundred at one time, and there must have been at least three times that number. So long as we kept to the boat there was little to fear from these brutes, though the wild lashings of one of the crocodiles we wounded very nearly upset our little craft, and once in the water we should have had a very bad time of it.

It was by no means easy to capture one of these creatures, in spite of their size and their proximity, as our shot-guns had seemingly no effect on them, and even

the bullets from our rifles glanced off their thick hides.
One point in the neck and another near the eyes seemed
more vulnerable than the rest of the armor, and it was
only after we had learned to shoot at these that we managed to add two or three of the reptiles to our collection.

On one occasion I was the witness of a tragedy
caused by these creatures. On the way back from
Manacapuru, we stopped at a tiny settlement where one
of my boatmen had a hut. During our stay there one
of his children, a boy of about fourteen, who was
bathing in the river, suddenly gave a shriek and was
dragged under the water. Several men rushed to his
rescue, but he never appeared again. In all probability
he was carried away by one of the crocodiles.

Once back in Manáos I was soon able to complete
all the necessary preparations for the expedition.
Money would be utterly useless when we got really
into the wilderness; therefore I had to secure huge
quantities of goods for barter. Foodstuffs were also a
necessary consideration, for in many parts of the jungle
food is absolutely unobtainable. Finally came the problem of servants, for, although I hoped to secure porters
and canoemen from the Indian tribes through which we
passed, it was advisable to have a small group of men
who would do the whole journey with us and upon
whom I could rely in case we had any trouble with the
natives.

It proved far more difficult to get men to go along
than I had supposed, because of the dread of the jungle
which seems to fill the hearts of most of the citizens
of Manáos. I had to fall back on men of a rougher sort,
half-breeds and *caboclos* or civilized Indians who had
learned to take life as it came. It is men of this type
who act as pioneers in the opening up of the jungle

and who in general serve as intermediaries between Manáos and the wilds.

Eventually I picked two men and a boy. One of the men was a Venezuelan who had made his own country too hot for him, and who had fled to the Amazon region several years previously. He was to act as general foreman to the party and was to see that my orders were carried out. He had changed his name several times in the course of his wanderings, but was most commonly known by one not of his own choosing, namely, the Scorpion. The other man, a hideous, faithful, and simple-minded *caboclo* named Joaquim, was to act as cook, though I had been warned that his cooking was decidedly of a jungly nature. The boy, a quick-witted, cheeky youngster, was to act as a jack of all trades, though as a principal duty he was to carry and nurse my cameras and scientific instruments. He was the proud possessor of six names, given him in honor of various historical worthies, but I dubbed him Pequenino (little one), and Pequenino he remained.

The custom-house at Manáos gave me a great deal of trouble, and very considerably delayed our departure for the interior. The customs charges in Brazil are absurdly high. In most cases one pays in customs dues twice the total retail value of the article. For this reason it was to cost me well over a hundred pounds to clear the few things which I had brought with me from England. The interventor was kind enough to telegraph to the federal minister of finance at Rio de Janeiro asking that in my case the customs duty be waived, in view of the scientific character of the expedition.

For weeks I waited in vain for an answer. The next day a little river steamer was to start out up the

Rio Negro, the next stage of our journey. Another steamer would not leave until a month later. Rather than be delayed another month, on the very day of departure, at ten o'clock, I went down to the custom-house and paid the money demanded in order to secure my boxes. Scarcely an hour later the answer came back from the capital, stating that my things were to be allowed to enter free. I hastened down to the customs and tried to get the money refunded. But the sum had been entered up in the books, and I was told I would have to make a long official appeal in order to secure repayment. Being of Scotch descent I did not fail to do so, but although a year and a half has elapsed since then, the appeal is still going the rounds of the higher officials, and not a penny has been returned.

At least I was now able to start out on the next stage of the journey, which in a way was to be the real beginning of the expedition. In the Amazon basin unexplored jungle is not difficult to find. It lies around one on every side, but one particular field of research had long caught my fancy. The northwest Amazon basin, the district lying between the Rio Negro and the main Amazon stream, has long been known to contain a wealth of wild primeval life. As far back as 1914 Sir Everard im Thurn, the famous anthropologist, emphasized the importance of studying this region and declared that it was less known than any other equal area of the surface of the globe.[1] This is undoubtedly true in spite of the extraordinarily valuable work done by Dr. Hamilton Rice, by Koch-Grünberg, and by Captain Whiffen in isolated parts of the region.

I was determined to carry on in a very humble way the work initiated by these men. I was fully aware of

[1] "Geographical Journal," 1924, p. 146.

the enormous difficulties which lay before me. The people in Manáos were particularly pessimistic about our prospects. I was told again and again that the obstacles which lay in the way of a journey through the forests were insuperable, and that moreover we should certainly be killed by the savage tribes through which we should have to pass. But in spite of these Job's prophets I was determined to go on as far as possible, and trust to luck to bring us through safely.

I knew that the first part of the further journey, in any case, could be got over without much difficulty, as the little river steamer was to carry us as far as Santa Isabel, some four hundred and twenty miles further up the Rio Negro. Along each of the main tributaries of the Amazon there was a stretch of semi-civilized territory that kept in touch with Manáos by means of little steamers subsidized by the government. Beyond the last port of call, usually marked by a cataract or rapid, there is a further stretch of river-bank, which might be called the pioneer country, very sparsely settled by a small number of adventurous spirits who work the district for rubber. Beyond this region, and everywhere in the surrounding jungle, there is the Great Unknown. The river steamer was to take us up the Rio Negro to the pioneer country. After that we were to fend for ourselves.

CHAPTER IV

THE RIVER OF VANISHED GLORY

WE eventually departed on July 3. We were
due to start at 10 A.M.; but knowing local
custom, I did not turn up at the wharf until
noon. I then learned that our boat, the *Inca,* was not to
leave until sunset. In reality it was long after midnight
before we at last got under way; but *paciéncia* is something one soon learns in this part of the world.

Once free of the harbor, we started on our long
journey up-stream. Opposite Manáos, the Rio Negro
was about four miles broad, but when we awoke on the
following morning we had reached a point where the
river had widened out very considerably and measured
more than fifteen miles from bank to bank. It gave the
appearance of a veritable sea containing an archipelago
of islands. At this point and at many others the Negro
was far broader than the upper waters of the main
Amazon stream.

Violent wind-storms are by no means infrequent.
These give rise to huge and dangerous waves which are
much feared even by experienced navigators, and from
time to time even the larger river steamers are lost in
these Amazonian gales. The aftermath of a storm which
we just escaped caused us to rock and roll about far
more than we had ever done on the long journey across
the Atlantic.

class passengers, but as there were fifty such passengers and only four tiny cabins most of us spent the entire time on the open deck. The after part of the deck served as a community dining-room, smoking-room, and lounge. It was also the chief bedroom, as at night hammocks (which take the place of beds all over the Amazon region) were stretched crisscross in every direction. Shoes were pulled off, and the evening toilet was complete. The place looked like a menagerie.

The lower deck really was a menagerie. There was no cabin of any sort, and most of the space that was not taken up by the engines, fire-wood, and cargo was occupied by the cows, pigs, and turtles we were transporting to settlers up the river. Suspended between or above the various animals and the engines were the hammocks of the deck-passengers. On one occasion two of the cows got into a row and succeeded in bumping my boy Pequenino very neatly out of his resting-place.

We had only one pilot to guide our course, and he, poor man, had such long hours that I was scarcely surprised to see him on one occasion fast asleep while on duty. The sailor at the wheel, who knew the river well, did not trouble to waken him.

In spite of sleeping pilots and general wheeziness, we continued to make progress. On the third day we crawled into Moura. It was a drab enough little place —a collection of mud plastered huts with thatched roofs, but the settlement was famous because of the fact that not many years ago it had to stand a serious siege.

Almost opposite Moura, on the left bank of the Rio Negro, is the mouth of the little explored Rio Yauapery, which was and still is inhabited by tribes of mysterious, pugnacious, and reputedly cannibalistic Indians. Living as they did on a side stream, they were left unconquered by the advancing Brazilian colonists. Various attempts to exploit the river ended in disaster. But the natives were so alarmed at the coming of the whites that they swept down in their war-canoes upon Moura and tried to wipe out the whole settlement.

The little colony of whites was in fact forced to abandon the settlement and to take refuge on an island in the river, where they maintained a hot defense. News of the attack spread down to Manáos, and it is said that the citizens of that proud metropolis shook in their shoes lest they too be subject to an Indian raid. Eventually reinforcements were sent up the river. After hot fighting the settlers were relieved and the Indians driven back to their native jungles.

Since then these tribes have never again ventured upon so bold an attack, but they are still far from subdued. I was told that even in the last three years several rubber men who had ventured into their territory had been killed.

Two or three hours after leaving Moura we came to the mouth of the Rio Branco or White River, the largest of the Rio Negro's tributaries. Its light color was in marked contrast to the blackness of the mother stream. In its lower part it is bounded by vast regions of swamp containing many curious forms of bird and other animal life, but for the most part it has as yet been impossible to collect these on account of the terrible fevers which haunt the zone.

Higher up, the Branco is not only perfectly healthy, so I was told, but it is also one of the few places in the Amazon basin where European settlement on a large scale could take place. The thick jungle disappears—no one knows why—giving place to open plains, useful for cattle breeding. The natives of this region bring down to the outpost stations, from time to time, diamonds and gold-dust. I saw specimens of both, which our pilot had secured in some roundabout way, and certainly they seemed to prove that the region contains great hidden wealth. But this wealth must be well hidden, since the well organized and well equipped Rice expedition saw nothing of it.

We stayed only an hour or two in the waters of the Branco, but even this fleeting visit left its mark. The next day several of the passengers were down with fever; and as there was, of course, no medical man on board, I had to open up the well filled medicine-chest which Messrs. J. D. Riedel had given me and try myself to render aid.

This brought me into even closer touch with my fellow-passengers. They were a curious collection. There were several monks and nuns on their way to the missions far up the river. There were one or two pioneers of pure white descent who were on their way back to "the verge of beyond." Many of the other passengers were half-castes, with hard-seared features, free-lances, ruthless and dauntless in the search after rubber. Most curious of all were two or three Turkish traders, peddlers of all imaginable things to the settlers and natives of the outlying settlements. The lower deck contained, for the most part, natives of almost pure Indian extraction, men who had nearly forgotten their ancient freedom of the jungles, and who had become wage-slaves of the white man in return for a pair of cotton trousers or an iron knife.

The journey on the *Inca* gave me further opportunity to accustom myself to Brazilian food. The Brazil-

ian, like the Continental European, eats practically no
breakfast. He contents himself with coffee and a roll
smeared with the worst butter in the world. At eleven
o'clock comes *almoço* or breakfast, the principal meal
of the day. So much food is tucked away on this occasion
that it is generally necessary to sleep off some of the
effects. One awakes at two to have afternoon coffee.
At five o'clock comes *jantár,* another heavy meal, followed at eight by evening coffee. Shortly after this the
human constitution, refusing to be further stuffed, is
put to rest.

Rice and beans formed the staple article on our
menu. Equally common was *farinha,* literally flour,
which was in this case the meal made from the poisonous
mandioca root. The secret of removing the poison and
preparing the meal was learned from the Indians.
Farinha is a food with a romantic history, but to the
inexperienced palate it tastes like sawdust.

Fresh meat was scarce. Our living provender on the
lower deck was too valuable to be fed to the passengers,
and so we had to content ourselves with dried meat,
carne secca, which was of a consistency that rendered
it more suitable for hammering over leaks in the boats
than for human consumption. As occasional treats we
were fed with the flesh of the cow-fish, and of the
tartaruga or Amazonian turtle. The cow-fish tasted like
very greasy and rather coarse beef, but I found the
flesh of the turtle extremely appetizing. I was
astounded to find that it smacked of turkey.

Although the Amazon basin is an angler's paradise,
it was very seldom that we were given fresh fish. To the
Amazonian mind it was too much trouble to secure fresh
supplies each day, so that we were fed at every meal
on salted *pirarucú.* To catch one of these huge monsters

is one of the finest sports in existence, but as an article
of diet the *pirarucú* was far from enjoyable; it savored
too much of rancid soap. I was soon forced, however,
to become an expert in *pirarucú,* learning to detect it
in various guises. We had it broiled, boiled, baked, fried,
raw, and in various intermediary stages, no one of which
seemed better than the others.

At last we came to the little settlement of Barcellos,
the very picture of a jungle tragedy. In the old days
of Portuguese rule, Barcellos was the capital of the
whole province of Amazonas. History would have us
believe that it was a city of villas and palaces, churches
and courts of justice. Here came chiefs of powerful
tribes to deliver tribute. Haughty cavaliers and high-
born ladies thronged its streets.

It is hard to give evidence to the tale. The glory
of former days has completely vanished. The jungle,
jealous of intrusion, has had its vengeance. Strange
tropical maladies killed off the descendants of the early
settlers. The very buildings have been lost to view in
the new growth of the forests. The covered-up ruins
serve only as a lair for jaguars and for bats. Barcellos
is now but a miserable collection of huts.

We are told that in the old days there were many
plantations on the Rio Negro, where coffee, sugar,
cotton, and anil were grown. These have completely
disappeared. The scanty population of to-day prefers
to eke out a hand-to-mouth existence by tapping the
rubber-trees which nature has produced, rather than
by planting and cultivating. The Amazon basin could
increase its rubber crop a thousandfold if only rubber-
trees were planted and cared for. All of the rubber
plantations of the East were started with shoots brought
from the Amazon. The Amazon has a climate and a

soil better fitted for rubber than any other region, and yet in the natural growth of the jungle there may be a mile or two between the rubber-trees from which the settlers secure their living.

But to establish plantations requires too much time and too much trouble. Above all, it would mean too much labor, and labor is what the Amazon most lacks. The early explorers tell us that even the banks of the main rivers were thickly populated with Indians, and for this reason in the early days there was little scarcity of native laborers. But if the jungles proved fatal to the white man, the white man proved fatal to the native. Thousands upon thousands of Indians died soon after coming into contact with European civilization, and even to-day the coming of the white pioneers seems to spell death to the wild tribes of the inner jungle.

From the anthropological standpoint it is interesting to observe which native peoples can stand contact with the white man and which cannot. For the most part it seems to be a matter of previous culture rather than of race. It would seem to be the law that when the white man comes into permanent contact with a people of very simple culture, that people is doomed to extinction, but when a native people has already produced a highly organized civilization of its own, the people continue to exist even when the older civilization is destroyed.

Neither India, China, nor Japan, three centers of ancient culture, seems to be in any danger of "racial extermination"; but the Manchurians, Mongolians, and Tibetans, with a lower indigenous culture, show much less resistant powers. The South Sea islanders and the primitive inhabitants of Australia with still simpler

altar with images of various Holy Saints; but the alcove was screened off with a sheet so that the Holy Ones should not see the frivolity of their devotees. Later the curtain was pulled aside, and a curious little religious service was performed. There were no priests, and the service was but the wailing chant of a people calling softly upon the invisible powers of the heavens. Eerie and other-worldly was the rise and fall of the voices. Under their influence I forgot the modern clothes and the modern setting. The haunting refrain seemed to affect even the people themselves, for afterward quite other dances were danced to the pounding of a wooden drum of old Indian design and to the scraping of bamboo reeds. These were instruments of earlier times, and the dances were of long ago and portrayed the primitive enticement of woman by man, and of man by woman.

The lights burned lower and lower. Led on by the throbbing rhythm of the music, the men and women dropped the cultural mask which they had worn during the day. The brooding spirit of past generations was awakened, and many of the older women had tears streaming from their eyes.

When we had left Barcellos behind us we continued up-stream on the last stage of the steamer journey. The river alternately broadened and narrowed, and at times seemed lost in a world of islands. Although the surrounding country was flat, the river was flanked by high sandstone banks. We were no longer in a mere maze of swamps.

Once or twice great rain-storms blew up accompanied by marvelous sheets of lightning which illuminated the whole sky. The rainy season, which was over in Manáos, was dying more and more slowly further

to the west, and in its death-throes brought tempests
which hurled at us, not drops, but layers of rain. As
if to mark the approaching change of seasons, we experienced several days of marked chill, during which
it was necessary to don heavy coats.

This chill is an interesting phenomenon of the Amazonian climate. Each year at the beginning of the dry
season (usually in July) and at the beginning of the
wet season (usually in January) a few cold days set
in, caused, it is believed, by the wind changing its direction and sweeping straight down from the glaciers of
the Andes. At this time it is supposed that many of the
weaker animals of the jungle and even many of the
fishes die, and certainly we saw a number of dead fish
floating by in the water.

Although our hammocks were unprotected by nets,
we were troubled comparatively little by mosquitoes.
For some reason these insects are not so common on
the Negro as on other Amazonian tributaries. But their
absence was more than made up by other insect pests,
which annoyed even the well seasoned settlers, and
drove the new-comers of the region nearly to distraction.

The most obvious of the insect pests were the little
piums or midges. These swarmed about us in thousands.
Their sting gave more than a momentary discomfort,
for it left little blood-pockets, not mere mosquito-
bite lumps, which continued to irritate for many days.
But it was at this time I discovered that the
piums have powers of discrimination. When I was alone
I was driven frantic by their attacks, but if I could
induce Mannling, the camera man, a very plump and
well rounded-out person to sit by me, the midges would
concentrate nearly the whole of their attentions upon
him. I developed at this period a marked fondness for

long conversations with my companion, preferring him to my Brazilian attendants, who were rather a scrawny lot.

Unfortunately an equally common pest, the *mucuims,* were not so discriminating, and we all suffered equally from their ravages. The *mucuim,* not unlike the harvest tick, was a microscopic spider entirely invisible to the naked eye. Millions of them lay in the low grass, and every time we left the boat at a landing-station, even for a few moments, we were certain to bring back with us large numbers of these invisible enemies. The pests crawled up our legs and burrowed beneath the skin, particularly underneath our garters and belts, and at other places where there was especial pressure.

The irritation caused by the little ticks was a source of great annoyance. At the end of three or four days, they died, and were absorbed into the system. I found that the microscopic spiders had to be left strictly alone. Scratching only made things worse, and in the end relief came automatically. The most I could do was to secure a small amount of rum from the copious supply we had on board, and rub it on the affected areas. The alcohol seemed to allay the itching.

There was no lack of other undesirable guests. One day as I was writing up my diary I suddenly became aware of a huge centipede nestling on my knee. By a bit of luck he had crawled up my leg, outside and not inside my trousers. Consequently I managed to have him scraped off without damage to myself, although Pequenino, who did the scraping, was stung by the insect and gave out a yell which vied with the ship's siren.

Pequenino incidentally turned out to be a remarkably bright youth, well able to fend for himself. I had of course procured for him a third- and not a first-class passage on the *Inca*. But as he was dissatisfied with the lower-deck fare he managed to worm his way into the affections of the ship's cook, and in return for doing odd jobs in the scullery he was allowed to eat first-class food.

For some unknown reason all the maps give the insignificant settlement of Thomar as the limit of navigation on the Rio Negro. But we were to find that the real limit was Santa Isabel, more than a hundred miles further up-stream. At length we crawled under the banks of this little settlement and there disembarked. We had entered upon a new phase of our long journey.

CHAPTER V

IN THE PIONEER COUNTRY

IN reaching Santa Isabel we had come to the frontier of the pioneer country. The settlement itself consisted only of two or three huts. Most of its inhabitants were frankly "aborigines"—and no longer pseudo-Brazilians. By contact with white men they had indeed lost their status of "sons of the forest wild and free." They had abandoned most of their old tribal organization and many of their ancient customs. They had learned to drape themselves with clothes. But the veneer of civilization was very thin.

The use and value of money was almost unknown, and all business was carried on by barter. Every white man was still regarded as a feared and hated intruder. The natives had not yet mastered Portuguese or any other European language. Curiously enough, however, the idiom which they spoke, although of purely Amazonian origin, owed its existence in this region to the activity of Europeans in the days long gone by.

In the early colonial days the Jesuit missionaries, who were very eager to convert the natives of the newly discovered world to the Christian faith, found that a large number of tribes on the Brazilian coast spoke a variety of languages which could be reduced to one

63

common basis known as Tupi. This again differed but slightly from the Guarani dialects spoken further to the south.

In order to facilitate intercourse with the natives, the Jesuit fathers adopted a standardized and somewhat simplified form of the Tupi-Guarani language. This idiom, known as the Lingua Gerál (the general or common language), gradually spread over the whole country and was used as a medium of communication even with tribes whose dialect had no connection with the Tupi-Guarani group, as all the natives found it easier to learn this indigenous language than the complicated Portuguese.

The Jesuit missionaries are long since dead, and their work is mostly forgotten. Portuguese has prevailed in the more settled parts of Brazil; but in the border regions, between the colonized sections and the untamed tribes of the great jungles, not only does the Lingua Gerál still serve as a means of communication between the whites and the natives, but also between many of the various native tribes speaking divergent languages. In fact in many places, including a great part of the upper Rio Negro, the Lingua Gerál has entirely supplanted the earlier idioms and has become the mother-language for a vast number of half-civilized natives.

The day after arriving in Santa Isabel we made our first long excursion in the forests in order to accustom our hands to jungle shooting. Our day's bag consisted chiefly of a number of smaller birds, many of them song-birds. It gave me my first acquaintance with the most common bird of the upper Amazon region, a beautiful, yellow-breasted, black-coated creature, called by the natives the *piripipi,* from its warble. Even now when I sit and dream of the many months I spent in the jungle, I seem to hear the *piripi-i-pi* whistling far away in the distance.

This little excursion also gave me a good idea of the nature of the jungle which we were later to know so intimately. The word "jungle" usually brings to our minds a picture of palms and ferns. There are, to be sure, in the Amazon forests palms and ferns in abundance, but the vast majority of the trees appear, at first sight, similar to the deciduous trees of the forests of Europe, and one must look closely to realize that one is gazing at members of very alien families.

To a person as little versed in botanical lore as myself, the most striking difference from the sylvan scenes of Europe was the fact that the tree-trunks were all linked together by vines, lianas, and parasitic creepers through which we were able to crawl only with the greatest difficulty. By steady pushing and hacking we eventually got far enough away into the woods, but with our inexperience it was impossible to keep a sense of direction, and when our bags were full and we set out on the return journey we found that we were lost. It was only after we had roamed around for some hours that we came to a trail which led us back to the settlement.

The *Inca* had already departed on her return journey, and I was rather worried as to how we were to get ourselves and our somewhat bulky baggage on the next stage of the journey, through the pioneer country to the head-waters of the Rio Negro. At first I thought we should have to take to canoes immediately, but at last my letters from the all-powerful interventor helped us out of our difficulty. Colonel Rudolfo Gonçalves, one of the principal traders on the upper Rio Negro, and the proud possessor of a motor-boat, had arranged

to take the monks and nuns, who had come with us on
the river boat, on to the mission station of San Gabriel,
another two hundred and fifty miles up-stream. In spite
of the scarcity of space it was agreed that my little
party should also be tucked away in the launch.

The night before our departure, we were given a
farewell carousal by the white settlers at Santa Isabel.
There was always a little excitement when men set out
for the upper reaches of the river, and it was necessary
to absorb enormous quantities of beer to celebrate the
event. In this part of the world beer is considered a
very elegant drink, and it is little wonder, as each bottle
costs a small fortune. The native element did not take
much part in the festivities. They stood round in silent
groups staring vacantly at the amusements of their
masters. Apathy seems to be the characteristic note of
Indians under white domination.

At last the little launch started out. It chug-
chugged over the rapid which had barred the way to the
larger river steamer, and soon got into the smoother
water beyond. The launch itself, called the *Onça* or
Jaguar, a tiny thing of fifteen horse-power, was filled
to the brim with cargo for Senhor Rudolfo, who
smacked his lips at the bartering he was going to do
up the river. The passengers had to find quarters in two
barges which were tied to the launch, one on either side,
although these too were heavily loaded with boxes.

One barge was for the servants; the other, provided
with a wickerwork cover for the after part, was allotted
to the gentry. But as the gentry were nine in number,
and the boat only thirteen feet long, even the gentry
led a very higgledy-piggledy life. The population of
the boat was greater than of many hundreds of square
miles of Amazonian territory.

Because of the difficulties and dangers of navigation
on the turbulent waters of the upper river, the motors
were kept going only as long as we had daylight to
aid us. At night we moored ourselves to the nearest
bank. Occasionally we spent the night near a little clearing made by some adventurous settler. At other times
we had only the unbroken forest around us.

The first night out, near a long deserted hut, we
had an interesting experience with a magnificent *gavião*
or Amazonian hawk. Our first shot partially disabled
him, but instead of attempting to get away he flew
straight for our little party and with his beak and claws
managed to scratch *five* of us rather badly before we
could give him a *coup de grâce*.

Each day was marked by long battles with the raging waters. The placidity of the lower river was a thing
of the past. Our little craft was knocked about like a
match-box. In places the current was so strong that
for hours we would stay in one spot even with the
engines full on until the pilot succeeded in finding a
weak point in the surging stream, a counter-current
where we would at last slowly but surely push forward.

At one point, however, on the second day of the
journey, where the current was particularly strong and
where we were having great difficulty in making headway, the engines of the launch must have been over-
taxed, for they suddenly stopped, and we were knocked
and hammered back by the rush of the waters. Our
hearts were in our mouths for a moment, for we were
drifting helplessly among whirlpools and scarcely submerged rocks; but the boatmen rushed to get out some
oars, and eventually succeeding in guiding our craft to
the bank. Here we stayed for several hours while the engines were overhauled. At last the popping of the cyl-

inders told us that all was well again, and soon we were once more under way.

On the journey from Manáos to Santa Isabel the land had all been of sedimentary formation, a thick layer of clay over a sandstone foundation. The river had had little difficulty in wearing out an even bed for itself, and the whole country had been comparatively level. But we were now entering a far more rugged region, one marked by misshapen hills and rugged irregular mountains. In many cases naked rocks peered through the seared side of these forested hills, rocks formed at the first cooling of the earth's surface, rocks hard and resisting. We had left the region of the old inland sea and had come to the western flanks of the old Guiana continent.

So old was the country through which we were passing that the waters had eaten away any covering of softer rock which may once have been there, leaving the enduring primeval rock exposed to the surface. The hills and mountains did not form ranges running in parallel lines, but stood curiously alone. They were not the result of any buckling of the earth's surface, as are most mountains. From the flat surface of many of the hills around us, it seemed probable that at one time the whole country had been one great table-land, which had been gradually eaten away by the erosive waters, leaving the mountains as isolated fragments behind.

In spite of its great age, the granite plateau through which the river had forced its way was still so resisting that the waters had been unable to dredge out a level bed. The current was everywhere swift and powerful, and every few miles we came to rocky barriers marked by dangerous rapids and low waterfalls, termed by the

Brazilians *cachoéiras.* These formed the principal obstacles on our journey up-stream.

Occasionally we came across tiny settlements perched on the bank, each settlement consisting for the most part of a number of semi-civilized Indians ruled over by a white pioneer. In this far-away corner of the world every white man could act the part of a princeling, dealing out law and justice as he saw fit to the Indians whom he had gathered under his control, doling out cheap knives, cotton cloths, and rum in return for the rubber which they had gathered from the forests.

I calculated that in the whole of the vast region watered by the upper Negro there were only fifteen or sixteen pioneer families. The head of many of the families bore the proud title of colonel, a purely honorary rank, conferred by the government upon persons in official favor, and one in great esteem all over Brazil. The Brazilians have a great sense of the importance of titles—and of names. The Portuguese proper have but a scanty selection of Christian names. Every other man is either Carlo, Manoel, or João. But the Brazilian goes in for higher things, and among the dreary, shambling settlers lost in the forest I found a Felycinthe, a Mercurio, an Agamemnon. One man who spoke not a word of English flourished under the name of Shakspere. And it is the Christian name that counts, for it is always used in conversation even between chance acquaintances.

The settlers led a hand-to-mouth existence. Their dwellings were miserable huts of wattle plastered with mud, but they were deservedly content. For were they not officially officers of rank, and unofficially rulers of little kingdoms?

At each of the settlements we passed, we found the Indians more and more primitive. Nominally they

were all Christians, but for generations they had been
without priest or chapel, so that our good friends the
padres devoted much time to re-instilling in the natives
religious ideas. To their joy they secured a number of
infants to whom they could administer baptism. I
noticed they seemed far more shocked at finding that
five strapping youngsters had not been baptized than
at the fact that the parents of the youngsters were living
together without the formality of marriage.

Each day it rained, not once but many times. On
one occasion, in spite of the frequent heralding of the
coming of the dry season, we were treated to a real
Amazonian storm, wind, thunder, a world of lightning,
and sheet after sheet of rain. Our little craft, the launch
and its two attendant boats, were tossed to and fro by
the waves. The decks were swamped with water, and all
of us had to push into the tiny hold at the rear, which
was so crowded that we were almost suffocated, and had
to take turns at the door to catch a waft of air.

But after the storm was over, and the sun had again
put in an appearance, we were rewarded for our trials
by the sight of millions of butterflies which came in
swarms out of the forest. They seemed like clouds of
grasshoppers. Senhor Rudolfo, our host, informed us
that the butterflies swarmed thus one day a year, more
or less at the beginning of summer.

Each day our journey became more difficult because
of the increasing strength of the currents and rapids
through which we had to pass. A strong spice of danger
was added by great rock boulders, which frequently
lay only a foot or two below the surface of the water.
A crash against one of these rocks would inevitably
have sent us to the bottom. Many of the rocks would lie
fully exposed in the dry season, but the river was still

high enough to conceal them, and our pilot, a wary old Indian, had constantly to be on his guard to avoid them. In the smoother stretches of the river a superficial tremor of the water told him of submerged rocks, but with a sharp breeze blowing, or with bright sunlight ahead, his task was more difficult, and in the rougher portions of the river, near the cataracts, it was largely hit or miss.

In places where the current was especially strong the little launch found it impossible to drag along both of the dependent boats. So one boat had to be tied to the bank, while the other was rushed through to the comparatively smooth water beyond. The first boat was then left while the launch went back to bring up its companion.

On more than one occasion this expedient also proved fruitless. So great was the counter force of the water that the launch with even a single boat was slowly but steadily pushed back. The bank on either side was flooded, and it was impossible for the crew to get out and tow. Even so our sailors proved equal to the situation. Two men jumped overboard with a tow-line. With almost superhuman strength they swam for some distance up-stream, making their way from one flooded tree-trunk to another, which supported them against the oncoming rush of the waters.

They eventually tied the tow-rope to a forest giant some distance ahead. It was now our turn to toil. Crew and passengers pulled for dear life on the rope, while the engines continued to pound away their hearts. The addition of muscular to mechanical energy saved the day. By repeating the rope trick two or three times we at last got into water smooth enough to allow the engines to function once more unaided.

The towing process brought us against the flooded jungle at the side of the river. To help matters along we frequently seized hold of a protruding branch in order to give an extra pull. This was a rather dangerous pastime. On one occasion one of the crew just escaped placing his hand on a poisonous little coral-snake, the American cousin of the cobra, which was lying on the branch. On another such occasion a frightened spider ran across my hand, leaving a trail of poison, which caused not only an intense burning sensation but severe inflammation as well.

The other insect pests, particularly the *piums* or stinging gnats, were more maddening than ever, though I observed that unlike the mosquitoes the *piums* disappeared at sunset, so that we could sleep in peace, even without nets. Whether it was because of insects or of the general living conditions I do not know, but on the fifth day of the journey several of my companions fell ill once more, and I was forced to resume my duties as amateur nurse. For some reason I remained immune.

The journey was not without minor mishaps. All manner of things were dropped overboard. Mannling lost his best hat in this way, and I my favorite pipe— a much more important matter. The food question continued to be troublesome. Fresh fish was scarce, and we had continually to rely on dried *pirarucú*. There were no plantations of any size, and I found that the pioneers spent a good deal of the money they had gained in rubber-gathering upon the purchase of supplies from the lower river. This was a fact which gave me cause for foreboding, as I had brought with me very scanty food supplies, hoping to live as far as possible off the country, and we still had months ahead of us in the jungle.

The unbroken jungle indeed stretched around us on both sides of the river, but primeval jungle has very little to offer in the way of food. Very few indeed of its trees produce fruit fit for human consumption, so that the most we could hope was to shoot some of the animals that roam through the forest. Once or twice we were lucky enough to capture some *inambú* or forest fowls, and once an armadillo. I was surprised to find that this curious heavily armored eater of ants could be made up into a very palatable dish.

In the course of our journey we passed the mouth of an important northern tributary called the Canabury. Although rich in rubber and balata, it remains virtually unexploited, because of the ferocity of its native inhabitants. Unlike the half-civilized or rather quarter-civilized Indians on the banks of the main stream, the wild aborigines who dwell on the Canabury have steadily refused all contact with Europeans. They abandon their homes at the approach of any stranger and fly into the heart of the forest, until the pioneer, lured by the supposed absence of all danger, relaxes his guard, with the usual result that he is taken by surprise attack and murdered.

Many were the gruesome tales concerning this dread river which were poured into our ears by our host. He ticked off the names of various rubber prospectors who had gone up the river, never to return. The few who had escaped from native attacks had brought back stories that the Indians of the region were virtually white (strange, this ever recurring story of white Indians) with semi-European features, although their mode of life is most primitive.

A few days later we came to another important tributary, the Curicuriary or Parrot River, which flowed in from the south. Along the eastern bank of this river, for forty or fifty miles, ran a long narrow range of mountains, the most imposing mountains we had seen anywhere in the Amazon basin. Strange tales are told of the river—many of the natives are afraid to go near it. Stranger tales still are told of the mountains, for the Indians believe that near the highest peak is a magic lake where live the ghosts of the departed, and that on the banks of the lake are boats and many strange animals carved in stone.

A few miles further up the main stream we came to the great cataract of Camanáos, beside which those which we had previously passed sank into insignificance. It was impossible for our little launch, stanch though it was, to pull the two dependent boats any further. Consequently the boats were unloaded and the boxes carried overland for more than a mile to a point beyond the cataract. Most of the passengers preferred to accompany the baggage, but I determined to risk the journey in the launch, which had also been eased of most of its burdens. We took aboard as special pilot an old Indian who knew every rock in the river, and then with rather tremulous hearts started on our race through the surging torrent.

High dashing waves, violent whirlpools, and rocky snags made the passage of the long cataract very thrilling. It was necessary to thrust our way between the waves, whirlpools, and rocks. Again and again we seemed on the verge of destruction. The force of the oncoming waters threatened to hurl us upon a snag, and to avoid this the launch was wrenched into a vortex that sent her spinning round and round and promised every moment to engulf her.

We were all in a fever of excitement, ready to jump

into the foaming water in a desperate dash for safety—
a hopeless dash—should the launch founder. The
wizened Indian pilot alone remained calm. With death
at arm's length, ahead and on both sides of us, he seemed
to hold listlessly to the wheel, but each turn on the rud-
der was timed to the fraction of a second—and at last,
breathless, gasping, we pushed our way through to the
calmer waters ahead.

We ran into the bank to take on our fellow-passengers again. The baggage we had to leave behind to
be brought on by the launch on a second journey, for
the whole of the next few miles was far too dangerous
to permit of overloading.

The part of the river which followed was certainly
the most beautiful of all. For the next eighteen miles
the river was almost one continuous cataract. The
stream was frequently broken up by small islands of
the hardest granite, but covered by majestic trees.
Penned up by the islands into a number of narrow channels, the river seethed and boiled with doubled energy
and power.

It was necessary to tack from bank to bank in order
to avoid the most dangerous points. All of us were instructed to reduce our clothing to the minimum and
to dispense with shoes and stockings, so as to be ready
to swim in case of accident. But the skill of the pilot
was once more triumphant, and late in the evening we
came unscathed to our immediate goal, the little settlement of São Gabriel, the last outpost of the Brazilian
government. It was here that the monks and nuns who
had accompanied us disembarked. We too had to halt
at the settlement for several days, waiting for our baggage to be brought up, and making our last preparations for the journey into the unknown.

São Gabriel is the capital of the huge municipal department which includes the whole of the northwestern section of Brazilian Amazonas. But in reality governmental control extends only along the banks of the main river, and even there to only a limited extent, as the pioneer families in their own domain have things very much their own way. But little of this enormous department is mapped, and more than two thirds of it is still unexplored.

The power of the government we found to be represented by three individuals: a *superintendente,* a sort of civil governor; a *deputado da policia,* who had charge of the garrison; and a *juiz,* in whose hands lay the power of the law. High-sounding titles, all of them, but the three officials eked out a miserable existence, as they were seldom or never paid. When we arrived, the "municipal palace" had caved in, and its place had been taken by a miserable one-roomed mud hut.

The garrison consisted of four soldiers with about one complete uniform between them. Incidentally these soldiers could seldom be found when they were wanted, as they were forced to secure their livelihood by fishing. The *juiz* spent his mornings administering justice and his afternoons extracting teeth.

Altogether São Gabriel was a forlorn little outpost of empire, as forlorn as the ruins of the fort, which had been built long ago on the hill overlooking the settlement, and of which only a few broken stones and half-buried cannon remained. But the "government" was very friendly and accorded me an official reception, attended by the whole community in the one-roomed mud "palace."

Somewhere in the municipal cellars, the *superintendente* found a bottle of most excellent old port, which he brought up to do honor to the occasion. But unfortunately there was not enough for every one, so the bottle was carefully secreted behind a large desk which cut off one corner of the room. In the course of the proceedings, the head of the mission, Mannling, my camera man, and I were invited to inspect the old municipal charter on the desk. We failed to see the charter; but once safely out of sight we were given a glass of the precious wine, with whispered orders that we were to drink it silently, so that no one should know that it was there.

In spite of the cordial welcome they gave us, the officials regaled us with very gloomy stories regarding our future prospects, emphasizing the natural difficulties, the huge cataracts, the dense jungles, and the treacherous swamps which would confront us. All sorts of tales concerning the ferocity of the wild Indians were added, but the most disquieting remarks I heard were those in connection with the terrible jungle fevers. I learned for the first time that only three or four months before our arrival two Swedish scientists had passed through São Gabriel on a journey up the river, but that inside of a few weeks one had died of some mysterious illness, and the other had been forced to turn back.

I listened carefully to all this pessimism but refused to be deterred from my project. I found that it would be possible to use a motor-boat for another few days up the river, to the place where we should meet the "wild" Indians; so that as soon as the little launch had returned from Camanáos with the luggage I went down to see its owner with a view to using it for the further journey. We soon came to terms, but it was found that on the last journey the launch had been so badly buf-

feted by the waves that it would require a thorough over-
hauling before we could embark once more.

This meant a halt in São Gabriel for several days
longer, but I found more than enough to occupy my
time. I managed to have several long talks with some
of the older Indians of the settlement, and I soon discovered that underneath a superficial layer of Christianity and civilization there persisted a strong race consciousness and many traditions of the past.

In addition to the ordinary dwellers of the settlement, there were many other natives, more especially
children who had been brought to São Gabriel from all
parts of the surrounding district by the fathers of the
Salesian mission, who were zealous in winning the Indians to the "true faith," so that I had an excellent
opportunity of studying various types, though my
native friends seemed more than a little frightened at
my keenness in measuring their faces and skulls.

There were also several shooting parties. Because of
the thickness of the forest through which we had to
make our way, each excursion took up a whole day. In
spite of the great number of different species which
exist, we were to find that no species is very prolific and
that the jungle teemed with life, or at least larger animal life, in no such way as is generally supposed. At
first we fought our way through the thick forests for
hours on end without catching sight of anything except
insects, though this was largely our own fault, as we
had not yet mastered the secrets of Amazonian wood-
craft.

We soon began, however, to make progress. We
learned to discard our heavy tramping-boots, which
gave warning of our approach, and took to tennis-shoes.
More important and more difficult was the art of

tearing our way through the network of undergrowth and creepers without making a sound. But a few lessons sufficed to prevent our returning home with empty bags.

Among the first-fruits of our shooting excursion was an opossum, a sloth, and an ant-bear, or *tamenduá*. I had met the opossum before in North America, but I found him of renewed interest, as he is one of the best examples of the marsupials, which represent a stage of animal life when egg-laying was first abandoned, and the young, born prematurely, are nurtured for some time in the maternal pouch. It is curious that marsupials are found only in the New World and in Australasia, and one is set wondering how these animals got from one continent to the other. My Brazilian friends did not show any great knowledge of the denizens of the forest which surrounded them. The learned *superintendente* upon seeing the first opossum I caught assured me that it was a fox.

The ant-bear and the sloth were even more interesting to me, because they are only to be found in the Amazonian jungles. Although the sloth outwardly resembles a great, clumsy, slow-moving monkey, and both he and the ant-bear with its lightning tongue are provided with shaggy hair instead of a coat of mail, zoölogists tell us that both animals are closely related to the armored armadillo. All three animals belong to the same order, the *Edentata,* and have presumably developed from the same ancestor. Even in long past geological times, this group of animals was restricted to the South American continent, though fossil remains tell us that in the days of long ago, there existed alongside of the present species several other gigantic forms.

The skins of all these animals were added to the collection which I was making (I was now getting fairly expert at the skinning game), while the flesh went into the cooking-pot. These outlandish dishes were thoroughly enjoyed, by me at least. Poor Mannling was shy with culinary novelties and preferred to fast on these occasions.

At last the holes knocked in the launch were repaired, and everything was ready for a continuation of the journey, when one of my teeth decided to set up a disturbance, and began to expostulate about its place in the solar system. I was in no mind to face the terrors of the jungle and a continuous toothache at the same time, so I hied me to his Honor the Judge, during the time when he was accustomed to lay aside the burdens of state and handle the drill.

Our interview caused the whole community to assemble, as operations were conducted without anesthetics, and in addition to a sensitive tooth I was possessed of a hefty pair of lungs. It was decided that the troublesome tooth must be extracted. But twice in the excitement of the moment, or perhaps because the dentist's mind wandered astray into judicial fields, the wrong tooth was seized and pulled lustily, before a more than usually loud squawk told my tormentor of his mistake. When eventually the forceps were adjusted to the right tooth, it took three of my servants to hold me down—and even so the tooth refused to budge. Finally I managed to loosen a hand from the cook's grip and in anguish struck out at the poor judge. He jumped back to avoid the blow, and with this added impetus the tooth came out.

CHAPTER VI

BEYOND THE LAST OUTPOST OF CIVILIZATION

THE following day, long before daybreak, we once more stowed ourselves and our baggage inside the launch and started out on the next stage of our journey. For many miles the river continued to be broken by an almost constant succession of cataracts. Those through which we had already passed had seemed sufficiently terrifying, but the further we went the more stupendous the force of the waters became.

Rocky islets, seething currents, and spinning whirlpools more than ever marked the order of the day. Time and again our little launch trembled under the impetus of an oncoming wave which seemed determined to cast us back on some rocky crag. On each such occasion there was a shivering second of expectancy when the boat was brought to a standstill, and we waited to see if the engines were strong enough to drive us forward, or whether the force of the waters would be triumphant.

Even where the river was free from rocks the current was so strong that it was utterly impossible to keep to the center of the stream, and we had to hug the banks and take advantage of every counter-current. At that, the impetus of the rushing river was frequently so powerful that the engines were unequal to the task, and we were forced to resort again to the tow-line attached to a tree ahead of us, so that we could pull ourselves along the flooded bank.

When the current along one bank proved irresistible it was necessary to fight our way over to the other side in order to try our luck there. Each time we crossed the river the enormous energy of the river in the center of its course drove our launch back many hundreds of yards. This fact had always to be taken into account, so that we could only cross where there were no rocky crags for some distance down-stream.

Because of the skill of our pilot and the strength of our engines we were fortunate enough to meet with no serious accident, although the force of the battle which we were waging caused some of the recently repaired seams to open up again. We were able to appreciate our good luck all the more because we witnessed the disaster which befell another boat, which was unaided by engines.

This boat, while trying to cross the stream, was caught by the full force of the current. The pilot seemed powerless, and the boat was swept back more than half a mile and at last hurled upon one of the rocky islands in the center of the river. The boat itself was knocked to splinters, and though most of its occupants managed to save themselves, one man had a leg and several of his ribs broken. We did what we could to help these people and then pushed on our way again.

From time to time we stopped at some little settlement. The settlements were more and more primitive in type. They contained no white colonists; their inhabitants were pure-blooded Indians, whose only contact with white men was the occasional passing of some missionary or rubber man. In addition to one or two rusty and almost useless shot-guns, picked up through barter, the huts contained a number of bows, arrows, and blowpipes—relics of the old primeval culture.

The natives, however, were obviously used to white domination. When we stopped to rest for the night, the inhabitants of the principal hut without a word abandoned the main room to us for sleeping quarters and huddled into a little outroom next door. Food was brought to us as a peace-offering, and the villagers seemed filled with anxiety because their woebegone curs insisted upon barking at us.

They appeared astonished at my friendly overtures, and even distrustful, but I eventually managed to have long and interesting talks with them. All of them understood and spoke the Lingua Gerál, but though the old tribal organization had largely broken down, they retained a knowledge of their tribal languages and their tribal traditions. My mastery of the Lingua Gerál was still very scanty, and so I had one of the boatmen act as interpreter.

To the anthropologist the racial history and classification of the indigenous peoples of South America presents a very interesting and intricate problem. There are still enormous loopholes in our knowledge. But even with our fragmentary information, it is obvious that the South Americans, though of very mixed stock, with marked differences in physical characteristics among themselves, belong essentially to the Mongolian group of peoples.

In many cases the Mongolian character of the South American Indian is very marked, even to the obliqueness of the eyelids. I had already seen hundreds of natives whom, in spite of the several years that I spent in the Far East, I could have easily mistaken for Celestials. Curiously enough the natives of South America have greater points of obvious similarity with the Mongolians than have most of the North American Indians, although it is generally conceded that the South Americans must have reached their present abode by passing across the Bering Strait and down the western coast of North America and then over the isthmus of Panama.

Even among the pure-blooded Indians I frequently noticed markedly different types. This would tend to prove that the invading Asiatic peoples were mixed with some alien stock, but no one has the slightest information as to what this alien stock can have been. In any case the Asiatic migration must have taken place at a very early date, before the Mongolian culture proper had had time to develop, as there is little trace of it in the indigenous American civilizations.

Although they all belong to one large racial group, it is possible to make a threefold division of the aboriginal peoples of South America, even as regards their physical characteristics: the inhabitants of the Andean highlands of Colombia, Ecuador, Peru, and Bolivia form one group; the dwellers of the plains of the Argentine a second; while the Indians of the Amazon basin, and of the Guiana and Brazilian highlands, those remnants of ancient continents, a third.

The pampa dwellers are nearly extinct. In any case detailed reference to them lies outside the scope of the present book. The Andean peoples are to be considered hereafter, but it would be well to survey briefly what is known concerning the natives of the Amazon basin. At first sight there is a confusing multiplicity and complexity, with many hundreds of distinct tribes. A single small river may have on its banks thirty or forty groups bearing different names. But explorers of the past have discovered that it is possible, from the linguistic and cultural standpoints, to group most of these tribes into larger divisions. Three large groups are of especial importance. Their ramifications cover the greater part of the Amazon basin and the two ancient highlands. These are the Tupi-Guaranis (or better Tupi-Waranis), the Arwaks or Aruaks, and the Karibes.

None of these groups occupy isolated regions. They are, in fact, all inextricably mixed up; but, in general, it may be said that the Tupi-Guaranis occupy a large part of the territory south of the main Amazon stream. Beginning their career somewhere in the southwest, they seem to have moved slowly down the Rio de la Plata to the Atlantic Ocean, and then gradually to have spread up the sea-coast. The inhabitants of Paraguay still speak Guarani as their mother-tongue; and, as we have seen, the early missionaries who landed on the coast of Brazil found the allied Tupi language so common that they made a simplified form of it the general medium of communication with all the natives.

The Karibes and the Aruaks have their chief center north of the main Amazon River, though many isolated tribes from both groups have spread far to the south of the dividing line. Scientific inquirers who have managed to push forward to these regions tell us that along the Rio Branco and in the southern portions of the Guianas the native tribes are chiefly of Aruak stock. To the northward lies the domain of the Karibes, who incidentally gave their name to the Caribbean Sea. The whole of the northern portion of the Guianas seems to have been conquered from the Aruaks by Karibe invaders, who gradually moved southward through the ancient domain of their more civilized but weaker neighbors.

Considering the close affinity which persists between the widely scattered forms of the Indo-Germanic languages, it is remarkable that the various language groups of the South American Indians are so utterly distinct. Within each group the linguistic similarities are obvious, even between tribes thousands of miles apart. Aruak languages spoken on the Andean slopes are closely akin to the dialects which prevail in the far-away Guianas. But the Tupi, Aruak, and Karibe languages are so different from one another in structure that it seems difficult to believe that they ever had a common origin.

The secret of the origin of the various linguistic and cultural groups can only be solved by years of research among the tribes concerning which there is still little or nothing known. Lines of migration would thereby be traced, with the hope of ascertaining where the original centers of culture can have been. The difficulty of the problem is heightened by the fact that many tribes speak languages which cannot possibly be associated with any of the larger groups.

I was enormously interested in getting the natives to talk about their old tribal customs. I listened with fascination to the tales of old days when the whole of the Rio Negro had been dominated by the great native tribes known as the Manáos, the Bares, and the Baniwas. Although their descendants had now come to look upon the Lingua Gerál or Tupi Guarani as their mother-language, it was obvious from the ancient words and phrases which had persisted that all of these tribes were of pure Aruak stock. The dreaded tribes on the tributaries of the Negro belonged to some alien group, but on the main river we were in the heart of the ancient Aruak culture, a culture which is slowly but surely vanishing as the white pioneers make their way up the river.

Our long hard fight with the cataracts continued until we came to the mouth of the Uaupés River, the most important tributary of the upper Rio Negro. Beyond this point, both on the main river and on its tributary, the stream seemed to flow in a fairly smooth course. The river was resting between its various stages of violence.

Our boatmen told us that were we to keep to the main river, we should come in a few days to the wonderful Cassiquiare, the natural river canal which joins the Rio Negro with the Rio Orinoco. By keeping to the main river we should also keep within the Aruak domain. But I was determined to explore the upper reaches of the tributary, as I had been told that it was on this river and its feeders that some of the most interesting tribes of the still untamed Indians were to be found.

Since leaving Manáos, though the main course of the journey had been westerly, we had been slowly making our way to the north, and we found that the mouth of the new river which we were now entering lay directly on the equator. We were later to discover that this river zigzagged across the equator for a good part of its course, so that by journeying up-stream we had the amusement of crossing and recrossing the equatorial line many times; and yet on no occasion were we seriously inconvenienced by the heat.

We felt a certain thrill as we left the Rio Negro and turned into the Uaupés. We had now definitely left the country of the pioneer settlers behind us and were in the domain of the true Indian. We heard, however, that the river is yearly visited by rubber men, as the upper waters are noted for their richness in balata. Not all of the rubber men who go up-stream return. Many of them are killed off each year in Indian fighting; disease carries off many of the others.

Not long after entering the Uaupés, we came upon a poor wretch of a half-caste huddled in a rude hut built on the left bank. He was in the last stages of some wasting disease. He told us that he was a rubber man who had been abandoned by his companions when his illness had rendered him useless to the party. There was no bitterness in his story. Accustomed as he was to the wild law of the jungle, it seemed only natural to him that he should be left behind when he had been struck down by a fatal disease. He had strength enough to add, from time to time, fuel to his fire; but in addition to his other troubles, he was actually starving to death. He had been given a rifle, but this he was too weak to use, and his stomach was incapable of digesting the coarse *mandioca* grains, the only food that had been left to him. So we won the eternal gratitude of the poor devil, who was soon to enter upon eternity, by giving him a few tins of condensed milk which we brought with us. There was nothing else we could do. In a few days, in a week or two at the most, he must die, and he knew it. It was a lonely death, far away in the wilderness; but he seemed to accept his fate stoically, or rather apathetically.

For many miles after we left him there was a complete absence of cataracts, but the current was still dangerously swift. I was reminded of this fact in a rather terrifying way. Early in the afternoon of the second day after entering the river, we brought the launch to a standstill near a bank, and all of us jumped overboard to have a swim. I was foolish enough to strike out further from the shore than the others, and was soon caught by its strong current, which carried me with such force to the middle of the river that I was unable to fight my way back. In desperation I exerted all my strength, but it was a hopeless struggle, and I was soon so much exhausted that I had to abandon myself to the whim of the stream, contenting myself with an effort to keep afloat. Fortunately the others, seeing my plight, scrambled back into the launch. This was soon turned around and sent flying after me. Eventually I was caught and pulled out of the water, just as I was beginning to think my plight was hopeless. I was so weakened by fright and by my struggle with the current that I lay in something of a stupor the rest of the day.

By the next morning, however, I could once more take a keen interest in everything that went on. In the absence of cataracts and fellow-passengers, I devoted myself to a study of the crew. For the most part they were pure-blooded Indians, but there were two negro youngsters among them. It was interesting to notice the world of difference that lay between the effect produced by the black and by the redskin. For some reason there is always something comic about the negro, particularly the negro youth. It was so on this journey. Our ship-boy had only to roll his eyes, to stare, to move, and we were forced to smile. His tantrums with the cook were uproariously funny. With the Indians this comic element was entirely lacking. Even when they were at play or joking, they were invested with an air of soft melancholy. They were strong, robust, and energetic; but there was always a certain something about them that marked them as a dying people, and in the presence of the dying even humor is overshadowed by pathos.

All the Indians of the crew were of Aruak stock, and on talking with them I found that they had been filled with secret fear since we had left the Rio Negro behind us. The Uaupés River was inhabited by Indians who were strangers to them, who came of a different race, and who spoke a totally different language. They told many stories of the ferocity of these Indians, of their cunning, and of their mysterious knowledge of all manner of poisons.

As I was talking to them there was a sudden shower, a flash of lightning, and a distant roll of thunder. As if startled by the storm, a number of the strange toucan birds, with their monstrously huge beaks and black plumage, flew slowly across the river.

"Look, look," one of the Indians cried; "we have come to the land of the Tukanos." It was almost like an omen. For the most powerful and feared of the tribes into whose territory we had come claim descent from these strange birds and call themselves Dagse, or Tukanos. The Tukanos are only one of many tribes which inhabit this region. But in culture, in tradition, in language, these tribes are much alike. They are grouped together and called the Betoya tribes.

I was told then, and I was later to find for myself, that the region inhabited by the Betoya tribes is immense. It was all the more strange therefore to find that the language of these people bears no resemblance to that of the Aruak, the Karibe, or the Tupi-Guarani groups. These Betoya peoples are no mere subdivision of one of the greater groups but form an individual group which must be added to the others. Where they came from, what their origin or their racial history, is unknown.

I was told that on either side of the river-banks were

a large number of Betoya Indian settlements, Tukano
for the most part. Most of these settlements were
hidden far away in the forests, and we saw nothing of
them as we passed up-stream. From time to time, however, we could see the roof of one of the great tribal
dwellings which was nearer the river-side. We had gone
beyond the region where the Indians were content to
dwell in tiny huts, and could see something of indigenous
architecture. We stopped at two or three of these native
settlements. In each case the Indians were obviously
leading a more and more primitive and natural existence. Articles secured from white traders were more
and more rare, and there was a corresponding decrease
in the amount of clothing worn. We were rapidly approaching the territory of the "Naked Sons of the
Jungle."

I should have liked to stay longer in these outpost
communities, but it was necessary for us to hasten on.
There would be time to dally and investigate when we
were safely off the launch and on our own in canoes. At
last we passed the mouth of the Tiquié, one of the most
important tributaries of the Uaupés and one of the chief
centers of the Tukano tribesmen. I knew that there
would be much of interest to see on this river, but the
tributaries further up-stream promised an even greater
yield and so we continued along the main stream.

An hour or so later we came to the settlement of
Taraqua. Here we were forced to disembark, as only
a few miles ahead was the gigantic Ipanoré Cataract,
through which no launch could hope to pass.

Taraqua marked an important stage in our progress.
From this point we should have to rely entirely upon
the Indians for assistance in getting from place to place.
It was our last point of contact with "civilization" for

many months. The settlement itself was purely Indian, but about two years earlier Padre João had come from São Gabriel to this extreme outpost in order to convert the untamed Indians. His post was a difficult one, with a strong spice of danger. A few decades ago another mission had flourished here, but it ended in disaster when the padres attempted to interfere with certain of the strange religious rites of the Indians. Two of the missionaries were killed by the wrathful natives. The third had been forced to flee precipitately back to the Rio Negro.

For years no priest had dared to come near the place, and even Padre João found it necessary to be very cautious in his interference with native customs. I noticed that he was careful to turn a blind eye to many "heathenisms" and allowed the Indians to follow their ancient traditions. The stories we heard here regarding the murder of the former priests were not altogether auspicious omens for us, as I was particularly eager to study some of these strange native rites, and it seemed not at all unlikely that the Indians would fiercely resent any attempt to penetrate behind the veil.

But though Padre João was full of the gloomy stories—as was only natural, for it was here that the Swedish explorer had died, and several Indian attacks on rubber men had taken place near this spot—he was the soul of hospitality and insisted that we stay with him until we could proceed with our journey.

The day after our arrival he took us down to the great *maloka* or communal house at the foot of the slope and introduced us to the *tushawa* or chief, a great strong husky Tukano. Most of the Tukanos we found undersized but muscular and swarthy. It was obvious that in spite of two years of Christianity European customs had not entirely prevailed. As we entered, the noble chief beat a hasty retreat in order to don a pair of trousers, which he wore only when the padre was about. When this was accomplished, and he was thus in court attire, he appeared smiling before us and showed us over the *maloka*.

The housing arrangements form a very important factor in a study of the cultural relations of the various South American tribes. There are tribes with no settled abodes who wander perpetually hither and thither in the forests like the wild beasts upon which they prey. There are others which dwell in houses of thatch, shaped like beehives. Other tribes again build for themselves square or rectangular homes. Among most of the tribes south of the main stream it is the custom for each family to have a house to itself; but in the northwest, as we have seen, the whole of each clan or subtribe, which usually numbers well over a hundred persons, is housed in a single rectangular edifice. This edifice consists of but one room—but what a huge room it is! The *maloka* in Taraqua, by no means one of the largest, was ninety-five feet long, sixty-two feet broad, and at its highest point eighty-seven feet high, although at its outermost point the sloping roof was scarcely three feet above the ground.

The whole middle part of the great house was a sort of public reception-room reserved for dances and other festivities. I wondered where the individual family life came in, or whether the Indians, in common with some of our ultra-moderns, had given this up. But as we peered further into the gloom—and it is always gloomy in a *maloka*—we could see that along each of the two sides of the great house were rows of fires, family hearth-fires, one for each married couple. There was a row of pillars supporting the roof, and from each of these pillars we noticed a frail cross-bar to the outer wall. Each family had then a well defined compartment —or shall we call it an apartment?—of its own. Each apartment was of exactly the same shape and size— a great advantage this, for there could be no boastfulness and no "swank" as to the choice of "suites." Even the timid *minoiniya* whom a Tukano warrior had just brought home as a bride had a residence as large as that of her stout and rather headstrong mother-in-law. The chief occupied one such compartment at the rear of the great house. There was, to be sure, a certain airiness about these compartments. On one side they were bounded by the outer wall and on top by the roof, but there was nothing more than a narrow bar between the various suites. In the *maloka* every one was called upon to lead a "public life." One could see (as far as the dusk permitted) and hear from one end of the *maloka* to the other. I should pity the poor man who in such a house would try to confide a secret in his wife; but would a wise man do that in any part of the world?

After our tour of inspection we returned to Padre João's abode and tried to make more definite plans for the immediate future. Our launch had already returned down-stream. We were now in need of a new boat and of good stout arms to row it. Our new-found friend, the chief, had promised to secure for us the arms and the accessory human bodies, but the acquisition of a suitable boat turned out to be a more difficult problem.

The Tukanos and their neighbors are expert navigators, but their boats—consisting of carved-out and expanded tree-trunks—are usually very small, and none of the native craft we found in Taraqua answered our purpose. Padre João had an old but serviceable *mon-*

taria, a very popular conveyance on the Amazon, which consists of a native *uba* or canoe, with planks nailed on to heighten the sides. This I purchased on the spot; but it would carry only half of the cargo. The chief said he would try to collect a number of smaller boats from neighboring villages, to carry the remainder of our luggage. But this, we knew, would take several days, and pending their arrival we had to wait patiently at Taraqua.

During this period of delay my little party nearly met with a fatal accident. Mannling, my operator, and the inquisitive Pequenino thought they would take a trial trip in a native craft which was already at the settlement. But an *uba* with its round smooth bottom is not easy to handle, and they had scarcely gone ten yards when suddenly the *uba* decided to turn turtle, depositing its two occupants very neatly in the water. Mannling was smoking a pipe at the time; and even in the danger and excitement of the moment the fear of losing this precious and irreplaceable possession was uppermost in his mind, and his teeth gripped it harder than ever, much to the astonishment of all beholders. The situation might have been very serious, as the current was strong, and both men were fully clothed and wore heavy boots. In the end both were pulled out without mishap, but they spent the rest of the day roundly rating one another, each accusing the other of causing the accident.

Before all the boats were got together there appeared one day out of a blue sky another *montaria* commanded by a *balatero,* Dom Manoel de Silva—he had four or five high-flown middle names, but these I have forgotten. Senhor Manoel had led a roving adventurous life, full of interest and excitement, and at this time was determined to make a balata-collecting expedition in the upper waters of the Uaupés. The river is known to be rich in balata trees, but the fear of attack from the natives who have wiped out several exploring parties has prevented more elaborate exploitation. Senhor Manoel's boat was nearly empty, and he agreed to accompany us as far as the Yawarete, ten days' journey further up the river, and to take in his boat all our surplus cargo. This arrangement made the small boats unnecessary for the time being, much to the relief of Mannling and Pequenino.

The next day our fat friend, the chief, gave orders to six of his henchmen that they were to act as our paddlers (in this part of the world even *montarias* are paddled and not rowed). They also were to go as far as Yawarete, where I was told there was another great chief who would give me men for the further journey. All was now well and good; we were ready to start, and the whole community came to see us off. But before embarking on the proud vessel of which, by purchase, I had become captain, I desired to know her name. By some oversight, it seemed that she was nameless. I felt that would never do, so, in the absence of champagne, we filled a broken bottle with river-water, and re-breaking it over the ship's bows, I christened her the *Bella Tristeza,* or *Beautiful Sorrow,* in virtue of the air of sad resignation and dilapidation which the boat had acquired through many years of service.

At last we set out once more on the long journey up-stream. We had left every trace of civilization behind us. The banks of the river on either side were covered with primeval forest, the secrets of which were known only to the Indians. There was now a thrill about our journeying, greater even than that which we had known before. We felt that we had emerged from bondage into freedom. Mannling and I sang wild hilarious drinking-songs, intoxicated by the romance of the tropical jungle, into the very heart of which we were now making our way.

Even the Indian settlements were few and far between. Only twice on the first day of our wanderings in our *montarias* did we come across human habitations. These lay well hidden from the river, and we should never have found them had it not been for our guides. Neither of them was large enough to be worthy of the name of *maloka,* and I found they were really offshoots of the Taraqua *maloka,* and obeyed the orders of the same fat *tushawa.* Thus we could see even at this stage that the *tushawa,* or chieftain, system was somewhat complicated and that we had still much to learn concerning it.

CHAPTER VII

LIFE AMONG THE INDIANS

THE evening of the next day brought us to an entirely new territory. We arrived at Ipanoré, just underneath a great cataract, the noise of whose tumbling waters we had heard for hours. We found Ipanoré to be a very extensive Indian community consisting of three large *malokas* and several other scattered huts and houses. The inhabitants were not Tukanos, but belonged to a very different tribe, the Tariano. I had only to listen to their speech for a few moments to realize the truth of the report I had heard, that the Tarianos were intruders from the north, that they belonged to the great Aruak family which we had already met on the Rio Negro. For generations the Tarianos and the Tukanos have intermarried, so that it was not always easy to tell the difference between them. In general the Tariano seemed to be characterized by a coppery red color, a long face, and frequently a prominent —even a hooked nose.

We arrived in Ipanoré just a day too late. On the preceding evening a magnificent wake had been held, in honor of the chief who had died a week before. Native beer, *kashiri,* a thick, milky, sour-sweet mess, had flowed like water, and everybody had been content. When we arrived we found that some were wishing they had not taken quite so much—or been quite so happy.

The old chief had ruled over the whole community at Ipanoré. As the old man had died leaving no near relative except a boy of about twelve, we found that until the boy was grown the unofficial regency was to be exercised by one of the leading commoners. It was interesting to see how closely the Indians of this region keep to the distinction between noble and commoner. Among many savage peoples, when the chief is a child or weakling, his place will be usurped by a strong warrior, and not infrequently the unfortunate heir is put to death. But among the Tarianos, heredity seems to be deeply respected.

The next day brought a cloudburst, and we could make no further progress. But what matter? I was quite content to swing in my hammock and ask the Indians all manner of foolish questions, only half of which could they understand, while only half of their answers were intelligible to me. But I felt that bit by bit my knowledge of the Indians was growing.

The day was rendered exciting by the advent of two *balateros* who came from up river. They reported that further up-stream they had found the natives so hostile that they had been forced to give up their expedition, and they strongly advised us to turn back also. But I was firm in my intention to continue. In this part of the jungle there is almost constant hostility between the whites and the reds. The occasional white who has won his way through the Indian settlements has not infrequently raped the women, taken away the men to do forced labor, and stolen all he could lay his hands on. It is not surprising therefore that the Indian kills any white he finds off his guard.

It was slow work, but I felt the natives were already beginning to know and like us and I hoped that in the end we should be able to win their affection.

I was much helped by the fact that I found ample use for my medical chest. An epidemic of influenza was ravaging the native settlements. I am not a medical man, but I punched and probed and felt pulses and looked wise—and gave two or three pills—preferably of different colors, and assured the patient that in the morning he would be better. Above all, when in doubt I would give a dose of salts, or a tablespoonful of castor-oil, and I soon found that I was performing marvelous cures. [1]

We were lucky at one other point. We found here an Indian called Nicolao who, it seemed, was the chief of the numerous Tarianos who dwell in Yawarete, far up the river. He was returning from a long journey down-stream and had stayed on at Ipanoré to attend the funeral festivities. After some difficulty we persuaded him to add his native craft to our fleet, and to act as our pilot and guide as far as his home.

The next day, in spite of continued rain, we made the passage of the mighty cataract. It was certainly the most terrible of all the cataracts we had so far seen. The thundering of the water against the rocks gave rise from time to time to a low musical note. The Indians believed that this was the voice of the demon of the waters calling for sacrifice. Innumerable lives have been lost in this cataract, and it certainly marks the limit to all navigation.

[1] In the course of the journey I found that various skin diseases, rheumatism, tuberculosis, and above all malaria constituted the staple illnesses. Venereal diseases were unknown among the Indians who had not come into contact with the white man. Beriberi was not uncommon. Large numbers were infected with hook-worm.

The cargo had to be unloaded and carried along the bank through the jungle. The empty boats were pulled from point to point along the bank, and in the worst places we had to push them over great rocks to avoid the pounding of the waters. Our Indians worked well. They were smiling and cheerful through all the difficulties, but I was struck by the fact that they did not sing as they worked, as do the boatmen of so many nations. I was to find that the Indian sings only at his great feasts. Even the women knew no songs with which to croon their bairns to sleep.

The task of getting our boats over this cataract was so great that after it had at last been accomplished we had no time to reach the hospitable shelter of a *maloka*, and so we had to build a *barraca* or hut on the river-bank. In the forest hut-building is only a matter of a few moments. A few poles, spliced together by means of lianas or vines, formed a framework which was soon covered with palm-leaves. Hammocks were hung inside, and, as we foolishly say, there we were!

Yes, there we were, snugly tucked in. Protected from the steady drizzle, we smoked our pipes and talked in peace and contentment. Senhor Manoel was the star performer on this occasion. He told us of the many strange things he had seen, and of many hair-raising things he had done, in the most casual manner in the world. He was the best representative of the *balatero* type that I ever saw. It is the *balateros* who have gone into the unexplored forests, canoed on unmapped rivers, come across many an unknown tribe. The *balateros* are the true explorers of the Amazon basin, but unfortunately what they see and what they discover, never becomes known to the world of science.

Senhor Manoel, unlike most *balateros*, had learned

that it was advisable to treat the Indians well. He was a past master at handling them. His dry ironic humor pleased the natives immensely. But he had had long schooling. A victim of the softer passions, he had managed to combine love with business and had amassed a harem of nine wives, each wife from a different tribe, so that in addition to being a spouse each lady could be of use as an interpreter. But I was rather glad that none of the interpreters were with us on the present journey.

The next morning, when we started out, we began a routine of travel which was to be little altered during the many months that followed. To a certain extent, one day was much like another. After an early cup of tea, we paddled (or allowed ourselves to be paddled) until about 10:30 or 11, when we came to a new *maloka*. Here we "brunched," chattered with the people for an hour or so, and then pushed on again until dusk, by which time we arrived at another Indian settlement, where we could spend the night. A simple dull sort of routine, you will say; but it was far from dull. Each day brought something fresh to see and hear. Usually travelers are very wary about sleeping inside the great *malokas,* fearing treacherous attack in the night; but I felt that if we were really to get to *know* the Indians, it was necessary really to live among them. Consequently, though we sometimes had to erect a hut for ourselves when no *maloka* was within reach, for the most part we spent the night inside of one of the huge community houses. I was, however, always careful to take all possible precautions. We slept with our pistols at hand and the baggage so heaped as to form a fort behind which we could flee at the first sign of attack.

The hospitality which we sought at the hands of the natives was quite a simple one. In the language of a

London landlady, it was "unfurnished lodgings." There is always a compartment or so lying empty, and we were told that we could use it. Into this we would bring our hammocks and a certain number of our boxes from the boats, and we were ready for the night. The next morning the river was waiting for us to come and have a dip, so that even in the land of the Far Away we had no difficulty in finding bed and bath; from the Scotch point of view, our lodgings were, best of all, without price. The Indians expected nothing, not even a "present" in return.

We found the "wild savages" extraordinarily hospitable, even to the hated foreigner. Among themselves, at least among friendly and allied tribes, the hospitality goes even further. We found that families would take their hammocks with them and go on a round of visits that lasted for weeks. They were everywhere fed and lodged with the greatest good-will; only their hammocks they bring with them.

For many days after passing the threefold cataract at Ipanoré, the river was once more as still as a lake. Ipanoré itself is so terrible that it acts as an effective bar to the influx of the white man and his ideas. Here we could see how the Indians dressed, unaffected by alien influence. The washing-list was not long or difficult to remember: for the man a G-string or loin-cloth; for the women a short skirt. But it was enough. There was not a particle of immodesty about this natural scarcity of clothing. The men particularly had splendid physiques, and to see these "naked" savages silhouetted against the water was indeed a treat to the artistic eye.

The men wore their hair cut short. The women had not yet succumbed to bobbing, and curled, twisted,

twined—heavens! I am helpless in trying to express
what any lady does to her hair—let us say, did up their
hair behind, and kept it in place, and well in place, with
one comb, without a single hair-pin!

In spite of the great difference between chief and
commoner, the chiefs wore no badge or mark to indicate
their rank. Their G-strings were as scanty as those of
the common herd. There was a sort of proud healthy
democracy about this Indian hereditary aristocracy.

All that I have been describing constitutes the
everyday working attire. Each day when we entered
a *maloka* and looked up we could see a long oblong
wicker basket suspended from the roof. We had seen
it many times, but it was only after we had been journeying many days that we persuaded a chief to lower the
box and show us its contents. It was a communal treasure vault; or, to be more exact, the box contained the
feather ornaments, and the bracelets, necklaces, and
girdles of bone with which the Indians make themselves
splendid on the occasion of the great feasts: but let it
be remarked, it is only the men who may preen themselves in this finery; the women may have none of it.
And the feathers are all of the most beautiful, plucked
from the egret, the *arara* or macaw, and the toucan.

The next day we discovered that there is another
factor which plays a great part in dress on these occasions. We had left the Tarianos behind us, and we had
come upon the Woodpeckers, or Kolea, as they called
themselves. In their first and chief *maloka,* we found
the skins of the people, both men and women, painted a
dark blue, in semigeometrical designs. This, we were
told, was *genipapo* painting. We soon learned that the
Indians paint themselves with red *uruku* and dark blue
genipapo whenever feasts occur; but whereas the red

washes away in a day, the blue lasts many days longer. It was pleasant to know that even the ladies were permitted to paint and that they did so quite openly.

The time went by very agreeably as we journeyed slowly up the river. It was well that Chief Nicolao was accompanying us. Whenever we arrived at a new settlement, he executed what Mannling called a song and dance, which was really a long explanation of who and what we were and why we were there. The natives appeared to be duly impressed. I could hear them whisper, "Dotoro—dotoro" (doctor); the title in their minds carried with it something awe-inspiring. When I think what lopsided fools many of my "doctor" friends are— but that is another story.

But verily my new Indian friends spoke a language which was devilish. The Lingua Gerál or Tupi language was comparatively simple, but I was determined to study the language group of this region, which is unique. The Aruak group, represented by the Tarianos, was bad enough, but it was "French without tears" compared with the Betoya languages. This, I found, contained guttural sounds which not even a German or a Scotsman could pronounce, and nasal sounds which neither a Frenchman nor an American could push through his nose. There were at least four vowel sounds which even phoneticians would have no means of representing—or pronouncing—and the grammar was as impregnable as the rock of Gibraltar.

For many days I could not even hear the same sound as the same word; and my ideas about a "Grammar and Vocabulary of the Betoya Languages" began to appear rather ridiculous. But at last came the day when an Indian to whom I spoke gave a sickly grin. He almost deluded me into believing he might have understood what I had said to him. From that time I began to make progress, but, oh, so slowly!

It was at least a blessing that all the Betoya languages are vaguely similar, and moreover that throughout the region of the Uaupés and its tributaries Tukano, the language of the great warrior tribe, is the universal medium of speech. Even the proud Tarianos spoke Tukano, though they pronounced it abominably.

After staying two or three days in the Kolea territory, where they spoke a dialect of Tukano, we found ourselves once more among the true Tukanos. But we had already discovered that in this region the culture was remarkably uniform, irrespective of tribe, a most interesting fact. It was in its own way a high culture, and we were set wondering as to where it could have come from. Was it indigenous to the Betoyas, or brought by the Aruaks or others; and in any case who are the Betoyas, and what was their origin? Profoundly interesting questions, but we found them amazingly difficult to answer. We could only hope that as we penetrated further into the country we should be able to solve these problems.

As a traveler with a scanty food supply, I was particularly interested in one aspect of this native culture; namely, the way in which the Indians secure and prepare their provender.

Life in the jungles is not the thing of milk and honey that most persons imagine. In fable one takes up one's residence under a fruit-tree and opens one's mouth at auspicious moments to receive a ripe fruit which drops automatically into it. In reality there is in the primeval forest a perpetual fight with nature to acquire sufficient food.

We soon perceived that the division of labor was not

between the classes but between the sexes. As among many other savage tribes, the men were charged with the gentlemanly occupation of fishing and hunting, while the women did the agricultural work, which entailed an enormous amount of physical exertion. Even in the Amazon basin hunting and fishing are precarious, and many a time we saw the men return with an empty bag. But no woman ever dared to return from the plantation until her harvesting-basket was full.

Living as we now were among the Indians, we soon learned what these plantations produced. There was no rice, no wheat, no barley, oats, beans, or vegetables, only various sorts of tubers. The best of the tubers was the sweet potato. When we could secure this there were shrieks of joy from all my party. But the delicacy was rare, and consequently our shrieks were very seldom heard. It has probably been imported from the Tupi Indians of the south, as its very name *yapi* is of Tupi origin. We found no trace of the true potato, but there were two very tasteless and inferior substitutes, *makashera* and *kara;* the latter was by far the more common and the more positively tasteless.

Every day we watched the women come home to their *malokas* from the plantations; but unless, as frequently happened, we had bribed them to bring back some sweet potatoes or *makashera* or *kara* for us, we found that the heavy baskets they carried on their backs, supported by a band from their foreheads, were entirely filled with *mandioca,* by far the most important of the Indian agricultural products.

Mandioca is first cousin to the *makashera,* not altogether unlike a long fibrous potato. But it differs from *makashera* in one most important point. While *makashera,* Heaven knows, is tasteless enough, it is at least harmless, but the precious *mandioca* in its natural state is a most deadly poison, containing a large quantity of cyanic acid. But the good ladies staggering home under their burdens were not in the least worried by this fact. They knew that in preparing the tuber for consumption the poison would be forced out by natural evaporation.

That is all very well and good. But the question at once arises: how does our much vaunted science of anthropology explain the fact that these primitive, simple, scarcely rational savages, without chemistry or chemical experiment, have learned that it is possible to extract the poison, leaving a wholesome food? The answer is simple: it doesn't; any more than this science can explain why in other parts of South America the natives cultivated the real potato, which in its natural state is poisonous, until it became harmless. One would have thought that after the first gatherers of wild plants had eaten, for experience' sake, the *mandioca* and potato, and died, their friends and relatives would have declared these things taboo for all eternity thereafter.

Whereas, ordinarily, we boiled the *makashera* and *kara* we acquired (and then heaped on salt trying to give them a taste), the preparation of *mandioca* was much more complicated, and we had to rely upon the Indians to cook it for us. By grating and straining and squeezing them through a sieve, the tubers were reduced to a fairly dry paste. Most of the poison was squeezed out with the juice. The paste was placed on a large earthenware pan, under which a hot fire was kept, and the heat-waves drove out the rest of the poison by means of evaporation. By continued baking, the paste was transformed into a hard gritty wooden flour, if it were constantly stirred about; or else it congealed into huge flat pancakes if left to itself.

The flour, or *farinha* as it is called by the Brazilians, is used by the Indians chiefly on journeys, as the pan-cakes—called *beijú*—do not keep. But on all ordinary occasions the *beijú* pancakes form the principal article of diet. Getting dinner ready consists of making *beijú* (it is a lengthy process); and if there is anything else, so much the better, but if not, never mind.

I have no doubt that *beijú* is a wonderful dish, a monument of achievement; but it needs an Indian palate to appreciate it. For us it was always gummy and taste-less. I imagine that even the Indian must suspect its tastelessness, as he invariably dips it in a boiled solution of jungle pepper (*pimenta*), which we found was more than strong enough to give taste to anything. We tasted nothing except pepper for hours after each such meal.

We found little variety about the Indian diet. Game, when there was game, fish when there was fish, but in any and all cases and always *beijú* with *pimenta*. It was not an inspiring diet, and I was glad that we were not yet entirely reduced to it, as we had brought fairly plentiful supplies along with us. There should be more than enough, but I had not reckoned on the habits of Brazilian servants. Where Mannling and I took one instead of two teaspoonfuls of sugar, trying to save for the morrow, our friends ladled it in by the table-spoonful. "There isn't enough for long," they said; "let's see that we get our share before the others eat it"; and so our stores dwindled rapidly away, and we had still a long, long journey before us.

Bit by bit, however, we learned to live more and more upon the country. Even *kara* became eatable, and we soon discovered that by piling jam on it, *beijú* could be made into a substitute for bread. When by chance our Indian hosts had fish or game, they shared it with us.

Above all, we acquired from the Indians, from time to time, two items of food highly prized by us, though regarded with disdain by our hosts: chicken and pineapple.

The pineapple, though cultivated, was seldom or never eaten raw by the natives. The squeezed-out juice was sometimes put into the *kashiri* beer and fermented along with the numerous other ingredients, but our friends were astounded at the way in which we devoured the fruit in its natural state.

As for the chickens, it is a miracle and a mystery how they came here, and having arrived here, why they have remained. Their ancestors must undoubtedly have been the property of Europeans, though there is a wild jungle look in their eye. Some of the tribes lower down the river, in more direct contact with the whites, must have acquired the first pair, and then by intertribal barter have passed on the offspring to tribes further up in the wilds. It is just so with dogs. Chickens and dogs— dogs of unknown race, and of uncertain relationship— are the only two European things which seem to have the power of spreading, spreading, far into the jungle where never a white man has been seen.

This is in itself perhaps not very remarkable. But why is it that chickens have everywhere been so eagerly accepted, when no use is made of them? The Indians with whom we came into contact ate neither the chickens nor the eggs. The sole purpose in life of these fowls seemed to lie between the functions of house scavenger and house pet. Even when game was scarce, it never seemed to occur to the Indians to eat the domestic supply. In most cases we procured specimens for ourselves without great difficulty.

I use the word "specimen" advisedly: many were more fit for sending with my other birds to the museum than for consumption; but I knew that mastication was good for the health, and steady and prolonged chewing usually masters the toughest fowl. More mysterious still, we never saw any eggs, and could only suppose that in the enchanted Amazon region chickens grew on trees.

On the whole we were content with our larder, but it took weeks for our phlegmatic cook, Joaquim, to learn to obey orders as to how the food should be prepared. To me the boiling of either fish or flesh means its ruin. In Joaquim's eyes boiling was the only civilized way of preparing food. Day by day I gave orders that the meat should be grilled or fried, and day by day he brought it stewed. Here in the wilds he was trying to convert me to civilization. Eventually I was forced to show him a hefty stick and threaten to use it on him if he brought me a boiled mess again. It then slowly dawned upon his dim intellect that I meant what I said, and thereafter he condescended to pamper my degraded tastes.

CHAPTER VIII

A FEAST OF WELCOME

EVENTUALLY we arrived at Yáwarete, "the place of the jaguar," the capital of Nicolao's native kingdom. The settlement lay near the mouth of the Papuri, the river we intended to explore, and underneath the second great cataract of the Uaupés. It was thickly inhabited by Tarianos. In a radius of a few miles, there were at least five and twenty *malokas,* each with its own *tushawa;* but friend Nicolao was overlord over them all.

It seemed strange that this branch of the Tarianos should be separated from the branch in Ipanoré by hundreds of miles, with other alien Betoya tribes settled in between. It seemed strange, too, that the Tarianos should have taken possession of just these two places, Yawarete and Ipanoré, for they were ancient strongholds, almost sacred places of the powerful Tukanos. The Tarianos are certainly intruders from the north. They are conscious of their alien origin. It is the Betoyas who were the original possessors of the whole of this region. At first I thought that the Tarianos were conquering invaders who had driven the Tukanos out of their ancient domain, but the lively respect which even the Tarianos showed for the Tukanos was hardly consonant with this idea, and at last I wormed it out of Nicolao that his ancestors, coming from the north, had found Yawarete and Ipanoré deserted, and had calmly taken possession.

There was some mystery wrapped up in this. I was puzzled to understand how it was that the Tukanos had deserted the seats of their ancestors, places which they still regard as holy. I could get no explanation out of Nicolao; but I hoped that later, when we came to some of the old Tukano chiefs who had retained the ancient tribal traditions, we might find a solution of this problem.

We halted for some days in Yawarete. Nicolao granted us a corner in his mighty central *maloka,* and we ensconced ourselves in it most comfortably. The paddlers who had come with us from Taraqua now wished to return home, and it was necessary to pay them off, trusting to Nicolao to provide us with fresh men when we were ready to move on again. Payment was somewhat complicated, as money, of course, was unvalued and unknown; cloth, mirrors, fish-hooks, knives, tobacco, matches, and beads had to take its place.

I was much puzzled as to how the payments were to be reckoned, particularly as each man had his own tastes and wanted different things. For simplicity's sake I adopted the customs in use on the main rivers, where the whites come more in contact with the natives, and employ them for gathering rubber, but where payment in specie is equally unknown. I assigned to each man a theoretical wage of three milreis (thirty-five cents) for each day he had worked, so that each man had some forty-odd milreis owing him for the journey from Taraqua to Yawarete. We displayed our goods, and each man took what he wanted until we stopped him, telling

him he had had the full amount. The reckoning was
easy. We had the invoice for each article, and we "sold"
each article at cost price plus 50 per cent to cover cost
of transport—most of the Brazilian traders reckon cost
price plus 300, 400, or even 500 per cent. Our Indians
were more than satisfied, though they had not the slightest idea how the thing was managed. We found the Indians lacking in any mathematical sense. Ordinarily
they could count to five; with difficulty they could be
driven to understand ten; but anything beyond that was
"many." An Indian worker only knows that he can pick
and choose good things until his patron says stop. It is
small wonder that the Indian is consistently exploited by
the white.

We had intended to stay as short a time as possible
in Yawarete, wishing to push on into the "uttermost beyond," but we heard that Nicolao intended to give a
great feast, a *dubukuri,* in order to celebrate his return
from down river. To this feast many men from far and
near were to be invited, and as Nicolao thought the
presence of the great doctor and his companions would
add luster to the occasion, he urged us to stay, and we
were delighted to fall in with his suggestion.

Nicolao turned out to be a pleasant surprise. In spite
of his famous journey to Manáos (a journey almost
inconceivable to his fellow-Indians), he was no great
lover of the whites and had frequently turned them back
from his territory. But he suffered from rheumatism,
and my quackery had given him temporary relief. Furthermore the fairness with which I had tried to treat the
Indians made him believe that my claim to be "the
friend of the Indians" was well founded. Finally, for
mysterious reasons, he believed me the special emissary
of the far distant but much feared white government,

and he dreaded a punitive expedition in case I were not placated.

For the ordinary dwellers in the Yawarete and all the surrounding *malokas,* the days that followed were days of toil in preparation for the great feast and dance, but even we found the time busily occupied. Each day I rummaged around the various near-by *malokas* and dragged out all sorts of interesting things from dark corners and from the rafters—weapons and pots, baskets and other products of Indian craftsmanship. These things the Indians never dreamed of bringing to us, but in most cases they were willing to part with them in exchange for our trinkets, though they could not imagine what in the world I wanted with them.

Then there was the language question to be attended to. I wished to make an analytical study of all the languages of the region. But it was not only the Tariano language which I could study here, for among the women-folk we found representatives of five or six different tribes. It was the fixed and highly important rule in this part of the world that *no man could marry a woman of the same tribe.* To these people all members of the same tribe were brothers and sisters, however distant their actual relationship might be, and marriage inside the tribe was consequently equivalent to incest.[1] Outside the tribe the choice was free. A Tukano might marry a Tariano, a Kolea, a Waikano, or a woman from any other tribe, but in no circumstances another Tukano. As each tribe was possessed of its own language, this rule meant that the mother-tongue of each woman was different from that of her husband. In most cases the

---

[1] Incidentally relationship among these Indians is counted entirely on the father's side. The mothers, brothers, and sisters are not uncles and aunts—in fact are not considered relatives at all.

woman soon picked up the language of her husband's tribe, but I noticed in Yawarete that many of the Tukano women made their lesser halves carry on the family conversation in Tukano.

The preparations which were being made for the *dubukuri* were interesting to watch. Special messengers had been sent to all the near-by *malokas,* but, in addition, there was another way of announcing the forthcoming event. Almost in the middle of the *maloka* was a great signal-drum. It was a huge log of special wood, with a tiny slit along its length, and in three places the slit was widened into a hole of the size of a fist. Through these holes, with infinite care and patience, the interior of the log had been hollowed out. It was suspended by native rope from four poles to increase its sounding power. The drum was beaten, not on the ends, but on the sides. Two clubs served as drumsticks. The ends of these clubs were covered with rubber—this is the only way in which the natives ever seemed to make use of rubber.

The drum was beaten only at night, usually close on midnight. Both doors of the *maloka* were carefully closed, and the Indians asserted that the whole *maloka* served as a resonator, helping to carry the message far and wide. Strangely enough, inside the *maloka* the low booming note did not seem very loud, but its carrying distance must have been immense, as we could hear the answering signals from *malokas* situated many miles away.

It was obvious from the nature of the preparations that the feast was to be more liquid than solid. No attempt was made to amass foodstuffs for the forthcoming occasion, but a positively alarming amount of *kashiri* or native beer was brewed.

The preparation of *kashiri* was simplicity itself. A

large number of *kara, makashera,* sweet potato, and *mandioca* pancakes were baked—and this time over-baked, so that they were almost burned. The women of the establishment then set to work to chew up the pancakes, but instead of swallowing them they spat them out into a number of large jars. The saliva served as a ferment, for within two days a powerful form of home-brew was ready for consumption.

In addition to the staple constituents such as *mandioca, kara,* and sweet potato, a good deal of "flavoring" was poured in. The juice of *pupunha,* a native palm fruit, to which the natives are devoted, but which was horrible to our palates, was added according to taste, along with the juice of pineapple and of sugar-cane. The amount of sugar-cane used was enormous. It was interesting to note that whereas it was the women-folk who had to attend to everything else, the men, and more particularly the boys, gathered the fruit and squeezed out its juice, as well as that of the cane.

At last the great day arrived. Soon after sunrise numerous canoes appeared on the river and made for the little harbor which lay at the foot of our *maloka.* Men, women, and children, they were all there, and each canoe was loaded almost to the sinking-point. Contrary to native etiquette, I went down to the waterside to watch the visitors as they landed. As luck would have it, this allowed me to be the spectator of an interesting little drama. As one of the canoes neared the shore, a boy jumped into the water in order to guide the canoes through the rocks. Suddenly he gave a yell and became stiff and motionless in the water. He was soon hauled ashore, but in the meantime one of the men in the canoe, seizing bow and arrow, peered into the limpid stream, and almost immediately shot an arrow into the water.

There was a short swift turmoil, and then a long sinuous
fish came to the surface. It was one of the famous electric fish for which the Amazon is noted. There must
have been several in the water, but the others soon made
off. The Amazonian waters contain several species, both
of electric fish and of electric eels, but they must be
comparatively rare, as this was the first that I had seen,
although stories about them had been common enough.

In the case of children the shock of one of these creatures frequently causes death, so that I was anxious to
see what became of the boy. After vigorous slapping and
massaging he gradually came back, more or less, to a
normal condition, but he was badly shaken and took virtually no part in the festivities that followed. The accident, however, seemed to have no effect on the others,
who continued their festive preparations with unabated
zeal.

More than two hours were taken up with formal
greetings of the various parties as they arrived. The
women-folk, old and young, with the children, scuttled
immediately into the central part of the *maloka,* where
they squatted in two rows. The women of our *maloka*
came to them and shrieked out inquiries as to their
families, their journey, and the state of their health.
The answers to all these questions were duly yelled back,
although the interlocutors were not two feet apart. But
the more noise, the more politeness.

With the men it was even worse. The male visitors
remained near the front door squatting on the two long
benches of ceremony that are always placed on either
side of the main entrance. The younger men squatted
on the ground, behind. Each group of arriving warriors
was welcomed individually by every member of the host
maloka. First came the chief, then the other male hosts

in decreasing order of importance, with two or three minutes' interval between them. Then came the chief's wife, then the other women. With each person the same ceremonial conversation was gone through, voices steadily *forte crescendo*. Owing to lack of space at the front, the men of closely related *malokas* squatted on benches at the back of the house and shared in the function of hosts.

I thought that the home-brew of *kashiri* was enough to lay out a regiment; but, in addition, many of the visitors brought huge jars of the precious liquid to add to the general supply. The *kashiri* was soon put into general circulation. Huge calabashes of it were emptied at each gulp by the men. The women were much more moderate, but they also had their fair share. The huge quantities of spittle which this home-brew contained did not prevent even me from enjoying it. It was very refreshing, and not at all bad in taste. Its alcoholic content was fortunately small.

Soon afterward the real business of the day began. Both men and women had to array themselves for the dance. First came the important matter of paint. In small groups the men disappeared behind the *maloka*. Their women-folk followed them. First of all the whole face and body of each man was smeared by one of the women with a dark red powder, prepared either from the *uruku* or the *carujuru* plant. The powder from the carujuru has very peculiar properties. With it the Indians preserve and mummify small animals, and its astringent qualities make it prized by the Brazilian as a tooth-paste and mouth-wash. The Indians frequently smear themselves with it to ward off the rays of the sun, and as a cure for headaches and light fevers. But no one has ever been able to find out how the

Indians prepare this powder. When all the bodies had been smeared red, small earthen bowls containing the dark blue *genipapo* dye were brought forth. With this the women began to decorate their husbands, using little twig brushes which marked three parallel lines at each stroke. Arms, legs, the lower part of the face, and the whole of the chest and stomach were thus painted in more or less geometrical design.

The transformation caused by the paint was tremendous. I could scarcely recognize my friends. They seemed suddenly to have stepped back fifty years, and I felt for a moment that I was really lost among the wild denizens of the forest. But I was not to be outdone. At the urging of my Indian friends I too stripped to the waist and let myself be painted along with the others.

After the men had been attended to, the women were able to look after themselves. They painted their bodies with the same red and dark blue paint, and with designs almost identical with those of the men. The adornment of the women-folk consisted only of paint, but in this part of the world it was the men and not the women who were supposed to be the ornaments of society. It was therefore necessary that they dress to fit the part. To the Indians dress means of course simply adornment. Their G-string was *clothing* enough for all occasions. But the men from each *maloka* had brought various adornments with them, and I watched them as they proceeded to put these on. The women were not even allowed to touch such things, so that at this stage the men were forced to look after themselves. Each man donned a girdle of beautifully curved and polished bones, a necklace of jaguar teeth, and a string of polished nuts tied around the left ankle, to serve as a rattle and so mark time when dancing.

Finally came the marvelous feather head-ornaments, weirdly complicated and composed of the plumage of all the most beautiful birds of the jungle, including delicate egret feathers, worth a fortune in Europe, and the gay tints stolen from toucans and macaws. All these things seemed the same, irrespective of tribe; there was, however, a marked difference between the feather ornaments of the younger men and those of the older, more seasoned warriors, the latter being more complicated and more spectacular.

One man, curiously enough *not* our Tushawa Nicolao, played the rôle of master of ceremonies. He was especially elaborately adorned and carried a lance and a shield of state.

Now that every one was ready, the dances could begin. There were two main types of dances, "private" and "tribal." In the case of the "private" dances, three men, usually members of the younger generation, held in their left hands bamboo Pan-pipes. These consisted of an indefinite number, usually nine, of simple bamboo tubes beautifully bound together. The tubes were closed at one end, and were of different lengths so as to give variations in note. The right hand of each man rested on the left shoulder of his neighbor; the man at the end of the line of course had his right hand free. Thus linked together the men began to play upon their pipes and then proceeded solemnly to prance to and fro across the *maloka*. The Pan-pipes shrilled higher and higher, and once the tune was well under way, at every second step each man gave a heavy stamp with his left foot, causing his anklet rattles to reverberate. The young bucks did not even glance at the women-folk, but before many minutes had elapsed three husky damsels arose of their own accord and added themselves to the prancing male

trio, tucking their necks underneath the linked arms of
the men. In this way the girls followed, or rather were
dragged along by the men, who otherwise paid no attention to them. The music became wilder and the pace
faster, until the exhausted men decided to stop, and the
dance was at an end. There were numerous such trios or
sextets dancing at the same time in different parts of the
maloka.

As a mere man I should like to recommend this or a
similar system of dancing to our dancing-masters at
home. In it each man provides his own music and does
not have to keep step to somebody else's noise. Each
man dances around until some girl jumps up of her own
accord and becomes his partner—this saves an enormous
amount of bother in obtaining partners. Finally, the
women, who in any case know perfectly well where
their seats are, get back to them unescorted, and the man
does not have to follow and pick up fans and go to endless trouble trying to get refreshments.

The "tribal" dances were much more complicated.
In this case all the male dancers of the assembly formed
a long row which filed around the four central posts of
the *maloka.* The Pan-pipes were left behind, and the
dance-music was entirely vocal, all the men joining in a
long, wailing, melodious chant led by the master of ceremonies. In their right hands the dancers carried great
bamboo pounders, with which they stamped the time;
the left arm of each was on his neighbor's right shoulder.
With long elaborate forward, side, and back steps, and
with rhythmical swaying of the body, the dancers filed
round and round the four central posts. At a given point
all the women rose and joined them, each woman again
choosing her own partner—by no means always her own
husband, as one might have expected. The long slow-

moving chanting file, which now consisted both of men
and women, went on and on—I was almost hypnotized
by the music—until, presto! the women broke away—
the men continued their chant a few moments longer—
and the dance was at an end.

These "tribal" dances took place about every forty-
five minutes. The intervals between them were occupied
by the "private" dances.

Early in the evening, Nicolao, who up to this time
had taken little part in the festivities, prepared, with our
assistance, a great surprise for his people. On the occasion of his visit to Manáos some one had had a stroke
of genius. Here was a powerful chief on or near
the frontier. Brazil had never surveyed the frontier,
much less put soldiers or frontier officials in this far-
away jungle spot. It was well therefore to make Nicolao
serve as an amateur frontier guard. He was carefully
told the difference between Brazil and Colombia, and
was told never to forget he was a Brazilian. This
was comparatively unintelligible to Nicolao, but in the
end he was given the rank of colonel. He was on the
unpaid list, of course, and though he received a mul-
ticolored commission, a sword, and a pair of epaulets, no
one thought to give him a uniform. Thereby arose the
present difficulty. Apart from his breech-clout, Nicolao
possessed a pair of trousers, but no other clothing in the
wide world. In order to make his memorable visit to Manáos he had borrowed a coat from a relative down the
river, but the coat had been returned long ago. Nicolao
was anxious not only to tell his people of his new and
scarcely known honor, but, much more to the point, he
wished to show off his sword and epaulets. He found
it impossible, however, to put the epaulets upon his
naked shoulders. Eventually I learned of his awful

quandary, and after carefully screening off his compartment (so that no one was let into the secret) I rigged him into one of my khaki outfits, to which his military trophies could be fastened.

But more dramatic still, through the orders of his sons, all the visitors were ordered into the open space in front of the *maloka,* and the great hanging door closed behind them. A few minutes later it was suddenly opened, and Nicolao, in all of his glory, strutted forth. It was a master stroke. What a producer has been lost to the world far away in the Amazon! He made a little speech in which he tried to explain his new position in life, and then he added a few words recommending me to all the surrounding tribes. This little speech was later to be of the greatest benefit to my safety. After this affair, the dancing and festivities began again with double vigor, and the *kashiri* bowls again began their rounds. Hour after hour the din went on, and the people showed no signs of tiring, although they had not eaten a mouthful since their arrival.

One remarkable fact struck my attention. All of the women were naked to the waist, but most of them retained the little skirts which constituted their sole garment. Four of the women, however, reverting to the older customs, divested themselves of this adornment, and donned a tiny little bead apron about four inches by three. The whole of their bodies was carefully smeared red by means of *karajuru.* These damsels took an important part in all the dances, but I was much amused to notice that two older women were constituted guardians of public morality, or tribal chaperons, and kept the naked dancers under a very strict eye, walking by them while they danced and carefully observing that nothing untoward should take place.

At first these four were alone, but as night drew on, the call of ancient days grew stronger, and many of the younger women followed their example and removed their skirts. The music grew wilder, the dancing more ecstatic. Even the children warmed up, and the little boys, previously shy, who had fled into the corner at my approach, grew more and more friendly, and we played all sorts of childlike games, unmindful of the din that was going on around us. It was here that one of the brats christened me "Papu"—"Daddy"—a nickname that was to stick to me all through my forest wanderings.

When at about half-past eleven I crawled into my hammock, the merriment was at its highest. A few of the younger Indians likewise laid themselves down in their hammocks, but the excitement was too much for them, and in less than ten minutes they were up and at it again.

In spite of the din, the heavy pounding of feet, the shrill piping of the flutes, the low resounding chanting, and the steady booming of the drum, I slept perfectly in my little corner of the great *maloka*. When I awoke early the next morning, I found there was still no sign of abatement. It was nearly nine before the first departures took place, and it was fully two hours later before the *maloka* was once more in peace.

For four and twenty hours on end had the Indians drunk and danced. There now followed the inevitable reaction. Like heavy corpses they lay in their hammocks or stretched out on the ground. In such a condition the place would have been helpless against an enemy attack; and in fact, when the occasional intertribal warfare takes place, the enemy nearly always chooses such a moment to make a surprise attack. The Indian knows nothing of open warfare; his methods are ambush and surprise—a few hefty, well dealt blows, and then back into the jungle.

On this occasion we were spared an attack, but late in the afternoon the *maloka* was aroused by a messenger who brought news which for us was of very ominous portent. It seemed that the Indians up the Papuri River, where we were heading, had risen and slain a party of Colombians who had managed to force their way through the jungle into their territory. These Indians had further sworn to kill any other whites who came near.

Personally I put the whole story down to Indian imagination; the Indians can, with profound conviction, tell some most beautiful yarns. But the news had a very bad effect upon the members not only of my party but upon that of Senhor Manoel. Two of my servants, Scorpion and Joaquim (the cook), begged to be allowed to return to Manáos. Senhor Manoel's men also opposed any further advance into the jungle.

In the end a compromise was made. It had been previously agreed that Senhor Manoel should accompany us only as far as this point, but neither he nor I was anxious to conduct expeditions with only half-hearted support. Senhor Manoel therefore decided to give up his own undertaking, and allowed the major part of his men to return down-stream. But with his boat and his one faithful retainer, a man called Miguel, he agreed to join my party for the whole of the journey. Without many scruples I likewise allowed the Scorpion to return, but as I had wasted so much time and breath on Joaquim in the way of free culinary advice, I was loath to let him go, and eventually got it into his thick head that he would do better to remain with me.

Next day the chicken-hearts took leave of us and, embarking in a native canoe, set out down the river. I heard months later from Manáos that the little party never reached there. In some manner and at some place they must have lost their lives on the way.

I was now not merely the captain of a ship but with the purchase of Senhor Manoel's boat had become the admiral of a navy. With all of a new admiral's zeal I was anxious to start maneuvers, but it was another day before the Indians had sufficiently recovered from the effects of the festival to be able to serve as paddlers.

Our old paddlers had long since returned to Taraqua, but Nicolao eventually assembled another crew who were to accompany us for the next two or three weeks. When at last everything was ready, I sent the boats on ahead. They were to continue up the Maupés to the mouth of the Papuri, and then to ascend this tributary until they met me and the other white members of my party, because, hearing that there was a short cut through the forest, I decided to make the initial stage of the journey by land.

CHAPTER IX

SNAKES—AND INDIAN CUSTOMS

IN my march through the jungle I managed to bag several birds for my collection, chiefly different species of parrots. But I made the great mistake of trying to cook the flesh of one of these birds for lunch! We boiled, broiled, fried, roasted, and then re-boiled the carcass, trying to reduce its percentage of toughness. Even so, our teeth made only an unappreciable dent in it, and what morsels we did tear off were absolutely tasteless. It was a useful lesson; and in future, for culinary purposes, we left all members of the parrot family strictly alone.

At the mouth of the Papuri, there were a number of ugly rapids to overcome, and it was some time before the boats came up where we were. Even here the current was so strong that the *Bella Tristeza* was swept away from the shore just as Pequenino was trying to embark, so that he was thrown into the water and we had to haul him out by the hair, much to the amusement of every one except himself.

Slowly enough, working steadily against the racing torrent, we pulled ourselves up-stream. The Indians paddled frantically to prevent us from being carried back, but in many cases paddling proved useless, and we had to steer to the nearest bank and then pull ourselves along by clasping the overhanging boughs.

At this point the river was broken up into a number of arms separated by islands, usually huge granite blocks, with a top-dressing of earth, covered with forest. It was extremely difficult to estimate the real width of the river because of the islands, many of which were scarcely recognizable as such, but the main stream could not have been more than three hundred yards wide. It was an indication of the distance we had traveled from the majestic breadth of the main Amazon River. Incidentally the broken-up nature of the river seemed to be typical of all the regions near rapids and waterfalls, where the powerful waters break through many channels trying to find an easier outlet to the lower level.

In one of the smoother stretches of water I suddenly caught sight of a huge anaconda (or water boa-constrictor) coiled on a bush overhanging the water. He was sound asleep as we came upon him, and like most of his kind seemed deaf to boot, for he made not the slightest motion in spite of our noise. The head was invisible, but when we were scarcely three feet away I fired into the center of the coil, hoping to inflict some mortal injury. It was a rash thing to do. The snake dropped like a shot into the water. I could see that he was badly injured; the lower jaw was shot away, and one eye blinded, but he began to lash around in his agony, and eventually, perceiving the cause of his trouble, shot out at the boat. We received a bump that sent us back several feet. Had we been in an ordinary Indian canoe we should inevitably have upset and been in serious trouble. But the very impact had for a moment driven us out of the serpent's reach, and before he could come up to us again I fired the remaining shot from my gun. I immediately got out my pistol in case of further trouble, but the second shot had done its work.

The anaconda retreated under the bushes, where we could hear him wildly lashing about. I felt that we had had quite enough excitement for the time being, and we pushed on without waiting to renew the fray. Needless to say the snake was in no mood to have his size in skins measured by the tape-line, but he was certainly well over twenty feet in length.

The pilot of our boat took this occasion to clear his chest of a long discourse upon snakes in general and upon anacondas in particular. According to his own account he must have been a past master in snake lore, though the only part he had taken in the recent encounter was to yell at the top of his voice. I could only understand about one word in five, but it was easy enough to gather from his remarks that the Indians were even more afraid of the anaconda (called *sukuruju* in the Lingua Gerál) than of the real boa, his cousin of the forests. The boa is the smaller of the two species, but both varieties of snakes figure very largely in native mythology. In this the serpent plays the rôle of a demon of the first order, sharing the highest honors only with the jaguar, and in part with the crocodile.

It is well known that neither the boa nor the anaconda is possessed of poison fangs. They kill their victims by coiling themselves around them and crushing them. The pilot moreover added confirmation to a story which I had already heard, that these snakes need to wrap their tails around a tree-trunk in order to get the necessary support for their squeeze, if their victim be of any size. According to the pilot, in case a child were caught in the coils, it was useless merely to shoot the snake or to cut off its head, as the automatic contraction of the muscles would still go on. It was necessary to cut off the part between the tree and the coiled body.

In this way the serpent would be rendered powerless to contract and could then safely be killed. The story all sounded very well, but personally I was inclined to nominate the pilot for life membership in the Ananias Club.

Late in the afternoon we came to the end of our day's journey. We were again underneath a huge waterfall, and it was necessary to make a long portage overland through the forest, though the boats had to be dragged along the river-bank.

While the boats were being unloaded, Mannling and I went on ahead, following a narrow and almost invisible path. As was to be expected, we took a wrong turning, and arrived, to be sure, in a *maloka,* but one far in the forest, instead of one on the river above the *cachoéira.* Seeing that we were not permanently lost, I was quite content to stay where we were, as the *maloka* was one of the most interesting I had seen. We were still in Tariano territory (we had passed by three other Tariano *malokas* in the course of the day), and several of the inhabitants had attended the *dubukuri* in Yawarete, so that they knew at once who I was, but here everything was even more primitive and aboriginal than in Yawarete. There were virtually none of the occasional European knickknacks I had seen on the main stream of the Uaupés.

I was so much interested in examining the many new things I saw that I quite forgot to send word to Manoel telling him where we were; and he on arriving at his goal, the other *maloka,* and finding that I was not there, immediately concluded that I was lost in the forest, and with the Indians started a long search for me. It was some time before everything was straightened out and our little party assembled again.

The whole of the next day was devoted to getting

the boats over the series of *cachoéiras* of which the water-fall was the center. The fall itself was about twenty feet high, the first real fall we had seen. The roar of the surging waters could be heard for many miles around. To each place in the river where the water was disturbed by rocks, or where the current was unusually strong, the Indians had given a special name, so that from the mouth of the Papuri to the waterfall, according to native reckoning, we had passed more than fifty cataracts.

While the men were busy attending to the portage of the boats, I spent the time among the women-folk trying to solve the mysteries of native cooking. I had been eating Indian food for some time without becoming at all familiar with the finer rites of their culinary art. Apart from the special luxury of fresh fish and meat, the standard Indian dishes, it will be remembered, consisted of *pimenta,* or pepper-sauce, and *beijú,* or *mandioca* pancakes; and I stared for hours at the busy women and girls preparing these delicacies.

The fair females were more than a little taken aback at my attention, but I learned what I wanted. The preparation of *pimenta* was simple enough. The pepper-pods, brought in fresh from the fields, were placed in a long open oval basket, and allowed to roast over a fire until they were thoroughly parched. They were then pounded into powder in a stone mortar with a wooden pestle. The powder was then boiled in a fair quantity of water, with a number of pieces of old, moldy fish added according to taste. This mixture, when boiled down to a syrupy consistency and allowed to cool, was the hottest thing I ever tasted. Even the fish maggots—and there were a fair number of these in the pieces of old fish—were unable to stand the strain and ceased to make themselves noticeable.

The preparation of the *mandioca* was much more complicated. I had noticed a remarkable difference in the taste of the various *beijú* cakes served to us—which showed that we were becoming really Indianized, as at first all kinds of *mandioca* seemed absolutely devoid of taste. I was now to see that this difference in taste was due to the different ways of preparation, and to the different parts of the *mandioca* meal which were used in baking the pancakes. It is hardly likely that the present volume will be used as a cookery book by en-. terprising young housewives seeking to learn Indian recipes, but I cannot resist the temptation to describe a little of the process of the concoction.

It was already early afternoon before the women staggered back from the plantation carrying huge baskets of the heavy roots. The baskets weighed from one or two hundred pounds, but no Indian man would dream of carrying this load for his wife, not even for his fiancée.

On the way back to the *maloka* the roots had already been cleaned and washed in the river (at the same time the women had taken one of their several daily baths), and so by the time they came within my ken, the tubers were all ready for peeling. This was rather a difficult process, as the women had only wooden knives or scrapers, and so in many cases the ladies helped matters along by using their teeth. In case this was done it was necessary carefully to spit out all particles of skin so as not to allow them to come into contact with the tongue, as the roots still contained the deadly cyanic acid. In the Amazon, in skinning a potato, one is playing with death.

The roots then had to be rubbed or grated into a sort of mash. This mash was placed in a wide shallow basket supported on a wooden tripod, and then squeezed dry, the basket tray acting as a sort of sieve or strainer. The juice which was squeezed out, however, was very carefully collected in a jar, because it contained a large portion of the *mandioca* starch, which gradually settled at the bottom when the liquid was allowed to stand. When this poisonous liquid had been carefully poured off, the precious starch or tapioca flour at the bottom of the jar could then be collected.

But to return to the bulk of the mash, which was unable to get through the sieve. In order to wring out the last atom of moisture, the mash was shoved into a long thin cylinder of basketwork, which, when forcibly lengthened, contracted, squeezing out all the remaining juice. The forcible lengthening of the basketwork cylinder was accomplished by hanging one end on a peg, and having an Indian woman sit on a pole inserted through the other end. An Indian woman weighs a good deal, and when she sits on anything it bends. This may be one of the reasons why the Indian maidens do not sit on their lovers' knees.

The juice which trickled out through the cylinder was likewise collected in a bowl, but it contained little or no tapioca. If an Indian woman be in a bad mood she attempts to feed the raw liquid secured in this way to one of her friends, knowing that the friend will pass into another sphere. But otherwise she boils it for some time until the poison is evaporated, and the liquid is then drunk under the name of *manikoera*. This is sweet and sickly, but it is sometimes rendered delicious by having pineapple juice poured into it.

The mash or flour inside of the cylinder had by this time nearly all its water and poisonous juice squeezed out of it. The flour could now be extracted and placed

over a fire on one of the huge open Indian ovens and
so made into *farinha* or *beijú*. But in many cases the
dried tapioca flour was remixed with some of the mash
before the mash was baked. According to the quantity
of the mixture, the *beijú* acquired a distinctive taste.
Another type of *beijú* was prepared from tapioca flour
alone, while others preferred to boil the tapioca
with water and make it into a sort of a gruel called
takaka.

This is only a brief epitome of the many uses to
which *mandioca* could be and was put. *Farinha, manikoera, takaka, kashiri,* and all the myriad varieties of
beijú are only a few items on the *mandioca* menu. But
with the possible exception of *kashiri,* all of these put
together were not worth a loaf of bread.

Late in the evening when the work of the day was
over I moved on with my little party to the *maloka* on
the banks of the river, so that we might start the next
morning without delay. This *maloka* was the last of the
Tariano settlements. We were now to enter new territory. For the next several days' journey, the river was
said to be free from *cachoéiras.* It seemed strange to
us that all the Tarianos preferred to live by foaming
broken waters. It was at Yawarete and Ipanoré, two
of the worst cascades, that the Tarianos had made their
chief homes. On the Papuri, their *malokas* extended as
far as the first great chain of *cachoéiras* and no further.

It was at this outpost *maloka* that I purchased my
first *paca* from an Indian—as usual when buying animals, with the double purpose of mounting the skin and
eating the flesh, though the little brute scarcely appeared
appetizing. At first glance he looked like a huge tailless
rat; a better look reminded me of a guinea-pig, because
his coat of reddish brown was lighted with gray stripes.

He was indeed a rodent, and the distant cousin of a rat, but his flesh, a creamy white, turned out to be the most delicious I had ever tasted. Even Mannling, pig-headed as he was about food as about other things, went into raptures over the flesh.

Now that we were leaving the Tariano territory where we were well known, I ordered a somewhat stricter watch to be kept, though I had few fears for the immediate future. But in any case it was arranged that at least one man was to sleep in each of the boats, so that these could not be stolen in the night; and in the corner of the *maloka* allotted to us, I had everything so arranged that we could not be taken by surprise. These precautions were repeated every night thereafter.

The next day we got into our real traveling stride. The day was typical of most of the days that followed. I woke about six or half-past to find that all the Indians had long been up and about, for the Indians always awake long before the sun is up. Then there followed a dip in the river, which took some time, as even in the Amazon I found the water cold and had to hang on to the bank for several minutes screwing up courage enough to get in. At the time that I took my first bath, several of the Indians took their second, for every Indian splashes around in the water at the slightest excuse. To be sure, he is possessed of neither soap nor towel, but he requires neither. Among my trade goods were both of these articles, which I gave away from time to time, but the soap was used only for washing clothes (the only "clothes" of course being the skirts of the women), and the towels I could never get them to use. Although so cleanly about their persons, none of the Indians cleansed their teeth, not even rubbing them with their fingers or a twig, and yet in the vast majority of cases the teeth remained beautifully clean and white.

A little after seven breakfast was served, consisting of tinned *café au lait*—an invaluable aid to every traveler—and a slab of *beijú*. It was etiquette that Mannling and I were to be served first, followed by Senhor Manoel and all the Brazilian servants. Theoretically there was a third call for breakfast for the benefit of the Indian paddlers (such is the social scale in Brazil), but for the most part the Indians ate when and what they pleased. I provided them with *farinha,* the coarse *mandioca* flour. The rest of their food they found for themselves, though after the Brazilians had finished eating, a pot with anything that was left (and Pequenino took care to see that there was very little) was pushed by Joaquim, with his *foot,* toward the Indians. In his opinion to have *handed* them anything would have lowered his dignity. I could never instil into my Brazilian attendants any of my enthusiasm for the sons of the forest. With the exception of Manoel they were all too busy trying to cover up their own almost pure Indian ancestry to allow them to sympathize with their cousins of the jungle.

About eight o'clock everything was packed up and stowed away in the boats, but not until after the natives had been paid for the *beijú* we had consumed, and the various trophies (specimens of Indian arts and crafts) which we had acquired. Immediately afterward all of us went down to the river-side, a quarter or half a mile away, followed by the whole population of the *maloka,* who thus gave us a formal send-off. The front part of each boat was taken up by the Indian paddlers, who were exposed to sun and to rain; but the rear part, covered by an arched mat of bamboo and palm leaves, protected the more valuable baggage; and when the baggage was well packed, there was still room under the awning for two persons, though it was a tight squeeze. Mannling and I shared one boat, and Senhor Manoel and Pequenino the other, though why the little brat had more claim to cover than Joaquim was more than I could see. But when an arrangement works smoothly it is well for an admiral to have a blind eye for discrepancies.

Once we were off, a wild race sprang up between the two vessels of the fleet. Considering that it was incredibly hard work to pull our heavy craft up-stream, and in many cases against a torrential current, I was surprised that the Indians did not prefer to take it easily. But their pride in their prowess on the water, and the spirit of competition, urged them on. Shamefacedly I must admit that my flag-ship, the *Bella Tristeza,* being more heavily built, lagged behind, until I suddenly hit upon the idea of transforming the Indian paddles into English oars by means of poles tied on to the handles, so that my crew were able to row and not merely paddle. I was surprised to find that they not only entered into the spirit of the thing but rowed remarkably well, considering that they had always paddled and had never rowed. With the greater driving-power of the oars we soon overtook and passed our rival amid loud hoots and jeers.

Hour after hour we continued on our journey with the virgin unbroken forest on either side. In the heat of the day we passengers dozed for a minute or two, but the journey was never wearying; there was too much to do and to see. Apart from reading and study, my note-books and diary had to be attended to. Each day brought new facts, new words, new impressions to be entered up. The compass had to be watched almost constantly, as I intended to make a compass survey map of the country through which we passed, particularly of the Papuri of which so little is known. The existing maps of the region flatly contradicted one another, and none of them were within a hundred miles of being correct. The size, extent, even the direction of the Papuri was guesswork, and very bad guesswork at that.

Finally the shot-gun had to be kept closely at hand. The Indians had remarkably sharp and observant eyes and ears. The slight cracking of a twig, or a tuft of color, told them of a bird or beast not far from the river-bank; this meant a stealthy stalk, a quick shot, and not infrequently another addition to my zoölogical collection. Then came the long wearying work of cleaning, stuffing, and mounting the skins. In the case of the smaller birds this was particularly nerve-racking. So delicate were the skins that the slightest false movement rendered the whole thing useless.

Fortunately during most of the journey up the Papuri the *malokas* lay three or four hours apart, so that by noon we had arrived at a new settlement. We stayed there for an hour or two, while Joaquim cooked the midday meal and I had occasion to examine every one and everything in the huge house. Then early in the afternoon the journey was continued. Sometime before sunset we arrived at a second *maloka,* where we stayed for the night. Almost every day of our journey brought us to two new centers of Indian life, and day by day I could thus increase my knowledge of Indian lore.

On the first day after leaving the Tarianos behind us, we came toward noon to a new and especially spick and span Waikano *maloka.* The Waikanos here were

no longer the half-subject people that we had met on
the Uaupés itself, but representatives of a proud and
independent tribe. We were gradually approaching the
great center of the Waikano peoples from which the
colonists on the Uaupés had emigrated, usually because
they had made things too hot for themselves at home.
In this *maloka* I was struck by the skin color of several
of the inhabitants. It was almost a pure lemon yellow,
without that tincture of dark brown that makes us speak
of the "red" Indians. Under ordinary circumstances
one might suppose that this difference in color denoted
a separate racial origin for the Waikanos, but one
has to be extremely careful of drawing general con-
clusions about racial matters in this region. Where the
mothers of the tribesmen come for countless generations
from alien tribes, each tribe is necessarily of exceedingly mixed stock, and it is now virtually impossible
to refer any physical characteristic to any tribal group.
The language of the people, however, showed clearly
that we were away from the intruding Aruak stock,
represented by the Tarianos, and were now back among
the Betoya peoples.

In view of what our "pilot" had told me about the
Indian worship of snakes, I was particularly interested
in the decoration of the four chief wooden pillars supporting the roof of the *maloka*. Each of the two rear
posts was decorated with a representation of a long
winding boa, done in black and white. On the two front
pillars the fingers were a little more anthropomorphized
and represented something half-snake, half-man. They
were portraits of the demonic King of the Snakes. The
coloring was more varied than on the rear posts, and included red, white, black, and yellow. All these colors
consisted of thin layers of colored clay.

These fantastic portraits were not the only signs of artistry and craftsmanship in the *maloka*. I found several of the women busy with the making of pottery. Pottery is one of the chief interests of all anthropologists. It is by a study of the various stages of pottery that a great deal of the early history of the human race has been traced. I was therefore to be excused for neglecting much of the interminable palaver with the chief that was customary on our arrival at a new *maloka*, in order to devote all my time to the women who were hard at work with their fingers.

It is probable that pottery was one of the earliest of human inventions. There are a number of still existing tribes which have never reached the pottery stage, but the use of cooking-pots has according to one school of anthropologists, usually come a long time before the use of clothes or the knowledge of any form of weaving, even that of basketry, and may therefore be considered the first stage of civilization. Beyond a doubt, it is the women who have been responsible for this development, and in the northwest Amazon, as in several other parts of the world, pot-making is still a female monopoly. This is likely due to the fact that the women have charge of the family cooking—or rather of the family *boiling*, for the northwest Amazon is once more true to type in that all food, when boiled, is prepared by women, but when it is roasted or smoked (the only other types of cooking known) its preparation is undertaken by the men.

In the pottery, we had another very strong evidence of the cultural unity of the whole of the region watered by the Uaupés and its tributaries, as the pots that were made here were almost identical with those I had seen everywhere else. They were of all sizes and shapes, from huge basins for holding *kashiri,* into which a man could have crawled, to tiny little jars containing the blue-black *genipapo* body paint. In shape and size, the pottery of this region was similar to that of the Aruaks to the north and east, but whereas the Aruak pottery was colored, and was frequently painted with an elaborate design, all the Betoya pots I saw (with the sole exception of the mysterious *kaapi* jars to be mentioned later) were finished with only a uniform black glaze. They were usually without ornament, though occasionally simple geometrical designs, such as lozenges, had been pressed into the sides with the fingers or a stick. The black color was given by applying a mixture of soot and a sticky semi-resinous juice from a certain tree.

It is obvious from the uniformity of the pottery of this region that not only were women its inventors, but they were the agents of its universal spread. In a land where every woman must marry outside her own tribe, it is obvious that when she makes her home among a new people she brings her knowledge of ceramics with her, and it is certain that many tribes first acquired their acquaintance with pottery through the women they had begged, borrowed, or stolen.

Concerning the simplicity of their apparatus it was remarkable what artistic results these women could attain. Nowhere in the New World was that most useful of all simple inventions, the potter's wheel, known or even dreamed of. Everything was entirely done by hand. Clay of course is very common in the Amazon, but clay suitable for pottery is comparatively rare and is highly prized. It is nearly all of a rich fatty quality, blue gray in color, and when by careful kneading it has been more or less refined and cleared from pebbles and other impurities, it is at once mixed with the ashes of a certain kind of bark to give it greater tenacity.

The prepared clay is then rolled into snake-like coils. These coils are placed on top of one another in such a way as to give the pot the desired shape and size. A wooden scraper then smoothes the coils to a uniform mass, and the pot is ready for drying.

Work on these pots had evidently been going on for some time, as there were a good number in various stages of preparation, some fully baked, others just drying. Pequenino, as might have been expected, managed to make a fool of himself by picking up one of the largest of the half-baked jars, thereby allowing the bottom to fall out, and causing a good ten days' hard work to go for nothing.

After leaving the Waikano *maloka* behind us, we pushed on until sunset, when we reached the first important tributary of the Papuri, which flowed in from the south. During the whole of this journey the river had continued free from *cachoéiras* and consequently was a single stream several hundred yards broad unbroken by islands.

CHAPTER X

CONFERENCE—AND A PEACE-PIPE

AT the junction of the Papuri with this tributary we found a large Indian settlement inhabited by our old friends the Tukanos. Here we settled down for the night. Our supply of fresh meat was exhausted, and I at once attempted to buy from our hosts something in the way of flesh or fish. But we had come at an unlucky time. The Indians themselves had only *pimenta* and *beijú,* except for a huge *barrigudo* monkey, which one of the hunters had shot that afternoon, but this was good-naturedly offered us. The Indians were surprised that I did not at once jump at their offer, as monkey was considered a great delicacy; and indeed after thinking the matter over the prejudice against the eating of monkeys, for the most part extremely clean eaters, seemed absurd. Consequently, after a moment's hesitation, I gladly accepted the offer, and a few minutes later the carcass was roasting away on the spit.

In contrast to our experiment with parrots, the monkey feast turned out to be a great success. Mannling, of course, rather than eat this outlandish dish, went supperless to bed; but I only smacked my lips and ate his portion as well, though I must admit that when

Joaquim handed me an arm with the hand still on it, it looked too much like an infant's hand to be entirely pleasant.

But there are monkeys and monkeys. Some species are particularly tasty; others are almost uneatable. This is rather remarkable, when we remember that all of the American monkeys belong to one suborder, the *Platyr-rhinæ,* or broad-nosed monkeys, in contrast to all the monkey families of the Old World. Undoubtedly the New World monkeys are much more primitive than their African or Asiatic cousins, or perhaps it would be better to say they are more unlike man. An instance of this is the well known fact that whereas none of the Old World monkeys have prehensile tails (in many cases, in fact, the tail has virtually disappeared,) many, though not all, of the American monkeys are able to use their tails almost as an extra hand. Again, whereas the number and the arrangement of the teeth among the Old World monkeys is exactly the same as among human beings, the New World monkeys have three premolar teeth instead of two.

Among the monkeys of South America, the *barri-gudo* species plays the part of the proud and pompous gentleman. As the name implies (*barrigudo* means fat-bellied in Portuguese), he is possessed of an enormous pot-belly, so swollen that at first he looks diseased, while his chest is narrow and thin.

As luck would have it, not only was the chief of the settlement present, but the overlord of all of the *malokas* on the tributary happened to be on a visit; and as he was an exceedingly shrewd and capable old man, I got him into a long conversation on the surrounding country and its inhabitants after our roast monkey had been consumed. By way of payment for his garrulity, I gave him a package of cigarettes (always a welcome present with the Indians), but following good native etiquette he preferred to seize at intervals the pipe which I was smoking. He would take a few puffs and then return it unwiped to me.

In this part of the world it did not pay to believe in germs, and so we continued to puff at the same pipe until far into the night, chatting meanwhile concerning all manner of things. I was eager to learn from the old chief something about the tributary river on which we were, which, though a large and important stream, was not marked on any of the maps I had with me. He told me that the river was called by the natives Turi Igarape, and that it maintained its southerly direction from its very source. From this source a path led in one day to the Yapo Igarape, a direct tributary of the Uaupés, while another path led in two days to the river Tiquié, the other direct tributary of the Uaupés, which we had passed three weeks earlier. The Turi Igarape itself, I was told, was the seat of five Tukano *malokas* over all of which my fellow pipe-smoker was overlord. My noble friend informed me, with a certain air of disdain, that for many days further up the main Papuri River we should be inside the Waikano territory, but that eventually we should once more come upon the Tukanos. He spoke as if meeting the Tukanos again was to be a long-looked-for pleasure. I could always tell a Tukano in three seconds by his sinful pride, for in this quality the average Tukano comes second only to the average Englishman. Only those acquainted with the expression, "It may be all right, but it isn't the *British* way of doing things," could have understood what a Tukano meant when he said that he was a *Tukano*.

When he was busy sucking my pipe and I had a

chance to slip in a word edgewise, I asked my new friend how it came about that the various Tukano *malokas* were so widely scattered, instead of being grouped together, as was the case with the settlements of most of the other tribes. I was told that in the old days the Tukanos were in sole possession of all the lower Uaupés, and of the Tiquié and Papuri rivers as well, but that gradually other tribes had filtered in, forming settlements between the various Tukano groups. The Tarianos had come from the north, and the Waikanos from the northwest. Formerly the Waikanos had lived on the upper reaches of the Uaupés, in close union with the Wananas, but subsequently the Waikanos had broken away from the Wananas and wandering down the Maku Igarape had eventually occupied long stretches of territory along the banks of the Papuri.

This story coincided with what I had heard earlier from the Tarianos, but I was still puzzled as to how it was that the proud warlike Tukanos had allowed these intruders to settle in their territory. To my inquiries the old chief could only reply that "once upon a time," long ago, many, many Tukanos had gone away—all at once —leaving much of their old territory deserted. This was gradually filled by the overpopulated tribes of the adjacent regions. I felt that I was at last on the track of some historical fact of great interest, of a great exodus or migration that would throw a light on the development of the whole of the northwest Amazon; but many weeks were to elapse before I could learn more of this migration and of its causes.

On this particular occasion I was diverted from the subject by the old chief's account of a strange mysterious people called the Maku or Pogsa. I had already heard various wild stories about this tribe, but it had been difficult to get confirmation, so that I was particularly interested in what my friend had to say. He seemed to regard the Pogsa as the old-time white slave-owner regarded the negro, as something scarcely human. From the old chief's account it was obvious that the Pogsas stood at a much lower cultural stage than any of the Betoya or Aruak tribes. Unlike the Aruaks, the Pogsas, according to the old chief, were possessed of no tribal organization. They were without any settled abode, wandering in small bands through the forest, never staying longer than a few days in any one place. They were acquainted with no form of agriculture, eating only the wild fruits and roots of the forest. They were ignorant even of the use of the canoe, and lived in the heart of the forest, far away from the rivers. Although the Tukanos were bound to take their wives from some alien tribe, under no conditions could intermarriage between a Tukano—or a member of any other Betoya tribe—and a Pogsa take place.

On the other hand, I was told that the Tukanos from time to time made long raiding expeditions into the forest, captured some of the younger Pogsas, and brought them up as slaves. My old friend had previously had several such slaves, but two had escaped, and the others had died. He was now preparing for another slave-raiding expedition to recoup himself for his loss. I was impatient to learn more of these utterly primitive people, but the old chief told me that further up the Papuri I should probably have an opportunity of seeing them, at least in captivity as slaves in some Tukano *máloka.*

By the time we parted for the night the old chief and I had become firm friends. Early the next morning he tried to persuade me to make an excursion up the Turi

Igarape and visit the other *malokas* under his jurisdiction. This would have been very pleasant, but as it was necessary to push forward as rapidly as possible, I was forced to refuse.

Seeing that we had paid well for all the provisions we had bought here, the overlord offered to send a special messenger to the next *maloka* to bring us some pineapples and chickens. Living as we did from hand to mouth, I was very glad to accept the offer, and instead of moving on, we spent the whole morning in the same place.

The time was very pleasantly spent. I showed the natives my books containing animal pictures. Every picture was greeted with shrieks of joy. Particularly was this the case where the pictures represented animals that were well known locally or associated with a tribal name. Thus, for example, a picture of the monstrous-beaked toucan bird was the particular joy of the Tukano people.

I was, however, surprised to find how slow the Indians were in recognizing the pictures of familiar animals. In many cases I had to tell them what some very passable likenesses of common animals were supposed to be. This I think was due to their entire ignorance of pictures of any sort. At first they could only see meaningless black and white lines on a piece of paper.

The old chief was an even more excited spectator than the children of the tribe. He was visibly upset when I refused to sell him my books of wonders. Failing to secure these, he was eager to purchase one of the mouse-traps which the museum had lent me in order to secure specimens of the Amazonian rodents. It was not so much that his *malokas* were plagued with mice (in spite of constant setting, I managed on my whole journey to secure only some dozen specimens), as that he regarded the traps as the most magnificent playthings he had ever seen. To set the trap, and then to spring it with a stick, or on the finger of one of his unsuspecting tribesmen, was the summit of his joy.

I managed to find almost equal amusement in an Indian invention, a combination baby-chair, carriage, and cradle. A small wooden hoop, through which sagged two bast bands, was suspended by a cord from one of the beams. It came within a few inches of the floor. A baby was then placed within the hoop, the bands acting as a sort of chair. The infant could just reach the ground with his feet, so that he could either sit or walk as he pleased. If he walked he could not fall, as the hoop supported him; nor could he walk far, for after going a certain distance his feet could no longer reach the ground, and he automatically swung back. It was a really wonderful idea. The infants were kept out of harm's way while the mothers were busy. The children were prevented from crawling around in the dirt, and yet they were kept constantly amused.

The Indians had as much hesitation in disposing of their baby-carriage as I of my mouse-trap, but eventually an exchange was agreed upon, just as the provisions arrived from the neighboring *maloka*. Now that everything was in order, we ate an early lunch and set off on our journey once more.

I had been so much pleased with the monkey meat of the preceding evening that when, later in the afternoon, I heard the chattering of a band of monkeys in the jungle, I ordered the boats to stop while we went on a foraging expedition. This and other similar hunting raids were rendered extremely difficult because of the denseness of the jungle. Not only was speed out of the question, but the necessity of hacking our way through the undergrowth made it almost impossible to maintain the necessary noiselessness, and at the slightest alarm the intended prey was off and away. This time we were comparatively lucky, for we managed to shoot three of the monkeys before the whole band with loud screeches took to flight. Only two of the victims could we salvage; the third had been caught by the branches high up in the air and was out of reach. One of the two seemed only slightly injured, and I hoped by careful nursing to bring him back as a captive, but later the same evening our poor little victim died. Unlike the paunchy *barrigudo* of the previous day, the monkeys we shot on this occasion were thin, wiry, extraordinarily long-armed little creatures. My Tukanos called them *waki,* and I have never seen the exact species before or since. I can give them no other name.

Not long afterward we passed by a deserted *maloka.* I asked one of the paddlers why its inhabitants had left a house that still seemed to be in good condition. He told me that it was because the chief of the place had died. This was well in accord with native customs in many different parts of the world. In many places (I remember the head-hunters of Formosa in particular) the whole house is abandoned on the death of any person. This is done obviously to avoid being haunted by the ghost of the departed. But in the Amazon basin the spook of an ordinary person did not seem to be considered very dangerous, for I learned that although it was the custom to bury all bodies in the earth inside the *maloka,* in the case of an ordinary tribesman the other inhabitants did not feel impelled to shift after the funeral. A nonentity in this world was supposed to be a nonentity in the next and not likely to cause harm. A

powerful chief, however, and even more a notorious
medicine-man, was likely to prove more troublesome;
and after the death of such a person the other tribesmen
preferred to erect a new abode, thinking that the ghost
would never have sense enough to follow them to their
new residence. I was told that at other times a move
was made to a new locality because the ground in the old
plantation had been exhausted and it was necessary to
clear a new fertile section from the virgin forest. As far
as I could make out, the life of a *maloka* was only about
twenty years.

As it was nearly sunset we tried to find the *maloka*
which had been erected to take the place of the deserted
building, in order to rest there for the night. But the new
maloka must have been well hidden in the woods, for
though we followed various trails for over an hour, we
could not find it. Unfortunately there was a heavy rainfall while we were searching, and all of our party were
soaked. In the end we abandoned our search and rowed
on to the next settlement. This was only a few miles
away, but before we could get there Senhor Manoel and
Pequenino had become thoroughly chilled. We did at
last arrive, but the damage had been done, and by nightfall both men were suffering from high fever. I was
afraid that serious complications might set in, but I
could not do more than wrap both patients up in their
blankets, and fill them full of quinine.

I too felt wabbly, but it was necessary for me to sit
up far into the night to prepare the skins of the monkeys and birds we had secured. It is difficult to conceive
how much time such work entailed. By now I had passed
beyond the novice stage at this work, but still it took
half an hour to prepare each bird, and more than an
hour to prepare each monkey.

tedious work enabled me to observe how
...ly broken the sleep of the average Indian
...raor... though the natives are expert at hammock-
was. ...ing, they have never learned the weaving of blan-
mak... ...ly ...ights, even in the Amazon (and here we
and so, to ... ...nder the equator), are distinctly cool,
hammocks, during the night. The Indian therefore is
or ... place more wood on the fire, and then crawl
back again. During the long hours that I was awake
this took place several times, and not infrequently on
such occasions two or three would squat for a few
minutes over the fires, smoke a communal cigarette,
gossip for a little while, and then go back to sleep
again. It is remarkable that the Indians have the gift
of waking and sleeping when and as often as they
please, as this is in marked contrast to many primitive
peoples, particularly in the wilds of Africa, with whom
a deep long unbroken sleep is an absolute necessity.

By morning the two invalids were much better, but
as they were not yet fully recovered, I decided to make
once more only a half-day's journey, so as not to overtax
their strength.

We eventually got under way, however. An hour or
two later we again came across an anaconda, curled on
a bush projecting out of the water. Warned by our
previous experience, we were more careful in aiming,
and fired two quick shots one after another into the
center of the gleaming coils, which immediately fell a
writhing mass into the water below. This time the great
snake was done for, and a minute or two later we were
able to haul him into the boat. He was smaller than the

one that had escaped us and was only abo[...]
feet in length. Even this, for a boa-constrict[...]teen
have been enormous, but it is generally believe[...]
some anacondas grow to more than twice [...]is size. [...]
hor Manoel swore that he had seen one [...]was more
than forty feet long, but as h[...]
ing only when t[...]
statement had to be taken with a grain of salt.

In accordance with our plan we sto[...]
settle[...] the afternoon. [...] land[...]
two or three of the men were outside the ma[...], but
these rushed inside as soon as they saw us. This seemed
to be an act of unfriendliness, but actually it was only
in accord with native ideas of etiquette. When a guest
leaves, the whole population comes down to the bank to
see him off, but when he arrives every one must scurry
inside the *maloka* and wait for the visitor to present
himself formally at the doorway of the community
house, when if he be of importance every one, one by
one, with brief intervals, comes forward to meet him.

Although we were now well beyond the limits of
Nicolao's jurisdiction, and in the heart of the Waikano
country, I found that the news of my little party had
already spread far up the river. The chief of this new
maloka was anxious to know which of us was *dotoro*.
The friendliness these Indians displayed became in
fact a little embarrassing. As it was obvious that
no one could be shocked, and as the afternoon was op-
pressively hot, I stripped down to my bathing-shorts.
This brought about little cries of excitement—not, as I
thought at first, on account of my lack of clothes, but
because of the paint which had been applied to my skin
for the dancing in Yawarete, and which had not yet
worn off. The natives seemed to be astonished to see a

I called out to them they came down to us and began
a long but entirely friendly powwow. It was evident
that they had some curious suggestion weighing upon
their minds, which they were timid about expressing.

Eventually they unburdened their souls to my Indian pilot. It seemed that here, as elsewhere, the natives
had heard of the coming of the strange white man,
supposedly possessed of magic powers. The *maloka* of
these Indians, which lay hidden far away in the forest,
had recently been visited by an illness which affected
nearly all the children, so that they were anxious for me
to perform on the children the mysterious name-giving
ceremony of the white men in order to prevent further
evil.

It was some time before the real meaning of their
request penetrated my thick skull. The pilot, seeing my
perplexity, assured me that I had only to pour water on
the children and give them a name; they were asking
me to perform the sacrament of baptism! These Indians
did not pretend to be Christians. They had not the
slightest interest in the white man's religion. Many of
them had never even seen a white man before; but no
doubt, as the result of the missionary activity on the
far-away Rio Negro many decades ago, the news had
spread, in the strange fitful Indian way, of a magic rite
which could be administered only by a white man, and
which brought good luck, especially to children.

I was so astounded at the request that at first I
thought of refusing it; but at the thought of the simple
faith of these dwellers in the forests, I was touched, and
leaving Senhor Manoel to supervise the work with the
boats, I set out with the Indians through the jungle,
accompanied only by Pequenino, who was burdened
with salt, candles, and the medicine-chest, as I had a

secret suspicion that the healing powers of baptism would be increased if a little quinine-giving were mixed up with it.

Eventually the settlement was reached, and the children were brought forward for my inspection. They ranged from infants in arms to youngsters well in their teens. There then came the troublesome business of choosing names. I wished to preserve the euphony of the Indian names and to baptize the children with names originally given them by their parents. But this was impossible, because even to me, the baptizer, the parents refused to reveal the native names of their offspring. In this part of the world, as in many others, a name is something profoundly secret and sacred. A name is part of the soul, and a stranger by magic rites can bring disaster upon a man if he but possesses the secret of the name.

Strangely enough this applied only to native names. A name given them by a white man was rendered safe by the magic power of baptism and could be freely employed. For this reason I was forced to fall back on names from the far-away land of the white man. But I was not anxious to increase the already huge crop of Pedros and Joãos, and so I dubbed my male patients Plato, Diogenes, and Cicero. In one case, being at a loss for a name, I must with shame confess that I christened one innocent youth Anonymous, but this name seemed to meet with especial appreciation.

With the girls my task was easier. I revenged myself upon the various young ladies of Europe whose hand I had sought (and who had rejected or jilted me) by giving their names to the maidens of the jungle.

In spite of my inexperience in sacramental matters (at my own baptism I was too busy trying to kick the clergyman to remember much of the minor details), the

Nicolao, the Tariano chief (in uniform), who acted as guide to the party

The two *montarias* which constituted the expedition's "fleet"

Basketry, and the weaving of fish-nets

Pottery—a female monopoly

ceremony went off in great style, except for one untoward accident. The *maloka* possessed two or three huge *japo* birds as pets. During the ceremony they were busy among the rafters, with one eye on the strange happenings down below, and the other for any insect prey within their reach. Suddenly one of them lunged out at a huge spider—and just missed him—but the spider in fright fell down upon my neck and then dropped to the ground. The pursuing *japo* had secured and gobbled him before he could escape, but not before I gave a sharp yelp at the sudden interruption. I could only hope that the Indians did not consider this an integral part of the baptismal ceremony.

By the time all the children had been suitably christened and I had made my way back to the river, the boats had been safely brought above the rapids and we could go on our way again. From this time I frequently took a hand at paddling, in order to harden my muscles in preparation for whatever ordeals the future might bring us. I knew that our crew would only go to a definite point, and that beyond this it was uncertain whether we should get sufficient men to handle the boats.

Late in the afternoon we came to the mouth of a large tributary flowing in from the north. On the main river almost opposite the mouth of the tributary we saw a huge *maloka,* the whole front of which had been adorned with elaborately painted geometrical designs. Here we halted for the night, and I found that we had reached the very center of the Waikano territory. The chief of the *maloka* was the overlord of all the Waikano settlements on the Papuri and its tributaries. We had once more come to the seats of the mighty.

Soon after our arrival we went to bed, as we were worn out by the day's exertions; but the next day, in-

stead of continuing the journey, we stayed on, largely
in order to cultivate the chief's acquaintance and to see
how he governed his jungle kingdom. The chief was
really a most impressive figure. There was an air of
quiet forcefulness, of concentrated and controlled energy, of reserved dignity about him that would have
made him a noticeable figure even among European
potentates; and indeed the territory over which he ruled
must have been equal in size to some of the smaller
European states. Though he was but a "naked savage,"
he made his plans and delivered his decisions with a
laconic decisiveness which could only be based upon long
administrative experience and an assured sense of
power.

In all minor matters, every *maloka,* with its local
chief, appears to be more or less autonomous. Many of
the individual *malokas* we visited seemed to be quite
independent of all outside control. But for the most
part, a powerful chief exercises a certain control over
all the surrounding *malokas.* The extent and nature of
his control depends no doubt upon the power and forcefulness of the overlord, but should the overlord be a man
of character, he seems to exercise a great deal of influence throughout the vast tribal domain.

I found in this *maloka* two or three chiefs from other
Waikano settlements, who had come to talk over matters of policy with their suzerain. A cousin of Kandi—
this was the overlord's name—had just returned from
a visit to various other *malokas,* and I heard him give
his august relative a detailed account of all he had seen
and heard.

Almost as interesting as the overlord was the witch-
doctor or medicine-man, who also exercised many of the
functions of tribal high priest. Nominally each tribe,

in most cases each *maloka,* possesses such a personage; but further down the river the medicine-men had been less conspicuous, and the practice of their art more secret. The medicine-man in this *maloka* was so skilful that his fame had spread throughout the district. He was a near relative of Kandi, and obviously, next to the chief, the most important personage in the "kingdom."

Just as we arrived at the *maloka,* however, this tribal wizard was faced with an ignominious failure. The aunt of the chief was hopelessly ill—she was in the last stages of beriberi—and had wasted away until she was a mere bundle of bones. The old wizard openly confessed that he could not cure her.

Although the old dame was still very much alive, the chief had shown his bent of administrative efficiency by having a coffin prepared and placed beside her hammock. The coffin consisted, as was usual in this region, of an old dugout canoe, which had been sawed through in the middle so that the two ends could be placed together.

The witch-doctor was rather shocked at the old lady's refusal to die after he had given her up. He and the chief came to me and held a long consultation. After I had confessed that even my medical powers were useless in this case, they asked that at least I give the old dame a dose of poison to help her out of this unhappy world. They were, I think, astonished at my refusal, but at the same time I was equally astonished that the medicine-man thought it better to call in outside aid; for it is certain that the Indian medicine-men possess the secrets of a number of mysterious poisons, some of them unknown even to Western science. It is probable that the wizard wished the direct responsibility for the death of the old lady to fall on some one else's shoulders.

Kandi, the chief, was possessed of a stern relentless countenance, and he was so unrelaxing in his dignity that I had a secret idea that we were not in reality very welcome guests, and that he resented our intrusion upon his private domain. I was therefore somewhat astonished when early the next morning he came to the "apartment" which we were occupying and announced that he was setting out on a tour of the territory which lay on the tributary the mouth of which lay just opposite the *maloka*. He suggested that we accompany him, so that we could see more of his domain.

His invitation was rather startling, but thinking that in this way I might have an unusual opportunity of observing certain aspects of Indian life, I finally accepted, particularly when I heard that the tributary bore the name of the Pogsa or Maku Igarape, because of the fact that its upper waters flowed through a country inhabited by a number of the Pogsas, or "wild men of the forest," about whom I had heard so many mysterious stories.

I left the major part of the luggage, some of the crew, and one of the boats behind (under the guard of Miguel, the man Senhor Manoel had brought with him), and in light marching order we set out on the new adventure. Kandi himself acted as pilot, and his two stalwart sons were pressed into service as chief paddlers.

The tributary up which we went came in long winding bends from the north. It was broken from time to time by rapids, but we were used to rapids by now, and they did not mar the idyllic tone of our journey. Perched on the surrounding trees were numerous birds, including three or four kinds I had never seen before, and I soon added these to my collection.

Once or twice Kandi proved his supremacy over the

whole of the territory through which we were passing by stopping and robbing some of the fish-traps that we found on the way. These consisted of long screens plaited from strips of bamboo, with which the entrance of some smaller stream or back-water had been fenced off. Kandi assured me that at night-time the fish tended to leave the main stream and enter the back-waters, so that at dusk the screen would be left open. At dawn, when the fish wished to return, the barrier would be closed, and the fish would find their retreat cut off. Huddled up in the narrow space, crowded around the screen as they were trying to get out, the fish could then be easily caught, either by nets or by spearing. Kandi's sons thought that it was even greater sport to catch the fish with their hands. It was remarkable to see one of them dive into the water, remain there for what seemed an eternity, and then emerge with a struggling fish clasped between his fingers.

The *malokas* of the Waikano Indians were at least three or four hours' journey apart. Between them lay the unbroken forest, and yet even inside one tribe there seemed to be very clearly defined boundaries. Kandi would point out a little back-water or a curiously shaped tree and tell me that the territory of a certain chief began or ended there.

The idea of property and the division of property was therefore well understood, even in the heart of the jungle. Yet in other ways much of what one saw in each *maloka* was common property, owned by the tribe or subtribe, and not by any individual. The *maloka* itself was common property, as it was erected by the coöperation of all its inhabitants under the direction of its chief.

At one of the first *malokas* at which we stopped on our journey up the Maku Igarape I saw that the same communal enterprise was employed in clearing and preparing a new plantation. Here the older plantations were rapidly becoming impoverished (*mandioca* is a great drain upon the land), and a new clearing had to be made from the virgin forest.

Early one morning the local chief gathered all his men together. Armed with axes they set out for the selected spot. Several of the ax-heads were made of polished stone bound by thongs to wooden clubs. These, of course, were a product of the ancient Indian industry. I was surprised to see how expertly the Indians could hack down huge tree-trunks with these stone implements. But in addition to the stone axes the tribe was the possessor of two iron axes which had been obtained by intertribal bartering from Indians further down the river, who had no doubt obtained them, directly or indirectly, from the whites. It is the craving for iron and steel which binds the Indian to the hated white man.

Even with the aid of the metal axes I thought it would take weeks to clear a space large enough for the plantation, so thick was the forest, and so great the number of trees. But it was here that the Indians showed their skill. A dozen particularly large trees were singled out, and these were cut and made to fall in such a way that they tore down a large number of small trees which stood around them. A single day's work made a marked effect upon the forest, and it was clear that in another two or three days the first stage of the work would be completed.

I was told that the trunks were to be left alone for two or three months after they had been felled. By this time they would be dry enough to burn easily, and a huge bonfire would then take place. The ashes would be left as fertilizer upon the ground, and *mandioca* planting could then begin. The newly cleared plantation would belong to the community as a whole; but to each person, or rather to each woman, a plot would be allotted, upon which she could grow *mandioca* enough to support herself and her male attachments.

Although house and garden among the Indians rested upon so communistic a basis, I was soon to see that tribal socialism had by no means wiped out the feeling of attachment to private possessions. The next day brought us to a *maloka* which was particularly rich in baskets, pots, and beautifully woven hammocks; and I set about adding to my collection by barter. I saw that everything belonged to one person—and to one person alone. The owner of a certain very beautiful basket was away, and neither his brother, his wife, nor the chief could sell me the basket in his absence. The idea seemed to be that the *maloka* and the plantation had been made by collective labor and remained general property, but what was made by individual work belonged strictly to the individual.

The personal quality of property, I was interested to see, held true even as regards the women. I cast a covetous eye on a trinket worn by a woman standing near, and thinking it would be better form to do so, I tried to barter for its possession with her husband. But I found that wisdom lurked in the husband's breast. I was told to do my bargaining direct, and a very expert trader I found the lady to be. Equally interesting was the fact that it was the women and not the men who arranged to sell things belonging to the children.

In this, as in many other lands where the women are supposed to be without rights, I found on more than one occasion that the wives know how to shove a very effective finger into the family pie. The husbands wisely allowed their wives to drive their own bargains, but when I strove to secure things which belonged exclusively to the men, the women-folk frequently broke in with all sorts of irrelevant advice, and demanded of their husbands that they take this or that from my spread-out stores. More than once a man came to secure fish-hooks and went away with beads.

Whenever it came to bargaining I had to call in Senhor Manoel. My eager interest in the Indian *objets d'art* was too apparent, and the women particularly went soaring up in their demands. So I contented myself with roaming around the *maloka* poking into odd corners and peering under the rafters. Invariably I found something of interest, and as the Indians never dreamed of bringing anything to me of their own accord, I would seize all my trophies without more ado and deposit them in a heap in the center of the *maloka*. The owners would squat around the heap, and the stage was set for Senhor Manoel to appear. He would nonchalantly stroll up, give a disdainful look at the booty and at its proprietors, turn away and gaze vacantly into space, expectorate slowly but voluminously, and, in an absent-minded, uninterested voice, inquire if the owners would not be glad to get rid of this useless lumber. The battle royal had now begun. At the end of an hour a handful of beads, a few fish-hooks, a packet or two of cigarettes, would be handed out, and the trophy heap would be carted away to my boats. The worst customers were always the old women, who never could make up their minds what they wanted in return for their treasures.

Three days we continued our journey up the Maku Igarape. It was in the nature of a triumphal procession.

Kandi, the great overlord, had arrived, bringing with him the much-talked-about, mysterious white strangers, who neither robbed nor shot the Indians. Kandi's invitation to us to visit his dominion was obviously a very shrewd political move. His prestige increased enormously, particularly after the medicine-chest had eased the pains of some of the ailing tribesmen.

Now that my relations with Kandi had reached such a friendly and almost confidential stage, I ventured one evening, as we were sitting around the fire, to ask him about the mysterious religious rites of the Indians of the region, concerning which so much has been rumored and so little is known. Kandi was obviously more than a little startled at my questioning, and at first tried to turn the conversation into other channels. But I stuck to the point and repeatedly assured him that I was the friend of the Indians and that no harm would come of my being initiated into the secrets.

Kandi, after careful consideration, seemed on the point of embarking on a long explanation, when suddenly he broke off and said that if I would wait long enough for all the preparations to be made he would order one of the mysterious ceremonies to be performed, on which occasion I myself would be initiated. At last I should be able to peer behind the veil which shrouded the intimate beliefs of the Indians.

It was to take many days before my curiosity was satisfied. Kandi had long powwows with the local chiefs in order to win them over to the idea of initiating a white man. Then messengers were sent to all the surrounding *malokas* to supplement the summoning pound of the drums. Perhaps even the magic drums could not cope with a long explanation of allowing the white man to share in the mysteries. Finally the instruments for the ceremony had to be secretly prepared, far away from the *maloka* and from all women-folk.

These preparations dragged out over many days—and purposely so, because the ceremony could not take place until after a certain number of days of partial fasting had elapsed, during which time none of the men partook of fish or flesh. As an aspirant for initiation, I too was supposed to go in for training, but I must confess that a diet limited to *beijú* gave me an altogether too ethereal feeling, and so, late one night, when all the world was asleep, I stole to the provision-box and secretly opened a meat tin.

This led to rather tragic results. Pequenino, the boy, had long shown a liking for the good things of life, and had been caught several times delving into forbidden food. Joaquim, the irreproachable cook, noticing the disappearance of the meat, thought quite naturally that the boy was at the bottom of it, and soundly boxed his ears. Pequenino in a vent of righteous indignation seized a knife and made a jab at Joaquim, and if I had not stepped in and stopped further contention the magic rites would have been performed over very bloody ground.

Early each morning the older men solemnly and silently disappeared into the forests, and I had to amuse myself with the younger and more frivolous members of the community. Even these were very industrious. The youngsters would gather the long, thin, pointed leaves of the *tucum* palm and extract from them the fine tough fibers. The women pulled up their skirts so as to show a good six inches of hip, and on this excellent foundation they rolled the fibers into very serviceable thread. The thread or string, which was thus prepared, was used by the men in knitting their fish-nets and hammocks.

Other and more valuable hammocks were not knitted but woven, in this instance by the women, on a curiously primitive but very effective loom.

I spent a good part of my time skinning and stuffing some of the beautiful birds which are to be found only on this river. The work turned out to be more than usually troublesome. The heat made clothes highly superfluous, and I had long accustomed myself to a one-piece costume of bathing-shorts, a very effective uniform except when I had to sit huddled up for hours almost without moving, trying to remove intact the filmy skins of humming-birds. On these occasions countless gnats, mosquitoes, and blood-sucking flies would gather for an orgy on my unprotected skin, so that I had to learn to skin birds with one hand and slap insects with the other.

Even more troublesome than the insects were the women, as these could not so easily be slapped away. At first the maidens of the jungle proved extraordinarily shy and kept themselves hidden in the darkest corners of the *maloka;* but eventually they must have seen what a harmless person I was, and while I was busy with my skinning, they would gather around me and, though going on with their *mandioca* kneeding or thread making, would seek to engage me in conversation. They wanted to know the name of everything in my language, and what the women were like in my country, and whether they grew beards also, and if I had a wife, and if not, why not. They were particularly shocked to hear that in the far-away land of the white man men and women of the same tribe could marry one another, and that it was not necessary for a German to marry an Englishwoman, or vice versa.

An intolerable nuisance they were, to be sure, but good kindly souls, with not a particle of impropriety in

their pressing attentions. I was particularly struck by
two or three of the women who came of Desano stock.
The Desanos are a tribe that have usually but little to
do with the other Indian tribes. They live apart, cut off
from the others. The Tukanos, in fact, will almost never
marry a Desano, though the Waikanos were obviously
more lax on this point.

The appearance of the Desano women was different from that of the others, and when I learned that
further up the river there were two or three *malokas*
belonging to this tribe, I determined to occupy the
period of waiting by making a little excursion on my
own. I left Mannling and da Silva behind with Pequenino, and accompanied only by Joaquim and five Indians I set out once more up river.

CHAPTER XII

THE BEAST MEN OF THE JUNGLE

AS we came toward the head-waters, the river broke up into a number of small turbulent streams. Up one of these, the Piripini, we pushed our way, continuing always in a northerly direction. Every hundred yards or so we met some obstacle, either in the way of rapids, a rocky snag, or a fallen tree-trunk, which completely blocked the stream. The tree-trunks had to be hacked through in order to get our boat past. We had now passed beyond the domain of the Waikanos, and it seemed likely that the Desanos had purposely felled a number of the trees as a protective barrier. The political frontier was something more than an imaginary line.

For many miles the jungle was unbroken by human habitation. In the evening we came to a place where the river fell over a rocky precipice, forming an imposing waterfall. Further progress in our boat was impossible, and there was still no sign of the Desanos; but one of my Indians landed, and after carefully scouring the neighborhood he came upon a tiny path which led to the rocky cliffs that overlooked the waterfall. Pursuing this path we at last came to the Desano *maloka,* where, after the usual ceremonies, we established ourselves for the night.

The Desanos belong to the same northwestern or Betoya cultural group as the Tukanos and the Waikanos, but I found many points of marked difference. Nearly all of the Aruak and Betoya tribes of this region are essentially river Indians, living on or near the banks of the larger tributaries and very seldom attempting to penetrate into the center of the jungles. The Desanos, on the other hand, have settled at the extreme headwaters of the various subtributaries, where the rivers are little more than forest brooks, continually broken by cataracts. They are essentially forest rather than river dwellers, and they have the reputation of possessing more of the secrets of the forest than most of the other tribes.

This *maloka* I found to be cruder and less extensive than those I had hitherto seen. It had none of the palatial air and appearance which, for example, Kandi's dwelling possessed. To make up for this architectural deficiency the Desanos showed me samples of weaving and basketwork finer than I had seen anywhere else.

Most important of all, perhaps, was the fact that in spite of the constant racial mixture to which the Desanos as well as the other tribes have been subjected, the Desanos, more than the others, seem to have preserved a more marked physical type. Nearly all the tribesmen here had huge broad faces, with conspicuous "Chinese" cheek-bones. The forehead was retreating but did not betray any lack of intelligence. Most striking was the bodily color. There was not the least suggestion of "red" or copper color in their pigmentation, which was a pure light yellow or lemon color.

Even according to their own traditions they are strangers to this region, as they declare that they formerly lived far to the north and west, but that they were driven out by the invading Aruaks, and they still seemed to live in fear that the Aruaks would pursue them even to their present places of refuge.

In view of this tradition I was interested to see that the Desano language presents as complicated a problem as does their true racial relationship. A large number of words are similar to corresponding words in the Tukano and Waikano languages, including such key words as those for water and fire. At first, therefore, I thought that Desano was but another Betoya dialect, but I found a large number of common words of obviously non-Betoya origin; and these words belong to no other known Amazonian language group. Who and what the Desanos are, therefore, remains a problem for the anthropologist of the future.

The language question was more than a theoretical problem that night, as I sat for hour after hour conversing with the Desanos. Tukano was here, as elsewhere, the language of diplomacy; but I found that most of the Desanos were as cramped and uncertain in their Tukano as I, and so when there was something of importance to be discussed I found it necessary to go to work more indirectly. I expounded in the simple Lingua Gerál to one of my Tariano boatmen, who would render the sense into Tukano. The Tukano was rendered into Waikano by one of my Waikano paddlers for the benefit of one of the women of the *maloka,* who had come from Kandi's domain. She finally would change the flow of wisdom into Desano for the benefit of the assembled multitude—and when the answer came it had to go through the same lengthy channel.

Finally, in order to make the communication more direct, I got out my zoölogical atlas, with its pictures of the strange animals of the jungle, and the men and

women shrieked with joy when they recognized their
four-footed acquaintances. But when we came to the picture of the dreaded jaguar, one of the men pointed to the
chief of the *maloka,* who in the meantime had fallen
asleep. Whereupon the others laughed—and at the same
time looked afraid—for the word *iya* in all Betoya
tongues denotes both jaguar and medicine-man, and the
chief was the tribal medicine-man as well. In the old
days there had been another chief, but he had fallen foul
of the wizard, and the demons of the forest had carried
him away, and now the wizard himself ruled in his stead.

Medicine-man and jaguar—to the Indian mind they
are the same thing, strange mysterious powers, sinister
and unaccountable in their actions, before whom all
other creatures quail. When a wizard dies he is
transformed into a jaguar and continues to prowl
through the forests; and even during his lifetime many
a wizard has the faculty of assuming the form of a
jaguar and of wandering at night through the jungle,
even when his human body lies fast asleep. Who knows?
Perhaps, as we saw the chief fast asleep in his corner,
his ghost was abroad roaming among the trees, whose
rustling we could hear around us.

The Desanos have far closer relation to the Pogsas,
the strange dwellers of the heart of the jungle, than
have any other tribe; and the next morning I devoted all
my attention to the wizard chief, and tried to persuade
him to take me to the wild men of the forests. He did his
best to distract my interest and desire, and spoke of the
great difficulty of penetrating into the center of the
trackless jungle, and of the difficulty of finding the
Pogsas even were we to get through.

But I would take no refusal, for I saw that my
friend knew more of the strange tribe than he cared to

admit. Eventually I found that some time previously the chief had possessed a Pogsa slave, who had been with him for several years. Subsequently the slave had been the means of saving his life, after a hunting accident, and had therefore received his freedom. The Pogsa had then gone back into the recesses of the jungle, but he had learned enough of the benefits of a settled existence to induce him to erect a small tribal hut of his own, to which he invited a number of his wild homeless companions.

The Desano chief therefore suggested that we try to reach this center, as it would at least give me the opportunity to study the Pogsa types. It would be necessary, however, to pay a surprise visit, for otherwise the Pogsas would certainly run away at our approach. I had to leave even Joaquim and my Indian paddlers behind, and trust myself to the guidance of the chief and five Desano warriors. At first our way lay once more on the water. It would have taken too long to get my boat above the waterfall, and so we went in one of the tiny dugout Indian canoes. This was the first time I had ever embarked on a real journey in one of these craft, and during the first few minutes my clumsy movements very nearly upset our party four or five times. The canoes are made out of a single hollowed log, and have perfectly round bottoms with no keel. Obviously the slightest motion to either side upsets its balance and deposits its occupants in the water. Worse still is the fact that the boats all lie so deep. There is never a hand's breadth between the water and the rim of the boat, and with six men in the canoe this space had diminished to less than an inch.

It would have been bad enough in perfectly still waters, but to make matters worse we had to pass through several small rapids, and it seemed a miracle that we were not swamped. Through my clumsiness we did ship a little water, but it was soon bailed out. I apparently had only to raise a finger and the water came in; while the Indians could stand and move about in the canoe with perfect safety. Once I felt a strong inclination to sneeze; and I made the chief put into the bank, so that I could be near dry land before daring to do so.

The stream eventually broke up into three branches, tiny brooks, on each of which was a Desano *maloka*. Up one of these streams we paddled past the *maloka,* and at last we reached a rocky gorge where the stream was so small and so turbulent that even our little canoe could not get through. We had now to abandon the boat and continue the journey by land.

The chief gave me strict instructions that I was to be absolutely silent, as otherwise the whole journey would be in vain. It was therefore impossible to walk in boots. Even I noticed the thud and the crackling noise they caused when I stepped on a leaf or twig. In spite of possible snakes, insects, and thorns, it was necessary to go barefoot, and even then warily and cautiously.

It was extraordinary to see how noiseless the Indians could be in their progress through the jungle. When I closed my eyes, I could hardly believe that five human beings were jogging along in front of me. There was no sign of a path, and I was astonished to see how quickly and adroitly the natives managed to make their way through what seemed impenetrable jungle. The Indians are really remarkable woodsmen, and I was now to find that many of the popular legends about them were true. In accordance with Leatherstocking traditions, my companions would frequently stop and point at what were, to me, invisible marks, and from these they knew what animals had crossed the track, and how, and at what time. From a trampled leaf they were able to assure me that a band of Pogsas had been in the neighborhood within the last two hours.

Hour after hour we stole through the forest. It was rough irregular country, occasionally broken by little ravines. These we crossed by walking over some fallen log which spanned the chasm; and when I saw the thin slippery nature of the bridge it was only with difficulty that I could force myself to try the passage, which seemed a good imitation of tight-rope walking. The thick undergrowth, and the trailing vines that hung from every tree, made progress difficult, and for me noiseless progress was almost impossible. Yet each time I slipped or made the slightest noise, the chief would give me an angry look and caution me to be on my guard.

At last we came to a little clearing in the forest, which had obviously been made by human hands. In the midst of it, but partly hidden by bushes, stood a roomy but ill made hut. This was the dwelling of the Pogsas. The four Indian warriors hid in the woods at various places around the clearing, so that the inhabitants of the hut could not get away without being noticed. Then the chief and I hurried on to the dwelling and made our approach known.

A general squealing and wailing went up when the Pogsas became aware of our surprise visit; but eventually they were made to understand that my intentions, at least, were friendly, and they settled down enough to allow me to observe something of their appearance and customs. I was astounded to see how different these primitive savages were from the Indians of the higher cultures. They were smaller, and for the most part in-

credibly ugly—particularly the men—for some of the
girls were rather pretty. Huge protruding jaws and
retreating foreheads were characteristic, and there was
a look of furtive cunning in their eyes such as I had
never seen before. Their long unkempt hair, their wizened haggard faces, and the bony angularity of their
bodies rendered their appearance all the more remarkable. In spite of the cunning, there was also a good deal
of apathy and dullness in their expressions, and they
contrasted with the other tribes with which I had come
into contact by showing very little curiosity or inquisi-
tiveness.

It is probable that much of the haggardness and
ugliness of the Pogsas comes from lack of proper and
consistent nourishment. Living as they do far from all
large streams, fish is an almost unknown luxury with
them; and though the Pogsas are renowned as hunters,
surpassing all other Indians in their skilled use of blowpipe and bow and arrow, the supply of game in the
Amazon forests is very irregular, so that it seems certain that between great feasts, celebrated when monkeys
and wild fowl are plentiful, are interspersed long
periods of famine rations. Among the settled Indians the
mandioca plantations give a steady supply of food, but
the Pogsas have not yet reached the stage of agriculture
and are forced to rely upon the wild roots and fruits of
the forests. This sounds all very fine. One has usually
the idea that the primeval jungles abound with edible
delicacies, that they are a sort of wild fruit garden. But
this unfortunately is pure illusion. The bananas, the
pupunhas, and the other fruits of the Amazon are only
to be seen where they have been planted by the hand of
man. The only food I could see in the Pogsa settlement
was a large number of fruit-seeds from a certain kind of

wild palm, which the other Indians use only for obtaining a dark purple dye.

Culture so primitive I had never seen before. Neither man nor woman wore a stitch of clothing. Both sexes were as naked as on the day on which they were born. There were no signs either of weaving, basket-making, or pottery. Even the ever present hammock was lacking. A heap of leaves served as a bed. Canoes were, of course, unknown. Most curious was the absence of any means of personal ornamentation that I could see. There was no paint with which the men and women could render themselves beautiful, no feather ornaments to be donned at tribal festivals—indeed among the Pogsas tribal festivals were unknown.

Is there any other people in the world, I wonder, where the peacock instinct remains equally dormant? Where neither man nor woman attempts, by queer devious means, to make him or herself more beautiful than he or she is? Is it possible that vanity is only achieved at a certain stage of evolution?

In view of the primitiveness of the life of these strange people among whom I found myself, I was interested to find evidence of two things without which human life scarcely seems possible: fire and music. Even the Pogsas, most of whom are homeless wanderers, who prowl like wild beasts through the forests, and whose very habits and instincts seem to resemble those of the animals—even these seem to have possessed the marvelous secret of fire from time immemorial. It is so here, and it seems to be so everywhere else. No traveler in any of the far-away corners of the world has found a race of men without a knowledge of fire.

And though the Pogsas possess neither gala dress nor dances nor festivities, I found in their hut a flute

made of bone (a human bone, it seemed to me). No
instrument could be more primitive. It was merely a
hollow bone with five holes in it, but when I eventually
got one of the men to play on it there welled from it
a hidden world of melody, and in the strange high notes
I seemed to hear the mournful wailing of the strange
phantoms of the jungle. The music told the story of a
race, forlorn and fleeting, groping blindly for a soul and
for expression.

The knowledge of fire, music—and laughter. These
are the three things that distinguish even the most primitive of men from the highest of the animals. The most
important of all is laughter. Even animals appreciate
warmth and respond to the appeal of music; but no
animal can laugh; and when at last these strange shy
people of the forest forgot their shyness and joked and
laughed, I realized that they and I belonged to the same
family and to the same primordial race.

The Pogsas are supposed to be without tribal organization. There is certainly not among them the hier-
archy of chief, nobles, and commoners to be found among
the other Indians. They seem to have no elaborate codes
and customs, but the reliance of the many upon the one
was to be seen here as elsewhere. The ex-slave, who had
learned during his years of slavery something of the
secrets of "civilization," who had learned to build a house
and to plan and execute, was the leader to whom the
others looked for support. He was the prophet who was
leading his people out of darkness into light.

In view of the promiscuity theory which in the last
century played such an important part in anthropology,
and according to which, at the lowest stages of human
development, the institution of marriage was unknown,
free and indiscriminate intercourse between the sexes

taking its place, it was interesting to observe that among this people marriage, and in fact monogamy, was as much the order of the day as in modern Europe. Not only so, but there seemed to prevail the same rigid rule that a man must marry outside of his own tribe which is observed by the Indians of the higher cultures, for although the higher Indians throw all these primitive savages together as Pogsas, it was obvious that the Pogsas themselves were divided into a number of tribal groups, and all the men and women I found in the hut belonged to different groups. It was obvious to me, therefore, that the mysterious Pogsas must be considered not a primitive tribe, but rather a survival of an exceedingly ancient racial group.

The language of the Pogsas I found most extraordinary. It bore no resemblance to any of the ordinary Indian dialects and contained many metallic clucks which I found it impossible to transcribe. It was therefore all the stranger to find the familiar sounds "pa" for father and "na" or "ma" for mother. These sounds almost seem to belong to a primordial universal language.

To me it seemed fairly clear that the Pogsas are the remnant of the original inhabitants of the Amazon—and probably of South America. Ages ago they were scattered all over the continent and were doubtless divided into innumerable tribes. The higher tribes of Indians, whether Karibe, Aruak, or Betoya, represent a later invading race, which has pushed this primitive people back into the heart of the jungle. The name "Maku" or "Pogsa," it is true, is confined to the wild tribes between the Rio Negro and Rio Japurá, but from various other parts of the Amazon travelers have brought back stories of fleeting homeless savages of peculiar appearance, and it is probable that all these peoples can be assigned to the same cultural stage.

In almost all cases there seems to be a wide gulf between these primitive tribes and the other Indians. Between the members of the higher tribes there is enmity and scornful disdain. The Aruaks despise and hate all Betoyas, and the feeling is heartily reciprocated, but the Aruaks have no hesitation in seizing a wife from the Betoyas, and vice versa. Marriage between a Betoya or an Aruak, on the one hand, and a Pogsa, on the other, is a thing unknown, something to be regarded with horror. Even my Desano friend went into hysterics when I vaguely repeated a Tukano canard that the Desanos had once or twice contracted such a mésalliance. The marriage of an English peer with a kinky-haired negress would cause less scandal, for even the most stubbornly conventional regard the negroes as human, while the cultured Indians look upon the Pogsa as completely animal.

The interesting question now arises: is the insuperable barrier between the Pogsas and the other Indians due entirely to cultural differences, or can it be traced back to racial differences? It is almost beyond dispute that the ordinary South American Indian is of Asiatic origin, that he is in fact a distant cousin of the Mongols. But what of the Pogsas? Are they to be derived from the same source, or from another? It is difficult to decide. There is, to be sure, in *some* ways, a general racial similarity between the two groups of Indians, at least by comparison with other races; but in other ways the appearance and physical characteristics of the Pogsas are so distinctive that one is led to presuppose a different origin. Whereas most of the Amazonian Indians have retained the broad face and round heads of the Mongolians, all of the Pogsas in this little forest settlement had thin tapering faces and markedly long heads. In many ways the heads of these living Pogsas correspond closely to very primitive skulls which have been dug up in Patagonia and other parts of South America, and which are supposed to represent an extinct race. Several scholars, including Joyce, believe that this race had its origin in Europe.

At present it is wise to avoid any sweeping statement or high-flown theory; but at least it is a remarkable fact that, whereas most of the ordinary South American Indians are brown or copper-colored, the Pogsas whom I saw were either much darker or much lighter. I could observe two distinct types among them. One was almost black, though apart from color this showed little or no negroid characteristics. The other resembled the Desano shade, a very light lemon color; in fact it was even lighter than that of the Desanos, and was scarcely darker than that of the average Latin. From time to time various well known travelers have come back with stories of white Indians in the depths of the Amazonian forests, although details have always been missing. No settlement of these Indians has ever been found. A few white faces have been seen in the depths of the forests, and these have quickly disappeared. It is quite possible that many of these stories may be traced back to casual encounters with wandering hordes of this primitive people.

All day I remained among the Pogsas studying their language and their customs. Gradually their shyness wore off. In the afternoon two or three of the hunters set out with their bows and arrows and blowpipes in search of booty. In spite of their greater primitiveness in many ways, the weapons of the Pogsas are equal in

workmanship to those of the other Indians. They are
particularly noted for their skill in the use of the blowpipe, and the poison used to tip the tiny arrows shot out
by the blowpipes is supposed to be most efficacious. The
Desano chief assured me that even he had never been
able to discover the secret of the Pogsa poison, and he
added that in the ancient days all the Betoya tribes—
Kaikanos, Tukanos, Desanos, and the rest—had known
only the bow and arrow, and that they had learned the
use of the blowpipe from the despised Pogsas, though it
seems likely that the Pogsas themselves had borrowed
the blowpipe from the Baniwa or Aruak tribes to the
north. The blowpipe seems therefore to be an Aruak
invention.

Toward evening the hunters returned with two monkeys. In the absence of pots in which to boil them, the
carcasses were laid on the fire to roast, and we all sat
down to a feast—though I noticed that the Pogsas did
not dare eat a morsel until all the Desanos had finished.

Early next morning I prepared for the return journey. Shortly before we started the Desano chief held a
long powwow with the ex-slave and the other Pogsa
notables, in the course of which he informed the poor
frightened savages that he and his Desano warriors
would leave them in peace provided they would assist
him in the preparation of a new plantation. To this,
after some murmuring, they agreed, lest a worse evil
befall them. In the Amazon, at least, the day of the
robber barons is not yet over.

We returned the same way we had come. This time
it was not so necessary to observe absolute silence, and
consequently we made much quicker time. But when at
last we reached the canoe and set out down-stream I
became a little too bold. It began to drizzle, and a heavy

storm seemed in the offing. In order to get more quickly under cover and avoid a drenching, I began to paddle along with the Indians, but I had hardly given two strokes when my clumsy motions upset the boat, and all of us were spilled into the river and were carried some distance down-stream by the force of the water before we could recover the canoe and get inside again. Fortunately this occurred in a fairly safe part of the river, or it would certainly have proved disastrous; but it was rather comical that my desire to keep a dry skin had given us all an involuntary bath. For the rest of the journey I was content to let my Indian companions do the paddling.

We returned to the Desano *maloka* early in the afternoon, but in view of the thunder-storm which had at last broken loose, it was necessary for me to wait there another day before returning to Kandi and the Waikanos.

For the preceding two or three days I had been troubled by a pain in my feet; the long march through the forest had aggravated the trouble, and I now could scarcely stand. One of the younger Desano warriors, the eldest son of the chief, seeing my difficulty, came over and gave the offending members a careful examination. He at once realized that the trouble was caused by a large number of invading sand-flies or chigoes. Why they should be called flies I cannot make out, as they have no wings and can neither fly nor hop, but lie on the surface of the ground and attach themselves to any flesh which touches them. Although they are microscopic creatures, they are able to bore deep under the flesh of the foot, particularly under the toe-nails, and there deposit their egg-sacs, each of which in time swells to the size of a pea.

Realizing what was the matter, I began excavation with a penknife, but my friend imperatively stopped me, as in my clumsy efforts I was breaking the egg-sacs. Once the sac has been broken, it is almost impossible to extract all the eggs individually. The Desano youth, seeing my inexperience, gave me an exhibition of forest surgery. With my knife he cut away a good deal of flesh around the egg-sacs, and then with a long thorn pushed and pried the remaining flesh away from the intruding bodies, so that they could at last be extracted in one lump. As a primitive but very effective antiseptic, he rubbed the wounds with strong tobacco-juice.

Altogether it was a very creditable performance, but after it I retired to my hammock and for some hours was more interested in my feet than in all the rest of the universe put together.

Even before the thunder-storm had subsided the *maloka* had begun to fill with Desanos coming from the other settlements. The news had spread that I was staying in the *maloka,* and the inquisitive neighbors had called for a friendly stare. The chief was a perfect host and master of ceremonies. He must have anticipated this coming, as the women of the *maloka* had in the meantime prepared a huge tub of *kashiri* in honor of the occasion. The whole affair seemed like a nightmare version of a very stiff European reception "to have the honour of meeting H.H. the Prince of Belgravia," but I am afraid that with my wild beard, tattered clothes, and bandaged feet I was a very poor imitation of a visiting foreign prince.

Most of the guests had, of course, never seen a white man; one young man, however, I remembered having seen several weeks before on the far-away Uaupés River.

The Indians are, within small geographical limits, great travelers and are constantly paying and receiving visits, but I was still very much struck by the fact that a Desano had strayed so far afield, particularly into what must have been, for him, hostile country; I eventually managed to worm out of him that he had undertaken his long journey with matrimonial intentions. Being forced by custom to marry outside the tribe, a young man desirous of matrimony, and eligible for it, is forced to wander abroad to secure a helpmate. But these scouting expeditions are not always successful. In spite of a journey which had lasted well over a month, my young friend had not managed to "catch" a bride. (I noticed he used the same word for catching a bride that is used for catching a fish. He had therefore returned home to rest for a few weeks, before continuing his search in another direction. The way of the lover is indeed hard, even in the land of the Amazons.

The crew I had brought with me must have tapped the *kashiri* tub earlier in the day, and finding it to their taste had emptied calabash after calabash with record speed. As a not very surprising result, my conversation with the Desanos concerning the trials of courtship was suddenly interrupted by the sounds of a battle which had broken out between two of the Tariano paddlers, who were now industriously trying to break their paddles on each other's heads.

I was amused to find that the cause of the turmoil was that one of the topers had called the other *caboclo*. Now *caboclo* is a term used by the Brazilians to denote a "civilized" Indian, one who has been duly clothed and converted, as opposed to the wild Indians of the forest. To find therefore that the free and wild Indians looked upon their civilized brethren with contempt, and that the very word *caboclo* was the most exasperating term of reproach, was not a little surprising.

The Desanos and I tried to smooth the feelings that had been ruffled, and when this proved unavailing we separated the combatants by force; but as soon as we set them free, they were at each other's heads again. After three or four encores of this tragicomedy, I had to have the two strapped and tied to their respective hammocks, from whence, being physically incapacitated, they took refuge in a long wail of mutual abuse which lasted over an hour.

The next morning when I freed them from their bonds each was much too worried about the state of his own head to concern himself about that of the other man.

Early in the day we took our departure from the home of the Desanos and toward evening reached the Waikano territory again, and the expedition was once more united. Mannling was, I think, even more delighted to see Joaquim, the cook, than me. Pequenino had been doing the cooking for him with disastrous results. To save himself the trouble of boiling two pots of water, he had used the water in which he had boiled the sweet potatoes for making the tea, and had so overloaded everything with the strong native pepper that Mannling had spent the last few hours gulping down river-water trying to find relief.

CHAPTER XIII

INITIATION INTO THE HOLY OF HOLIES

PREPARATIONS for the great ceremony were rapidly being completed. Nearly all the instruments had been made in the forest, far away from the women and from the uninitiated. The next day the last preparations were to be made, and I was eager to accompany Kandi and the other past masters to see exactly what was done, but this was denied me. I was not yet initiated and was therefore barred from witnessing any of the sacred rites. As far as I could learn from the accounts Kandi later gave me, the heart of the ceremony lay in the solemn pulling off of bark from the trees. The trees which gave the bark were regarded as holy. Humbly would the older Indians invoke the true spirits, and ask permission to remove the sacred bark from which the instruments were to be made. Tobacco-smoke was blown over the part of the tree which was to be robbed of its covering, and then, amid more incantations, long cuts were made, and the necessary amount of bark pulled off. The religious and sacramental use of tobacco was particularly interesting. It is possible that in the Indian imagination tobacco is a narcotic which prevents the sacred tree from feeling the operation that is performed upon it. When the

instruments were at last ready, they were buried deep
in the waters of the near-by river.

At last the day of days dawned. Hundreds of
visitors arrived from all parts of the Waikano domain.
Many of them I had already seen; but some faces were
new to me. The guests all gathered inside the great
maloka and gossiped and babbled at great length,
while the men were busy putting on the gala feather
adornments and having themselves painted by the
women. When everything was ready, Kandi, with
his two sons and a dozen other young men, unobtrusively disappeared in the direction of the river. Here
they rescued the instruments from the river, and from
the water's edge they blew a long deep note upon them.
There was an air of eerie melancholy, of far-away melody, about the music; but the effect upon the women
in the *maloka* was startling. It was as if a sudden panic
had broken loose. Seizing their children in their arms,
they rushed through the rear door of the *maloka,* far
away in the forest. A very real terror seemed printed
on their faces, though they must have known that the
ceremony had long been in preparation.

Two or three men followed the women, to keep
guard over them and to see that none of them desecrated
the sacred rites by their presence. To make surety
doubly sure, another four men, one at each corner, were
placed outside the *maloka* to act as sentinels, and the
rear door was solemnly closed and sealed. All my Brazilian servants were forced to remain with the women, as
they had not been chosen for initiation. But Senhor
Manoel and Mannling were allowed to remain. All the
Indians had an unholy awe of the genial Brazilian adventurer and dared not exclude him; and as I was
extremely eager to secure some pictures of the great

festival (they would be the first that had ever been taken), I eventually persuaded the Indians to allow Mannling to remain as well. It was just as well that none of them understood what he was doing with his queer box!

Once the *maloka* had been cleared of all save the initiates and the candidates for initiation, the ceremonies began. A number of the men went down to the river to join the others who were already there, and after a long incantation had been performed, Kandi and all his followers came back to the *maloka* in slow and solemn procession. Fourteen of the men arranged in seven pairs played upon the magic flutes of the demons, while others bore on their shoulders great bundles of freshly gathered fruit.

It was a festival of virility, of life-giving, of creation. To the Indians it is the man who is the creator and the life-giver, and so it is only the man who can share in the rites; and likewise, to the Indians, it is the dark mysterious spirits of the jungle—above all the great ghostly spirit of the Earth and Jungle itself (to the Indian these two things are one)—which has produced the fruits and flowers of the forests, and it is in their honor that the rites are performed.

The nature of the mysterious spirits of the jungle is profoundly obscure. The spirits are at once the creators and the destroyers, the givers and the takers of life. They breathe, and the jungle shakes with the tempest; they dream, and the trees are covered with leaves and flowers. Hence it is that the rites are strange, eerie, obscure, performed in awe and regarded with dread.

When the procession came at last into the *maloka*, the great door or entrance was also closed, and in the

dusk of the huge building it was at first difficult to see
the men or the trumpets, but the strange rising and falling notes of the music told me of their presence. The
music was deep and mysterious. Even upon me it had a
curious psychological effect. It seemed as though I
were transported from the world of everyday reality into
a land of sinister shadows and far-away echoes. Gradually, as my eyes became accustomed to the darkness,
I could make out the size and shape of the instruments
which were being played. They were really trumpets,
each with a mouthpiece made of hollowed *pashiuba*
palm, lengthened by rolls of bark. Each of the seven
pairs was of a different size and gave out one distinctive
note, but the concord between the seven pairs was such
as to produce a harmony of sounds that seemed to strike
some hidden chord of emotion. Each of the instruments
had a special secret name which might never be publicly
spoken. Each represented, and was supposed to em-
body, a special spirit of the jungle possessed of peculiar
powers.

It was clear that to the Indians these strange trumpets were no mere dead instruments of sounds but the
jungle spirits themselves, and that in breathing through
them they were directly in communion with the ghostly
beings who ruled over their destinies, who at all
ordinary times are invisible to the fleshly eye.

Inside the *maloka,* long and elaborate ceremonies
were carried out. Many of these I could but imperfectly
understand, and in any case it would be impossible to
describe them here. But a word must be said of the rites
of initiation. No woman is ever permitted to attend the
ceremonies under pain of death; but the boys, when
they have reached a certain age and have undergone
certain tests, are allowed to participate in this strange

native ceremony, which may be compared with the ceremonies of freemasonry.

On this occasion two boys were to be initiated. In addition to their long fast, these boys had been filled up with the extraordinary native drug called *kaapi*. This drug, in the form of a liquid solution, was also handed to all the other participants of the rites, and had obviously a very strong effect upon them, working them up into a sort of ecstatic delirium. Naturally enough the effect of the *kaapi* upon the two youngsters was even greater, and they declared that they saw all the demons in whose honor the ceremonies were conducted. I too received a bowl of the weird preparation and naturally had to swallow it, though the drug was so bitter that I could scarcely get it down; but curiously enough, on this occasion, it seemed to have little or no effect on me.

At a certain point in the ceremony the two youngsters were placed in the center of the *maloka*. A staff was placed in their hands, and on this they leaned, with their heads against the hilt. While the trumpets continued to play, a number of the other men seized curious dance-rattles formed from hollowed gourds, filled with acorn-like nuts; and shaking these rattles with a certain peculiar rhythm, they marched round and round the neophytes. When the music and the rhythm of the rattles had reached a point of wild abandon, the master of ceremonies stepped into the circle and rhythmically but forcibly struck the youngsters, with a long plaited whip, round the back and stomach, producing long wounds from which the blood soon began to trickle. The boys gave no cry, nor did they in any way cringe. Rather they seemed to regard the pain as an ecstatic pleasure. I must confess that I saw this procedure with ominous foreboding. I had not had enough of the magic *kaapi* to reduce me to the state where the flogging would have been an exhilarating thrill, and yet, as I was classed as a candidate for initiation, I had qualms that I too should have to undergo this ceremonial, but very real, whipping. A special exception, however, was made in my case and in that of my two white companions, and our frail skins were left untouched.

The Indians have a firm belief that the sacred *juru-pari* rites not only banish all evil influences but bring about all manner of cures. I was therefore interested to see that one old tribesman, whom I had plied with pills in vain, trying to cure him of a rheumatic fever, and who could scarcely move, was now dancing, stamping, and rattling as wildly as the others. Whether this was due to the weird music, or to the *kaapi,* or to the influence of the spirits of the jungle, is more than I can say.

After the ceremony of initiation was over, the trumpets were blown in every corner of the *maloka* lest some lurking evil should remain. Then the dregs of the *kaapi* drug were solemnly played out of the *maloka* and thrown amid wild incantation into the great square outside. With this the rites were at an end. The fourteen players once more formed a procession and to the last long wailing notes marched down to the river, where the instruments were again buried underneath the waters.

The doors of the *maloka* were now opened, the sentinels set free, and the women allowed to return. As they came in I was surprised to see that many of them had tears streaming from their eyes. Far away in the forest they had heard the wailing tones of the instruments they were never allowed to see, and so haunting were the tones of this strange melody that, as one old lady informed me, memories of old forgotten days, of children who had long been dead, and of the dreamy days of their own childhood, had welled up within them.

Even now that I had witnessed the famous *jurupari* rites, rumors of which had reached far down the river to distant Manáos, I was left with a sense of mystery. What was the real meaning and the origin of the rites which I had seen? The *jurupari* rites are the peculiar property of the forest dwellers of the northwest Amazon basin. They are not found anywhere else in the South American continent, and yet inside this region they are common to all the tribes, both Aruak and Betoya. The Indians cling tenaciously to the mysteries, even if they cannot understand their ultimate import. I could not forget that the Catholic missionaries had lost their lives as soon as they had attempted to interfere with this performance.

The exclusion of the women appears to be very strict. Kandi came to me again and again and implored me to say nothing to the women about what I had seen, and above all not to reveal the secret names of the trumpets which I had been taught; for if, even by accident, a woman were to see the festival or any of the instruments, or even to hear the name of the instruments, she must die. Senhor Manoel, experienced in these matters, told me of a number of cases where such a death had taken place. The unfortunate woman is supposed to die automatically, that is, to be killed by the forest spirits; but I have a strong suspicion that if the spirit declines the task the lady is given some secret slow-working poison by the medicine-man.

Soon after the return of the women, the air of mystery completely disappeared. We were at the beginning and not at the end of the festivities. The women soon covered themselves with a coat of paint, the harmless Pan-pipes took the place of the deep sounding trumpets, and the ordinary dancing began. These dances were much the same as those which I had seen in Yawarete, but this time they did not appear so strange, and I was able to appreciate and enter into their melody and rhythm; and whereas in Yawarete I was forced to remain a mere spectator, on this occasion I joined in the dances myself. Mannling and da Silva at first held aloof, but it was not long before even their reserve melted, and they participated in the dances as heartily as I.

The private dances proved somewhat difficult. It was not easy at any time for me to extract any noise, much less a tune, from the primitive Pan-pipes; and when in addition I had to join arms with two youngsters and stamp wildly around the *maloka,* it was impossible for me to produce any noise except an occasional squeak from one of the higher notes. But it made no difference. The rhythm was there, and the pace, and the shrill notes of other Pan-pipes from every corner of the crowded *maloka*; so hour after hour I stamped and ran, and panted with the rest. There was indeed a lively rhythm about the dances, far more than with most of the other exotic dances I have seen.

The Chinese, the Japanese, the East Indian dancing is impressive but slow, and to our minds lifeless and rhythmless. One watches, but the feet do not instinctively keep time. One must go to the negro before one finds a tempo that is as contagious as this in the Amazon jungle. And yet—and yet the rhythm, the melody, is curiously elusive. Hour after hour through the long night I listened and danced to the music. I had heard

it before in Yawarete, and was destined to hear it time
and again in the many months that followed; yet
neither Mannling, who possessed a musical ear, nor I
could ever impress the melody or the tune upon our
memories. As soon as we tried to whistle it, it was gone.

The "tribal" dances, which were interspersed between the trios danced by the young men and women,
were more formal and stately. They were attended by
much of the ceremonial courtliness of the ancient
minuet. Here, as in Yawarete, all the women were
gathered in the center of the *maloka,* with the male hosts
at the rear, while the male guests were seated on long
benches at the front of the great tribal dwelling. Before each of the communal dances, the master of ceremonies would strut to the front of the *maloka.* On his
left arm was a shield, beautifully woven from bamboo,
and hung with feathers. In his right hand was held the
lance of state, a long, splendidly rounded and polished
war-lance, with a shaft which formed a rattle. As he
struck the lance against his shoulder, the sound of the
rattle reverberated through the whole company, com-
manding silence. Then to each one of the male guests
he would go inviting him to dance the dance of the
elders. One by one the men would rise, seize each his
wooden pounder, and join in the procession led by the
master of ceremonies.

In a long line the men would march around and
pound the four central pillars of the *maloka,* forming
a circle around the assembled women-folk. Then,
prompted by four of the men in the middle of the line,
who acted as dance leaders, the men began a long melodious chant. Accompanied only by the pounding of the
dance-drums, the voices rose and fell in perfect accord.
The words were very old, so old that the meaning of

many had long been forgotten, but the meaning of the song as a whole was clear. It was a chant of enticement, of invitation, to the women:

Come, little sister, come.
Our faces and bodies are painted with beautiful colors and
    designs.
Come, little sister, come.
We have donned the plumage of all the wondrous birds of the
    forest.
Come, little sister, come.
Our shoulders are covered with the teeth of the jaguar, who
    prowls through the forests at night.
Come, little sister, come.
The birds and the beasts of the jungle could not escape us.
    They flew, or they ran, but our arrows were quicker.
Come, little sister, come.

When the long recital of their prowess and of the items of their dance regalia had come to an end, the women rose and accepted the very pressing invitation of the men to dance with them. Each woman picked out her own partner, and, as in Yawarete, the married women by no means always chose their husbands. The young dame who had perpetually pestered me with questions as to my family status shoved her head under my shoulder in five out of the seven tribal dances in which I joined, and I could not say her nay.

As in Yawarete I saw that four of the women had divested themselves of their skirts and were clothed only with paint and a bead bangle. These I found were the female dance-leaders, who invariably danced with the four males from whom the others took the time and steps. The "morals police," were once more in evidence. They remained standing inside the circle, keeping their eye on the long swaying procession and occasionally letting out a long wavering cry.

Round and round we went, but it took ever so long to complete the circle. Three long steps to the left, two steps marking time, three short steps backward, two short steps to the right, three steps marking time, and then again three long steps to the left, and so on indefinitely. Whenever I made a false step my fair partner would give me a nudge, and under her careful tuition I was soon dancing with the best of them. As soon as the women-folk had joined them, the men started another song, this time a long chant of triumph which lasted until the end of the dance.

When at last the dance did come to an end, the sexes were once more separated, the women squatting in the middle of the *maloka* and the men resuming their seats on the benches toward the front. There were, however, two great exceptions to this rule. Da Silva and Pequenino found the society of the males rather tame and preferred to remain with the ladies, rather to the scandal of the morals police. Da Silva, undeterred by their dismay, proceeded to have a violent, even though harmless, flirtation with both the police women (each of whom was old enough to be his mother), and so managed to maintain his ground. Pequenino was less careful in his choice, and, to my delight, the dusky damsel to whom he paid attentions soundly boxed his ears, so that he was forced to retire from the fray.

I, for my part during the interludes, sat in state among the visiting elders. After every dance copious drafts of *kashiri* were brought, and so by nightfall even the elders forgot some of their formality and began to recite wondrous tales of their youth, of the hunts for the wild boar (peccary) and the tapir, and of the wars

and battles in which they had been engaged. I could
understand only one of their words in ten, and to them
my descriptions of the wondrous white man's land were
equally unintelligible. But all of us sat content and at
peace with the world. Every few seconds my neighbor
on my right or left would seize my pipe, take a few
puffs, and then hand it back. Sometimes it would go
down the whole line of warriors on the bench before it
came back to me. Not very hygienic, perhaps, but it was
the pipe of friendship and of peace, and in return I was
expected to puff at the great native cigars that were
handed down the line.

Nightfall was no hindrance to the festivities, for
the Indians have learned that splinters from the wood
of a certain tree burn very slowly and give ample light.
In addition to these wooden candles, huge masses of
pitch were placed on poles driven into the ground at each
corner of the *maloka,* and each of these gave out a blaze.

Kandi's two sons played an important part in the
festivities, both of them acting as dance-leaders, but the
chief himself kept serenely aloof. He had not donned
either paint or feathers, but, adorned only with a huge
straw hat he had woven for himself (a curiosity this, as
the Indians ordinarily wear no head-covering), he
moved solemnly through the company, critically in-
specting the whole proceeding.

I could not fail to be amused at one of the curious
aspects of Indian etiquette. In the course of the many
long hours of the day and night, it was of course necessary for the men to go outside to perform a natural
function; but far from making an unobtrusive exit,
each man would ceremonially stand before every other
occupant of his bench and would announce to him formally what he was going to do. From each the answer

would come, "May you do so mightily." On his return
he would once more go the round and announce to each
person, "I have done so mightily," which evoked the
invariable refrain, "It is good that you have done so."

As is usual, the festivities lasted all through the
night and far into the next day, with no intermission
for food or sleep. In the early dawn, the men, spurred
on by the *kashiri* which they had steadily imbibed, hied
themselves in thought back to the days of warfare and
glory, and, armed with javelins and shields, executed a
long and elaborate pantomime dance, illustrating the
stealthy attack on an enemy settlement, ending in a
wild shout as the enemy's *maloka* was taken by storm.
So realistic was this performance, and so wildly passionate were the performers, that for a bit I imagined
they might take it into their minds to have an encore,
with my little party representing the enemy. I wakened
Mannling and da Silva, who had both in the meantime
fallen asleep, and warned them to look out for trouble,
particularly as I knew that several of the fiercer tribesmen had been very much opposed to our initiation into
the *jurupari* rites the day before. But as luck would have
it, the dissatisfied warriors had so thoroughly drowned
their dissatisfaction in *kashiri* that they had not held
out until this dance, and so everything passed over
smoothly.

When at last the festivities came to an end, there
followed two days of aching heads and swollen tongues,
in which nothing could be done. All my crew were temporarily *hors de combat*—and *hors de travail*. Kandi,
as was natural, was the first to recover, and so I utilized
the enforced idleness trying to persuade him to let me
have the *jurupari* instruments, to be added to my collection. For hours I met with stubborn opposition. The

instruments were sacred and must not be parted with. The generous offers I made him only awakened his scorn. To Kandi, savage though he was, the things of the spirit were beyond price, and he refused uncompromisingly to barter them. I had to play upon his finer feelings, and picture to him the despair of my white subjects (to all the Indians I was a great chief), who would have to continue to live without the sacred trumpets that enabled one to have direct communication with the mysterious spirits; and eventually he consented to *give* them to me as a special mark of honor and esteem.

I had, however, most solemnly to promise that I would never allow any woman to see them, and now that I have brought the instruments back to Europe, this same promise troubles me. In view of my promise, dare I give these strange trumpets to a museum for public exhibition? I should like to have some good casuist give me advice.

The preparation of the instruments for transport caused no little trouble. All the women had to be kept with various excuses away from the water's edge, while the youngsters dived down once more to rescue the trumpets from under the rocks where they had been safely tucked away. Fortunately I had with me a good deal of sacking, and I had the instruments carefully wrapped up in this. To my mind the women were now safe from the lingering death which would be caused by a view of the trumpets, but Kandi was not yet satisfied. The women could still see the sacks in which the trumpets were hidden, and even this might cause disaster. The smaller instruments had to be tucked away under all the other baggage, and the sack containing the larger trumpets had to be tied underneath the boat, as a sort of

keel. Even the freemasons of Europe do not guard their
secrets more carefully.

During the succeeding day Kandi kept hovering
around me, fixing me with a peculiar glare, and several
times he seemed to be on the verge of bursting into an
oration, but each time he checked himself, and beat a
retreat. I was afraid that he had repented of his rash-
ness in giving me the instruments and wished to get
them back. In spite of his friendliness I still had a
healthy respect for Kandi, mingled with a little fear,
and so I was rather troubled as to what was going to
happen next.

Eventually, supported by his two sons, he came once
more to where da Silva and I were sitting and proceeded
to unburden his soul. To my astonishment and relief,
no word was spoken concerning the *jurupari* affair. He
had heard of the titles and honors which old Nicolao had
received from the Brazilian government, and his soul
was eaten up with the desire to receive similar honors
for himself. After speaking, therefore, of the great difficulties which we were likely to meet on our further
journey through the jungle, of the danger of becoming lost and of the hostility of other tribes, he at length
proposed that he and his two sons should accompany
us as guides on our long wanderings through the wilderness back to civilization, asking in return only that
I should request the governor of Amazonas to give him
official recognition and a military title.

This proposition was, I think, almost unique in the
history of South American Indians. To Kandi it meant
leaving his forest kingdom for many months, passing
through the territory of many tribes which were bit-
terly hostile to his own, and finally venturing into the
white man's land, before which every Indian stands

in breathless awe and fear—and all this for an empty
name! The Indians of the forest are as human as the
European who gives away half his fortune for a title.

Needless to say, I accepted Kandi's offer with
alacrity. His help would be invaluable, particularly
when the time came for my crew to return to Yawarete.
It was very doubtful whether we should be able to get
other Indians to take their place, and to be left stranded
in the heart of the jungle would be more than a passing
joke. Kandi and his two sons were all stalwart fellows,
and with them and the Brazilian servants, I thought it
would be possible to maneuver our boats unaided, if the
worst came to the worst.

Kandi's packing did not take long to accomplish.
He and his sons had only to roll up their hammocks and
select a good bow and a dozen poisoned-tipped arrows,
and their equipment for the long journey was ready.
How much I wished that we could travel with an equal
scarcity of luggage! But the ceremonial leave-taking
was to occupy much more time. Kandi's cousin, the
medicine-man, was to act as regent, and with elaborate
ceremonial Kandi handed over the reins of authority
in a long singsong chant. Every *maloka* in the domain
was mentioned by name; the names of all the subordi-
nate chiefs were recited, as well as the names of all the
dwellers in Kandi's own *maloka;* and after each name
came the invariable refrain: "This lies within thy domain. This must be guarded and ruled."

When this important devolution of power had been
attended to, we were ready to depart. All the tribesmen gathered at the water's edge to see their chief start
off on his long journey with the strange white men,
and they no doubt wondered if he was ever to return.

CHAPTER XIV

INTO HOSTILE TERRITORY

THE first couple of days we had to retrace our path down the Maku Igarape. At last we reached the main stream of the Papuri again and halted at Kandi's *maloka* to secure the heavy baggage, the boat, and the portion of the crew that I had left there. When this was done we set our faces once more up-stream.

Kandi chose to be the pilot of the *Bella Tristeza,* and his two sons turned out to be my most zealous paddlers, in spite of their princely rank. Through their zeal we were now able to make quicker progress.

For several days we were inside the Waikano domain. As most of the inhabitants of the *malokas* had assembled at the *jurupari* festival, I could now greet them almost as old friends. The chief of one of the *malokas* had, however, been prevented by age from coming. He was a hoary old gentleman, and must have been well over ninety years of age, but was still in perfect possession of his faculties, and laid about him with a stick, when any of the younger tribesmen were not quick enough in executing his demands.

The Indians seem generally to live to a fairly advanced age. Men and women of eighty (as far as one can estimate age, for the Indians have no native method of calculation) are by no means uncommon. This may well be due to a sort of survival of the fittest. Infant mortality is high—the women are always bewailing the loss of their children—and those who survive infancy must be pretty sturdy.

It is remarkable how many of the modern advocates of eugenics revert to principles which have long been practised by savages. In Europe one hears long-winded discussion of the desirability of sterilizing unfit stock. The Indians of the Amazon have a sweeter and shorter method of keeping the species up to standard. Struck by the marked absence of all deformed persons among the tribes I had visited, I asked two or three of the chiefs about it. The others evaded a direct answer, but Kandi, direct and outspoken as ever, declared that imperfect babies were killed at birth. This certainly would appear to be the general if not the invariable rule. It was interesting to see that Kandi shared a common primitive belief that twins were monstrosities and should likewise be removed from existence. Among certain tribes in the northwest one of the twins is allowed to survive—the healthiest looking. The Waikanos seem to support the doctrine that both infants should be made away with.

One of the Waikano *malokas* we visited made a very peculiar impression upon me. In the first place I was struck by the fact that I had seen none of its inhabitants at the great *jurupari* festival; and furthermore, wandering around the *maloka*, I could find no trace of the paint-box and feather adornments which are almost invariably to be found in a large basket suspended by a cord from one of the beams of the *maloka*. Equally remarkable was the curt and peremptory way in which Kandi addressed the head of the establishment, and the servile manner in which he was answered.

After much questioning I eventually wormed out of my friend the meaning of all this. We were in a colony of the vile proletariat. Whereas the Tukanos and the Desanos are in the habit of catching or trying to catch the roving Pogsas, and forcing them to do all the heavy and obnoxious work, the Waikanos consider the Pogsas so low that they will not even have them as household slaves—the very presence of the Pogsas meaning pollution. But the Waikanos seem to be in need of a working-class, as much as the other tribes, and so they have solved the problem by declaring the inhabitants of one *maloka* outcasts, and forcing these poor unfortunates to aid them in carrying out all sorts of heavy work. At ordinary times these semi-serfs are allowed to lead their own life in their own settlement undisturbed. But when Kandi wishes to build a new *maloka,* or to clear a particularly large area of jungle, a summons is sent to the wretches, and they are forced to render unpaid assistance.

Not only are these serfs not invited to attend the great tribal festivals, but they are forbidden to institute such affairs among themselves. Dances, feather ornaments, and *jurupari* ceremonies must be limited to their social betters. There must be a reason for this social outlawry, but I was unable to discover it. The outlaws appear to be of as pure Waikano descent as their more fortunate cousins. This was admitted even by Kandi; otherwise I should have imagined that they were the descendants of captured and tamed Pogsas. At some time in the distant past their forefathers must have done something to win tribal contempt, and the sins of the fathers have been visited upon the children and grandchildren.

Perhaps they can consider themselves fortunate that

at ordinary times they are left to themselves, and that they are allowed to profit by the harvest of their own plantations and the booty of their bow and arrows, without being forced to render tribute to their masters. They appear, at any rate, to have learned the art of industry. When we arrived the men were busy finishing two native dugout canoes. I was particularly interested to hear from them that they were making these canoes, not for their own benefit (they had already enough for their own use), but for the purpose of barter. They were hoping to dispose of their two boats in return for an ax from some of the Indians down the rivers.

In spite of their complete ignorance of mathematics, and in spite of the absence of money or any other medium of exchange (even Kandi could not understand my repeated attempts to explain to him the nature and use of money), the Indians of the northwest Amazon have a thriving system of intertribal commerce. To be sure, each tribe, each *maloka,* is very nearly self-supporting. There is no export or import of foodstuffs, and at a pinch each tribe can, and does, make its own pots, build its own boats, and weave its own hammocks and baskets. But it is only natural that each tribe should achieve preëminence in some one line, and that these especially well made products should be desired by the other tribes.

The Tarianos and the Waikanos are the most expert potters: the Tarianos, being Aruaks, have better coloring for their pots; but the Waikanos have invented more graceful shapes. The Desanos excel the other tribes in the art of basket-making. The Tukanos are the inventors of the beautifully carved and decorated stools upon which the Indians are accustomed to sit. It is therefore not infrequent that a Tukano will dispose of one of his stools in order to get Desano baskets or Waikano pots. More curious still was the origin of the beautifully worked *mandioca* graters which I had seen everywhere since entering the domain of the Indians. These consist of rounded boards into which sharp tiny stones have been inserted in such a way as to form elaborate geometrical patterns. Nowhere on the rivers along which we had passed had I seen any stones corresponding to those in the graters, but it was only at this point that I solved the secret which seemed to shroud this matter. All of these graters had come from the Baniwas, the Aruak tribes which dwell on the Isana River, which lies many hundreds of miles north of where we were. None of my friends had ever seen a Baniwa or ever been to the Isana River, but by constant bartering and rebartering, the graters have spread over a territory five hundred miles and more in diameter. Not a bad achievement for a people who have no medium of exchange, and who can only with difficulty count up to ten.

Are the philosophers right? Is mathematical knowledge really inherent in every human mind? Kant with obscure polysyllables assures us that arithmetic, algebra, and geometry are *a priori* postulates, innate to man, and not learned by experience. Plato in more charming language tells us the story of Socrates's conversation with an unlettered youngster who is yet under the master's influence, able to work out for himself the principles and problems of geometry. A very fine story, but I should like to have seen Socrates conversing with an Amazonian Indian on the subject of conic sections. Had he done so I think we should have had a much revise version of the dialogues.

After we had continued our voyage up the main

Papuri River for several days, we once more came to
a series of very troublesome rapids known as the Beijú
Cachoéira. Here we had the usual trouble of unloading and carrying the baggage through the forest to a
point higher up the river, while the boats themselves
were hauled over a very trying series of rocks. Very
appropriately the Indians had chosen this natural barrier as a territorial frontier. The Waikano domain ruled
over by Kandi came to an end here, and we found ourselves once more among the Tukanos, the largest and,
in many ways, the most powerful group among the
natives of the northwest Amazon basin, even though
they are more disintegrated and less efficiently organized than the Waikanos, who had been bullied into
efficiency by Kandi.

In former days the Tukanos formed a unified whole
and were not broken up into isolated groups, but even
to-day, in the period of Tukano decline, they continue
to exercise a great deal of prestige. Even Kandi and his
sons were affected. They seemed to regard the Tukanos
as the Goths must have regarded the magnificent
Roman civilization after the fall of the imperial city;
and the Tukanos, in spite of their formal politeness,
were not modest in showing their disdain for members
of every other tribe.

The Tukanos I had met further down the river had
given me a very cordial reception, but in this the very
heart of the proud and arrogant tribe the welcome accorded us in the first instance was distinctly cooler.
Their distrust of the white man was obvious, and
I felt it necessary to double all my ordinary precautions. On no account was I prepared to turn back; but
I was beginning to feel a little anxious as to what was

to become of us, when I was once more helped by a curious bit of luck.

Two days after entering the Tukano territory, while we were busy paddling our boats up-stream, a terrific thunder-storm broke loose. It was accompanied by such a strong wind that it was impossible for us to make any further progress, and we had to lie under a bank for about two hours. Even here we did not feel very safe; ominous cracks and the sounds of heavy falling told us that the gale was throwing down many of the aged giants and weaker brethren of the forest, and we did not know when the trees beneath which we had taken refuge would fall upon us. In our own case our fears proved unfounded, but when at last the storm was over and we could make our way to the next *maloka,* we found that others had not been so fortunate.

A girl who had been gathering fire-wood in the jungle, when the gale broke loose, turned to fly back to the *maloka.* The wind blew over a great palm-tree, which fell upon her head; knocking her senseless. When we arrived on the scene we found the inhabitants of the *maloka* gathered around what they took to be an inanimate corpse. I made a careful examination, however, and found that the palm must have fallen on her in a slanting direction, and that, though it had split open her scalp, producing a terrible wound which reached from low in the forehead almost to her neck, she was only stunned. The flesh had been cut and jammed aside, leaving the skull exposed to view (not a pleasant sight), but the skull itself by some miracle had not been broken or even cracked.

As soon as the *maloka* chief saw us approaching, he began the long greeting ceremony which Indian etiquette demanded, quite as if the accident had not occurred, but I deputed Kandi to fulfil all the social obligations while I proceeded to do what I could for the unfortunate girl. The palm that had caused the damage was one of the numerous species which are guarded by innumerable small, black, hard thorns all along their trunks. A large number of these had found their way into the lacerated flesh, and it was first of all necessary to remove these. After this, it was fairly simple work to stitch the scalp together, though it is extraordinary how tough human flesh is, and how much force is needed to drive a needle through it. When this was done, I poured some stimulants down the girl's throat and was delighted to see that after a few minutes she began to recover consciousness.

Her return to life made an enormous impression upon the Indians, who by this time had fulfilled the demands of social etiquette and had once more gathered around the victim of the accident. It was obvious that the spectators labored under the delusion that I had resurrected the girl from the dead. As the result of this little occurrence, the tone of hostility which I had observed among the Tukanos seemed to vanish, and I was assured of a certain amount of respect, not only among the dwellers in the *maloka,* but throughout the Tukano territory, for I was later to find that the news of the "miracle" had spread like wildfire to all the other *malokas* of the surrounding region. As long as we stayed inside the Tukano territory, we had no fear of attack.

If I was able to teach the Indians something in the way of sewing up wounds, the Indians were able to teach me something in the way of a cure for toothache. All the way along the journey Pequenino and I had taken turns at the toothache. This time it was his turn to possess a smoldering molar, and as I had been foolish enough to bring no forceps, I could only fill him up with various pain-killers, which came nearer killing him than the pain. In this *maloka* one of the women, who noticed the fond way in which Pequenino clung to his own cheek, brought out a curious sort of resin (in Lingua Gerál called *caranha*), which when placed in the tooth cavity caused the pain to vanish almost immediately. This appears to be the only way in which the Indians treat toothache. They seem to have invented no substitute for forceps (tooth-filling is of course unknown), and they wait until a bad tooth is sufficiently loose so that it can be extracted with the fingers. The native medicine-men are able to massage the jaws in such a way as materially to lessen the pain, but they have not added dental surgery to their accomplishments.

The old dame who brought the resin saw that I was interested in her remedy and gave me a long lecture on its qualities and uses. The quarter of the lecture which I was able to understand sufficed to inform me that the resin was used also on sores of every description in order to render them antiseptic; more important still, it was the native substitute for a safety-razor. The Indians made a great point of keeping their faces and bodies free from hair. Fortunately for themselves, they have, like the Mongols, a very scanty natural growth of facial and bodily hair, but what little fuzz does appear had carefully to be removed. As their knives were not sharp enough for the purpose, they smeared their fingers with the resin and seized the intruding hair. They then forcibly pulled their hand away—and the hair was gone. It was rather drastic treatment (the lady experimented with a part of my beard, so that I know by personal experience), but it was very effective.

CHAPTER XV

VAMPIRE-BATS

JUST as it was necessary to go about the *malokas* and seize everything that looked interesting— as the Indians never dreamed of bringing anything forward of their own accord—so was it also necessary to peer and probe and interrogate interminably in order to secure any information regarding native customs and beliefs; almost no information was volunteered.

A day or two after the episode of the broken head, I had a striking instance of this reticence. On arriving at a new *maloka,* I noticed that one of the "family apartments" was screened off by mats. This desire for privacy was so unusual that I was curious to find out its cause, but my eager questioning met with apathy. Senhor Manoel refused to take any interest in so small a matter as a few feet of matting, and I was forced to do all the questioning myself. The only explanation I could elicit was that one of the young men was ill.

In the drowsy tropical twilights, one does not feel inclined to press issues, and for a time I let the matter drop. But after I had been strengthened by dinner, I returned once more to the fray. Why should the Indians screen off one sick man and leave others exposed to public gaze? Could it be that the natives had a primitive manner of isolating infectious diseases?

With the aid of Senhor Manoel I broke through the matted barrier and examined the young man who lay in the hammock, discovering that he was suffering from excessive loss of blood caused by the attacks of vampire-bats. Twice in the last few nights he had been visited by these malignant creatures, and was now so weak that he could not stand. The Indians assured me that the vampire always came back to the person it had once attacked rather than pick out a fresh victim. The youngster had been screened off by mats largely in order to protect him from a fresh attack, which in his weakened condition might prove fatal.

I remarked that although the *sides* of the apartment were screened off, there was no covering *above,* except the great roof of the *maloka,* inside which the bats could find their way. I was assured, however, that vampires never descend directly upon their victims, but swoop in low circles just above the ground until they have smelled out the object of their attack. Altogether it seemed that the Indians had made a profound study of the psychology of bats. No doubt they had had ample opportunity for gathering data. I had long since heard that the region was notorious for vampires, although this was the first direct evidence I had come across.

Seeing my interest in the subject, the father of the youngster begged me to give him a meter of good stout cloth, so that he could prepare rough slippers for the boy's feet. The bats, it seemed, almost invariably made for the toes, though they would occasionally alight on the fleshy part of the nose. If the nose and the toes were protected, a man was supposed to be immune from attack, even though the rest of his body were uncovered.

I was quite willing to part with the cloth, and we soon had the youth's feet and nose suitably swathed. During the process I had occasion to observe the nature of the wounds the bat had inflicted. They consisted of four narrow but deep holes where the fangs had entered the flesh. In view of the depth of the wounds, it seemed almost impossible to believe that they could have been made without awakening the victim. Bats are believed not to possess any saliva which could act as a local anesthetic; and yet it is a fact that they can insert their long teeth and suck out the blood of their victims without awakening them. Not a single case is known in which a sleeper has awakened while the vampires were at their work. It is also very curious that bats never attack a person who is awake, however silent and motionless he may be. Consequently it is still a profound mystery exactly how the bats carry out their bloodthirsty work.

To me it is equally mysterious how the vampires continue to keep alive if it be really true that they live solely upon blood. Special regions of the Amazon forest contain hundreds of thousands of these creatures. The human life in the forests would certainly not suffice to keep a hundredth part of them alive. Contrary to popular belief the ordinary animal life in the jungle is far from rich, and it would certainly not be sufficient to provide nourishment for the vast numbers of vampires. It seems certain that the vampire-bats must be able to go for long periods without food; or else they, like their less interesting cousins, the ordinary bats, must also be able to assimilate fruit and insects.

The Indians gave me such graphic descriptions of the vampire-bats and their bloodthirsty habits that I had great difficulty in falling asleep that evening. Although our stock of petroleum was getting very low, I kept my lantern burning all night, as I was assured that the light would keep the bats away. As an additional precaution (such is the cowardice of even a professional "explorer"), I went to bed in my boots and tied a handkerchief around my nose. The next morning I found that the vampires had indeed revisited the *maloka,* but their only victim had been one of the scrawny chickens which had not been properly cooped up the night before. The carcass of this unwary fowl I secured as payment for my cloth sandals. Incidentally I had already noticed in many of the *malokas* through which we had passed that the Indians had an efficient way of protecting their fowls from bats and other nocturnal marauders. One of the huge *kashiri* pots turned upside down made an excellent chicken-coop, especially when a hole had been knocked in the side which allowed the hens to come in and out, but which was carefully closed every evening when they had gone to roost.

All the way along I found that the Indians were glad to get my cheap Brazilian cigarettes. This was rather surprising, as nearly every *maloka* had a small tobacco plantation. Tobacco appeared to be a really native product. It must have existed in this region long before the weed was known to Europeans. The quality of the Indian tobacco was good, although the method of curing it was primitive. The Indians would gather the raw tobacco leaves and dry them near a fire. The leaves would presently be moistened again and then pounded together so as to form a sort of cylindrical brick. From these tobacco bricks huge cigars would be made, averaging from two to three feet in length.

The cigars were usually reserved for festival occasions. One cigar sufficed for a whole community at a sitting. The cigar was usually held in a huge wooden prong or fork elaborately carved and decorated. The local chief took the first whiff of the cigar, which was then handed around to the other male members of the community. The cigars were frightfully strong, as I learned to my cost. I too was forced to take a whiff from the communal cheroot, and although I had long been accustomed to the rankest shag, I was nearly bowled over by this Amazonian substitute for a peace-pipe.

I think that even the Indians must have found the cigars very strong, as they were reserved for high and solemn moments when the natives did not mind getting dizzy. This would account for the popularity of my cigarettes. Tribal etiquette prohibited the women from smoking the huge cigars, for the cigars had almost a religious significance, and the women of the Amazon basin were not permitted to have anything to do with religion. But I found that the ladies could and would puff away at my cigarettes as well as any male.

The Indian males seemed to think it even better to get a whiff from my pipe than to receive a whole cigarette for themselves. I am sure that my poor pipe was shoved into at least a thousand mouths besides my own before I lost it.

Tobacco appears to be known to all the tribes of the Amazon basin, though the method of smoking varies slightly from tribe to tribe. My Tukano host told me with much merriment of a strange custom practised by the Witoto Indians, who lived many hundreds of miles to the south. According to my informant the Witotos never *smoked* tobacco, but preferred to boil the tobacco-leaves to a thick juice, which was placed in a special jar in the middle of the *maloka*. Of an evening when the men were gathered together to discuss affairs of state, a warrior would put forth some proposition and then dipping a stick into the tobacco-juice pass it over his tongue. All who agreed with him would follow his example as a token of assent.

My host told me many other stories concerning the Witotos, whose customs seemed to be fairly well known in this region, in spite of the great distance that separates the Witotos from the Tukanos. The Witoto women, I was told, wore no clothing at all but were very fond of painting themselves with elaborate designs, designs much more elaborate than those executed by the Betoya tribes. Painting of some sort seemed to be common to all the Amazonian Indians, but I could find no definite trace of tattooing.

I had seen tobacco everywhere among the Indians from the very beginning of my journey, but it was only after leaving the Waikano territory that I first came into contact with the extraordinary stimulant known as coca. It is from the coca-leaf that the Europeans prepare the insidious drug cocaine. But as prepared and used by the Indians, coca appears to have a much less dangerous effect; some would even ascribe to it a beneficial action. Even so, there appears to be a sharp boundary line between the users and non-users of coca. To the south and west of where we were, stretched the coca territory, almost without a break, to far-away Peru. To the north and east, in the country through which we had passed, I had found no trace of it. The Waikanos looked upon the drug with disgust, and even the Tukanos on the main Uaupés River seemed to be unacquainted with its use, but the Tukanos on the Papuri were coca addicts. This seemed to argue for a spread of the coca habit in this region at a comparatively recent date, certainly after the break-up of the Tukano nation into a number of different groups.

Coca was one of the principal drugs at the ancient court of the Incas in Peru. It is very probable that the knowledge of the drug has gradually spread eastward through the jungle as a posthumous working out of Inca influences, for coca could not have reached this region until long after the downfall of the Inca Empire.

In the course of coca's progress through the jungle, the method of its preparation seems to have undergone a good deal of modification. Ancient chronicles tell us that the subjects of the Inca emperors were in the habit of chewing coca-leaves. This was simplicity itself compared with the work my Tukano friends had to do before the drug could be consumed. On several occasions I watched some of the younger tribesmen go through the stages of preparation. First of all, the leaves would be plucked from the coca-bush and then dried or roasted in a pot over the fire. The dry leaves would then be pounded in a mortar into a rough powder. To this powder would be added the ashes of burnt begonia leaves, and the mixture then placed inside of a sack attached to a long pole. The sack was pounded against the walls of a wooden cylinder until the refined coca-powder gradually seeped through the sack, leaving the impurities inside. The coca was then ready for consumption.

By means of a special spoon or ladle made of bone, the coca-powder was scooped into one side of the mouth and there gradually allowed to dissolve, whereupon it was automatically swallowed with the saliva. A coca taker always looked like a man with an abscessed tooth.

The effects of the drug are remarkable. It allows a man to go for days and nights on end without either eating or sleeping and to accomplish marvels of physical exertion while under its influence. When famine comes or when a long journey has to be undertaken, the Indian has only to swallow his drug to be prepared for all emergencies. But unlike cocaine, coca does not seem to have any markedly deleterious effect upon the body. Even habitual users seem to live to a great age with unimpaired physical powers, though I noticed that coca users were usually not so clean personally as those who avoided the drug. I also noticed that coca seemed to produce flatulence in a marked degree.

In our case coca proved a distinct help. Soon after entering the Tukano country I let most of my Tariano paddlers return to Yawarete and took in their place a number of Tukanos. Whenever food supplies ran low and I was worried over making two or three fish answer for the whole party, the Tukanos would voluntarily waive their claim to a share in the evening repast, assuring me they were perfectly content with their coca-powder, although in many cases they had paddled ten hours up-stream. I too tried a bit of the magic powder but could not become enthusiastic about it. On me it had chiefly a nauseating effect. Worse still, half an hour after the coca had been swallowed I found that I was still quite prepared to eat a hearty meal. It was remarkable to see what different effects a drug could have on different persons.

To a certain extent coca seemed to have the same effect upon the Indians as a good mellow bottle of wine upon Europeans. Frequently of an evening I would chat with the chief of whatever *maloka* we were visiting, and after he had consumed a certain amount of coca, he would usually unlimber a bit from his dignity and tell me some of the old legends and traditions of his tribe. One or two of these legends were, to me at least, so interesting that I reproduce them here.

According to one quaint legend, long, long ago the tribes in this region were unacquainted with the use of fire. But fire was then sent by God to the earth. It was first given to the Tarianos, who at that time lived on the Ariari River, far away to the north. All the other tribes sent representatives to view this new wonder. At last the *jacaré,* the crocodile, offered to take the fire and distribute it to all the various tribes so that every man could have the benefit of it. The owners of the fire were foolish enough to give it to him. When the *jacaré* had swum to the middle of the river, he sank, and the fire disappeared. Mankind was disconsolate at the loss and sought the aid of other animals in order to get back the precious gift from the gods. The frogs gave a great banquet to which they invited the *jacaré,* but the sly *jacaré* came only to the door, and when the frogs croaked in premature exaltation over their success the *jacaré* went quickly away.

Mankind then sought the aid of the wise old lizard who acted as medicine-man to the *jacaré.* The lizard went to treat the crocodile, and in the approved fashion of all medicine-men blew and sucked all over the *jacaré's* body, pretending to treat him for an illness, but in reality trying to find out where the *jacaré* had hidden the fire. As the result of this treatment, smoke came out of the *jacaré's* body, but the lizard could not find out where the fire itself was hidden. Mankind then went to the white *japo* bird, who was known to be very wise; but although the white *japo* bird searched everywhere even he could not find it.

At last, in despair, mankind went to the black *japo* bird, who was, and still is, possessed of a curved beak;

and by means of the curved beak the black *japo* found the precious fire in the very tip of the *jacaré's* nose and restored it to human beings. Since then mankind has been much more careful with the gift of fire, and in no *maloka* is the fire ever allowed to go out.

Even more interesting to me was the story concerning the origin of man in this part of the world. I was eager to find out if the Indians had any traditions as to whether they had come from the east or from the west. After I had tried unsuccessfully to solve this problem by questioning various Tukanos, my friend Kandi came forth one evening with the following legend. According to him all the Indians of the Amazon came, not from the far-away mountains to the west, but from a great sea to the east. Once long, long ago a great sea-monster who lived at the mouth of the Amazon River built a vessel and ascended the stream. In the vessel there also came a number of birds. Finally the vessel was stranded on the Jacaré Island on the Uaupés River and was there shipwrecked. The birds flew away and were eventually transformed into Tukano tribesmen, while the fish monster (*wai*) gave rise to other men, the Waikanos.

This childish legend may contain a grain of truth. It has long been a disputed point whether the Indians of the Amazon came from the Andes or from the east. Personally, as the result of months of study of this question, I am convinced that the following process must have taken place. Originally South America was peopled by a very primitive race now nearly extinct, of which the Pogsas are quite likely a remnant. The typical South American Indians are of Asiatic origin. They probably came down the west coast of North America and passed over the isthmus of Panama to the

South American continent. From the northernmost part
of South America there must have been two different
migratory waves. One was along the west coast and
resulted in peopling the Andean regions, where the
Inca culture was later destined to arise. The other migration was along the east coast, from which the Indians
gradually penetrated westward into the heart of the
Amazon jungle. The invaders killed off most of the
original inhabitants but probably married some of the
women.

It is impossible, of course, to give any precise date
to this migration, but it was probably comparatively
recent. We all know the marked difference there was,
certainly as regards Europe, between the paleolithic
and neolithic cultures. The stone implements of the
older period were only roughly hewed and chipped.
Those of the later period were carefully polished. It is
curious that until now no paleolithic or rough-chipped
stone implements have been found in the jungles of
South America. As far back as we can go, even the
most primitive of the tribes possessed polished stone
weapons. It seems therefore probable that the tribes
which invaded South America had already passed beyond the paleolithic stage before they reached their new
habitat.

CHAPTER XVI

HUNTING WITH POISONED ARROWS

FOR the most part our daily routine continued to be much the same as earlier in the journey. Each morning and each afternoon we spent on the river, in constant progress up-stream. All the *malokas* that we passed along the banks of the main river were inhabited by Tukanos; but my Indians said that far up the various rivulets we passed there were Desano settlements, and that beyond the Desanos, in the virgin forest, there were roving hordes of Pogsas.

Portions of this so-called virgin forest must have been fairly well traversed. The Tiquié River, also inhabited by Tukanos, ran almost parallel to the Papuri four or five days' journey to the south, and I was told that the dwellers on the two streams paid one another frequent visits, cutting across the jungle in order to do so.

Kandi and his two sons were followers of the old school and believed in endless ceremonial. Whenever we arrived at a new *maloka,* instead of the few words of greeting which I had been in the habit of giving when we were traveling alone, Kandi would start a long sing-song incantation with our hosts which lasted nearly an hour. He told me that I was supposed to do all this, but that he would act for me because of my ignorance of etiquette and good manners. It was interesting to see his belief, a belief shared by all the natives, that it is the Indians who are cultured, and the whites who are barbarous in their manners.

As we continued up-stream I was pleased to find that the hostile attitude at first assumed by the Tukanos wore off and that I was a more or less welcome guest. I found that in every case the Indians knew of my coming beforehand, and that contrary to all native usage they had stretched a hammock near the entrance to the *maloka,* in which I was invited to sit as soon as I arrived. From this point of vantage, and consoled by my pipe, I could listen to the ceremonial pandemonium which was carried on by way of greeting. It was marked by endless repetition, in which each person echoed the last words of the previous speaker.

"We have come"; "You have come"; "We have come from down the river"; "From down the river"; "From down the river after traversing many, many leagues"; "Many, many leagues"; "Many, many leagues, and visiting many, many tribes, and many valiant chiefs"; "Many valiant chiefs"; and so on indefinitely.

When we had safely arrived at our destination each evening, I found this flow of words rather pleasing, but it had its disadvantages when, as frequently happened, we passed some canoe on the river coming from the opposite direction. Whenever this occurred we had to halt, while Kandi exchanged compliments with the occupants of the canoe. The result frequently was that we were an hour or so late in arriving at a place where we could prepare our midday or evening meal; and etiquette and an empty stomach make very bad companions.

In spite of their rigid adherence to all the rules of

etiquette, I noticed that there were two points on which my Waikano companions held fast to their independence. One was their refusal to take any coca; the other was their insistence upon sleeping outside the *maloka*. Each evening all the men of the *maloka* we were visiting would gather together in a circle, and in the center would be the local chief, da Silva, and myself. The women-folk usually squatted in the gloom behind the men. During the long-winded conversations which followed, a bowl filled with coca would go the round. Each man was expected to take a mouthful, but Kandi and his sons, with rather obvious disdain, would pass the bowl on untasted. On one occasion, to be sure, when Kandi was safely out of sight, I saw one of his sons try a small dose, but his expression indicated that he found the drug as unpleasant as I did.

In the same way, although, in most cases, there was plenty of room in the various *malokas* we visited, Kandi and his little party preferred to pitch their camp by the side of the river, in close proximity to the boats. Camp-pitching consisted, of course, merely in the hanging up of hammocks between the trees, and in making a fire. Even in the event of a heavy rainfall they preferred to take refuge in the boats rather than sleep inside the *maloka*. It was obvious that Kandi thought that the elaborate exchange of compliments was all very well, but he intended to see that the line of retreat was not cut off in case of a surprise attack.

I, for my part, continued to trust in our hosts and slept indoors, though I always kept a loaded rifle beside my hammock. Events showed that my confidence was justified, for I found that as long as we stayed in Tukano territory we had more to fear from the perils of hunger than from savage attack.

My scanty supply of biscuits had long since given out. Sweet potatoes and *macasheras* were much rarer than they had been further down the river, and I was forced to rely entirely on *beijú* as a substitute for bread and vegetables. *Beijú* could only be made palatable by the addition of jam; but the jam was fast disappearing, and it now became necessary to reserve it as a delicacy for rare occasions, and to take the sharp native *pimenta* as a substitute at ordinary times. I was luckier than many of my companions, as I had long been accustomed to highly seasoned dishes; but neither Mannling nor my Brazilian servants could stomach the "heat" of native seasoning. Once or twice we were fortunate enough to secure a bowl of specially prepared nuts, somewhat resembling our chestnuts. The nuts were mashed into a uniform mass, a little seasoning was added, and the whole mess was then allowed to go bad. At the end of about three weeks of waiting we then had before us a very excellent imitation of highly flavored Gorgonzola cheese.

Fortunately I found that our supply of tea would be more than sufficient to last us for many months to come, and I allowed my little party many a wild tea orgy when there was nothing else to be had, though with the tea it was necessary to take sugar and milk in limited doses. But as long as we had any tea I felt assured that Joaquim would be forced to follow my instructions and really boil all the water we were to drink.

I was interested to find that the Indians had no substitute for our ordinary beverages. Tea and coffee were of course unknown. Cocoa never spread from Ecuador to the Amazon basin. Even more surprising, the famous *mate* herb of the Guarani Indians, in the extreme south of the Amazon district, never found its way to the natives living north of the main Amazon River, although it has succeeded in becoming the standard drink of many parts of South America, even among the white population.

On special occasions my Indian friends of the northwest Amazon basin had recourse to *kashiri*. At ordinary times they were content with water, though, to be sure, in nearly all cases the water had *farinha* mixed with it, giving it a slightly sour taste. Considering the fact that the water was ordinary river-water and that it was never boiled, it was rather surprising that typhoid and other similar fevers were apparently unknown. I can scarcely credit the Indian assertion that the addition of the *farinha* or *mandioca* flour made the water harmless.

From the beginning of the journey until we were well into the Tukano territory we did a roaring trade in salt. Many of my most precious specimens of Indian handicraft were secured at the price of a handful of the precious saline, but our stock eventually became so depleted that I was forced to reserve the rest for our own consumption. Our supply of the other varieties of barter goods was also running low, and I felt some fear that we should have nothing with which to pay our way when we came to the tribes further up the river. On the other hand, we were helped by the fact that the further we traveled the more valuable our goods became. Further down the river a handful of beads or a mirror had scarcely been enough to secure us a day's provender, but already these things were considered the foundation of a fortune, and at this rate of progress I felt that in a month or two I could buy up a whole *maloka* with a pair of scissors.

As the Indians could no longer secure salt from us, I was curious to find out how they dealt with the need for salt when left to their own devices. The desire for salt seems to be a craving innate to the human race, far more universal and more pressing than the desire for sweets; and yet salt is almost unknown in the giant fresh-water basin of the Amazon.

Salt as such is almost unobtainable, and it seems to have been the desire for a substitute seasoning which has led the Indians into using their sharp *pimenta* in such vast quantities. It has been said that it is the desire for salt which has brought about the curious habit of earth-eating among the children, which is regarded as a special secret vice by the Indian parents. I have also heard it asserted that the cannibalism practised by several of the South American tribes is really due to a desire for salt, as human flesh contains a larger proportion of saline material than the flesh of most animals.

The natives of the northwest are luckier with respect to salt than are many of their cousins in other parts of the Amazon basin. They have discovered that a certain weed manages to extract a good deal of salt even from fresh water. This weed looks very much like European water-cress. It grows principally on stones which are subject to the constant pounding of falling water, such as the stones underneath the numerous *cachoéiras*. In fact I never saw this weed growing in still water. All so-called fresh water contains, of course, a minute quantity of salt, but the quantity is usually so minute that it is not noticeable. The weed of which I am speaking seems to have the faculty of extracting this minute quantity of salt from the water which passes over it, so that by eating the weed the Indians are somewhat able to palliate their desire for saline substances. I ate the weed on several occasions. It certainly had a bitter salty taste, though I could not be sure that the flavor was really due to the presence of sodium chloride.

As long as the tea-canister held out and we remained near a river, I knew we should have something to drink; and as long as we continued to come across *malokas* filled with busy women who knew how to prepare *beijú,* I knew that we should not actually starve. But in spite of what the modern food specialists tell us, a vegetarian leads worse than a dog's life (for even dogs are not vegetarians); and as we were forced more and more to live on the surrounding country, our little stops to try our hand at hunting or fishing became more frequent. But for a long time after entering the Tukano territory, there was a great scarcity both of game and of fish. This region was, for the Amazon, so populous, so filled with skilled hunters, that the forests had been largely thinned of suitable prey; and as we were still in the rainy season, most of the fish had retired to odd nooks in the flooded forests and were no longer swarming in the river.

We were extremely unlucky in one respect. In the Amazon region good fishing is to be had only in the dry season, but it was our bad fortune always to be a few weeks ahead of the dry season. When we left Manáos, the dry season was regarded as just beginning. But in the huge Amazon basin the seasons are not everywhere the same, and slowly as we had been traveling we had traveled more quickly than the seasons. Everywhere we went we were told that in another two or three weeks the dry weather—and good fishing—would begin.

But needs must when the devil drives. With hunger

pressing us, we redoubled our exertions, and in no case were we for long without sufficient food. As we could not rely upon buying fish or game from the *malokas* we visited, we ourselves had to see to it that the larder was regularly replenished. Kandi and the other Indians of the party were of great help in this respect, as they were all skilled hunters. And by watching them I gained an excellent insight into Indian methods of fishing and "shooting."

It was obvious that the Indians were originally entirely without knowledge of fishing by means of hook and line. This, no doubt, was due to ignorance of the use of metals, though occasionally I saw very ingenious bone hooks which had been recently made in imitation of the iron fish-hooks introduced by the white man. Isolated iron fish-hooks which made their way far into the interior of the jungle by means of intertribal barter served no doubt as models. But though the Indians have only recently adopted the hook, they have proved very apt pupils in the art of angling.

The fish-hook has not been able, though, to oust the older indigenous methods of fishing. These consist either of catching the fish in specially constructed traps or nets, or by shooting with bow and arrow, or by means of poison. I had heard a good deal of the art of fishing by archery, but it was Kandi who showed me the perfection to which it could be brought. He would stand alert with drawn bow and arrow while we slowly paddled along some likely place, such as where a sand-bank lay only a few feet underneath the water. The sand-bank served as an excellent background, as we could see everything that passed over it in the water below. Usually a flash of silver was all that told of the presence of a fish, but immediately upon seeing the flash Kandi would let fly the arrow. In almost every case the shot went home. His accuracy was all the more remarkable in view of the deflecting power of the water, but the wily Indians have learned carefully to allow for the deflection when taking aim.

This skilled process is, however, very slow when, as in our case, one has to provide constantly for fourteen hungry mouths. For this reason Kandi would not infrequently have recourse to poison. Where the water was turbid he would prepare little pellets consisting of tiny pieces of meat mixed with the chopped-up leaves of a bush which we found planted near many of the *malokas* and which contained some obscure poison. The pellets were thrown into the water and soon disappeared, but should any fish be present they would almost invariably swallow the poison pellets, and a few seconds later they would become stupefied and rise to the surface of the water.

Even more effective was the method of fish poisoning which was employed by Kandi when we came to some back stream where the water was comparatively calm. He would cut the stalks of certain bushes we found growing wild in the forest, and when we at last came to a suitable spot in the river he would pound the stalks to a pulp and pour water over them. This gave rise to a thick milky-looking liquid which was then thrown into the river. I was surprised to see that even comparatively small quantities of the poison were sufficient to stupefy all the fish in the surrounding water. In a few moments the surface of the water would be covered with paralyzed fish, which we could gather in with no difficulty.

Hunting in the forest was a much more difficult problem. Not infrequently we would leave our boats by

the river-bank and roam for hours through the forest
looking for game. Mannling and I took with us shot-
gun and rifle. I may mention that we found the rifle almost useless during the whole journey, and I should
advise future explorers of the region to content themselves with fairly heavy shot-guns. The Indians, of
course, were unacquainted with firearms and took with
them only their bows and arrows and not uncommonly a
blowpipe. The blowpipe was used largely for securing
birds and the smaller varieties of monkeys, the bows
and arrows for the larger animals. On several occasions
I let Kandi shoot with my gun, but rather to my surprise he informed me after several experiments that
he thought a blowpipe or a bow and arrow the better
weapon, because the noise of one gunshot would frighten
away other game, while with the native weapons one
could make shot after shot without disturbing other
possible victims. The chief advantage of firearms was
of course their longer carrying-power, but in the thick
jungle, where one could scarcely see twenty paces ahead,
this was of little advantage.

Both the ordinary arrows shot from a bow, and
the long thin toothpick-like arrows shot from a blowpipe, were tipped with the deadly curari poison, so that
a mere scratch was certain to bring about death. The
preparation of this poison is a long and arduous process. In most cases it can be carried out only by some
important medicine-man who has been duly initiated
into the secret. I was never able to watch the exact
method of manufacture. The chief ingredient seems to
be a creeping vine which I saw not infrequently growing
wild in the forest. The vine is mixed with water and then
boiled down to a thick syrupy substance, but this is only
the beginning of the long method of preparation. Kandi

informed me that a great variety of other things are
added to the syrup to add to its potency, such as the
skins of toads and the hairs of jaguars. But according
to him, no doubt, it was the magic formulas muttered
by the medicine-men which really gave the poison its
death-dealing qualities.

No antidote to this poison is known ever to have been
discovered. Once one has been wounded with a poisoned
arrow, one must be content to pass on to a better life.
The action of curari, however, appears to be painless,
bringing about mere numbness and gradual suffocation.
I was also surprised to see how slowly the poison
worked. Some of the good old missionary fathers who
first explored the Amazon tell us that when a man was
struck by a poisoned arrow, "before he could utter the
name Jesus, he was dead." It seems to me that the
friends of worthy fathers must have been very slow in
uttering the sacred name, for even with small birds shot
with poisoned arrows at least three or four minutes
would elapse before they expired. In the case of larger
animals, it was not infrequently fifteen or twenty
minutes before death took place.

Although a full dose of curari is invariably deadly,
the natives have discovered that in diluted form it
merely numbs its victims temporarily. Making use of
this knowledge, the Indians are able to capture alive
any of the animals of the forest. This explains the existence of the many house-pets in the various Indian settlements I visited. Particularly common were *araras* and
other brilliantly colored birds, as well as several varieties
of monkeys.

In most cases, when the birds are caught young,
they are fed by hand; that is, they have food thrust
down their throats. For this reason the birds never learn

to eat unaided and would starve were they to fly away
into the jungle. The Indians therefore never have to
use cages for their pets, nor have they to clip their wings
to prevent them from flying away. The Indians seem to
show a real fondness for their pets. I remember seeing
in one Tukano *maloka* a tiny baby monkey which had
recently been captured, and as it was unable to take
ordinary food one of the women suckled it along with
her own infant.

The most frequent additions to our larder were
either monkeys or various rodents such as the *paca* and
the *cutia*. Once or twice our prey was delivered almost
into our hands. Twice we saw *cutias* trying to swim
across the river, and while they were battling with the
water it was easy to secure them. Why they should have
taken to the water I cannot understand, as *cutias* are
essentially land animals. Not improbably they had been
chased by some roaming jaguar and had taken to the
river in order to escape from him. I know of no flesh
which is more appetizing than that of these rodents, and
I would give all the beefsteaks and roast chickens in
the world in order to banquet off one once more.

Our search for larger game proved more difficult.
On one occasion, while we were stopping with a Tukano
chief, we heard that not many miles away there was a
swamp which was noted as a gathering-ground for tapirs
and deer. Mannling and I determined to have a shot at
them. At one o'clock in the morning we were awakened
by the chief's son, who was to act as guide, and we set
off on our long tramp through the forest. I found the
same difficulty in making silent progress through the
thick undergrowth as on previous occasions; but this
time the difficulty was heightened by the absolute blackness, which seemed only intensified by the lantern that

we took with us. For four hours we kept steadily on our way. Shortly before daybreak we arrived at a small stream. Our guide knew that we must be near the right spot, but in the darkness he could not find the way. We did not dare beat about the bush too much for fear of frightening the animals away, and I began to fear that our long march would have been in vain.

At this stage the chief's son remembered that not very far away was a *maloka* of Desanos, who were renowned as hunters, and he determined to go there and ask for aid. While he was away, I lay down on a rock in the middle of the stream and in spite of the uncomfortable position was soon fast asleep. Unfortunately I turned over in my sleep and woke up to find myself in the water. I had scarcely time to pull off my wet clothes when the Tukano youngster returned accompanied by a Desano. In a few moments the Desano guided us to the right spot. We were there indeed before we realized it and were startled by the sudden stampede of two tapirs and three Amazonian deer. We had scarcely time to raise our guns before they were away, but we sent a parting shot after them which must have told, for after following the trail for another mile or so we eventually came upon a wounded tapir that had fallen from exhaustion.

The tapir is the largest of the wild animals of the Amazon forest. He is really a small and very remote cousin of the elephant, though from a distance he looks like a huge boar. The flesh tastes something like beef but is rather fatter and richer, and the Indians have a belief, no doubt well founded, that it is not wise to eat much of it.

We were able to shoot a number of birds from our boats while we were paddling up the river, as many birds have the habit of perching on the branches of trees overlooking the water. The bird with the best taste was the huge-beaked toucan. Almost as good was a large bird which looked like a crow and which the Indian called *kaokao* because of the noise which he made. I was interested to see that the Tukanos had no hesitation in eating the flesh of the toucan birds, although they regarded them as their ancestors. When we shot our first *kaokao,* I was surprised to see Kandi squeeze out the fluid from the bird's eyeballs and pour it into his own eyes. The *kaokao* is supposed to possess unusually good eyesight, and Kandi assured me that by anointing his eyes with the magic fluid from the bird he could improve his own vision.

CHAPTER XVII

WIVES, SLAVES, AND KINGS

THE river continued to be beset every few miles with rapids and cataracts, but we were fast becoming masters in the art of dealing with these difficulties. My Indian paddlers seemed to hail each new rapid with delight, although it increased their work enormously. They appeared to enjoy battling with the elements; and I was more and more struck by their pluck, endurance, and cheeriness in the face of danger. Beyond question these cataracts did form a very real danger even to the Indians. Frequently they would point to some spot and tell me that it was here that the brother or the cousin of So-and-so was drowned.

We were very nearly the witnesses of one such accident. In the middle of a rapid our boat struck on a rock, and it looked as if it were going to be pounded to pieces. One of the Indians immediately jumped into the stream. Perched on the rock he succeeded in pushing the boat free, but before he could climb back into the boat, the force of the water had carried him away, and for a quarter of an hour he had to battle for his life with the waves. We, of course, had to undo an hour's work by shooting back with our boat to his rescue. Eventually we managed to get him safely on board again. My Indians seemed to regard the incident as a huge joke and

laughed and jeered at what they considered the carelessness of their poor comrade.

The accident caused such a delay that night overtook us before we could reach a new *maloka*. We were
forced therefore to camp in the forest beside the river.
Early the next morning I was awakened by the advent
of a small Indian canoe carrying only a young man and
a young woman. Both of them looked much frightened,
but I could secure from them no adequate explanation
for their arrival at such an unseemly hour. They cowered among my Indians and tried to make themselves
as inconspicuous as possible. A few minutes later a
larger canoe, commanded by a very irate chief, came
into view and landed at our camp. From the vehement
language which ensued, I discovered that I had just
been the witness of an interesting elopement.

The young man who had first arrived was a Desano
who had run away with the daughter of the Tukano
chief, who was now hotly pursuing him. The young
couple threw themselves on my mercy, and I had the
ticklish job of deciding whether they should stay
"eloped" or not. In this part of the world marriage by
robbery is still, theoretically at least, the rule. Even
when the father of the girl consents, the prospective
bridegroom pretends to capture the bride by force. But
in most cases the father is aware of what is taking place
and connives at the robbery, provided he receives a *quid
pro quo*. The young man either agrees to give his sister
in marriage to a member of the father-in-law's tribe,
following the principle that fair exchange is no robbery, or else he is forced to offer the parents of the girl
a suitable number of presents such as pots and baskets.

The young man who had taken refuge with me,
however, was too poor to pay the necessary tribute and

did not possess a marriageable sister. The fact that he was a Desano was also against him, as all Tukanos affect to despise the Desanos. But I felt a certain amount of sympathy with the course of true love, particularly as the girl seemed to be enamoured of the man who had stolen her. Consequently I agreed to give the irate father, out of my private stores, a sufficient number of fish-hooks, beads, and knives to induce him to consent to the abduction. Now that the young couple were free to continue their elopement, I wanted to see if a marriage ceremony would take place, but it seemed that such a thing was unknown. The young man told me that when the bride arrived at her new home his mother would ceremoniously show her her new apartment in the *maloka* and her allotment in the tribal plantation, and the nuptials would then be considered complete.

Even when the marriage takes place under more usual conditions, there is little deviation in the ceremony, according to my Indian friends. The young man brings presents to the bride's parents. The bride's tribe then institutes a great *kashiri* festival, in the course of which the father-in-law solemnly gives the girl to the prospective bridegroom. After this there is the pretense of robbery. The girl wanders down to the river-bank near the boats. The young man seizes her, springs into a canoe, and paddles away. The father and mother then rush down from the *maloka* and wail and howl over the loss, although they no doubt consider themselves very lucky to have got their daughter safely and suitably married.

A month or so after the nuptials, the father and mother of the bride pay the young couple a visit and in most cases give them a number of household utensils, so that when a young man invests his money in a wife he has a fair prospect of getting something in return.

After receiving such an unexpected insight into the method of marriage among the Indians, I naturally became interested in their ideas concerning divorce—marriage and divorce are such close corollaries in the modern mind. I was not lucky enough to witness a native divorce-court proceeding, but in the course of the next few days I managed to extract from the Indians their views of the divorce problem.

Theoretically the man and the woman are each free to get rid of the other, but there is this great difference in their position. The man *can,* it is true, send his wife packing off home at any moment, but this is considered a great insult not only to the woman but also to the woman's tribe; and without real justification such a proceeding is likely to lead to a tribal war, and consequently seldom occurs. On the other hand, if a woman, being dissatisfied with her husband, returns to her own people, no tribal offense can be taken, as it is considered that a man must be very wicked indeed to cause his wife to desert him.

So deep is the barbarism of the Amazon Indians, therefore, that a divorce is one of the rarest of events. So little are they accustomed to the benefits and usages of civilization that conjugal infidelity, one of the chief causes of divorce, is almost unknown. I remember reading in various learned works that in South America, "from the Fireland to the Isthmus of Panama," it is the universal custom of the natives to offer a daughter or a wife to distinguished visitors as a token of respect. I regret to say that, as far as my experience goes, this statement is entirely untrue. In no cases had I or any member of my party to suffer from the embraces of a fair dame or damsel who was flung at our heads. Pequenino, who no doubt would have welcomed these advances, invariably got his ears boxed whenever he sought to become affectionate. The only offer I got in this direction was from da Silva, who said he would be glad to turn over to me one of his nine wives as a keepsake, should we ever get safely back to civilization.

No, I lived for months among the Indians, sharing their homes and joining in their customs, and I am prepared to give them alpha plus in their record of conjugal fidelity whenever they may apply for it. Occasionally, very occasionally, I had reason to believe that among the younger unmarried men and women there was a little "carrying-on," but once the life-partner had been chosen, faithfulness was the almost invariable rule.

Because of the greater laxity among the unmarried girls, the men were frequently anxious to secure their wives as young as possible, and yet there was nothing approaching child marriage among the Indians. As far as I could tell from appearances, the average age for marriage among the women was seventeen or eighteen, and among the men from twenty to twenty-three.

Monogamy was almost the invariable rule among all Indians with whom I came into contact. Theoretically the chief was allowed to have more than one wife, provided the first wife consented to the taking of another one; but in the few cases where I saw supposed polygamy existing, I found that the additional wives were wives only in name. Where a warrior had been killed, leaving a widow behind, the chief "married" the widow in order to allow her to retain her status in the tribe.

The Indians have no idea of naturalization by marriage. A Tariano woman remains a Tariano even though she be married to a Tukano. If her Tukano husband dies a few years after the marriage, it is only natural that she return to her own people. If, on the other hand, she has lived for many years with her husband's tribe, the older ties and associations are broken, and she prefers to remain among her adopted people even after the death of her husband. In such cases she frequently becomes, in name at least, the wife of the chief; less frequently she is taken on as an additional wife by a brother of the deceased.

In dealing with so shy and reserved a people as the Indians, it is always useful to have some way of breaking the social ice. I found the best method was to devote myself to the children. By playing with them and talking to their mothers about them, or, better still, getting their mothers to talk about them (mothers are alike all the world over), I found that more could be accomplished than by hours of Kandi's ceremonial palaver.

This carefully thought-out plan of action taught me a good deal concerning the games that are played by the Indian children. The youngsters had the same delight in walking about on stilts as everywhere else. The girls particularly were fond of spinning "cats' cradles." But by far the most popular of the pastimes was top-spinning. The tops were made of either wax or baked clay, through which a small stick was thrust to serve as a point. Some of the tops were much like our own in appearance. Through others a hole had been bored which caused the tops to make a musical noise when they were spun.

On several occasions I tried to teach the youngsters some of our European games, such as tag and blindman's-buff, but without much success. They could never fathom the purpose of these complicated amusements. I was equally mystified by a game which seemed to give the younger Indian children particular amusement, and in which I was frequently persuaded to join. The children and I would sit on one of the long benches, arms around one another's necks. Then swaying rapidly forward and backward we would cry out, "Ai-ai-ai." When this had gone on for some time, we would rub one another on the head and say, "Mumi-mumi-mumi." This was the beginning and end of the game. What it could possibly have meant, I have no idea, but each time I played it there were shrieks of joy.

The only Indian game of this sort which seemed to resemble our own was one which the Indians called *anta,* or tapir. Two or three of the youngsters stood in the middle of a ring formed by all the other children with linked arms. The imprisoned tapirs would first go around the circle, touch each arm, and demand, *"Komenda?"*—(is it an) iron arm? To which the invariable reply was, *"Yapeda"*—(it is only a) sweet potato arm. Encouraged by this declaration of weakness, the imprisoned tapirs would then try to break through. Whoever was the first to give way was forced to take the part of the caged animal. The fact that the words *anta, komenda,* and *yapeda* were Lingua Gerál, and not Tukano, showed that this game must have come from the far-away south, but how and when it was introduced is more than I can say.

We had gradually come to the heart of the Tukano country, in which Indian pride reaches its acme. In many instances this pride naturally took the form of trying to lead as gentlemanly—that is to say, as idle— a life as possible. This was rendered possible by the fact that several of the *malokas* I visited possessed four or five Pogsa slaves, who had been captured by the Tukano warriors on some marauding expedition.

On the whole, the Pogsa slaves seemed well and

even kindly treated. This doubtless accounted for the fact that they made little or no effort to escape. There was nevertheless no doubt of the subservient position occupied by the slaves. They were not even allowed to sleep inside the great *malokas* but were forced to build for themselves little huts a few hundred yards away. In several cases Pogsa women as well as Pogsa men had been caught. The men and women were allowed to live a family life so that they could breed further slaves for their masters. The slave children seemed to be regular articles of commerce. On more than one occasion I was asked if I did not wish to purchase a Pogsa boy. It would have been rather romantic in this very dreary modern world of ours to be the possessor of a full-blown slave, but as I should not have known what to do with one, I was forced to decline.

I noticed, however, that the slaves were allowed to hold certain property of their own. Two or three Pogsas helped us to get the boats over a bad waterfall; I was not quite certain whether I was to pay them or their masters for their labor, but I found that the masters claimed rather less than half of the total wage and allowed their chattels to retain the rest.

In many respects the Pogsa was treated as a sort of household animal, as a particularly useful sort of dog, except that the Tukano children frequently played with the dogs, and a Tukano mother thought it very degrading if her offspring played with the Pogsa youngsters. But I noticed that the slaves were allowed their share of *kashiri* and even of the divine coca after their masters had had their fill, though on no occasion were they allowed to join in the general conversation. Nor were they allowed to wear any feather ornaments or to take part in the tribal dances.

The work required of the Pogsa slaves was not particularly arduous. The female slaves had to do most of
the work on the plantations, so that their mistresses
could lie at ease in their hammocks. The male slaves
helped in all the rougher work about the *maloka*. They
were also expected to use their almost animal cunning
in the trapping of wild animals. Altogether the slave-
owning Tukanos had a very fine time of it. I noticed
that several of the chiefs were too lazy to hold the huge
native cigars before their mouths; even this work had
to be performed by a Pogsa.

Yet the enslaved Pogsas seemed to be faring rather
better than their wild cousins of the jungles. They
looked better nourished and better groomed. Slavery
is not always bad for a people, at least from the material
point of view. There is no question that the majority
of the negro slaves in North America led a better life
than do the majority of their emancipated descendants. When one is a slave there is no unemployment
problem; one always knows where the next meal is coming from. When one is old or sick, one cannot be cut
off the employment list.

At the same time it must be admitted that there are
certain disadvantages about being a slave. In spite of
what I have said of the high morality of most of the
Indians, I noticed that a little affair with a pretty Pogsa
woman did not seem to be considered very seriously.
The slaves also had a bad time of it if an epidemic broke
out and the local medicine-man did not know how to
cure it. The Indians believe that no disease comes naturally. It is always the result of black magic on the
part of some evil wisher or of some malicious spiritual
influence. As far as I could gather from talking to my
Indian friends, when a medicine-man could find no

other obvious cause of disease and no reliable cure, he was apt to suggest that one of the slaves had been practising black magic and was therefore the cause of all the trouble. In such cases it was likely to go rather badly with the unfortunate slave.

Much to the astonishment and rather to the indignation of the Tukanos, I continued to devote a good deal of attention to the Pogsas. I think that to the Tukanos the study of monkeys would have been more intelligible than the study of Pogsa language and customs. Rather to my surprise, I found that to a certain extent in type, and to a larger extent in language, the Pogsas of this region differed very considerably from those whom I had visited several weeks earlier on the Maku Igarape. This seemed to add weight to the supposition that the Pogsas are the remnants of an old and almost extinct race and not merely a rather unfortunate tribe.

My interest in the Pogsas did not prevent my continuing to take a very active interest in the customs and traditions of their masters. Gradually, as the Tukanos became more and more accustomed to me and my ways, they began to tell me of their old tribal legends, and I began to get an insight into the soul of a people who must at one time have constituted a large and powerful, though now forgotten, kingdom. Most of the Indian tribes of the Amazon basin formed tiny isolated groups with almost no historical tradition. They were never able to build up any important political organization. Their own stories and the accounts of other tribes indicate that the Tukanos must have formed an exception to this rule, although the glory of the ancient Tukano kingdom has vanished forever.

Evening after evening, in the various *malokas* which we visited, I got the tribal elders to recount the days of long ago. Bit by bit I began to get an inkling of the history of this vanished empire.

All the Tukanos seemed to agree with the legend I have previously mentioned that they with the other Betoya tribes had come from the east, "from the great, great river." Whereas the smaller tribes confined themselves to the minor tributaries, the Tukanos populated the banks of the main Uaupés River and had built up two important strongholds, Ipanoré and Yawarete. In and around these two places the Tukanos waxed in number and in strength and gradually formed a fairly centralized political organization.

At that time the Papuri and Tiquié rivers were in the hands of various rival tribes, such as the Yurutis, Kobeowas, and Baras. Eventually a great war broke out between the Tukanos on the one side and the several rival tribes on the other, in which, after incredible bloodshed, the Tukanos emerged victorious. The Yurutis and Baras were reduced to a mere handful of men and were forced to retreat to the very head-waters of the Papuri and Tiquié rivers respectively. The Kobeowas were driven further to the north and west (where they still remain), occupying a territory which had been previously inhabited only by wandering Pogsas. For a long time the Tukanos held undisputed possession of the whole of the lower Uaupés as well as of the Papuri and Tiquié river systems.

At this period the Tukanos seem to have been ruled by various members of a special family, concerning whom many remarkable traditions still exist. This family was always referred to as the Waiyapisa, or the hairy ones; this is a very curious epithet when one remembers the hairlessness of nearly all South American Indians. The members of this family are also considered to have been much lighter in color than any of their tribesmen. Tradition says they were adorned with many golden ornaments; this is also worthy of note, as almost none of the other Amazon tribes were acquainted with the working of any form of metal, remaining entirely in the stone age until the coming of the white men. This was, of course, in contrast to the skilled metal-workers of the far-away Andean civilizations. The Tukanos have now entirely lost the art of gold-working, nor could I find out where their ancient rulers obtained their gold.

The memory of even the vanished fashions of the ancient days seems to remain very vivid in the modern Tukano minds. The women showed me how in the days of long, long ago the ladies did up their hair in a curious puff at the back of their heads unsupported by a comb. The men at that time wore their hair, not short as at present, but done up in a curious little pigtail, plaited at the back of the head. Why the pigtail should have been in the Amazon region is more than I can imagine.

After the great victory of the Tukanos there came a period of tribal, one could almost say, national, grandeur. But the day of reckoning was soon to follow. At the period of their greatest glory the Tukanos were ruled by four brothers, all great chiefs. The names of each of the brothers, the names and nationalities even of their wives, are preserved to-day, although these events occurred several centuries ago, and there are, of course, no written records. The fact that the wife of one of the great chiefs was a Tariano shows that the Aruak tribes were gradually seeping in from the north, although they did not yet dare to dispute possession of the Uaupés River with the Tukanos.

These four valiant chiefs sighed like Alexander of Macedon for more worlds to conquer. Their kingdom, great as it was, must be still further enlarged. This time, instead of going to the smaller tributaries to the west, the Tukano rulers determined to go back to the land of their distant ancestors, to sail down the Rio Negro back to the "mother of the waters," and there to retake the land from which their ancestors had migrated.

The four chiefs, followed by more than half of the Tukano population, set out on this voyage of migration and conquest. The great settlements at Ipanoré and Yawarete were deserted. Only a few *malokas* on the Papuri and Tiquié rivers were left undisturbed to serve as frontier posts against the defeated tribes. When the four chiefs went away, they left no unified regency but instructed the heads of the individual *malokas* to manage their own affairs until they, the supreme rulers, should return.

The main horde of the Tukanos swept down the Rio Negro and for a long time seem to have been triumphant everywhere they went. None of the other native tribes could withstand them. My informants assured me that the Tukano warriors of old did in fact reach the main stream of the Amazon and busied themselves there carving out a new empire. It was just at this time that the first white men made their appearance in the Amazon basin. A war broke out between the whites and the Tukanos for the mastery of the region. After a long contest, the superiority of the white man's firearms brought the period of Tukano mastery to an end. The Tukanos met with an overwhelming defeat. Great numbers of them were killed. Some retreated to the Rio Negro and founded a settlement there. A few stragglers made their way back to their homes on the Uaupés and brought tidings of the great tragedy.

After the migration, and the tragic defeat which followed it, great stretches of the original Tukano territory lay almost unpopulated. The remaining Tukanos could no longer maintain control over the huge territory which they had conquered. The Tarianos came in from the north and settled even in Ipanoré and Yawarete, the strongholds of the old Tukano régime. The Waikanos migrated down the Maku Igarape and took over even part of the Papuri. The remaining Tukanos were broken up into more or less isolated groups. The tragedy of a rising empire, crushed at its inception, had been played out. The present Tukanos have little more than memories to console them.

Many months later, on my return to civilization, I tried to check the story of the great migration from the white man's point of view by looking up some of the old Portuguese chronicles. I was unable to do so satisfactorily, but the accounts that I heard in the jungle were so clear and exact, so uniform, and so well confirmed by the members of other tribes, that I feel convinced that in its broad outlines the story must have had a historical basis.

The Tukanos have never recovered from the blow which they received long ago. It is probable from their present aristocratic languor that they will never again rise to real greatness. Under the able rulership of Kandi and his two sons (both the sons seemed to have inherited much of their father's organizing ability), it is possible that the Waikanos may have more of a political future than the Tukanos; but with the gradual advance of the white man into the recesses of the Amazonian forest, it

seems likely that any Indian kingdom would meet the
same tragic end as did that of the Tukanos.

It will probably be a long time before the white man
begins really to colonize the Amazon region and utilize
its enormous natural resources. But the richness of the
river-banks in rubber and balata are bound to bring to
them increasing numbers of rubber collectors, and with
the coming of the rubber men the simplicity and the independence of the Indian tribes are doomed. From time
to time, as we battled up the river, da Silva, an authority
on such matters, would point out to me some tree from
which one of the several varieties of rubber or balata
latex could be secured. His trained eye could tell approximately how much of the precious substance each
tree could produce. As he showed me this natural wealth,
I realized how great was the danger to which my wild
free Indian friends were exposed.

CHAPTER XVIII

THE PAGEANT OF THE DEMONS AND OF SEX

AT last we came to the place where the Papuri broke up into two smaller streams, called by the Indians Awa and Paka, and we had to decide which of the streams to follow. The Paka came in from the north, and though it was supposed to flow through very interesting country, it would have taken us out of our way. Consequently we made up our minds to paddle up the Awa so as to continue in a westerly direction. Before going further, however, we determined to eat our midday meal on the little spit of land which marked the junction of the waters.

Here we found not a *maloka* but a small and, for the time being, deserted hut. Small huts such as this are not altogether infrequent in the Indian country. They serve as shelters to little groups of natives who are forced to make long fishing and hunting expeditions, when the waters and the forest nearer their permanent homes have been too well exploited. These Indian groups generally choose a camping-ground where they can conveniently stay three weeks or a month before returning home. In certain cases these huts serve almost as week-end residences and are frequently visited by little fishing parties, although never permanently inhabited.

We installed ourselves in the vacant hut, and Joaquim was soon busy performing his daily miracle of producing a meal for fourteen persons from next to nothing. On this occasion our larder was more than usually scanty, and I was afraid our lunch would do little more than whet our appetites.

Scarcely had Joaquim got the water boiling, however, when two Indian canoes arrived bringing eight or nine natives. After the official greetings had been made, the new-comers got out several baskets from their boats. They had come, they said, in search of ants. As this seemed a rather unusual quest, I decided to follow the strangers in order to watch further developments.

A few minutes after leaving the huts we came to a series of nests made by the little *sauba* or leaf-cutting ants. As this ant is one of the commonest insect pests of the Amazon, I was surprised that my new acquaintances should have come so far to see so ordinary a sight. But soon I heard a low but long continued buzzing sound that eventually rose to a croon. We had arrived at the ant-nests at swarming-time. The Indians had timed their arrival very precisely, though how they were able to do so remains a mystery to me.

Thousands of young queen ants and drones crept out of the nests and began to fly away. At ordinary times, of course, one sees nothing of these ants, as they remain buried deep down in their nests. It is only once in their life that they are provided with wings; namely, at the time of their nuptial swarm.

The Indians rushed forward and placed their inverted baskets over the mouth of the nests, and the newly winged ants, in their passionate yearning for flight, flew upward only to be caught in a trap.

When the baskets were full, we returned to the little

camp. The Indians then proceeded to initiate me into the mysteries of ant-eating. The queen and drone ants were considerably larger than their ordinary working cousins. Even so they were scarcely larger than a thumb-nail, but I was to find that ninety or a hundred of these little creatures made a most sustaining and indeed a most appetizing meal. The Indians ate the ants both raw and roasted. When eating them raw, the Indians bit off the heads from the living ants. The heads were then chewed and swallowed while the bodies were thrown away. Those who preferred their ants roasted placed them in a huge earthenware pan over a fire and kept them there until they were crisp. In this case the whole body was eaten.

In spite of the novelty of the idea, I was glad to try the ants both raw and roasted. The zest of hunger caused even my Brazilian followers, after a little hesitation, to do likewise. Before long, we were all vying with one another in a race to see who could secure the most. I must confess, though, that I found the roasted variety preferable to the raw. When eaten raw, the ants had rather an unpleasant oily taste, but when roasted they reminded me very strongly of crisp bacon.

After eating them I could not understand why one should have an objection to ants as an article of diet. The prejudice against them is no doubt merely a matter of custom. It is not impossible that in years to come roast ants will be as fashionable in first-class hotels as is caviar to-day. There are, however, ants and ants. Not every species of ant is edible, and only two or three varieties recommend themselves even to Indian palates. It must not be thought, though, that the Indians are driven to eating ants by hunger or because of the absence of other food. My Indian crew assured me that they considered ants one of the greatest possible delicacies.

We were to find that ant-eating was not altogether without a spice of danger, especially when the ants were eaten raw. Pequenino, the irrepressible jackanapes, saw the Indians take the squirming ants in their hands and bite off their heads. He decided to follow the example set by the natives, but he forgot to move his tongue to the back of his mouth while doing so. Scarcely had he got an ant's head in his mouth than he gave a squeal of agony. The ant, resentful of the treatment it was receiving, had bitten Pequenino on the tongue.

An hour or two after the ant feast, just as we were thinking of getting on our way once more, another canoe put in an appearance. This one had but a single occupant, a man whom I remembered having seen some time previously at Yawarete. As the Indians were constantly traveling up and down their streams, on several occasions I met and remet old acquaintances. We soon discovered that this man lived in a *maloka* a little way up the Paka and that he had been sent with a special message to us from his chief.

He wanted to know whether it was up the Paka or the Awa that we had decided to go. Hearing that it was the Awa, he pleaded with us to pay his chief a visit before continuing our journey. He assured us that the chief had prepared a great festival in our honor. Our friend had brought with him four chickens and a duck, which the chief had sent as a present, by way of foretaste of the banquet which was to come. I was pleased at this sign of Indian good-will, but I much regretted any delay and hesitated about accepting the invitation. Seeing my hesitation, my friend gave an added reason why we should return with him, a reason which was very extraordinary, considering that it came from an Indian. He said that the women of the *maloka* had never seen a white man, and would never be content until they had seen us. He pleaded with me to satisfy the curiosity of the ladies.

This argument was overwhelming. Out of chivalry we postponed our journey up the Awa and paddled instead for an hour or two up the Paka until we came to a landing-place leading to the *maloka* to which we had been so pressingly invited. After reaching the landing-place we still had an hour's walk through the forest along an almost invisible trail before we came to the settlement itself. This was the first Tukano *maloka* we had found which lay so far away from the river's edge. Most of the Tukano settlements had been within a hundred yards of the bank. But we were now on the outskirts of the Tukano territory, and warfare between the Tukanos and their neighbors was, we found, still comparatively frequent in this region. The chief had therefor chosen the site for his settlement with an eye to strategic defense.

The chief himself, in spite of his hospitality to the curious white man, was obviously a strong adherent of the Conservative party. I noticed in his *maloka* a rigid observance of many old customs which had elsewhere fallen into desuetude. Not a single steel ax had found its way to this out-of-the-way corner of the world. The stone axes, on the other hand, were particularly well made and showed signs of very effective use.

It was not long before I discovered the real reason for the pressing invitation which had been extended to us. The chief of this settlement, Mandu, had seen the prestige which Kandi had secured by acting as our guide. For a long time he had wished to secure preëmi-

nence over the other Tukano *malokas* in his neighborhood. He now seemed to think that he could best do this
by following Kandi's example and joining my party.
Needless to say, I immediately accepted the proposal
he made me. From this time I had two very important
chiefs in tow.

It is not strange that one feels a sense of romance in
the heart of the jungle. At home a person like myself
is but a small, inconspicuous, and very much buffeted
member of society. Morning and evening one crowds
into a packed underground carriage and has one's toes
trod upon by costermongers. One is but a name in a
telephone-book, a figure of directory imagination. Only
the income-tax man shows any real interest in one's
existence.

In the Amazon it was all very different. From being
a plain ordinary man in the street, I had blossomed
forth into a mysterious personage whose coming was
heralded weeks beforehand, in whose honor great festivals were held, by serving whom chiefs hoped to develop
into kings. My very paddlers were princes of the
realm. What did it matter if I had only ants for lunch,
if the seat of my trousers showed two large holes, if my
beard and hair had not known scissors or even a comb
for many months? There would always be time to secure a comb and to buy a new pair of trousers—on
credit—when I relapsed into being merely a man in the
street again.

The banquet which my new camp-follower gave me
was worthy of all praise. *Kashiri* flowed once more
like water. Pan-pipes gave out once more the shrill high
melodies of the jungle. Dancers stamped and pranced in
marvelous rhythm after a manner which had come down
from a time immemorial.

On the occasion of this festival I was able to study the effect which the curious drug *kaapi* has upon the natives. I had seen it two or three times before, but it was only here that it seemed to play an important part in the ceremonies. Unlike coca, which is consumed in huge quantities every day, *kaapi* appears to be taken only at rare intervals and on solemn and ceremonious occasions. It seems to have great religious significance. Not only are women prohibited from drinking it, they are not even allowed to touch with their fingers the drug or the implements with which it is prepared.

Kaapi itself is a root. To prepare the drug for consumption, the roots are first pounded to shreds. Water is then poured over the shreds in order to extract the essence. When the liquid has been sufficiently brewed, it is placed in a special bowl of very curious design, used only for this purpose. Whereas the ordinary pots on the Papuri are nearly always of a uniformly black color, the *kaapi* bowls are invariably ornamented with red and white designs. Custom decrees that the bowls may never be washed or entirely emptied. When the time comes for the drug to be imbibed the bowl is brought with great ceremony to the middle of the *maloka*. With equal ceremony, the men go in pairs to drink the mixture out of tiny little cups made of gourd.

I found *kaapi* indescribably bitter, so bitter that it was difficult to swallow. Its effect was certainly most extraordinary, though it seemed to affect various people quite differently. I had heard so much of its potency that on previous occasions I had dared to take only a mouthful or two. As I had been unable to notice any effect from these small doses, I decided this time to keep pace with the Indian drinkers. Even so, the effect on me was not particularly striking. I was able to walk and talk in a perfectly normal way, though I felt a curious sort of mental numbness creep over me, as if my mind, floating somewhere far off in space, were giving distant orders to a body which remained far behind. I noticed, however, that the body seemed perfectly capable of carrying out these distant commands.

Upon the natives, although much more accustomed to the drug than I was, the effect appeared to be even more far-reaching. Why this should be so, I cannot understand. Even among the Indians, *kaapi* seemed to work in two quite different ways, according to the accounts given me by my fellow-topers. In certain cases it appeared to have an erotic action. The world and its inhabitants grew more and more beautiful. Some of the imbibers even had elaborate visions in which lovely forms floated before their eyes. In other cases the natives tended to go off into a hypnotic trance in which the conscious mind was somewhat stupefied and in which only the subconscious mind continued to function. Curiously enough, certain of the Indians fell into a particularly deep state of trance, in which they possessed what appeared to be telepathic powers. Two or three of the men described in great detail what was going on in *malokas* hundreds of miles away, many of which they had never visited, and the inhabitants of which they had never seen, but which seemed to tally exactly with what I knew of the places and peoples concerned. More extraordinary still, on this particular evening, the local medicine-man told me that the chief of a certain tribe on the far-away Pira Parana had suddenly died. I entered this statement in my diary, and many weeks later, when we came to the tribe in question, I found that the witch-doctor's statement had been true in every detail. Possibly all these cases were mere coincidences. In any case the exact nature of the drug and its effect upon the human constitution was most mysterious, and I am convinced that the matter is worth further investigation.

Under the influence of this unusual stimulant, it is small wonder that the Indians performed on this occasion a number of remarkable dances in honor of various jungle demons, all of whom were graphically represented. Curiously enough the women were allowed to remain in the *maloka* while these dances were being performed, although, as the dances were of a religious nature, no woman was permitted to take part in them.

All the demons of the Indians are forest demons. It was quite natural therefore that they should be represented in animal form. During the earlier dances little figures—usually though incorrectly called fetishes— were carried suspended by palm-fiber cords from ornamental drumsticks. These figures were mostly carved of wood and were ingeniously colored, and decorated with down and feathers. They represented, for the most part, various birds and fishes.

Later came other and even more elaborate dances, in which the chief performers were dressed in masks that had been specially prepared from pounded tree bast—bast is found in considerable quantities between the outer bark and the trunk proper of certain trees. The masks were really costumes that covered the whole upper part of the body, with sleeves through which the arms were thrust. The masks were elaborately painted and adorned, and they also represented various animal demons. Among them I noticed representations of butterflies (strange that butterflies should be considered demons!), lizards, and of course snakes and jaguars, the most important members of the jungle pantheon.

It was easy, in the majority of cases, to see from the decorations on the masks what each dancer was supposed to represent. Lest there should be any ambiguity, the mimic actions of the performers gave a very spirited imitation of the characteristic actions of the animals. The owl with huge yellow eyes fluttered awkwardly from post to post and gave from time to time a weird cry of "hu-hu-hu." The snakes and lizards squirmed to and fro with swift soundless motion. The jaguars made huge cat-like springs. The butterflies flitted aimlessly from one end of the *maloka* to the other. From the character of the dances and the demeanor of the performers and spectators, I realized that it was not merely hunted animals which were being represented. Each mask was the embodiment of a mysterious and powerful demon who had control over birth and life and death. We were back in the dawn of religious belief, where not only man but every beast was given a soul—and a dark and dreaded soul.

One of the dances was a vivid characterization of the triumph of death, given by people to whom death could never be natural but was always the result of dark magic and of the anger of the demons. In the last few months three of the tribesmen had gone to join the shades of their fathers, and their death had now to be ceremonially bewailed. Most of the masked dancers went outside the *malokas,* sang a long mournful song, and danced in an endless circle. Two of the performers remained behind in the communal house, but they too were destined to play an important rôle. For when the other dancers attempted to return to the *maloka,* the two who remained behind barred the entrance, and a ceremonial but very realistic fight broke out between the two groups. The dancers outside were the dark angry demons who were

attempting to storm the *maloka* and to bring disease and
death into its midst. The two dancers inside were friendly spirits who were determined to prevent the advent of
all evil. During the struggle several of the women-folk,
relatives of the dead men, raised a long wailing
croon. For a long time, in spite of inferior numbers, the
defenders put up a successful fight, but in the end the
spirits of evil broke through and obtained possession of
the *maloka*. The wailing of the women changed into a
chant of despair and ended with bitter sobs. I had witnessed the Indian equivalent of a mystery play, such as
is found in all religions the world over; but whereas
most mystery plays represent the eventual triumph of
good over evil, this Indian ritual showed with bitter
realism the overpowering victory of Death.

The Indians are wise enough not to classify their
deities as good and evil spirits. No demon is wholly good
or wholly bad. The same dark jungle spirits which bring
about disease and death are the producers of life and
fertility. This was very clearly—almost too clearly—
illustrated by the next dance which our hosts performed.
It was emblematic of the life-giving qualities of the demons and took the form of a phallic dance. Each of the
dancers took in his hands a phallus made of twisted bast,
to which were tied two cones, somewhat similar to pine-
cones, but filled with small red seeds. Holding, stroking,
and shaking these objects, the dancers, in wild excitement, stamped and pranced up and down the *maloka*,
running between the spectators, male and female, and
scattering the little red seeds right and left. It was obvious that the erotically exuberant effect of *kaapi* was
beginning to tell on all the performers; and yet there
was nothing inherently indecent in the dance or the actions of its performers. It was a symbolic representation

of all the fertilizing powers of nature—and as simple,
and almost as sublime as these. The dance was supposed
to bring fertility, not only to the women-folk, but to all
the beasts of the forest, and to the plants and trees from
which mankind gathered its food.

Two things struck me as particularly interesting in
connection with these masks. One was the fact that the
chief and his immediate relatives, who constituted the
local aristocracy, were not among the performers. Some
of the most important rôles were played by very insignificant members of the community. This, it seemed, was
done purposely. The *masks themselves* were supposed
to be the actual embodiments of the demons. They were
not mere representations. The masks therefore were
more important than the persons who wore them. The
performers were more or less insignificant mediums at a
spiritualistic séance.

The other significant fact was that after the dances
were over all the masks were carefully destroyed by
fire. The masks were the temporary homes of the demons
(the medicine-man and one or two of the other *kaapi*
inebriates swore that they could see the ordinarily invisible "spiritual substance" of the demons themselves), and
when the ceremony was over the spirits must be allowed
to return to their own abode, but they could only be
released by burning the masks. I wished to secure some
of these masks for my collection, but Mandu assured me
that the presence of the masks would bring trouble. The
spirits would be angry at their continued imprisonment.
It was only at special times that it was advisable to invoke the unseen powers and cause them to appear
among mankind.

After the spirits had been safely released and sent
back to their homes, some of the ordinary dances began

and, as usual, continued until dawn; but I was so worn out by my theological, or rather demonological, studies that I tucked myself in my hammock and was soon fast asleep.

CHAPTER XIX

CANNIBALISTIC ORGIES

AFTER so much festivity, it was natural that the next morning no one felt very enthusiastic about making an early start, and it was afternoon before we could get away. Several of our paddlers left us here, but with the aid of the Tukano chief, Mandu, we got other natives to take their place. I noticed that there was no great eagerness on the part of the volunteers, as we were now nearing the territory of tribes noted for their hostility. In fact, in order to secure a full crew, I had to accept two Pogsa slaves who were offered to me by their masters in lieu of their own services.

Mandu himself was the most welcome addition to my party. Although he had little of the energy and forcefulness which characterized Kandi, he was exceedingly shrewd, and his occasional words of advice were always very much to the point. He was particularly valuable, as he had once before been through the country which we were to cover in the course of the next few weeks.

We first made our way back to the junction of the Paka and Awa rivers and then started up the Awa once more. For the next two or three days we were still in Tukano territory, though we were rapidly approaching the tribal frontier.

It was in one of the last of the Tukano *malokas* that I first got detailed information of the trouble which had broken out between the whites and the Indians further up the river, of which I had heard extravagant rumors for several weeks past. It seemed that a Colombian rubber prospector had managed in some way to blaze a trail to this previously untouched part of the world. He had apparently come from the northwest, from the civilized portion of Colombia. He showed heroic perseverance and endurance in accomplishing his long journey. He must, however, have suffered from Westermarck's illusion of the free and easy nature of the Indian women, as he had awakened the jealousy and the wrath of some of the tribesmen a few days' journey ahead of us by paying too much attention to their wives. Not only had the Indians risen up and slain him by chopping him into small pieces with their knives (my informants gave me a very interesting and detailed account of the slaughter), but I was told that the wrathful natives had eaten him as well.

Despite many common and hair-raising stories, cannibalism is comparatively rare among the South American Indians, but it is by no means non-existent. In most cases it is prompted by a feeling of intense hatred and a desire for revenge, combined with the idea that by eating the flesh of a powerful enemy his strength and courage can be imbibed.

Prompted by the recent tragedy, I made inquiries among my new friends regarding cannibalistic orgies; and I found that the Indians of this region, though they but rarely eat the flesh of human beings, practise a very curious form of cannibalism. The bodies of certain chiefs and medicine-men are buried in the usual way for fifteen to twenty years, by which time the flesh, of course, is en-

tirely decomposed. The bones are then dug up, ground
into powder, and on special occasions added to the
kashiri, which is then ceremoniously drunk by the assembled tribesmen. The local chief who told me of this
custom dragged out a calabash or gourd filled with a
gray-looking powder. This, he assured me, was bone-
dust which had been prepared for the next such occasion.
He was kind enough to ask me whether I should like to
taste the powder. The invitation was no doubt a great
compliment; and I was willing to take it as such, even
though I felt it necessary to decline.

The eating of dried bones did not worry me, but I
was afraid that the far-away forest-dwellers up the river
might have found the Colombian such good eating that
they would wish to add another white man to their menu.
More important still was the fact that the Indians who
had been involved were probably suffering from an un-
easy conscience and would be likely to look upon any
white men who came into their territory as members of
a punitive expedition. Out of sheer panic, therefore, it
was not unlikely that they might attack us. Having
come so far, however, it was obviously impossible for me
to turn back; and so I encouraged my followers as best
I could, and incidentally tried to screw up my own courage at the same time.

As we were about to enter new territory, I tried
to complete my collection of examples of Tukano craftsmanship. I already possessed pots and baskets of a great
number of sizes and shapes. I had also secured various
types of bows, arrows, and blowpipes, as well as fish-
nets, fish-traps, and hammocks. I had now only to procure odds and ends, such as samples of native calabashes,
and last but not least some of the elaborate ornaments
and paraphernalia used at the great festivals.

The calabashes were very easy to secure. They were made from gourds cut in two and specially blackened and polished on the inside. They were the only drinking-cups known to the Indians; for curiously enough, in spite of their skill as potters, the natives have never learned to make drinking-cups or bowls of clay. The festival paraphernalia, since it was regarded as sacred, was much more difficult to procure. Some of the masks, in fact, I was never able to purchase. I had already secured at various times so many of the sacred ornaments that I was at last able to get hold of sufficient additional specimens to make my collection more or less complete.

At the same time I did my best to provide a larder sufficient to last us for another two or three weeks in case we should be unable to establish friendly contact with the Indians further up the river. For fish and game I hoped that we could rely on our own resources, but I bought huge quantities of *beijú* or *mandioca* pancakes, as well as several baskets of *mandioca* flour. These were our substitutes for vegetables and bread.

It was at this time that our sugar gave out. Joaquim, the cook, played a queer game with us for several days. Day after day he would dump a small handful of sugar before us and tell us that this was the very last of our stock. We economized accordingly, but when his handful had disappeared, he would manage to discover another. But all too soon his game came to an end. Our sugar supply was really exhausted, and we had to make up our minds to go without sweets until we could once more get back to civilization. We did indeed still have three tiny pots of jam, but I was determined to reserve these for some special occasion.

Poor old Joaquim had a very narrow escape at this stage of our journey. It was his duty each day to collect sufficient fire-wood to keep our cooking fire going. In most cases he was helped in his task by one or another of the Indians. On one occasion, while he was searching for dry branches, his Indian companion suddenly knocked the stolid Joaquim aside. Joaquim had trod on a *jararaca* snake, one of the most deadly reptiles of the Amazonian forest. The frightened snake immediately turned and struck. Thanks to the Indian's blow, Joaquim was knocked almost out of harm's way. The snake struck for the leg, but by great good fortune the fangs closed only on the cook's cloth trousers. Before the snake could increase its hold, the Indian was able to kill it. This incident was enough to shake any one's nerves, but Joaquim was so phlegmatic that he did not even flinch.

Joaquim also suffered a great deal in another way. In the jungle we found it necessary to examine our feet every day to see that no chigo or other insect had lodged there. If left alone, these little parasites multiplied very rapidly and caused untold damage. Joaquim was very careless in this respect, and an incredible number of chigoes had burrowed into his soles and toes before he noticed them. It was almost like conducting a major operation to cut out all the insect pests. When the task was at length accomplished, the poor cook's feet were so badly lacerated that he could stand only with the greatest difficulty. For many days thereafter he had to lie in his hammock even while he was trying to cook.

Eventually we left the last Tukano *maloka* behind us. Before us in the distance we could hear the dull booming of falling waters. We were approaching the huge *cachoéira* which marked the limits of Tukano influence. For many miles below the cataract, the river was covered with great masses of white foam. The white

froth on the surface of the dark red waters of the Awa
was a remarkable sight. The waters must have contained
some special mineral or vegetable substance which
caused it to become lathered when subjected to the stupendous churning of the cataract. The fact that the
foam had a distinct taste tends to confirm this impression. It may well have been the same substance which
gave the water its peculiar half-red, half-black color,
though chemical analysis has not yet been able to establish what the substance is.

At last we came in sight of the great cataract itself,
and it was one of the most impressive objects I have ever
seen. For half a mile the river was compressed by surrounding rocks to a tiny channel scarcely twenty yards
wide. In the course of this half-mile, the river fell several
hundred feet in a series of cascades and falls, each with
terrific force and splendor. The noise of the howling
waves was so great that we were almost deafened. My
Indians, who were always very susceptible to natural
phenomena, seemed to regard the great cataract as a
revelation of divinity. It would have been difficult to
imagine a finer natural frontier.

It was impossible to get our two boats through
the channel carved by the rapids. Portage was obviously necessary, but the rock walls of the gorge were so
precipitous that not even a single unimpeded man
could make his way along them to the untroubled
waters above. It was necessary for us to take our
axes and cut a path through the forest wide enough
to permit the passage of our boats. This proved a ter-
rifically difficult task and occupied two full days. When
the path was at last completed, we found to our dismay
that our united strength was not sufficient to pull the
heavy boats along it. We were in despair until we at

last thought of chopping off some of the round boughs from the surrounding trees. By using the boughs as rollers we eventually succeeded in dragging the boats through the forest to a point on the river above the cataract.

While we were busy with this task we pitched our little camp on the rocks overlooking the great cataract. Unfortunately our rest and even our work were greatly disturbed by the presence of large numbers of leeches, curious blood-sucking worm-like creatures which I observed here for the first time since our arrival in the Amazon basin. The leeches soon attached themselves to our skins and began to bloat themselves with our blood. It was highly inexpedient to pull them off, for when we did so they invariably left a nasty wound which for some reason refused to heal. In this quandary I remembered similar experiences which I had had in the jungles of India and astonished my companions by showing them that by smearing a little salt on the leeches they immediately shriveled up and dropped off.

We had scarcely got our boats through the forest when I became ill. It is possible that my illness was due to eating some of the stale *beijú* pancakes we had brought with us, though it may have come from other unknown causes. In any case a high temperature set in, and we were forced to halt for two more days while I kept to my hammock in order to give the fever time to work itself out.

The inaction was vexatious, but as soon as I began to recover I was kept in good spirits, first by an incident which occurred to Mannling, and secondly by long theological disputations carried on with my two attendant chiefs.

Early on the second morning of my illness Mannling

spent a full twenty minutes looking for his pipe. He ransacked all his pockets and opened up bag after bag and box after box with great perseverance but with no success. The pipe was not to be found. Eventually he discovered that he had had the pipe in his mouth the whole time he was looking for it.

The theological conversations furnished a more lengthy entertainment. So many of the religious dances which I had seen, and so many of the casual references to demons and deities which I had heard, remained so mysterious to me, and in part so contradictory, that I got Kandi and Mandu to sit by my hammock while I put them through an elaborate catechism.

By listening to their answers to my questions I found that the Indians had two entirely different types of deities. One consisted of the various wild spirits and demons of the forest, which I had seen so graphically portrayed, first in the *jurupari* festival, and subsequently in the weird ceremonies performed by the masked dancers. I was told that there were innumerable deities of this sort, but that there was a sort of king of the demonic pantheon called Wagti. As distinct from the jungle demons in general and Wagti in particular, there was also a more ethereal being called Wako. The early missionaries who busied themselves with native beliefs generally translated Wagti by "devil" and Wako by "God." Were this interpretation correct, most of the Indian religious ceremonies would have to be considered manifestations of devil-worship, as nearly all the native festivals were performed in honor of Wagti and his allies. But I soon found that both "God" and "devil" were words entirely inappropriate to any description of native beliefs.

Wagti, the "devil," was in no sense the eternal

enemy of mankind. It was Wagti who caused all the trees and plants of the jungle to grow. He was the mysterious creator and vivifier. His moods were, indeed, changeable. He could be irate as well as benevolent, but in no sense was he the enemy of Wako, the "good god." He was merely the dark and fearful spirit of the earth. Most human evils, such as disease and death, were according to the Indians caused by envious medicine-men of other tribes, and not directly by the demons, though, to be sure, the demons caused disaster when they were neglected by mankind. Thus, for example, should the ceremonies in honor of the jungle spirits not be performed, the harvest would necessarily be bad. For this reason the Indians could not understand why it was that the missionaries, who so tragically and unsuccessfully attempted to convert them, had tried to stop their sacred *jurupari* rites.

As Wagti was really only the creative spirit of the earth and the jungle, much to be feared but easy to placate, Wako on the other hand was a combination of the ideas of tribal hero and high good god. In all probability the Wako doctrine developed out of ancestor-worship and hero-worship, but by a process of sublimation and elaboration, Wako, the tribal hero, came to be regarded much as Christians regard the Supreme Deity, save that Wako was not supposed to trouble himself very much about the present state of the world.

Both Kandi and Mandu were willing to admit that Wako was the primeval creator of the world, though I found that many Indians ignored this aspect of their cultural divinity. According to Mandu, at the very beginning of all things, Wako created the earth, the sun, the moon, and lightning and thunder, but no living beings. One day thunder came to Wako and bewailed

the fact that the world was so still and empty. Thereupon Wako and the thunder together created a woman
out of tobacco-smoke. They placed her in a great canoe
filled with various kinds of animals; whereupon she
set out on a long journey from the Milky Way to the
earth. When the canoe reached the earth, the animals
became the ancestors of the various tribes of men. What
became of the primeval woman, a sort of Adamless
Eve, I could not find out. Presumably she went the way
of all flesh and died.

Wako, I discovered, was reverenced above all as the
giver of culture. It was Wako who gave to mankind
its laws and customs. It was Wako who taught human
beings how to prepare their feather ornaments, and who
told them how and when they were to dance. Wako
did not always give the same laws to all the tribes. To
the Tukanos he gave the coca-plant, so that they were
allowed to use this drug; but to the Waikanos he did not
give it, and so they are not permitted to indulge in its
use.

"How was it that Wako gave mankind its laws?"
I asked, and both of my chiefs told me a long story
about the incarnation of divinity. In the light of the fact
that in all probability Wako was originally only a tribal
hero, there is nothing very strange about the story of
his incarnation; it was certainly not due to missionary
influence. According to my informants Wako suddenly
appeared as a full-grown man among human beings,
first of all at Ipanoré, but subsequently at many other
places. Wherever he appeared a cataract sprang up.
Altogether Wako stayed on the earth a whole year.
During this time he particularly instructed the members of each tribe how they were to prepare *kashiri* and
kaapi.

All the Indians agreed that Wako during his stay on earth took unto himself a woman as a bride and that trouble ensued. It was also agreed that his bride was a Kole woman, though why this small tribe should have been selected for the honor I could not make out. Kandi and Mandu differed widely from each other, however, on the details of the story of the bride. Kandi said that the woman had been unfaithful to her divine spouse and had had an illicit affair with a forest demon. A bird had been a witness to it all and had informed Wako of it. Thereupon Wako made the first blowpipe and the first poisoned darts, and with these he killed the demon. He did indeed spare the woman, but he was so angry at her infidelity that he left the world forever. The woman later gave birth to the first snake and also to the first frog.

Mandu in his account of the circumstances was not quite so hard on the woman. According to him, soon after their marriage, Wako wished to test his bride and appeared to her as an old, ugly, and wrinkled man. The bride was disgusted with him and sent him away. Later Wako reappeared, bringing with him a *bacaba* fruit as an offering, and the two were reconciled. Wako then commanded a great feast to be made. This feast was attended not only by human beings but by all the beasts of the forest. More especially, great numbers of monkeys came, each of them bearing a *bacaba* fruit; but each of the monkeys magically had the same face as Wako, and the girl could not tell which of the multitude was her real husband.

The girl presently brewed huge quantities of *kashiri* for the assembled guests, and when she had taken the first sip of this drink, she was able to recognize her husband and brought him some of the precious *kashiri* to drink. Wako was thus appeased, but in any case he was determined to leave the world. He therefore gave long instructions to all the assembled men and beasts as to what they were to do and how they were to behave. He then ascended into the sky. As he disappeared, he sent down a pounder, or drumstick, which has ever since been used by the Indians in honor of their divine law-giver.

In due course the girl gave birth to a deer. The girl's mother used to take the deer to the forest to let it eat leaves, but one day it ran far into the jungle and never returned. Soon afterward the girl herself disappeared into the bowels of the earth.

One of my other paddlers joined in the conversation at this point and gave an interesting addition to the story of Wako's farewell banquet to all living beings. Before the banquet, so ran the tale, mankind had been immortal and had never known sorrow. When Wako informed the assembly that he was going to leave the world forever, men and women began to weep for the first time. Wako told them that they must not weep or they would surely die. The sorrow of the people was so great, however, that they could not stop weeping, and, as Wako had predicted, because of their tears death came into the world.

Since Wako disappeared from the world, he has continued to exist somewhere in the high heavens, but he has little or nothing to do with mankind in its present state. Men follow his precepts and are thankful for his teachings, but as he is good and friendly whatever happens, the natives do not trouble to make him offerings. It is the jungle deities who bring about evil and who must therefore be appeased.

CHAPTER XX

DANGER FROM BEAST AND MAN

PARTLY because of the medicines I took, and partly, no doubt, because of the exalted nature of our conversation, my illness completely disappeared the next morning, and we were able to continue our journey without more ado. Even above the cataract the current was extremely strong, and it took us several hours to cover the next four or five miles. The river was once more broken up into a number of narrow channels, and we could again see the great clumps of rocks rising out of the waters. But for the first time in months, the rocks were not granite but consisted of conglomerate and sandstone.

At last we came to a bend in the river. At this point we could see no sign of human habitation, but Mandu assured us that an Indian settlement lay not far away. True enough, we at length found a path which in about half an hour brought us to a large *maloka* which was particularly well hidden away in the forest. Its inhabitants I found were Pamoas, or Armadillos, so called from their supposed ancestor, the armadillo. In days gone by, the Pamoas must have been a numerous tribe, having control over several of the near-by tributaries, but sometime previously a mysterious malady had at-

tacked them. Hundreds of the tribesmen had succumbed, and the rest had fled to the spot where we found
them. The Pamoas differed considerably in appearance
from the Indians further down the river. I found, however, that their language belonged to the same Betoya
group and was not entirely dissimilar to the Tukano
dialect, although for many generations the Tukanos and
the Pamoas have been deadly enemies.

I was so interested in the physical characteristics of
the Pamoas that soon after arriving at their *maloka* I
got out my calipers and proceeded to make a number
of anthropological measurements. I found the *maloka*
dwellers so shy and frightened, however, that I thought
it better to measure some of my crew first in order to
show our new acquaintances that they had nothing to
fear from my strange activity. It was an interesting
commentary on the usefulness of anthropological measurements that by casually measuring my crew I discovered that one of my supposed Tukano paddlers was
in reality a Pogsa.

To the eye he appeared very much like his companions. I had noticed nothing peculiar about him,
but upon applying the calipers I found that the shape
and size of his skull agreed so closely with those of various Pogsas I had measured that I asked him if he did
not also belong to this tribe.

I soon discovered that my questioning had raked up
a family scandal. The man was in reality the illegiti-
mate son of a Tukano father and a Pogsa mother, but
by virtue of his father's "nationality" he claimed to be
a Tukano himself, and at first he would not even admit
that he could understand the Pogsa language. My discovery of his Pogsa affiliations by means of the calipers
seemed to make a great impression on my followers.

My stay in this settlement incidentally taught me two new possible sources of food. Shortly after my arrival, the Pamoas caught a number of small river-frogs and proceeded to prepare them in a very cruel way for eating. Long wooden prongs were stuck through the bodies of the frogs, and, though still alive, they were then slowly roasted over a fire. In our hungry condition, however, we could not be squeamish. Not only did we accept the frogs offered to us, but we found that they made very excellent eating.

The other new article of diet was even more remarkable. In spite of their very cleanly habits, the Indians, especially the women, frequently have a number of lice in their hair. Not uncommonly of an evening the women find amusement by forming a circle and picking out the lice from one another's heads. I found that the Pamoas not only engaged in this pastime but went a stage farther and ate the lice which they captured. In spite of my exploring zeal, I discovered that this was one native custom which I had no desire to imitate.

We were careful to inquire here into the truth of the story concerning the murdered Colombian, and we found it confirmed at every point. Such being the case, I was anxious to get one of the Pamoa tribesmen to go with us, or even ahead of us, in order to let the settlements further up-stream know that we were not members of an official avenging party. I found, however, that the Pamoas themselves were so frightened by the incident that they advised us strongly to turn back. When I insisted upon proceeding, they did indeed give us detailed information as to where each of the up-stream settlements was to be found, but they refused under any circumstances to accompany us.

The next morning, with a good deal of trepidation,

we set out once more upon our journey up the river. Needless to say, we maintained an unusually sharp lookout the whole day; and contrary to our usual practice, we kept our boats to the middle of the stream instead of hugging one of the banks, as we thought that in this way we should be less liable to surprise attack.

An hour or two after starting, we passed the mouth of an important-looking tributary called the Japo, which flows into the main stream from the south. The head-waters of this stream are supposed to arise in a huge morass, called by the Indians a lake, only a few miles south of where we were. This same morass is also supposed to be the source of the Tiquié River and of one branch of the Pira Parana, although the latter belongs to an entirely different water system and is in no way connected with the Uaupés and Negro rivers.

Far south of us, and no doubt overlooking a part of the huge morass, we could see a range of mountains. These I found were regarded by my Indians with superstitious awe on the ground that they were the abode of demons and of the spirits of the dead. My Indians also had a story to the effect that at the foot of these mountains, hidden in the mud of the great morass, were many strange animals of huge dimensions, animals such as are to be found nowhere else.

I was strongly tempted to follow the Japo up to its interesting source. But I knew that this tributary was entirely uninhabited, and as I did not want to flounder in the morass without local guides, I at last decided that we should continue up the main stream. Early in the afternoon we came in sight of a new *maloka*. Very cautiously we approached it, as we did not know whether or not we should be met by a rain of arrows. When we finally arrived, we found the place entirely deserted. It was obvious, however, that the Indians had been there only an hour or two previously, as the coals in some of the hearth-fires were still warm. Not only had the Indians decamped, taking their hammocks with them, which showed that they were not likely to return; they had also carried away all available food supplies.

For the first time I regretted the fact that we had no women, more particularly no Indian women, accompanying us. A plantation with plentiful *mandioka* roots was only a few yards away, but none of the men were capable of transforming the poisonous roots into a palatable food. For this reason I was doubly glad that we had a fairly plentiful supply of *farinha* along with us.

Unfortunately we could secure neither fish nor game. We still had half a dozen small tins of deviled meat, but in view of the long journey ahead of us we could only afford to consume one of these at a time. I soon found that one tiny tin of meat gave very scanty rations when divided up among fourteen people. The only thing to do was to boil up the contents of the tin with a huge mass of *mandioka* meal and cut-up bananas, so that each person could get a taste of the meat and imagine that he was partaking of a substantial meal.

The three other settlements we came upon in the course of the next day and a half were also deserted, so that it became necessary for us to make a strenuous attempt to secure food by hunting and fishing. This led to one or two unfortunate accidents. One of my Indians, while scouring the woods in search of game, came upon one of the miniature crocodiles which inhabit the upper waters of the Amazon basin. These crocodiles are much smaller than the huge caymans of the main stream, but unlike the larger variety, they are, at least by the Indians, considered edible. My Indian decided to add the reptile to our cooking-pot, but only succeeded in wounding him slightly. The hunter rushed forward to secure the prey with his hands, but not only did the reptile escape, he also succeeded in rather badly mauling the Indian's arm. Unfortunately crocodile's teeth are not the cleanest things in the world, and I had to take all sorts of precautions to prevent sepsis from setting in.

Curiously enough, it was on the same day that another of my Indians was stung on the instep by a venomous jungle spider. The sting of this insect has always very serious effects and is not infrequently fatal. On this occasion, not only the foot but the whole leg swelled up, and in a short time the man was in agony. I cut open the flesh and sucked out as much of the poison as was possible and then gave the poor Indian diluted potassium permanganate to drink, while I applied a stronger solution to the wound itself. The man eventually recovered, but he was ill for several days.

In the course of our slow progress up the river we came across several *malokas,* but they were invariably deserted. This fact gave us all rather an uncanny feeling. For all we knew, the Indians of the district, though invisible, might be near at hand. It sometimes seemed as if prying eyes were fixed on us from dark places in the surrounding jungle, and we feared lest we be attacked at any moment.

Undisturbed by this fact, however, we continued to stop at each settlement, in a vain attempt to reëstablish friendly relations with the natives. In each case it seemed as though the inhabitants had deserted their *maloka* only an hour or two before our arrival, but our protests of friendship shouted into the jungle failed to bring any response.

At one of the settlements at which we stopped I saw a very fine coca pounder and mortar. My collector's heart yearned to possess this trophy, and I was on the point of appropriating it as part of the spoils of war when Kandi stepped in and urged me to do nothing which the Indians of the surrounding district might consider a hostile act. I was a little ashamed of having to be reminded of the decalogue by a wild Indian, but I must confess that I still regret that Kandi happened to be looking just as I was trying to make away with treasure. I never saw so fine a specimen either before or afterward.

One of the last of the deserted settlements we visited gave us an especial thrill. We knew from the accounts given us by the Pamoa Indians that this *maloka* must have been the actual site of the murder of the Colombian. We therefore landed and approached the settlement with especial care. The same creepy silence and lifelessness awaited us, but we did stumble on two things which gave us a vivid reminder of the tragedy that had recently taken place. One was a blood-smear on one of the rocks outside the *maloka*. The other was a European felt hat hidden away in a corner of the huge tribal house. We could find no trace of any other article of clothing, but the hat I took with me as a ghastly memento of our visit to the house of tragedy.

It was already late in the afternoon, but none of us felt in the mood to spend the night in a place which savored so much of battle, murder, and sudden death; so we continued our journey up-stream and halted only when we came to a small island in the middle of the stream.   Here at least we seemed safe from secret observation.

The next day we came to a place where the stream was so small that it was impossible to follow it any further. We had now to abandon all attempts at navigation, for the time being, and attempt to hack our way through the jungle itself. By keeping due south we hoped eventually to fight our way through the forest to some river flowing into the Japurá, which at this time was our goal. We had, however, no idea of how long it would take to make our way through the jungle, nor what was the best route to follow. It was therefore urgently necessary that we find some Indians who could act as guides. All of the *malokas* we had recently visited had been deserted, and until we could once more establish friendly relations with the Indians of the district we seemed in a hopeless position.

Mandu, my Tukano chief, knew of a settlement miles away in the jungle, and we determined to get into touch with its inhabitants at all costs. We landed our boats on the banks of a little backwater which opened out on the southern side of the Awa River and there talked over the best plan of action. Mandu assured me that a path led from this point to the *maloka,* though the path was entirely invisible to my European eyes. After long consultation we decided to pitch camp where we were, while Mandu and two of the other Tukanos went on alone to the *maloka* in order to announce our arrival. Should all of us go together, it seemed certain that the natives would flee into the forests, and we should again find nothing more than a silent and deserted house; but it seemed possible that the Indians would be willing to receive two or three of my native followers as emissaries.

As soon as Mandu and his men had departed, we

Preparing for initiation into the *jurupari* mysteries

Tribal elders and Dr. McGovern in his initiation costume

Preparation of the mysterious drug, *kaapi*, the bitter "nectar of the gods"

The sacred trumpets of the *jurupari* ceremony, which no woman may see
under pain of death

began repacking and rearranging our luggage, so as to put it in fit shape for transportation through the forest. This task occupied us the whole of the afternoon. Scarcely had it been accomplished when Mandu suddenly reappeared and informed us that he had indeed been able to get in touch with the inhabitants of the forest *maloka,* but that they were in a very hostile mood and wanted to have nothing to do with us. This was no doubt due to the fact that among these Indians there were several who had been implicated in the death of the Colombian, and who had fled to this distant settlement in order to escape retribution. Not only were these forest dwellers loath to serve as guides through the jungle, but they were even talking of the advisability of attacking us.

In these circumstances, Mandu proposed that we stay where we were for the time being, while he returned to the *maloka* and tried to bring its inhabitants into a better frame of mind. I sent him back with a number of presents and told him to paint my character as Friend of the Indians in very glowing colors. The rest of the party settled down for the night, though it was agreed that we were not only to hold our weapons in readiness for an attack, but also to take turns in keeping watch so as not to be taken by surprise.

As luck would have it, we found that we had pitched our camp near a nest of *tukandero* ants. This discovery was made when one of these insects stung Pequenino, causing him to give a yelp of agony. Remembering his previous misadventures, I was struck by the uncanny predilection which all insects showed for his person. There was something comic about the situation, but it had its serious side, for *tukanderos* are not only the largest members of the ant family (measuring as they

do from an inch to one and one half inches in length),
but their sting is also the most painful and causes real
agony.

Spanish-Americans call the *tukanderos* *"veinte
quatro,"* or twenty-four (hours), because of the fact
that the pain from a single sting is supposed to last a
day and a night. It is even said that the bite of one such
ant may prove fatal, at least to a child. I could quite
believe this, for Pequenino had his whole arm swollen
and benumbed for several hours as the result of a single
sting.

Fortunately we found that *tukanderos* do not form
very large families and that there are seldom more than
a hundred or two of them in any one nest. Knowing
this, we tried to destroy the nest we had stumbled upon,
together with all its inhabitants, by means of fire and
smoke. We were not certain about the success of our
efforts to exterminate the tribe, though we managed to
kill off many scores of its members.

Later in the evening, in order to pass the time, Kandi
related all manner of hair-raising tales concerning demons and devils. So successful were his efforts that we
all felt very creepy and nervous, quite apart from the
constant fear of attack which haunted us. For this reason it was late at night before we could get to sleep.
After the camp had eventually quieted down, I kept the
first watch and then woke Kandi, who was to take the
second. Thereafter various other Indians took turns at
playing sentry.

About three o'clock in the morning we were awakened by a sudden shout from one of the paddlers who
was acting as sentry. At first we thought that the threatened attack had really materialized, but we found that
the alarm had been given only because a sudden but

very violent thunder-storm had occurred. In a few moments a deluge of rain descended. For strategic reasons we had not erected our tents but had merely slung our hammocks in the open between the trees. It was now necessary, however, to put up one of the tents as shelter.

Because of the darkness and pouring rain, this proved a very difficult matter. In the midst of our activity we discovered that all the *tukanderos* were not yet dead. The rain revived some of the smoked-out insects, and these succeeded in adding Mannling and da Silva to the list of victims. It is rather distressing to other persons when two men holding up tent-poles give a sudden yell and abandon the tent to its own resources while they nurse wounded limbs. It was particularly distressing to me, as I happened to be inside the tent when it collapsed. I struggled wildly for many minutes before I could extricate myself from the canvas, imagining all the while that *tukanderos,* Indians, and forest devils were making a special attack upon my person.

Eventually the tent was put up, and we cowered inside it until the rain subsided. Sleep was out of the question, and we could only wait patiently for the dawn and the return of the faithful Mandu. Unfortunately the rain had ruined our *mandioka* flour, so that we were forced to wait on empty stomachs.

At last, about eight o'clock, Mandu appeared, followed by a number of strangers. His diplomacy had won the day, but it was obvious that we were still faced by a difficult situation, for when I stepped forward to shake the hands of the new arrivals they imagined I was after their lives. Giving a shriek they disappeared into the forest, and it was some time before we could coax them into the open again. Eventually, however, friendly negotiations were concluded. We were at least to be allowed to go on to the native settlement. Once there, we could attempt to talk over the best means of continuing our journey.

The *maloka* to which we were going had obviously been intended as a place of refuge. The long trail leading to it from the river was carefully concealed by making it cross and recross a number of small streams, which meant that no footprints were visible, and also by felling huge tree-trunks so as to give them the appearance of having fallen naturally. When we at last arrived at the *maloka,* I sensed among its inhabitants such a feeling of scarcely suppressed fear and hostility that I felt called upon to make particularly friendly overtures. I found that this settlement, like the deserted *malokas* we had previously come upon, belonged to the Karapana (Mögtöa) or Mosquito Indians. It seemed fairly certain that a number of the gentlemen around me had banqueted on the murdered Colombian a few weeks previously, but I determined to omit all reference to this interesting meal and to the events which had preceded it.

It was necessary to get our friends into a more friendly mood before inquiring from them the possibilities of making our way through the jungle to the next river system. This meant that we had to embark upon the long and elaborate greeting prescribed by native etiquette. It was interesting to see that in this formal and diplomatic conversation, not only was Tukano the language employed, but also that Mandu, as a Tukano, was given social precedence over Kandi, even though Kandi was a much more forceful personality.

Even more important than the formal conversation, however, was the informal powwow which followed, and

in this Kandi played a leading part. He retired into one
corner of the *maloka* and soon had all the old women
gathered around him. These he managed to entertain
and enlighten far better than Mandu could have done.
In spite of his very dignified and rather martial manners, Kandi always seemed to have great influence among
the women-folk. Many a time we had twitted him about
his "conquests," but on this occasion his Casanova qualities were certainly of the greatest assistance.

CHAPTER XXI

THE MARCH THROUGH THE JUNGLE

GENERAL diplomatic negotiations took up the whole of the first day of our stay at this stronghold of the Indians. By the morning of the second day, however, we felt sufficiently secure of our position to broach the matter of our further journey. We found that the Indians did know of a river many days' journey to the south; but they assured us that it would be impossible for us with our heavy baggage to make our way to it, because of the density of the intervening jungle, and that in any case they would be unable to accompany us as guides, since they had recently been engaged in warfare with some of the tribes on the other river. Incidentally many weapons used in tribal warfare seemed more common and in greater use among these people than among any of the tribes I had hitherto visited. These were a sort of heavy wooden sword or club, battle-lance, and wickerwork shield.

Once we had overcome their initial fear, however, I felt we were on safe ground. Da Silva spread out some of our wondrous beads, cloths, and knives and allowed the natives to have a long envious look at them. He then informed them that this treasure would belong to them if they would only bring us safely through the jungle. In the end cupidity got the better of timidity. The Indians agreed not only to guide us to the far-distant river but to carry our luggage as well. This was an important point, as we needed every available man to bring my numerous boxes through the forest. The two boats we were forced to leave behind, and one or two of the heavier boxes; but it was impossible, of course, to part with the collections that I had made. Our trade goods would be imperative on the other river, and finally the film and camera were equally indispensable. Consequently I insisted even that my crew who wished to return at this point must accompany us until we could once more embark on the river, so that with the natives of the new *maloka* who were to go with us my little party had now swollen to fifty in number.

Early in the day on which we were to begin our new undertaking a number of the Mosquito Indians set out through the jungle, accompanied only by Mannling and Kandi; it was arranged that the remaining members of my party were to start half an hour later. Scarcely ten minutes after their departure, however, the Indians of this advance-guard came rushing back shrieking "Colombiano, Colombiano." Upon hearing these dreaded words all of the local Indians seized their hammocks and prepared to flee into the forest. I knew it would never do to let them disappear, as once they were out of sight we should never be able to get hold of our guides again. I therefore shouted to da Silva to close one entrance to the *maloka* and stand guard over it while I did the same at the other door, so that no one could leave. I then tried to find out exactly what had happened, but in their frightened condition it was almost impossible to get any intelligent explanation from the Indians, and we had to wait until Kandi and Mannling returned before we could secure this.

I then learned that two strange Indians had sud-

denly emerged from the jungle crying out that a band
of Colombians had arrived. Immediately afterward
these strangers had seen Mannling, and thinking that
they had jumped from the frying-pan into the fire, they
had once more disappeared into the jungle.

It was obviously impossible to continue our journey
before getting to the bottom of this story. I therefore
sent two of the native women into the jungle to find
the strange Indians who had arrived so inopportunely
and to tell them that they need have no fear of us.

It took the women nearly an hour to entice the messengers from their hiding-place. When they were at last
brought into the *maloka* I observed with much amusement that they had to go through the whole of the long
sing-song greeting ceremonial before they could tell
us their story. These Indians turned out to be members
of a tribe dwelling in the far-away south, who had been
driven by fear to make the long journey through the
jungle. They informed us that a band of marauding lawless Colombians had broken through the jungle at a
place where no white man had ever before been seen,
and that these outlaws were now ravaging a number of
Indian villages.

This news so frightened the Mosquito Indians that
for a time they gave up all thought of guiding us
through the jungle, but after much argument I managed to convince them that with our help they had
nothing to fear from any other white men, and they
once more agreed to accompany us. In fact I succeeded
in instilling such confidence in our prowess that even
the strangers from the south consented to return with
us to their homes. This was a real achievement, as these
strangers were likely to be the best guides of all. The
very fact that the southerners had made their way

through the jungle showed me that the forest could not be absolutely impenetrable. In fact it was obvious that there must have been some sort of intercommunication between the inhabitants of the two river systems, if only because of the occasional hostile raids which I was told had taken place.

After the excitement had quieted down we once more set off on our journey. It can hardly be said that there was a path. Communication between the two water systems took place probably only two or three times a year, and the quick-growing jungle soon obliterates every trail; but the Indians were obviously accustomed to follow a particular route, and as we advanced through the jungle I could occasionally see from an old knocked-off branch or a fallen tree-trunk that the jungle had once at least been visited by mankind.

The heavy tropical rains and the constant fertility of nature had caused fresh trees to grow up in the place of the old. Considering the density of the jungle and of the undergrowth, and also the presence of vines and creepers between the trees, it seemed almost a miracle that a man even without a load could get through, yet my Indians were hampered by carrying huge and weighty boxes. I was astonished at the load which each man could shoulder. Huge tin boxes full of films, each weighing nearly two hundred pounds, were carried hour after hour and day after day. I noticed that the Indians carried all the loads on their backs, but supported by a strap tied to their foreheads. Even the women had been pressed into service. It is probable that they wanted to visit their old homes and in order to do so had cheerfully shouldered burdens quite as heavy as those of the men and in addition had slung over their shoulders squawking infants.

Notwithstanding their burdens, the Indians continued to progress at what was really a remarkable rate. Two or three went on ahead armed with the long forest knives (machetes) I had given them and tried to hack out a free passage. Even so it was necessary to duck and twist and gyrate in a manner comparable only to the modern conception of dancing as exemplified in the Charleston. Worse still was the fact that we occasionally came across huge stretches of swamp and marsh where we sank up to our knees in mud. On higher ground we would frequently have to cross a ravine bridged only by the thin round slippery trunk of a fallen tree. The Indians have a remarkable facility in the use of their feet. Frequently I had observed that they would pick things up with their toes instead of using their hands. Consequently they were able to run along slippery tree-trunks by using their flexible toes to secure a hold where it was impossible for a shoe-clad European to follow. In spite of the thorns, the insects, and a fear of snakes, it was necessary to go barefoot; even so I had to bite my lip until the blood came before I could force myself to go over some of the slippery natural bridges which the Indians crossed without concern.

For many nights we had to camp in the forest. This meant that on several occasions we were wet through to the skin. I had purposely brought with me a very small tent large enough only to hold the more valuable and perishable part of our luggage. A larger tent would have increased the weight enormously, and in any case would have been useless, because of the density of the jungle.

I have always a distrust of large, elaborate, and well equipped expeditions. The better the equipment the greater the difficulty of getting through. I have generally observed that the explorer who gets anywhere goes out with next to nothing and usually dumps that down as useless somewhere on the way. Whenever it rained too hard we crowded together in the little tent for mutual warmth and shelter but returned to our hammocks as soon as the shower was over.

Far worse than the wetting of our persons was the fact that on one occasion the whole of our scanty stock of matches became so soaked as to be useless. We were rescued from a fireless predicament only by the skill of the two Pogsa slaves who were numbered among my attendants. I was surprised to find that none of the other Indians could compete with the Pogsa in fire-making, but this was no doubt due to the fact that the settled Indians always keep at least one fire going perpetually and so are able to start other flames from this central hearth. It is only the wandering home-less Pogsas who are forced to light a fresh fire each day.

My Pogsa followers were of course ignorant of flint and steel, but by boring one piece of a certain kind of wood (it looked like a thick rush) into another they at last secured a spark which was soon blown into a flame. I was surprised to find that both pieces of wood came from the same branch, so that one was not harder or softer than the other.

The jungle continued to be unfriendly as regards food, and we met with almost no game, but the Indians surprised me one day by collecting from the trees a large number of caterpillars. With these they proceeded to prepare their evening meal. I was interested to see how they set to work. The "innards" were carefully squeezed out, and only the skins were thrown into the cooking-pot. They were boiled for half an hour, and the banquet was then declared ready. I was surprised to find how tough these boiled caterpillars were. They required careful mastication, and both in consistency and in taste they reminded me rather forcibly of rubber bands.

I always tried to keep our party together, but Mannling and I got into the habit of going on ahead, and on one occasion during a blinding rain-storm we became separated from the others and were soon hopelessly lost. For hours we wandered aimlessly through the forest and then tried to retrace our steps. It is curious how the lost invariably wander in circles. Three times we came back to the same spot after hacking our way through the jungle for what seemed an eternity. We were without food, and in the absence of matches even our pipes were useless.

Mannling wanted to fire his rifle as a signal, but I prevented him from doing so lest the Indians think that the dreaded Colombians had come upon them. Had the shot been fired, the Indians would probably have scattered far and wide instead of coming to our rescue. To make matters worse we got immeshed in a large bog, and for a long time we could not find our way back to dry land. While we were struggling in the bog I must have been bitten or stung by some insect, as my right foot became very painful and proceeded to swell up enormously. At first the experience had seemed a joke, but as evening drew on we became really frightened. Night fell, and as we could still see no way out, we determined to crawl up into the boughs of some tree and wait for morning before struggling on further. Just then, however, I heard in the distance some one calling us. The Indians had noticed our absence, and the faithful Kandi and Mandu had headed a search party. There is no doubt that on this, as on many other occasions, the

Indians, though so often accused of treachery and faith-lessness, saved our lives.

On several occasions during our journey through the jungle we heard strange noises coming from the surrounding forest. Sometimes it seemed as if wooden rods were being beaten against one another; at other times I imagined that I heard some one cutting down a tree in the distance. These noises always seemed to frighten my Indian companions, and when I asked them about the cause of the mysterious sounds, they invari-ably replied that it was the demons of the forest at play.

After many days of wandering we came to another large swamp, which proved to be the source of a river flowing to the south. This turned out to be the Pira Parana, or Fish River, although on the maps the source of this river is erroneously placed about four hundred miles further west. At the point where we reached the river it was a mere brook, scarcely three feet wide, and covered every yard or two by fallen logs and overhang-ing vines. It was obvious that we could not attempt to embark here but would have to continue our journey overland until we came to a point where the river was more navigable.

On the way up the Papuri the insects had been a good deal of a nuisance during the daytime, but on no occasion had we found it necessary to use our mosquito-nets at night. Immediately on entering this new river system, however, we found that sleep was impossible unless we were well protected by nets every night. I noticed that in spite of the enormous number of insect pests in this region, the Indians had never learned the art of preparing any form of nets, and they were forced to protect themselves by keeping smoky fires burning under their hammocks all night.

One of the most troublesome of the insects was the *motuka*, a voracious bloodsucker, although it looked exactly like a large European house-fly. Unlike the vampire-bat the *motuka* inflicted a very painful sting. I was surprised to find that it was able to sting through my thick hammock and even through my clothes. On one occasion I thought that Pequenino was attempting a joke by sticking a long needle through the hammock in which I was sitting, and I yelled to him to stop his nonsense before I realized the real cause of the trouble.

For some extraordinary reason we were attacked early the next morning by a huge swarm of bees. These insects alighted in such numbers on our camp that we were forced to pack our things and continue the journey at an unusually early hour.

For the next two days we kept to the jungle and lost sight of the river, which at this point made a huge bend to the west. During this time we once more managed to lose our way, even though we were in the company of some of the Indians. They themselves were not over-sure of the proper direction, and we had to wait until the two Indians who lived on the river came up to us and gave us proper directions.

Just about this time, in falling over a stump I broke my watch. Mannling's timepiece had long ceased to function, so that we were forced to rely upon the sun as our chronometer, and as long as we were in the jungle even the sun was rarely visible. This troubled us very slightly, however. We had long adopted an almost Indian attitude toward time. The only important difference was between day and night, and our stomachs told us any further details of the passage of the hours which we required to know. Far more important than the destruction of the watch was the fact that Mannling lost his pipe shortly afterward and was accordingly forced to share mine.

From time to time we crossed over little forest streams which ran down to join the Pira Parana. The difference in the color of the water of these streams was remarkable. Some had the same black-red color of the Papuri, others were brown, while others again were perfectly colorless; and yet the streams ran through the same forest, and I could not observe any difference in the nature of the soil.

CHAPTER XXII

THE LAND OF NAKED WOMEN

IT was a welcome relief when a sudden break in the forest once more brought us in sight of a human habitation, even though this turned out to be of a very rough and primitive sort, quite unlike an ordinary *maloka.*

We soon found that we had come upon a mere haven of refuge. The regular tribal *maloka* was several miles away, on the banks of the Pira Parana, but fear of the Colombians had caused its inhabitants temporarily to abandon their home and erect this hut far away in the jungle.

We had, of course, come to an entirely new tribe of Indians, the members of which called themselves Tsönoas, or Inhambús.[1] Living as they did on a very different river system from the one on which we had hitherto been journeying, I was interested in studying these new natives in detail. Careful examination showed that we were still in Betoya territory, for as regards both language and general culture the Tsönoas were obviously affiliated with tribes of the Uaupés and Papuri rivers.

The Tsönoas were, however, far more primitive than

[1] The *inhambú* is a well known Amazonian wild fowl.

any of the other Betoya tribes we had hitherto visited. The women, for example, did not wear a stitch of clothing except for a pair of beautifully woven garters. These were for adornment only, as the ladies of course wore no stockings. Perhaps because of their nudity the women were more shy and reserved than any I had so far seen. It would seem that the less clothes women wear, the more highly proper and reserved is their conduct.

The men covered their nakedness with a bast loincloth similar to the one worn in the Papuri district; but unlike the tribes with which we had previously come into contact, the males of this region wore a long black wooden skewer through the nose and a feather-tufted bone in the lobe of each ear. A wooden button was thrust through a hole bored deep down in the lower lip.

Altogether the Indians of this region were a rather wild-looking lot, and I was tempted to be more afraid of them than of any marauding Colombians, but from their very friendly attitude I soon saw that fear was groundless.

Unfortunately, however, the absence of our hosts from their fishing-ground meant that they could not help us much with our food problem. This was particularly disappointing, as my native carriers were naturally exhausted from their long exertion in the forest and were badly in need of something more sustaining than *beijú*. I tried to console them for the absence of fish and game by giving them a soup prepared from beef extract, telling them it was the clotted blood of strong animals. The tale went very well with the Brazilians, but the Indians turned up their noses in scorn at the mess I offered them and preferred to stick to their diet of *mandioca* meal and water.

That same afternoon I secured from the Tsönoas

a bird which though unusable as food, provided me with a good deal of amusement. This was a *jacamin* or *trompetero,* which, although only recently captured, was already very tame. In size and appearance it was not unlike a large pheasant. The Indians regarded it as a bird of sorcery. From the curious ventral noises made by the bird when excited, the natives asserted that they could not only foretell the coming of friends or foes but also prognosticate any change in the weather. Certainly as to the latter point I must say that the Indians' interpretation of the bird's noises proved remarkably correct, and I should like to suggest that some of our weather observatories in Europe and America would do well to equip themselves with this feathered barometer.

To me the most curious thing about my newly acquired *trompetero* bird was the remarkable zest he showed in fighting and killing snakes. The Indians happened to capture a small snake that same afternoon, and instead of killing it immediately they threw it in front of the bird. A pitched battle ensued. The snake lunged out at the bird again and again, but although the bird looked extremely awkward and slow, he managed always to keep just out of reach. From time to time the *trompetero* succeeded in giving a sharp peck at the snake's neck, and at the end of twenty minutes the snake lay lifeless.

The hut was so crowded that my little party was forced to sleep once more in the open, but this proved no great inconvenience, as the night was marvelously clear and the stars shone down brightly upon us. I began to talk to my Indians regarding the stars and was surprised to find that they had a keen interest and a good knowledge of the various constellations. As they were unable to calculate periods of time, the Indians had

learned to make the stars serve as a sort of calendar;
the planting of the crops, the performance of certain
ceremonies, and the periodic wailing for the dead were
all attended to when the stars stood at a certain position
in the sky.

To the Indians, of course, as to all primitive people,
the celestial bodies were mysterious spirits, some good
and others evil. The sun, I was told, is a male spirit,
similar to Wagti, the high good God, but not to be confused with him. Every morning the Sun emerges from
his *maloka* through the front door, and every evening he creeps back to his *maloka* through the back door.
The Sun's rays are the festival adornments which he
binds to his head. Eclipses take place when the Sun
smears himself with dark *genipapo* paint. He appears
red whenever he paints himself with *karujuru*. The
Moon is the younger brother of the Sun-god. Because
of his youth, he is not yet allowed to don full festival
adornment. He is alternately lean and stout because of
his habit of alternately fasting and feasting.

The next day the Tsönoas guided us through the
forest to their abandoned *maloka* on the banks of the
Pira Parana. Here we found two canoes, so that from
this point we could continue our journey by water. We
found, however, that we should have to embark on this
new phase of the journey alone. Both my Tukano crew
and my Mosquito guides insisted upon returning to their
homes on the Papuri. Even the Tsönoas refused to accompany us down-stream, so frightened were they at
the prospect of meeting the Colombians; so that for the
time being Kandi, his two sons, and Mandu were to be
our sole Indian companions.

The returning Indians had to be compensated for
their services, and as some of them had been with us for

several weeks and had comparatively large sums owing
them, the process of paying them off proved a lengthy
affair and required the whole of the afternoon. Considering the strenuous work they had been called upon to do,
I was surprised to find how moderate they were in their
demands, but at the same time they were as "finicky" in
the choice of presents as any of the other Indians with
whom we had come into contact.

As there seemed to be a run on fish-hooks and knives,
of which we had only a moderate supply, da Silva and I
made an attempt to interest our men in other less popular trade goods, and in the end we were not altogether
unsuccessful. Our perfumes and mouth-organs had in
the past found a very poor market, and we made a special effort to get rid of them on this occasion. We opened
a bottle of most pestiferous scent, and by holding it
under the nose of each man until he promised to buy
some, we eventually got rid of several bottles.

Encouraged by this success, da Silva did his best
to coax a tune out of one of the mouth-organs. So great
was his musical genius that one youth was at last be-
guiled into taking one of these instruments as part payment for his services. We were so delighted at his appreciation of music that we gave him three other mouth-
organs as free-will offerings. But even this bonus failed
to induce any of the other Indians to follow his example.

I was particularly pleased to find that through a
little ruse of mine we were able to dispose of a large
number of red and green beads. All along these had been
very unpopular, the natives invariably demanding only
the blue and white varieties. This led me to try a social
experiment. For several days past, Mannling and I had
worn necklaces made from the large stock of green and
red beads, while under my orders Joaquim and Peque-

nino had adorned themselves with necklaces made from the blue and white ones. This fact had not failed to impress my native carriers; and when da Silva, carrying on the good work, gave a long lecture upon the social superiority of red and green, the Indians allowed their social ambitions to overcome their artistic preferences, and agreed to reduce our stock of the beads of the previously despised colors.

As soon as the payments had been completed, most of the Indians set out on their long journey through the jungle, but we kept the Tsönoa tribesmen with us for some time in order to secure from them detailed information concerning the country through which we were to pass. As we should be guideless, it was necessary that we be forewarned against all possible trouble. After much questioning we were told that on our journey down the river we should pass by two *malokas* which were so well hidden in the woods that it would be impossible to find them, but that at the end of a day's journey we should come in sight of a *maloka* near the water's edge. Here we should find a woman who had once been married to a Tukano, and so we should easily make ourselves understood.

Having secured this information, we were forced to allow the Tsönoa Indians to depart. By this time it was too late to make a fresh start, and we slept that night in the deserted *maloka*. Early next morning when we sought to continue our journey we found that the two canoes we had secured, our only means of transport, would not be sufficient to carry more than a quarter of our luggage. Consequently after much consultation it was agreed that our little party should break up into two detachments. Most of the luggage was to be left behind at the deserted *maloka*, Pequenino, Miguel, and

Kandi's two sons remaining with it as guards. The rest of us were to go on ahead to the next settlement, and from there, after securing additional boats, to send back for the others. Pequenino was at first rather frightened at the prospect of being left behind, but after I had given him a rifle and appointed him head of the camp he began strutting around as if he were the commander of a huge army.

We of the advance-guard at last started on our way, but we soon found that progress could be made only slowly and with great difficulty. The river was still little more than a forest brook, and it was completely blocked every hundred yards or so by some tree-trunk which had fallen across it. We had constantly to stop and hack these obstacles out of the way. In most cases after paddling only five or ten minutes we were forced to spend half an hour using our axes. Occasionally we found that by springing into the water we could pass the canoes under the tree-trunks without cutting the latter apart, and though this device necessitated a frequent bath, we adopted it whenever possible.

About three hours after starting, we came to a place where a small tributary joined the main stream. This rivulet we knew must be the Ambaiwa, the sources of which, we had been told, lay very close to the head-waters of the Ti Igarape, which in turn flowed into the upper waters of the Uaupés River. We were later to find that this fact was to have some importance for us.

We, of course, continued down the main stream. This maintained a southwesterly direction but with many bends and deviations. On either side of the banks we could see that the land was low and swampy, and obviously the whole region must have been under water during the rainy season. In this low swampy ground I noticed a much larger number of palm-trees, particularly of *kawai* palms, than I had previously seen.

Although we had once more been told that the dry season was about to set in, we were overtaken by a heavy thunder and rain storm early in the afternoon. The tiny open Indian canoes afforded no shelter whatever. We hastily cut long palm-leaves and laid them over the boxes in order to protect their contents as far as possible, but we ourselves were exposed to the full fury of the elements. There is no rain-coat in existence which can keep out an Amazonian downpour, and Mannling and I soon discovered that it was far better to follow the Indian example and strip to the skin, tucking our clothes inside one of the boxes in order to keep them dry.

Two hours later, when the rain had dwindled away to a drizzle, we solemnly donned our clothes and our rain-coats again. It seemed rather ridiculous to put on our rain-coats when the rain was over, but we needed them for protection against the cold. At ordinary times the temperature was about eighty-six degrees Fahrenheit. After the rain-storm the thermometer sank to about seventy-five, but we found that even this small change made an enormous difference to our comfort. We shivered and shook with cold and had eventually to stop and brew a pot of tea before we could warm up again.

An hour later, as we were vigorously paddling downstream again, we saw on a bough overlooking the river a large sloth. This we immediately shot in the hope of securing something for dinner. The wounded animal fell into the river, but when we paddled to the spot and I thrust my hand into the water to seize our prey, its strong iron-like claws closed around my wrist, and I felt that I too was being drawn irresistibly into the water. In my fright I struggled wildly to get loose and at last succeeded in doing so, but this meant that the animal was soon swept beneath the waters and out of our reach forever.

Early in the afternoon we came to the first cataract on the Pira Parana. This was sufficiently large to force us to unload the boats and carry them over the rocks. It was our first experience of trying to get over a *cachoéira* going downstream, and though it was smaller than many of the others, it gave us a good foretaste of what was to come.

After overcoming this obstacle we paddled on hour after hour. By evening the river had broadened so that we were only occasionally troubled by fallen tree-trunks. The low palm-covered bank and the gray-green water furnished us with a most lovely landscape picture, but we had little time to devote ourselves to its beauty. Dusk set in, and we could still see no trace of human habitation.

The Indians count distances on their canoe journeys by bends in the river. The Inhambú chief had tallied off ten bends on his fingers and had told us that the *maloka* must be found at this point; but we had already made more than twenty such bends, and the settlement seemed as far off as ever. Even my two chiefs began to fear that we must have passed by the *maloka* without seeing it. Our spirits sank lower and lower as night set in, but we continued to hold our course and were at last rewarded. A new curve in the river brought us in sight of a large *maloka,* where we made haste to land.

CHAPTER XXIII

A MEETING WITH OUTLAWS

THIS settlement was also inhabited by Tsönoa Indians, but through the presence of the very genial Tukano widow, we were able to converse with greater ease than at the preceding *maloka*. This good lady was very garrulous, and we soon learneb a great deal about her history. I was particularly amused at her complaints about the lack of clothes. While married to a Tukano and living on the Papuri, she had been in the habit of wearing a skirt, but since her second marriage, she had been living in a region where skirts were unknown, and as her new neighbors considered her dress scandalous, provocative, and in generally bad taste, she was forced on all ordinary occasions to go as naked as the rest.

It was well that we had some one here who would readily understand us, for I found that this was one of the *malokas* which had been visited by the dreaded Colombians, and the people were naturally frightened at the arrival of a second party of white men. We heard a long tale of woe about the misdoings of our predecessors. We found among other things that they had forcibly carried off three male members of the *maloka*. The grass-widows of these men were especially vociferous in their complaints.

That evening I heard Mannling and da Silva engaged in a long dispute over what day of the week and month it was, a dispute not helped by the fact that neither spoke the other's language. In any case we had all become very hazy about the passage of time, and I was rather astounded to see this renewed interest in the calendar, but it was not until the next morning that I discovered the reason for the discussion.

The discovery came about in a rather startling way. I was suddenly awakened by the sound of three pistol-shots, fired only a foot or two from my hammock. But when I seized my rifle, thinking that an attack had begun, I found that my little party had worked it out that this was the morning of September 28, my birthday, and that Mannling was only trying to celebrate the occasion in an appropriate way. Even the Indians seemed to understand that this was a day of great festivity, as they brought me as a present various fruits, among them a bunch of delicious palm-grapes. In honor of the occasion, Mannling and I allowed ourselves for breakfast the last remaining pot of jam.

Shortly afterward my two chiefs went away with one of the local tribesmen in an attempt to find more boats in one of the near-by settlements. During their absence, Mannling and I tried our hand at fishing in order to secure something for a birthday banquet; but our chief catch seemed to be some submerged logs, and in trying to detach my hook from one of these, I eventually upset the canoe in which we were sitting, so that both of us found ourselves in the water. This somewhat dampened our festive ardor, and when late in the afternoon my Indians returned and announced that they had been able to secure only one additional canoe, we all felt a great sinking of spirits.

But the day was to end on a more joyful note. Quite near the *maloka* was a heap of Amazonian acorns. In the evening we heard a curious noise coming from this spot, and rushing out with our guns, we saw a peccary or wild swine helping himself to a free lunch. We soon shot him, feeling that Providence was distinctly kindly in sending one of the wild beasts of the jungle to our very door.

The next two days were spent in collecting the men and the things that had been left behind. My Indians returned with the three canoes we now possessed to the deserted *maloka* far up the Pira Parana. By loading each of the canoes to the brim they managed to bring everything away at one time.

When at last our little party was once more united, I had a long talk with my two chiefs as to what had best be done. It was imperative that we have at least six canoes, but we had only been able to find three. There seemed little prospect of securing others. Kandi at last suggested that two old discarded canoes near our *maloka,* though full of holes, could possibly be mended sufficiently for us to use them. In the absence of any better plan, we proceeded to act on this suggestion.

Some trees from the near-by jungle furnished us with excellent pitch, and with this we managed to put the two old canoes into such a condition that we thought they *might* carry us on our journey.

Even so, we were one canoe short, so that it was necessary to set to work and build a new one. A tree was felled and the main trunk cleared of bark and branches and cut to a suitable length. A little groove was made along one side of the trunk, and a continuous smoldering fire was kept in this groove so as to burn out a great portion of the center. While the trunk was still pliable from heat, the two sides were gradually pushed apart by means of wooden bars thrust between them. When the cinders had been cleared out with an ax, the work of boat-making was complete, and the single tree-trunk had been transformed into a very serviceable canoe.

The South American dugout canoes were, however, much more difficult to handle than the birch-bark canoes of the North American Indians, and I had some fear lest one of the boats should suddenly capsize and thereby cause the loss of some of our valuable cargo.

The building of the new boat and the repair of the old ones occupied several days; and as this work was done almost entirely by my Indians, the rest of us had a long period of enforced idleness. This was almost ruinous for the white and half-white members of my little party. They became ill, discontented, and quarrelsome. Joaquim and Pequenino flew at each other's throats on two occasions, and even Mannling and Pequenino had private differences of opinion which they tried to make as public as possible.

Da Silva came to our rescue in this predicament and by recounting his literary experiences managed to while away the tedium. As far as I could make out, in the many years he had spent after leaving school, he had read only one book, but this was a novel in six volumes, and he proceeded to narrate to us the contents of one volume after another. The fact that he had forgotten the name of the book, of the authors, and of the principal characters, did not in the least mar our pleasure, and every day we listened for an hour or so to his thrilling narrative.

But even this was not enough. It was necessary to invent imaginary tasks for my followers, but I was delighted to find that the carrying out of these tasks restored peace and calm to our midst. Da Silva and Mannling were able to occupy themselves with a hunting competition. In this da Silva almost invariably won. Mannling, though a good shot, would scour the forest for hours and bring back with him only a long face, while da Silva almost invariably had some interesting trophy. Among the animals that we shot here for the first time were a number of different kinds of squirrels.

This forced activity was unnecessary so far as I was concerned. I am almost proud of the fact that I can do nothing in a better and more graceful way than any one else alive, but on this occasion I scarcely had need of the faculty. I had my books to read and my notebooks to write up. Material for study was everywhere around me. Last but not least, I was busily occupied with one of the most charming and harmless love-affairs in the world.

The daughter of one of the leading tribesmen, a girl of sixteen or seventeen years, had struck me ever since my arrival. Unlike the squat and rather dumpy figure of most Indian women, every line of her slender body was indicative of charm and grace. No longer did I have to spend hours trying vainly to extract from the Indians the native words for things, for this little girl undertook with great zest the task of instructing me in the Tsönoa vernacular. We would sit side by side for hours, and a hundred times she would touch my eye or my nose or my mouth, and each time I would have to repeat the native word for it.

Then, in true romantic style, of an evening we would sit under a tree and look up at the stars while she told me the Indian names of all the constellations. But when she turned the tables on me and asked me what they were called in the far-away land of the white man, I, being a wretched astronomer, had to invent new appellations to cover my ignorance of the real ones.

Poor little thing, she seemed to have great interest in the far-away land of the white man, and I could see that she longed to go there. Hidden as we were, in the far-off jungle, I began to dream romantic dreams and to think of a jungle mating, but the very sweetness and childish charm of the girl brought me back to the world of reality. She was of the forest, and her grace and beauty belonged to the forest, while I, for good or bad, belonged to the world of men, and to this I must return. So I contented myself with giving her a photograph of myself (it was a passport photo and revealed all my beauty) and—one kiss.

The completion of the boats brought an end to our romance. The evening before our departure we busied ourselves repacking and rearranging our things and trying to secure further information regarding the tribes down the river. My Tsönoa friends had particularly interesting things to say about the ferocity and bloodthirstiness of the Palenoa Indians, but I had heard so many similar stories regarding other tribes that I refused to be frightened.

Just as we were in the middle of our conversation, we were startled by the sound of distant paddling. A few moments later, three Indians suddenly appeared in the *maloka*. They were the natives who had been seized and carried off by the Colombians, and we soon found that the Colombians had returned and were now mooring their boats in the harbor.

It was a very interesting moment, this meeting of

white men far away in the jungle, men of the same color, and yet with a certain instinctive hostility between them. I heard from the Indians that the arriving party consisted of three Colombians and a number of natives who had been pressed into their service. It was necessary quickly to make up our minds what attitude we were to take toward them. The fact that the Colombians remained for some twenty minutes at the water's edge, before coming to the *maloka,* showed that they also must have been discussing what their attitude toward us was to be, as they could see from our boats and baggage that we were inside the house.

Eventually I went out to parley with the leader of the Colombian party. On seeing me emerge from the *maloka* he at once came forward to meet me. Both of us were ostentatiously unarmed, but both of us were protected by drawn rifles from behind. As my party was numerically superior, the Colombians did not venture an open outrage, and after a rather formal greeting, the leader merely asked if we had any objection to his party staying in the same *maloka* for the night.

It was, of course, impossible to refuse this request, and we more or less divided the *maloka* between us. My little party continued in possession of the front portion of the great house, while the Colombians hung their hammocks in the rear. The rightful owners of the *maloka* were forced to crowd together into whatever space was left. I noticed, however, that most of the women and many of the men fled into the forest and did not return. Several of the younger men came to me and asked permission to sleep in my part of the *maloka.* It was obvious that they were afraid lest they too be seized by the Colombians.

Later in the evening da Silva and I exchanged formal visits with the new arrivals. In the course of these, I managed to exchange some tea for much needed tobacco and matches. I also found out how our visitors had managed to find their way to this hitherto unexplored part of the jungle. They had come from the upper waters of the Uaupés to the mouth of the Ti Igarape, had ascended this river to its source, and had then made their way overland to the Ambaiwa, descending it until they at last came to the Pira Parana. On their first visit to this *maloka,* they had come in a small canoe, but had then seized in this and other settlements a sufficient number of men to enable them to go back and drag their larger boats over the watershed separating the Ti and Ambaiwa rivers.

The Colombians were a very rough lot, even according to their own account. Many of the tales they told regarding their exploits in the past would have made a degenerate Roman emperor green with envy. The civilized portions of Colombia had eventually proved too hot for them, and so for the last two or three years they had been forced to keep to the jungle, only occasionally emerging at some small outpost to exchange their rubber and balata for some luxury which the forest could not give them.

They were obviously gentlemen acquainted with, and accustomed to, the pleasure of life. They had brought with them a supply of rum sufficient to last them for many months—and, in addition, five Indian women to act as "lady friends" whenever there was a local shortage. How the three men divided the favors of the five women I could not make out, notwithstanding interested inquiries in this direction.

In spite of the formal exchange of visits which had taken place, and the seeming desire of the Colombians to maintain the truce that had been declared between us, I thought it better for my little party to go back to the custom of keeping sentry-watch throughout the night.

Once or twice my sentries heard noises indicating that some one was stealthily moving around the *maloka,* but otherwise the night passed off quietly, and when morning arrived we thought that we should be able to depart according to schedule, leaving the Colombians behind us.

We soon discovered, however, that the noises heard in the night had not been without significance. These had been caused, not by the Colombians, but by four of the natives whom they had brought with them. These poor wretches had been carried off, no doubt by force, from some other *maloka,* and they had at length decided to run away from their masters.

This fact alone would not have worried me very much, but I soon found that the runaways had stolen one of my canoes in order to make their escape. This meant that both the Colombians and ourselves were placed in an awkward predicament. Several of the Tsönoa Indians had volunteered to come with us down-stream, so that we had more than sufficient paddlers, but with only five canoes it seemed highly hazardous to attempt to continue the journey.

The Colombians, on the other hand, though possessed of only two canoes, were not troubled for boat-space, as both their craft were in the nature of *montarias* and were large enough to carry a party three times as numerous as theirs—it was no doubt the very size of these boats which had caused the runaways to take one of my canoes rather than one belonging to their masters. But now that four of their crew had deserted, the outlaws no longer had sufficient men to handle their craft, nor did they dare to seize any of our men by force.

Such being the case, I was not surprised when a little later the leader of the Colombians came to me with the proposal that we join forces. They too were making their way down-stream to the Japurá, and they informed me that we should be welcome to a place in their boats, provided that I lend them some of my paddlers. I considered this suggestion for some time. There was much to be said in its favor. We could not wait to build another canoe, and there was real danger should we attempt to pile all our cargo into the five canoes at our disposal.

But I felt that a journey with the wild and lawless Colombians would be equally dangerous. At any moment hostilities might break out between my party and theirs. Above all, I had come to the jungle largely in order to study Indian life, and I knew that the presence of the rubber men would seriously interfere with the pursuit of this object. It was more than likely that should we travel with these companions we should find all the down-stream *malokas* deserted.

Consequently I decided to continue the journey alone, even at the risk of shipwreck, and had all the cargo placed in our own canoes. They lay perilously deep in the water, and it seemed as if a single misstroke with a paddle would send them to the bottom of the river. But I was determined to rely on the skill of my native crew, and after bidding a formal farewell to the outlaws, we set out once more on our journey. They, we found, had decided to rest for a day or two before following in our wake.

CHAPTER XXIV

THE MYSTERIES OF BIRTH AND DEATH

PADDLING slowly so as to avoid an upset with our overladen canoes, we were able to appreciate to the full the beauty of the surrounding scenery. The region through which we were passing was certainly one of the most lovely I had ever seen. The stream had now widened considerably, and we no longer had to fear lest some fallen tree-trunk should bar our way. Soon after starting on our way we passed the mouths of two small tributaries, one coming from the west, the other from the east. On both these streams there were one or two Indian settlements, our Tsönoa guides told us, but we had to push on down the main river without making any detours.

The further we went the more difficult did our journey seem to become. The slightest movement on our part caused the canoes to ship water, so that we were forced to hold ourselves as rigid as possible. This meant, however, that all the white members of my party felt more and more cramped as the hours slowly crept by, and at last I for one was ready to cry out, in order to seek relief from the physical tension.

Our delight was unbounded, therefore, when we suddenly caught sight of an empty canoe slowly floating down the river. This, when overtaken and seized, turned out to be the very boat which had been stolen from us the preceding night. The runaways had no doubt only used the canoe to take them to a hidden path leading to some *maloka* far away in the jungle, and had then allowed it to drift away with the current. The finding of the boat made me doubly glad that I had refused the offer of the Colombians to join their party, for we soon managed to transfer part of the cargo and two of the men to the abandoned canoe, and thereafter we were able to progress in greater comfort.

Toward noon we came to another cataract, large enough to necessitate recourse to portage. After a frugal lunch the Indians began to unload the canoes in order to carry the cargo through the forest. I knew that this work would require some time, and as my presence was not necessary I decided to take advantage of the delay by making a short foraging expedition into the jungle. I was told that not far away was the site of an old deserted *maloka*. This I set out to visit, for though I knew that the house must long ago have fallen to pieces I hoped to find some sweet potatoes still growing in the adjacent plantation.

I reached the spot in about half an hour and was interested to see how clearly the limits of the old abandoned plantation could still be traced. The second growth of the jungle seems always to be of a peculiar and easily recognizable character. This fact, combined with the custom of the Indians of abandoning their homes every twenty years or so, means that the jungle appears to be full of places marking ancient settlements. The sight of such spots tempts one to believe that formerly the Indian settlements were much more numerous than they now are, but careful consideration tends to show that this belief is erroneous.

Unfortunately I was unsuccessful with regard to the main object of my search. Here and there the hardy *mandioca* continued to grow. Even the *maka-shera* and *kara* plants had not been entirely smothered by the return of the jungle, but of my beloved sweet potato I could find no trace.

Somewhat disappointed, I set out to rejoin my party, but instead of retracing my steps, I determined to make a short cut through the jungle, hoping to reach the river below the cataract where the boats were to be reloaded. As usual in such cases, the supposed short cut caused a long delay, as I soon got so immeshed in the forest undergrowth that I lost all sense of direction and wandered about for more than two hours without getting any nearer my goal. The situation might have had serious consequences, as I had not brought a compass with me, but I eventually hit upon a very simple way out of my difficulty. In the far distance I could hear a low, steady booming. This I knew could be caused only by the cataract. If I could only get to the cataract I should at least be on the river again, and no longer hopelessly lost; so I set out in the direction from which the booming seemed to come.

As the noise grew louder and louder, I knew that I was on the right path, but I was soon troubled in another way. I must have run across an army of ants on the march, for in a short time I found my feet and legs covered with the creatures, and as soon as I knocked them off, others took their place. I was so harassed by the stings of these insects that I was over-joyed when I suddenly came to a little brook running through the forest. Without waiting to take off my clothes, I jumped into the water and immersed myself up to the neck, thinking in this way to get rid of my tormentors.

The wiggling of a little water-snake, however, caused me to jump out of the stream even more quickly than I jumped in. For all I knew, the snake was harmless. It certainly wiggled away from me and not toward me, but I thought that even the stings of ants were preferable to the proximity to any serpent, and I started out through the jungle again. Spurred on by the presence of the ants and the fear of snakes, I tore my way through the undergrowth at record speed, and at last came to the cataract, the noise of which had acted as my guide. Thereafter I followed the course of the river down-stream and before long came in sight of my party once more.

By this time the work of reloading the canoes was virtually completed, but the boxes on one or two of the boats still had to be rearranged. While this was being done the canoe in which Pequenino was sitting broke loose from the shore and began to drift away. Pequenino of course immediately lost his head. In a wild attempt to stop his craft, he caught hold of an overhanging bough and held on for dear life. His clumsy movements caused the canoe to upset, and though the boat itself was soon recovered, two or three of the boxes were permanently lost.

These boxes contained the greater portion of our dishes and all of our knives, forks, and spoons. Thereafter we had to eat without the aid of these luxuries, but we had become by now so used to life in the wilds that we scarcely noticed their absence. Palm-leaves and Indian baskets took the place of dishes, and calabashes the place of cups. Our fingers proved excellent substitutes for knives and forks, and as we managed to rescue a pot in which to boil water for the tea, we felt we could be quite content with our lot.

We had almost forgotten many of the other amenities of ordinary social life. Our hammocks had taken the place of beds since the beginning of the journey; and as I had refused to take along any camp furniture we had come to regard a film-box as a perfectly suitable makeshift table, and the smaller box or logs equally good substitutes for chairs.

In spite of the delay caused by the accident, we made good progress that afternoon, but we failed to get beyond the long stretch of uninhabited country separating the Tsönoa and Palenoa tribes, and we had to camp in the open by the side of the river that night. The next day, however, brought us once more into contact with aboriginal life. Twice we came suddenly upon canoes filled with natives fishing in the river. The fact that one of the boats contained only women was rather surprising, considering that among most Indian tribes fishing is considered a very unladylike occupation.

The occupants of both canoes must have thought that we were the dread Colombians, for upon seeing us they immediately turned and fled. In both cases, however, shouts from our Tsönoa paddlers brought the Palenoa canoes to a standstill; and upon finding that we were not members of the party of outlaws, the strangers proved quite willing to exchange their fish for some of our trinkets.

The presence of these canoes showed that there were *malokas* on one or two of the various side streams, but the first settlement situated anywhere near the main river lay some distance further down-stream. Even this was well hidden in the woods, and it took us

some time to find it. No sooner had we arrived at the
maloka than all the younger inhabitants of the place,
both male and female, bolted into the forest, leaving
the older men and women to look after themselves. We
made no attempt to follow the fugitives but made a
point of being especially friendly to those who remained
behind. This did not fail to make a suitable impression,
and during the night a way must have been found to
tell the runaways of our harmlessness, as we discovered
on awakening the next morning that they had all returned to the *maloka*.

Now that all the members of this Palenoa settlement were reassembled, we proceeded to examine their
customs—and costumes—with some care. In most
ways the members of this tribe bore a close resemblance
to the Tsönoas. The women enjoyed the same state
of complete nakedness, even the natural covering provided by pubic hair being carefully removed. The
men made use of the same adornments, such as a
wooden button through the lower lip, a skewer
through the nose, and feather-tufted bones through the
ears.

But in addition the males beautified themselves in
a way which I had not observed elsewhere. On their
legs they wore the same well woven "garters" which I
had hitherto seen only on the women, and around the
muscles of their arms were bracelets made of rather
pretty small black nuts strung together. Finally on
some of them I noticed tight-fitting wrist-bands made
of snake-skins. My own Indians, Mandu, Kandi, and
Kandi's two sons, affected to despise most of the ornaments worn by the men of the Pira Parana, but I noticed that they were much struck by the snake-skin
wrist-bands. One of Kandi's sons, in fact, by carrying

on a little negotiation on his own account, secured a pair of these wristlets for himself.

I was interested to find that one of the young men in the *maloka* was not a Palenoa at all, but merely a visitor from the river Kananari, an important stream several days' journey to the west. His "dress" and general appearance were similar to the Palenoas, but I soon discovered that his language bore no relation to the Betoya dialects but was essentially Aruak in origin.

A long-winded talk with this man (a talk attended by the greatest difficulty, because of the need of several intermediary interpreters) convinced me that the river Kananari must mark the western boundary of Betoya influence. Only one of the tribes dwelling on its banks speaks Betoya dialect; the others have languages showing that they form part of the great Aruak migration from the north and east. From the tales told by this Aruak visitor I gathered that still further to the west was a vast region controlled by tribes of Karib origin.

The next day brought us to a second Palenoa settlement. Here too our arrival caused a good deal of alarm. This was somewhat surprising to me. On the Papuri, once we had made friends with one branch of any tribe, we found all the other branches of the tribe ready to receive us with more or less open arms. On the Pira Parana, methods of sending out advance information concerning the character of visitors did not seem to have been brought to the same perfection. The absence of the great signal-drums from all the *malokas* we visited on this river may have had something to do with it.

In spite of the fear which the Palenoas evidenced, my Tsönoa paddlers insisted upon regarding them as very ferocious persons, and invariably tried to win their regard by making particularly tedious and vociferous compliments at the time of ceremonial greetings. These greetings had been loud and long-drawn-out enough on the Papuri, but here they produced perfect pandemonium. Both the Tsönoas and the Palenoas shouted at the top of their lungs, although they were standing within a foot or two of one another. It seemed that the greater the noise the greater was the politeness.

My Indians from the Papuri took little part in this ceremonial greeting. The language and the etiquette in vogue in this part of the world, though related to their own, was sufficiently different to render them confused, and so they contained themselves with acting as interested spectators. It was they, however, who were of most use when it came to dealing with the food question. They pointed out to me a number of fruit-bearing bushes growing near the *maloka*. I had never seen anything exactly like them before but found that the little red fruit they bore was very similar in taste to a tomato. We pounced upon this fruit, for we had not eaten anything so closely resembling a fresh vegetable for many months.

We also secured a fair amount of freshly cooked fish at this settlement. I was interested to observe again, here as elsewhere, that the fish when boiled were prepared by the women, but when roasted or grilled were prepared by the men. So hungry were we, however, that the supply of fresh fish could not entirely allay our appetites, and I was delighted when my Indians, nosing around the *maloka,* found a hidden store of smoked fish, possession of which we soon secured by bargaining.

I, for my part, soon regretted the bargaining. Each of the smoked fish was of enormous size, representing types usually found only in the lower waters of the Amazon, so that as regards quantity we got more than our money's worth. But the quality of our purchase was more dubious. Such large fish, I discovered, could only be secured during the dry season, and these specimens we were told had been caught during the preceding dry season, since which nearly a year had elapsed.

The tales which we heard regarding the antiquity of our fish were amply confirmed by their condition. The process of smoking had been so well carried out that there was no sign of putrefaction, but a sort of dry mold had eaten its way through the flesh. In addition we found that a number of maggots had embedded themselves in all of our purchases, so that on the whole I could not regard them as particularly appetizing. My Indians were not so squeamish. They calmly knocked the maggots out, roasted the fish once more so as to counteract the mold, and set to with zest.

I noticed that the Palenoas were well acquainted with the preparation of the usual native stimulants, such as *kashiri, coco,* and *kaapi.* But in addition they possessed one delicacy which had not come to my attention before. This was snuff. The rank indigenous tobacco was pounded in a mortar to a fine powder. To add to its effectiveness, a small quantity of pepper was added. The method of taking the snuff was most ingenious. Two small hollow bones were cemented together by means of pitch, in such a way as to form a V-shaped instrument. The snuff was poured into the bottom of the V; then one end of the instrument was placed in the mouth, and the other in one of the nostrils. A short, sharp puff drove the snuff far up the nasal passage.

At the third Palenoa settlement at which we stopped we found all the inhabitants huddled together in a small hut. This was obviously a makeshift arrangement. The tribesmen had abandoned their old *maloka* and were busily engaged in building another one, using the hut as a residence only until the new edifice should have been completed. They had carefully leveled a large open space in front of their temporary home. On these were already placed a number of prepared tree-trunks which were to serve as pillars for their future residence. Three pairs of huge pillars, with connecting beams, were to act as the chief support of the roof. To the right and left of these were a number of smaller pillars, also supplied with connecting beams, which were to act as subsidiary supports and also as boundary-lines between the various family apartments. Needless to say, no nails of any sort were employed. The pillars and beams were lashed together by means of liana thongs.

As the supporting pillars had already been erected, the men of the settlement were now busy weaving the palm-leaf thatch which was to constitute the roof. This was a long and tedious task, and it was obvious that another month or two would elapse before the *maloka* would be ready for habitation, although it seemed probable that the community would move into its new quarters as soon as the roof was completed, without waiting for the front and back walls of the house to be added; this could be done later.

While the men were busy preparing the new tribal residence, the women of the settlement had their hands full working on the fresh plantation, which had been established a short distance away. I made it a point to follow them and see how they went about their task. The initial work of clearing the forest had been accomplished two or three months previously, so that planting could be begun immediately. Planting meant, of course, the planting of *mandioca*. The charred remains of the burnt trees acted as a sort of fertilizer, but in order to render the earth even more fertile the women and girls gathered twigs from a certain bush, and, after burning them, scattered the ashes over the cleared ground.

I was interested to find that it was impossible to grow *mandioca* from seeds, or from portions of the old tubers replaced in the ground. The plant, I was told, would grow only from shoots or portions of the stalk, trimmed of leaves, and thrust into the earth. There was no need for any sort of plowing. The ground was merely loosened by means of pointed sticks—wooden sticks without even a metal tip. These sticks were either straight, in which case they resembled a wooden sword, or else they were crooked and resembled an adz.

In spite of their preoccupation with *maloka* building, I got the men to go with me on a shooting jaunt through the forest, and with very successful results. Although inferior to the tribes on the Papuri in weaving, in pottery, and in general culture, the Tsönoas, and more especially the Palenoas, were certainly past masters of the arts of fishing and shooting.

They were far superior in this respect to any of the tribes I had hitherto visited, although their weapons were essentially the same. I noticed in this settlement for the first time that the bows were ordinarily kept very loosely strung, but when the arrows were to be sent a greater distance, the bowstrings were repeatedly twisted so as to shorten them, thereby increasing the tension and the power of the bow.

The blowpipes, here as elsewhere, were of two kinds. One was a simple piece of palm-wood through which a hole had been bored. The other consisted of two long pieces of wood with a groove down their center, which had been carefully bound together so as to form a long thin cylinder. The second type, I was told, allowed for a more certain aim. But whereas on the Papuri the blowpipes had seemed to be largely *maloka* ornaments, on the Pira Parana they were obviously in daily use.

My interest in the blowpipes caused me to see a new aspect of native mentality. In many ways I had been struck by the seeming callousness of the Indians, but I was to find that they possessed a streak of warm affection even for their animal pets. I was eager to get a moving picture of the way in which the Palenoas manipulated their blowpipes, but it was impossible to take such a picture in the forest on account of the surrounding gloom; and as the wild birds of the jungle naturally refused to pose for us in the cleared space around the settlement, I arranged that an Indian should shoot at one of the pet parrots which were to be found in the hut. The Indian was well paid both for the bird and for his services, and at first raised no objections to the proceeding, but as soon as he raised his blowpipe to aim he seemed overcome with compunction and eventually refused to injure the pet which he had so carefully reared.

For the last several days we had been traveling very slowly, so that I was surprised that the fast moving Colombians had not overtaken us, but when we were getting ready to leave this the last Palenoa settlement on the main river, we received news which accounted for their non-arrival. A man from one of the *malokas* we had previously visited suddenly appeared on the scene and told us that the band of outlaws had met their death while trying to get their undermanned boats over the large cataract near which I had been attacked by the ants. It seemed that the boats had been suddenly torn away from the banks by the force of the water and driven straight into the center of the seething rapids. This was a fine story, but as all the white men and only one of the accompanying Indians were said to have been killed, I had a suspicion that the force of the waters might have had a little human assistance in bringing about the accident. The dread of the Colombians on the part of the Indians was sufficiently great to make them go to any length to get them out of the way.

The news of the accident, though it did not upset me very much, caused a decided change in our program. Up to this time all of my Tsönoa paddlers had stayed with me, fearing that if they returned to their homes they would be seized by the outlaws; but now that they were relieved of this fear they refused to accompany me any further, though they arranged that an equal number of Palenoas should take their places.

I was not entirely averse to this change, as it seemed likely that the Palenoas would have a more intimate knowledge of the country through which we would be passing, but I was somewhat troubled by the thought of the language question. None of the tribes on the Pira Parana spoke the Lingua Gerál, so that this very useful dialect could no longer serve as a medium of exchange, and we had been too short a time in the region to have mastered any of the current languages.

Hitherto we had been greatly aided by the fact that the Tsönoa dialect, though radically different from Tukano in many ways, was yet sufficiently similar in others to enable Mandu, my Tukano chief, to make himself understood. With the Palenoas, on the other hand, direct communication was impossible, and I feared that we should have to rely entirely upon gestures when we wanted anything.

Finally we persuaded one Tsönoa youth to go on with us, even though his companions insisted upon returning. Fortunately the youngster possessed something of a language faculty, for not only was he able to comprehend in a general way whatever was said to him in Tukano (my smattering of Tsönoa helped us out at crucial moments), but he also spoke Palenoa and several of the other Pira Parana dialects.

In view of his potential usefulness, I eventually got this youngster to agree to join my party permanently, and not merely to remain with us for two or three days, as he had at first intended. I was a little troubled what to call the new recruit. Because of his new status, it was necessary that he have some appellation, and as he refused to confide in me his native name, I eventually dubbed him Ambiguous. This nomenclature seemed to please him and all my other Indians immensely.

The addition of Ambiguous meant that henceforward I had with me five Indians who had promised to see the journey through to the end. This was a great consolation to me, as I knew that at any moment it might prove impossible to secure any local assistance.

For the time being, however, I felt that I need have no worry on this score, as eight Palenoas had volunteered to act as paddlers. With them to aid and guide us, we started off down the river once more. But not long afterward we came to a new series of cataracts which delayed our progress for another day and a half.

This time the rocky walls encompassing the cataracts were so steep that we could not be content merely to push the boats over them. Each boat had carefully to be lowered by ropes, from one level to another. In view of what had happened to the Colombians, I was anxious lest the Palenoas try some treacherous trick on us, but I soon discovered that they worked with the greatest good-will in the world.

Once indeed a loaded canoe got away from its crew, just after they had finished sliding it over a dangerous reef, but two of the Indians, at imminent peril of their lives, swam after it and succeeded in rescuing both boat and cargo, as the seething waters were threatening to engulf everything.

We were forced to spend two nights in the open forest, one above, the other below the cataracts. On the second occasion we were again subjected to a great deal of annoyance because of the presence of a troop of *sauba,* or leaf-cutting ants. We woke up about one o'clock in the morning to discover that our hammocks were full of the little creatures. Even our nets had afforded the white members of the party no protection, as the ants with their sharp mandibles had gnawed through these, as through all other obstacles on their path.

We could kill thousands, but we knew that it was hopeless to fight against the millions which most of these ant troops number, and so we beat an invalorous retreat. Shaking off all the ants that had already attached themselves to us, we shifted our camp to a point two or three hundred yards away. But even this device proved useless, for in another half-hour the ant troop had caught up with us, and we were forced to take to our canoes and drift for the rest of the night in order to avoid them.

The next day brought us to a *maloka* inhabited by members of the Eruria tribe. It was in fact the seat of the overlord of all the Eruria settlements. The fact

that all Eruria *malokas* were subject to one overlord
was of great interest to me. A similar state of affairs
had existed among the Palenoas and the Tsönoas, but
no such unity had existed among the tribes on the Papuri and the Uaupés. Even Kandi, powerful though
he was, did not exercise control over the Waikano
malokas on the main Uaupés River. The Tukanos,
Desanos, and Tarianos were even less centralized than
the Waikanos. Among these peoples, the so-called
tribe was in no sense a political unit; it was merely a
name given to persons speaking the same language, and
professing a common ancestry on the male side. The
political unit consisted essentially of the individual
malokas, although it was the custom for a group of con-
tiguous *malokas* to recognize in a general way the
leadership of the most powerful chief of the district. The
inhabitants of each *maloka* may be said to have constituted a subtribe. Each such subtribe had a special name
of its own, but I was surprised to find that all such
names were kept as secret as were the names of individuals. A native was quite willing to say that he was an
Eruria or a Palenoa, but he refused to divulge the true
name of the subdivision of the Eruria or Palenoa tribe
to which he belonged.

The overlord of the Erurias was an interesting character, but the conversation which I attempted to have
with him was somewhat marred by the fact that I was
suffering from a combination of neuralgia and toothache. I stuffed myself with all manner of pills, but for
once the pills seemed to have no effect, and the pain
grew steadily worse. Seeing my trouble, Kandi eventually came to me and suggested that I call in the local
medicine-man to see if he could give any relief. I was
somewhat skeptical as to the powers of Indian witch-

doctors to cure toothache, but I decided to fall in with the suggestion. In any case such a treatment could do me no harm, and it would enable me to study more closely the methods the native medicine-men employed.

I found the local witch-doctor quite willing to undertake the case. He seated me in the open space in front of the *maloka,* and then proceeded to pass his hands lightly over my face, neck, chest, and back. He was, he said, drawing out the poison secreted in my body. Every few minutes he went through the motions of blowing and shaking away the poison which he had supposedly extracted with his finger-tips. Finding that this method alone was not likely to prove effective, he began to suck at the affected area, being careful always to spit out the imaginary malignant substance which he had absorbed. Finally by a clever sleight of hand he pretended to draw out of my neck three black thorns, which he said had caused the pain. I must admit that after his treatment both the neuralgia and the toothache completely disappeared.

The Indian medicine-men are no doubt charlatans in many respects, but many of them are certainly possessed of really remarkable powers. They appear to know a great deal more than most Europeans about massage, and they are unquestionably acquainted with the nature and use of many strange herbs, drugs, and poisons. It is also highly probable that these men are more than superficially acquainted with the principles of hypnotism.

In the course of our progress through the territory inhabited by the Erurias, we were destined to see a good deal more of the native witch-doctors and the work they carry on, which is not always of a purely medical character. In the second Eruria *maloka,* I noticed that one of the family apartments was screened off with more than usual care. Matted screens between the various family compartments were far more common on the Pira Parana than on the Papuri or Uaupés—and it was not unusual for the younger women to remain behind these screens upon our arrival at a new *maloka* instead of coming forward to greet us—but the way in which this particular apartment was screened on every side attracted my special attention.

Remembering my former experiences, I thought at first that the artificial isolation might be due to vampire-bats, but I soon discovered that it had an even more interesting cause. Four days previously a child had been born to the couple inhabiting the apartment, and in accord with native customs, both the father and the mother were now undergoing a short period of rigid confinement, during which time they were allowed to eat only *beijú* or *mandioca* pancakes and pepper. The fact that the father was forced to share in this temporary imprisonment, a relic of the widespread primitive custom of couvade, was of particular interest.

As among the Indians the ceremonial post-natal lying-in lasts only five days, the parents of the newly born infant were to be freed from their imprisonment the next day, and I decided to stay at the settlement until this should take place. Early the next morning the local medicine-man took charge of the whole *maloka.* Under his orders every piece of furniture was removed from the tribal house and carried outside. Even our boxes were not permitted to remain indoors. Then the witch-doctor, armed with a rattle, broke into the screened-off apartment and held a long incantation, the words of which I unfortunately could not hear, but which was undoubtedly meant to banish all evil influence from the infant and his parents and from the whole *maloka.* Soon afterward the father and mother emerged from their prison, carrying the child with them. They made straight for the near-by stream, and there proceeded to bathe themselves and their offspring at great length and with great care.

Later in the day the furniture and fittings were brought back into the *maloka,* but it was only after another long ceremonial incantation on the part of the medicine-man that the parents of the child were allowed to eat ordinary food again. We were told that three days later a name-giving ceremony in honor of the baby would be held, but for this we could not wait. In the afternoon of the same day we continued on our journey down-stream.

We had been present at the mystery of birth. A day or two later, at another Eruria *maloka,* we narrowly escaped being present at another great mystery, the mystery of death. Only a short time before our arrival one of the prominent tribesmen had died, and we found that the funeral ceremonies had just been completed.

I was sorry not to have seen them, but with the aid of Ambiguous, I managed to get a lengthy account of what had taken place. Immediately upon the death of the man, the whole tribe, or rather subtribe, had broken into passionate wailing, a wailing indicating not only sorrow but also a desire for vengeance; for according to Indian psychology, the death could not have taken place naturally but was due to the malign influence or secret poison sent by some other tribe.

The local medicine-man had indeed taken part in the wailing, but he was also busy with other things, for it was his business to drive the ghost of the deceased from the *maloka*, and not allow it to remain and haunt the living members of the settlement. But he had to attend to the body as well as the soul of the departed. Under his orders, the arms and legs of the corpse were closely bound together, so as to be sure that the ghost could not by black magic cause the decaying frame to get up and walk about.

Half of a large calabash was placed over the dead man's face. The calabash was obviously a sort of mask, as holes were cut in it to represent the eyes, the nose, and the mouth. The body was then laid away in a coffin. This, as usual among other tribes, consisted of a dugout canoe which had been sawed in two, one half being placed over the other. Unlike the custom in vogue amid many primitive peoples, the body was stretched out at full length and not forced into a sitting position. As far as I could find out, the corpse had been placed face downward, so that if after death it moved (observe the curious Indian belief in possible post-mortem activity), it would burrow deeper into the earth, and not emerge from its grave.

A number of the deceased's most prized possessions, such as his bow and arrows and his bone and feather adornments, were placed in the coffin along with the corpse; but seemingly no attempt was made to supply the ghost with food and drink for its long journey to the spirit world. After all crevices had been carefully filled in with broken earthenware and bast, the coffin was lowered into a deep hole which had been dug in one corner of the *maloka*. Then amid renewed wailing the hole was filled in, the earth being vigorously stamped upon to render it hard, and to make it level with the ground around it.

As long as the body was above-ground, none of the men and women of the *maloka* were permitted to eat anything at all. All eatables were, in fact, thrown away and the pots and pans carefully cleaned. Death had rendered unclean everything connected with food. Soon after the burial had been completed, however, the medicine-man had delivered another long incantation, freeing the *maloka* of all evil; and fresh food could then be prepared.

When we arrived on the scene, most of the ceremonial attendant upon the funeral had been completed. But the witch-doctor had one last task before him. A part of the dead man's possessions had been buried with him, but a number of other things remained aboveground, and these had to be parceled out between his relatives. Before these could be touched, however, the medicine-man had to exorcise them and render them free from all possible contamination. This he proceeded to do with a great deal of gusto. While he was busy with his task, a number of the other tribesmen began wailing once more. But as far as I could learn, this wailing was largely of a ceremonial nature and betokened no great depth of sorrow. The wailing, I knew from past experience, would be repeated at intervals for some time to come. I noticed incidentally that all the inhabitants of the *maloka* had streaked themselves with red *carujuru* paint in honor of the occasion.

Later in the day, I had a long conversation with the chief, through the usual long line of interpreters, and eventually managed to get a fair idea of the Indian beliefs concerning the future life. For a day or two after death, the spirit of the deceased was supposed to hover in or around the *maloka,* but before long it would find its way to the mountains far to the north. There it would abide with the other ghosts of the tribe for all eternity.

My Indian friend knew nothing of either heaven or hell. There was little or no distinction in the after-life between the good and the wicked. A man's position in the spirit world was much the same as in this. The dead dwelt in great but invisible *malokas,* hidden among the hills. Their mode of existence went on more or less unaltered. A great chief in this life was a great chief in the other world. An insignificant tribesman remained insignificant even after he had passed through the por-tals of death.

Occasionally the spirits even of living men went to visit the *malokas* of the departed. Such an event could take place only during sleep, or while a man was in a state of trance brought on by imbibing *kaapi.* In either case the soul was temporarily released from its body and enabled to wander abroad. At other times the spirits of the departed came back to their old homes. But this was something much to be dreaded. The spirits of medicine-men were particularly prone to return to the world of the living. In such cases they either hov-ered in the air around the *maloka* or else prowled through the forests in the shape of jaguars.

CHAPTER XXV

DA SILVA MAKES THE SUPREME SACRIFICE

SHORTLY after entering the Eruria territory, our Palenoa paddlers left us, but as an equal number of Erurias took their places we had for some time no difficulty in continuing our journey. Trouble arose, however, when we at last came to the southern limits of the Eruria domain. The next stage of our journey would take us, we were told, through a territory inhabited by two small but notoriously hostile tribes, known respectively as the Bees and the Wasps. It appeared that for some time the Erurias had had trouble with these tribes, and that there was more than one blood-feud waiting to be settled. For this reason the Eruria members of my crew showed a great deal of hesitation about accompanying us any further, but by playing upon their bravado and their cupidity I eventually succeeded in overcoming their qualms, and we set out on our journey once more.

The actual boundary-line of Eruria influence was marked by another cataract, but this was of no great size, and we experienced little difficulty in passing our canoes over it. The landscape below this cataract was of a rather peculiar type. The country appeared to be absolutely flat and level, and resembled a large even terrace. Lakes opened out from the river on either side, and even the main stream broadened out, and did not seem urged on its course by any strong current.

We saw a large number of wild fowl. Most of these we left unmolested, but we could not resist the temptation to shoot two ducks which flew only a few yards directly over our heads. These furnished us with an excellent midday meal, but we found that the noise of our shots was destined to bring us a good deal of trouble. The shots were heard for miles around and gave warning of our approach. They certainly must have frightened the Indians into whose territory we were coming, for shortly afterward we saw in a little back stream a canoe that had obviously just been deserted. Its occupants had fled into the forest in such haste that they had left all their paraphernalia behind them.

This, moreover, was only the beginning of things. About an hour later, as we rounded a bend in the river, we suddenly caught sight of three other canoes, but this time loaded with men. The occupants of these boats appeared to hesitate for a moment whether to await our coming or not. I shouted out to them what was meant to be a message of friendship and encouragement, but the strangers must have disapproved of the musical quality of my voice, for they turned their boats around and fled down-stream. It is possible that the Indians took us for the Colombians, the terror of whose name had spread far and wide. This in itself would have accounted for their flight, but it is equally possible that fear of the Erurias had something to do with the matter, for when my Eruria paddlers yelled to the fugitives to stop, they merely increased their speed in paddling away.

As I was eager to establish friendly contact with these natives, with a view to obtaining information concerning the nature of the country further down-stream, I ordered my little fleet to set out in pursuit. My paddlers obviously enjoyed the situation immensely. They set to work with furious energy, and our canoes were soon skimming through the water at a remarkable rate. Bit by bit we began to overtake the other canoes, and I hoped that before long we should be up with them. The fugitives, however, must have taken our pursuit as an act of war. Seeing that we must eventually catch up with them, they suddenly ran their canoes into the nearest bank, and then bolted into the jungle. Not to be outwitted in this way, we also beached our boats and attempted to follow them. But the runaways were now thoroughly alarmed, and before long we were met by a volley of arrows. Fortunately no one was hit, but I did not wish to expose either myself or my men to any further danger, and so I ordered my party back to the canoes, and we continued on our way without any further attempt at pursuit.

By this time I was somewhat alarmed at the prospect before us. Continued hostility on the part of the natives meant the frustration of all my hopes and plans. Consequently the next day I determined to try once more to establish friendly relations with one of the near-by settlements. There were no *malokas* on or near the main stream, but there were two tributaries of some importance in this region. One came from the west and had its head-waters, we are told, near the Kananari River. The other flowed from the east and was connected with the Tiquié. On the banks of both tributaries *malokas* were known to exist.

I decided to try my luck on the eastern tributary,

but this time I thought it better to go only with da
Silva and my Papuri Indians. The Erurias, and the
remaining white members of my party, I left on the
main stream. Only an hour or so after starting up the
tributary we came in sight of a settlement. Contrary
to usual custom, the *maloka* was near the water's edge.
Its inhabitants must have seen us approach, for upon
our arrival we found the place deserted.

After vainly searching the house for some sign of
life, we reassembled in the cleared space in front of the
maloka. Suddenly another shower of arrows descended
around us, sent from various hidden spots in the surrounding forest. This time we were forced to retaliate
with our rifles, as the continued proximity of the enemy
was likely to prove dangerous. Our shots must have
told, for before long the arrows ceased. It was obvious
that the Indians had retreated.

As we saw, however, that it was useless to continue
our journey up the tributary any further, we returned
to the main stream, and soon thereafter rejoined the
members of the party who had been left behind. We
could no longer hope to establish friendly relations with
any of the near-by settlements. There was nothing to
do but to continue our journey down-stream until we
came to a region inhabited by less hostile tribes.

With this end in view we increased our rate of
travel, and steadily put mile after mile behind us. The
next afternoon we came to the end of the terrace-like
land formation. The river was forced to make a sharp
descent, through a series of rapids. As these were rapids
and not waterfalls, we decided to race through them
in our canoes without taking the trouble to unload
and portage.

All my native paddlers and pilots were, however,

careful in choosing their course through the rapids. They kept the boats in the quieter waters on either side of the main stream, and painfully avoided the seething torrents which characterized the middle of the river. Pequenino, on the other hand, was not satisfied with this slow but sure method of progress. He and Joaquim occupied a small canoe by themselves. On this occasion Pequenino acted as pilot, and the cook was relegated to the post of paddler. Taking advantage of his command of the vessel, the youngster decided to forge ahead of the other boats by keeping to the swiftest part of the current.

It was another case of a fool rushing in where angels feared to tread. The Indians were aghast at Pequenino's bravado and shouted to him to return to safety. But it was already too late. The full force of the current caught the little craft and hurtled it down-stream. Piloting was out of the question; the foaming waters were free to execute their pleasure. Twice the canoe turned completely around, and we expected any moment to see it upset and sink, but in the end Fate decided to smile kindly upon idiocy. The boat shot through the last rapid almost without scathe, though it was some time before its two occupants recovered from their terror.

On some large bare rocks in the middle of the river, not far below the rapids, we saw a number of Indian "inscriptions." Several times before we had seen similar rock carvings, but never any executed on so elaborate a scale. Many of the figures were purely conventional, circles within circles being the favorite design, but others were definitely pictorial. Representations of men and fish were particularly conspicuous. Some of them were not at all badly done. Rock engravings of this sort are among the most characteristic and interesting expressions of Indian art. As they are made by rubbing stone blades against the smooth rock surface, the execution of each picture requires a great deal of time and patience.

An hour after leaving the inscribed rocks behind us, we came in sight of a small island in the middle of the stream. Toward this we headed our boats, thinking that it would be an excellent place to spend the night. We had no difficulty in reaching our objective, but were astounded to find perched on the lower end of the island a small Indian hut, crowded with people. In view of our recent experiences, I was at first somewhat frightened by this sudden encounter and at once reached forward to seize my rifle. I soon discovered, however, that there was no need for anxiety.

We had, in fact, reached a settlement inhabited by people whom we could almost regard as old even though indirect acquaintances. They, too, were but visitors to the Pira Parana, having come from the upper waters of the Tiquié, a region well known to my Papuri Indians. The men were all members of the Tuyuka tribe, but the wives of two of them were Tukanos and were well acquainted with the name and standing of Mandu, my Tukano companion.

I was much amused by one incident indicative of the fact that the people to whom we had just come belonged to the Uaupés type of culture. All the women were possessed of skirts. But being on holiday they had discarded these adornments, and at the time of our arrival we found that the chief, by way of joke, had tied around his body all the skirts the community possessed. He appeared greatly mortified at being discovered in this masquerade; and before even formal greetings could be exchanged he had to take off his many layers of female attire and give each back to its rightful owner.

In spite of the delay it was not long before we found ourselves on a very friendly footing with the strangers. From them we secured a good deal of information concerning the surrounding country. Not far away from the island was the mouth of another tributary, the head-waters of which also communicated with the Tiquié. Down this the Tuyukas and their wives had come for a lengthy angling expedition in the waters of the Pira Parana, reputed to be much richer in fish than the streams nearer their home.

I was interested to find that my informants had tales to tell concerning the great German explorer and ethnologist, Koch-Grünberg. Many years previously he had visited the tribes on the Tiquié River and had eventually crossed over to the Pira Parana by following the same small tributary down which these fisherfolk had recently come. He had always been a warm friend of the Indians, and the Tuyukas had many pleasant things to say of him. They seemed genuinely grieved when I told them of his death. The friendly reception accorded my little party was largely due, I think, to the favorable impression made by my distinguished predecessor. I could only wish that he had had time to visit the Bee and Wasp tribes.

As the Tuyuka hut, obviously a makeshift arrangement, was far too small to contain the members of my party, we slung our hammocks between the forest trees once more. It was, however, some time before we got to sleep. My Papuri Indians, stimulated by their conversation with the Tuyukas, continued to babble among themselves and with me until far into the night. Kandi,

I remember, was anxious to know if I would ever return to the Waikano domain. He and his sons tried to tempt me to come and live among them, saying that they would build for me a great *maloka,* greater than all the other *malokas* on the river. Simple kindly souls, they were. Whenever I hear tales of Indian treachery and worthlessness, I cannot but think of the long, loyal, painstaking service these men rendered me.

Early the next morning we set off again. Two of the Tuyukas came with us in the capacity of guides. With these men to aid us in choosing a course, we made rapid progress. In the morning we had to portage the canoes and their cargo through the jungle in order to avoid a waterfall, but otherwise the day passed off without incident until late in the afternoon. Then we again found ourselves confronted with a series of rapids. We raced our boats through the first rapid, but before attempting the second, a more dangerous-looking one, we held a council of war. Some of the Indians advised against making the direct passage, but it seemed to me that we should be able by careful steering to get through safely.

I was, however, unwilling to expose the other members of my party to the risk that was involved until I had myself shown that the task was possible. Ordering the other canoes to keep back for the moment, I set out with my boat accompanied only by Kandi. We experienced a very hectic moment. For a hundred yards, rocky cliffs compressed the river-channel to a narrow gorge. Through this the water angrily forced its way, venting its indignation by sending up high waves and spray. We shot through the gorge at lightning speed, but though covered with spray we eventually emerged safely at the other end.

Seeing the success which had attended our effort, a second canoe containing Mannling and two Indians set out to make the passage. This too emerged safely from the ordeal, as did three more canoes, manned only by natives. Thinking that there was now nothing further to be feared, I began paddling down-stream again, but soon a shout told me that something untoward had befallen the last boat to run the gantlet. This was in charge of my stanch Brazilian follower, Manoel da Silva. As I knew that his pilotage was likely to be far more reliable than my own, I had placed in his canoe the most valuable cargo. This included the greater part of the motion-picture film, a large number of my most precious zoölogical and ethnological specimens, and my papers.

The boat must have been overloaded, for when, half-way through the gorge, a wave struck it, water began to pour in on either side. We could see da Silva and his companion make frantic efforts to bail out the incoming water, but it soon became obvious that their efforts to save the canoe were doomed to failure. The little craft sank lower and lower, and before long another wave washed the boxes overboard. One or two of them immediately sank, but the others continued to bob along on the surface of the waves. Da Silva's native companion, Kandi's elder son, jumped into the water after them.

I was too far down-stream to be of any assistance, but the occupants of the other canoes at once turned around and at the peril of their own lives rushed to rescue da Silva from his plight. He, however, brave man that he was, thought more of his trust than of himself and shouted to his would-be rescuers to look after the boxes, adding that he could and would take care of himself. Unfortunately the men unquestioningly obeyed his orders. The floating boxes were caught and towed in to the bank. Kandi's son was also saved, but da Silva was doomed to pay for his fidelity with his life.

It was too late when he tried to free himself from the clutches of the current, which bore him gradually to the very middle of the torrent. By this time Mannling and I had our boats turned around and were rapidly approaching the spot where we could see da Silva tossed about upon the waves. For a moment we thought we could save him; indeed, Mannling had his hand stretched out to clasp the drowning man's arm. Just at this moment, however, da Silva was caught in a huge whirlpool. Seeming to realize that this meant there was no further hope for him, he raised one hand as if in despairing resignation, gave one shout of farewell— and then was sucked down by the irresistible force of the churning water.

It was the last we ever saw of him. I tried to probe the depths with the long blowpipe I carried in my canoe, but it was wrenched out of my hand by the whirlpool and failed to reappear. For three days we stayed at or near the spot where the tragedy took place, trying at least to recover the body. I and half the Indians camped just below the rapids, while Mannling and the remaining members of the party established themselves a mile further down-stream, in order to be sure that nothing should float past us unnoticed. Eventually the canoe in which poor da Silva had gone down was found, but for the body itself we watched in vain.

Three days we spent, filled with regret and despair. When at last it became evident that further search was useless, my Indians broke out into long ceremonious wailing, expressing deep wordless sorrow. Such a wailing is customary whenever a great and well-beloved chief dies, but so far as I know it had never before been used to mark the passing of a white man. It was a signal mark of esteem on the part of the Indians for a man who though a member of an alien and hated race had lived and died in accordance with their highest standards of honor. Hour after hour the sounds of the wailing echoed and reëchoed with an eerie note through the vast primeval jungle.

The white members of my party did not, of course, join in the elaborate chant, but their sense of sorrow was equally deep. Da Silva was a true knight-errant of the jungle, and, in spite of many foibles, had been faithful even unto death. The death of such a man could not but be a deep blow to all of us. I, for my part, felt more than ever steeled to carry the journey through to a successful conclusion. Da Silva had sacrificed his life in order that the fruits of our work should not be destroyed. It was my duty to see that his sacrifice had not been made in vain.

CHAPTER XXVI

THE RETURN TO CIVILIZATION

I ENCOURAGED my men as well as I could, and then gave orders to continue the journey. I soon found that by a sort of tragic irony the cataract which had been the cause of the tragedy was one of the last through which we had to go. For two days we paddled along in troubled waters, and then, shortly before reaching the mouth of the Pira Parana, came to a group of settlements inhabited by the Bugpumagsa, or Blowpipe Indians. Here our Eruria paddlers and Tuyuka guides left us, in order to return to their homes, and we were forced once more to stand on our own feet.

We did our best to ingratiate ourselves with the Bugpumagsa, but we found this a difficult task. There was no active hostility, but every one was markedly cold and reserved. For once even my animal pictures failed to awaken any enthusiasm, and we were made to feel that we were unwelcome guests. This was in great contrast to the friendliness which nearly all the other tribes had evinced after we had shown that we harbored no evil intentions.

I was particularly worried because my pistol disappeared while we stayed at this place, as I thought it might be used against us, but the thief evidently thought it better not to practise with his trophy until we were safely away. This, by the way, was the only time we lost anything through petty larceny. Everywhere else the Indians had showed themselves scrupulously honest, in spite of the fact that temptation had frequently been thrown in their way by our neglect to lock or even to shut our boxes.

Our attempts at friendly intercourse were again handicapped by the language difficulty. As even Ambiguous could make nothing of the Bugpumagsa dialect, we were forced to rely largely upon gestures. It was obvious, however, from the few words I picked up, that the language of the tribe was of Betoya origin, and certainly, as regard both appearance and culture, the tribesmen were markedly similar to the other Pira Parana groups among whom we had stayed.

One boy from a neighboring *maloka* was an exception to this rule. He was of so light a color and of such a semi-European cast of countenance that I thought at first he must be the half-breed son of some Colombian pioneer, but I at last found that he was a specimen of the light Pogsa type, one who had been captured from his wild roaring brethren several years before. I was interested to find that the practice of enslaving the Pogsas seemed as common in this region as on the Papuri.

In spite of the general ill will shown us, we had no difficulty in securing *beijú* and other food supplies. I also procured a couple of tame parrots and several specimens of local craftsmanship. For these I paid very lavish prices, hoping by a display of generosity to get the necessary number of paddlers to work for us. But on this point I was doomed to disappointment. Everyone evinced a strong dislike of venturing beyond the Pira Parana into the waters of the Apaporis. The men at the *maloka* in which we were stopping refused even to listen to the proposition. Four or five members of near-by settlements after much persuasion eventually agreed to come, but when the day of departure arrived they failed to show up. I felt myself in a desperate position. I dreaded embarking on the long journey through unknown territory without a guide. And in any case, without local assistance, we scarcely had sufficient men to propel the boats.

It seemed, however, that there was nothing to do but to go on alone. With sinking hearts we loaded our craft. Just as we were pushing off, however, a small canoe hove in sight, and we waited to see what it might token. A few minutes later the canoe pulled alongside, and we found that it contained only an old doddering man and the Pogsa boy whom I had seen a day or two before. The courage of the promised paddlers had failed them at the last moment, and they had sent these two persons along as substitutes. They were not very promising substitutes, but as they were better than none at all, we took them on board, and without further delay got under way. An hour or two later, they suddenly ran their boat alongside the bank and disappeared into the forest. It seemed like arrant desertion, but upon following them I found that they had merely gone to collect a load of delicious palm-grapes from a deserted plantation. Before long they returned, and after they had given us a generous portion of the fruit we set off down-stream again.

That same afternoon we emerged from the Pira Parana and began to paddle down the main stream of the Apaporis River. The Apaporis was of course much larger than the Pira Parana, and unlike the dark hues of the latter, its water had an iridescent green color of great charm. The Apaporis was certainly a beautiful river, perhaps the most beautiful in the Amazon basin, but to us it seemed the river of death and of desolation.

Mile after mile we put behind us, and nowhere was there any sign of life. Occasionally our aged guide would point out the site of some former human habitation, but these sites had long been deserted, and were covered with the second growth of jungle. It is on the Apaporis that innumerable battles have been fought between Colombians and Indians. Both have won Pyrrhic victories. The Colombians long sought to exploit the river and in their usual way wiped out innumerable Indian settlements. The Indians retaliated by exterminating the Colombians, but most of them died in achieving this object, and the rest have scattered to places far away in the jungle.

The silence, the desolation, were signs that we were gradually getting back to "civilization" again. What a difference there was between this stage of our journey and our progress through the heart of the untouched Indian domain! No longer were there friendly *malokas* at which we could rest at noon and in the evening. No longer were there pageants in honor of our coming. For hundreds of miles there was nothing but an echo from the empty jungle in answer to our calls.

No longer could we take life easily. In the absence of sufficient paddlers, every man had to do the work of two. The white members of my party formed no exception to this rule. Even Mannling and I were forced by circumstances to paddle as long and as hard as any one else. We found this task peculiarly difficult because of the necessity of keeping stroke with the Indians. The

natives could only work effectively when they were permitted to paddle in their own fashion. They could never
learn to give a long deep slow stroke. All their strokes
were short and quick, with the blade of the paddle
scarcely submerged beneath the water, but they seemed
able to keep up these strokes for hours on end without
tiring. Even so, all of us were exhausted each night, as
the result of our long continued activity.

As I could no longer devote any time to reading or
to writing, to relieve the monotony of the journey each
day I engaged in lengthy conversations with my Indians. Most of the time Ambiguous shared my canoe,
and I found my dialogues with him particularly entertaining. Mandu and Kandi were careful never to
mention any question of payment for their services.
They were seemingly content to receive anything I
might see fit to give them, but Ambiguous spent a good
part of his time dreaming about the treasure he was
earning by his daily labor.

He was particularly eager to secure a cap and a
jackknife, but confided in me the secret that he also
wanted some women's trinkets. Hitherto, it seems, he
had been something of a wallflower. None of the Indian
ladies had encouraged his advances. But he felt sure
that with the wealth he was now earning and with the
prestige of his travels he would have no difficulty in
landing even a chief's daughter upon his return to his
native territory. He was incorrigibly optimistic on this
point. I assured him that my wealth of fish-hooks,
beads, and looking-glasses and my travels in divers
lands had never helped me one whit in capturing a
bride, but he refused to be convinced that I was telling
the truth—and, alas, it was the truth!

It was while conversing with Ambiguous that I

knocked my pipe overboard. This was indeed a tragic loss, both to Mannling and myself, as we had been sharing this, the last remaining pipe, for some time. Urged on by our craving for a smoke, we succeeded, however, in constructing two makeshift substitutes. We bored a hole in the shells of two small palm-nuts, and then inserted in the holes two narrow hollow reeds. The reeds did not fit very well into the holes, but we got over this difficulty by cementing the nuts and the reeds with pitch. Every time we smoked, the pitch melted, and had constantly to be shoved back into place, but so small a matter could not detract from the pleasure of being able to smoke at all.

Fortunately our supply of tobacco held out, but we soon discovered that we were not so lucky as regards food. All of our tinned possessions had long since been consumed, and the supply of victuals we had secured from the Bugpumagsa lasted only a few days. Before long we had to rely entirely upon the surrounding country for means to keep body and soul together, and the surrounding country went back on us. The complete absence of native settlements meant that it was impossible to obtain *mandioca* or any of its preparations, and all of the wild fruits we came upon were poisonous. Fish and game were the only possible food sources, and for several days we found ourselves in a region where even these could not be obtained.

For hours at a time we cast our lines into the river, with not a single bite to reward us for our patience. Frightened at this, I sent Mannling and my Indian chiefs into the jungle to scour for game, but they returned without firing a single shot. Before long the state of affairs became positively alarming. We were reduced to famine rations, and as a result were so weakened that it became difficult to go on with the strenuous work of paddling. Each day our journeys became shorter and shorter, as our strength ebbed away, and at last we could only stimulate ourselves to further activity by copious drafts of strong tea.

We became desperate. We seemed so near the successful culmination of our journey, and yet doubted if we should be able to win through. Only a few hundred miles ahead of us lay an outpost of the Brazilian government, but it appeared that starvation would overtake us before we could reach it.

But the jungle is an erratic foster-mother. At times she refuses to provide anything; at other times she bestows gifts in abundance. Just as we were beginning to lose all hope we came to a stretch of the river where everything was to be had for the asking. We no longer dared risk delay by stopping to fish, but from time to time one of us would cast hook and line into the shallow water near the banks as we paddled down-stream, on the chance of catching something. Suddenly there was a bite, a second, and a third. Encouraged by this, we ceased our paddling and began to angle in earnest, and in the course of an hour or two caught 213 fish. It appeared almost a miracle specially arranged by Providence on our behalf.

We made up for our recent abstinence by consuming a great portion of our catch. I was astounded to see what an enormous quantity of fish the Indians were able to stow away inside of them. Even so, many were left over. These we cured by smoking, so as to be certain of something to eat for the next two or three days.

We found, however, that this precaution was scarcely necessary. Not only did fish remain plentiful, but we also managed to secure more than a fair quantity of game. In one day we bagged three monkeys, two *inhambús* or wild fowl, and best of all a peccary, or South American wild boar. The capture of the last trophy was attended by no little excitement. It was Mandu who monopolized the honors this time. While wandering alone in the jungle, far away from the rest of the party, he saw a troop of wild boars and shot in their midst.

One of the beasts was mortally injured, but the others, instead of running away, turned and charged the hunter, and poor Mandu had to run for dear life. It was only after the infuriated animals had given up the chase that he was able to return and secure his booty.

A day later we came to a spot on the southern bank of the river where, to our astonishment, we saw a broad path leading far into the forest. Never before in the jungle had I seen so well blazed a trail, and I wondered what its existence could mean. Our aged guide started along it without vouchsafing any explanation, and we all meekly followed him. For an hour we marched through the forest, and then suddenly found ourselves on the banks of another large river. The path had evidently been constructed to allow for the transportation of boats from one river system to another. I soon found that the river to which we had come could be no other than the Miriti, an important stream which is known to run parallel to the Apaporis for many hundreds of miles, although none of the existing maps show the close contiguity of the two rivers at this point.

Not far away from the banks of the Miriti, though carefully hidden among the trees, we came upon a large hut filled with men. It was the first human habitation we had seen since leaving the Pira Parana. I was somewhat surprised to notice that there were no women present. My curiosity was aroused by this fact, and I soon discovered that the hut was in no sense a *maloka* or settlement but a sort of "shooting-box" erected by some of the males of the Bugpumagsa tribes, who had been attracted to the spot by the abundance of game in the surrounding district.

The real home of these men was also on the Pira Parana, but I found them much more courteous and affable than their cousins whom we had visited some ten days before. They allowed me to join them on a shooting foray, and willingly shared with my party the game that was secured. They possessed neither shotgun nor rifle but showed more than usual ability in the use of bows and blowpipes. I got them to shoot one of my parrots in the open and in this way secured my coveted picture of Indian methods of hunting.

I had long been puzzled by the fact that the natives were able to eat with perfect impunity the flesh of animals shot with poisoned darts and arrows. No attempt was made to cauterize the meat or to remove the poisonous substance which had entered into it, and yet it was clear that the seemingly tainted flesh had no deleterious effect. It was at this hut that I got the explanation of this curious phenomenon. Seeing my hesitation to eat a piece of flesh that had obviously been pierced by a poisoned arrow, one of the natives sought to reassure me by picking up with his fingers a small portion of his stock of curari poison, rolling it into a ball, and swallowing it. From this I saw that the poison used on the darts and arrows, like many kinds of snake-venom, was injurious only if it entered directly into the blood by means of a wound, and that it could pass through the stomach without causing any harm.

This was so interesting to me that I next inquired

about the two substances with which I had seen fish poisoned. In this case the fish had died, or had at least been stupefied, not by a wound, but by swallowing the bait prepared for them. The Indians readily embarked upon a long explanation, but unfortunately I could not understand a word of what they said.

I was delighted to find that the hunters among whom we had so unexpectedly come were not only hospitable, but that some of them were also willing to accompany us a portion of the way on our journey down-stream. With this welcome addition to our party we returned without further delay to the Apaporis and embarked once more on our canoes.

The next stage of our journey was very agreeable. For many days there were, to be sure, no native settlements at which we could stop, but the extra paddlers meant that we no longer had to exhaust ourselves in order to keep our boats under way; and, most important of all, we found the river so full of fish that we had no worry in regard to food.

The presence of fish was not always an unmixed blessing. On one occasion, when our day's journey had come to an end, we jumped into the river and splashed about for several minutes. In the absence of anything better to do, I got out a hook and line as soon as our swim was over, although I feared that the noise we had made must have frightened all the fish away.

To my surprise, almost immediately afterward I made a catch, and this was followed by several others. I was horrified, however, to find that all these fish were *piranhas* armed with savage little teeth. I had not seen any members of this species for several months and had almost forgotten that such things existed. It was obvious that they must have been near while we were in the water, and I felt profoundly thankful they had not seen fit to tear us to pieces.

The fact that we had not been attacked added confirmation to a story told me by the Indians, that the *piranhas* are only aroused to action by the smell of blood. Had any of us had an open wound, however small, the bloodthirsty little fish would immediately have gone for us, but our whole skins had saved us our limbs and possibly our lives. Even so, I thought it better to give up the pleasures of swimming until we could get into safer waters.

It was about this time that I began to be troubled by the return of my toothache. For the most part the pain was quite bearable, but every time I placed anything warm inside of my mouth, the aching molar felt itself aggrieved and forced me to jump about in agony. As there was no medicine-man whom I could call in to render assistance, there was nothing to do except to alter my method of eating and drinking. Both my fish and my tea had to be left standing until they were perfectly cold and consequently perfectly nasty. It was rather trying for me, after a hard day's work, when I felt almost famished, to be forced to sit still and watch the others devouring their evening meal. Like a small boy being punished for some naughtiness, I had to wait until long after the others had finished eating.

Occasionally in the course of our journey we passed over a small rapid, or over a stretch of river troubled by concealed rocks, but for the most part the stream placed no serious obstacle in our path. It was against the sun rather than against the river that we had to guard ourselves. As long as the rainy season persisted, the sky was generally so overclouded that we scarcely noticed the sun, but the further we went down-stream the more evident was it that the dry season had at last set in, and with the coming of the dry season we were exposed for hours on end to the full force of the solar rays.

Fortunately we were able to substantiate the theory that sunstroke never occurs in the Amazon basin, for though we were now without hats (all our head-coverings had long since worn to pieces), we were never troubled even by headaches. But it was obvious from the sunburned skins of the white members of my party that the sun had not lost its potency. Mannling insisted upon going without a shirt and was soon burned as brown as any Indian, and even I began to wonder whether I could any longer claim to be a white man.

Whenever the heat became unbearable we would run our boats alongside the bank and seek shelter under the trees. In the shade it never became unduly hot. I kept a careful register of the temperature and found that away from the sun's rays the thermometer never registered more than 100 degrees Fahrenheit; 97 was the highest normal maximum. At night the temperature varied between 72 and 75. Only once, and that was after a rain-storm, did the mercury sink to 64. Even at 75, however, we found it necessary to make use of our blankets at night-time. The Indians, who did not have blankets, never failed to keep their hammock fires going from dusk until dawn.

Several days after leaving the path to the Miriti behind us, we again came to an inhabited part of the river. Most of the natives of the region, after their fight with the Colombians, had fled far into the recesses of the jungle and had never returned, but at two places we discovered that groups of Yahuna In-

dians had reassembled and were trying to rebuild settlements that had long previously been destroyed.

Our sudden arrival put terror into their souls. Seizing their hammocks, they rushed away into the forest
as soon as we came in sight, but my Bugpumagsa paddlers hurried after them and eventually persuaded them
to return. Even then the fugitives trembled whenever
we spoke to them, and it was some time before I could
persuade them that our intentions were entirely friendly.

Koch-Grünberg, who visited this region about
twenty years previously, speaks of the large well
equipped *malokas* of the Yahunas. Of such establishments we found no trace. The people were living in tiny
hovels, very flimsily put together. Most of the appurte-
nances of a typical *maloka* were lacking, and the people
seemed to have sunk below even the ordinary Indian
standard of civilization. The Yahunas were of Betoya
extraction, but in appearance and manner they reminded me strongly of the primitive Pogsas whom I
had found in the depth of the forest. Although living
within a few days' journey of a Brazilian outpost, the
community did not possess a single object of European
origin. The only things savoring of the dreaded white
man's civilization were a number of huge savage dogs,
vaguely related to the bloodhound family.

The men, timid though they were, eventually succumbed to my blandishments. Three of them consented
to act as paddlers, so that when we started off again on
our journey we had a crew more than large enough for
our requirements. This ideal condition lasted only a
day and a half. At the end of this time we came to a
huge waterfall, one of the largest in the whole Amazon
basin. All the Indians worked with a will, and we soon
portaged the boats past the obstacle.

In the troubled water below the waterfall we saw a number of enormous fish. Most of the Indians seemed nonplussed at the size of these creatures, but the Yahunas at once set about making a catch. Their weapons were, of course, bows and arrows, but the arrows were unlike any of the other Indian arrows I had hitherto seen; they were provided with detachable heads, secured to the shaft by means of a twine cord several yards long. With these they shot four or five fish as they rose almost to the surface of the water. The harpooned fish immediately sank and tore madly around the stream for several minutes, but the floating arrow-shafts allowed us to keep track of their movements, and when at last the poor things were exhausted from their struggles the Yahunas hauled them in without any difficulty. One of the fish thus captured, a *pirahiba,* was nearly six feet long, and must have weighed several hundred pounds. Like all the other Amazonian fish of great size, with the exception of the *pirarucú,* its flesh was not particularly appetizing, and many of the Indians refused to eat it, but this did not decrease their delight at having secured so magnificent a trophy.

The upper waters of most Amazonian tributaries contain almost no fish of larger size. The capture of these monsters therefore showed that our long sojourn in the little known and unknown upper reaches of the river was rapidly coming to an end. Ahead of us was the low-lying country characteristic of the main basin. In this country we should once more be within the white man's domain.

The Indians were well aware of this fact and acted accordingly. My faithful five, Ambiguous and the four Papuri Indians, steeled themselves to see the journey through to the end, but all the others, the Yahunas, the

Bugpumagsa from the Apaporis, and the old man and the boy from the Pira Parana, insisted upon returning to their own homes. Very unwillingly I paid them off and saw them depart.

Shortly afterward we ourselves set off again. Thrown entirely upon our own resources, we had a difficult task. Without guides and without sufficient paddlers, we were forced to keep ourselves alert and active the whole time. So great was the strain that even Mandu and Kandi, seasoned as they were, showed signs of exhaustion, but we knew that delay or relaxation was out of the question. At one point we came across the ruins of a Colombian settlement. This had long ago been razed to the ground by the Indians, and since then no white man, seemingly, had dared make an attempt to rebuild it.

The jungle, and the birds and beasts of the jungle, appeared to have forgotten the very existence of human beings. A bend in the river brought us upon a large colony of cranes. So unaccustomed were they to the sight of man that they allowed us to come near them and even to stand among them without making any attempt to fly away.

I had thought that the great waterfall was the last natural obstacle in our way, but two days later we found ourselves faced with another rapid. The river raced through a long line of naked rocks, rocks of recent volcanic origin, and it was necessary for us to get our boats through the passage as best we could.

It was a fearful ordeal. From a distance, the rapid had appeared trying enough, but when we got into its clutches we found it far worse than we had imagined. The onrushing water hurled about from rock to rock and gave rise to all manner of cross-currents and whirlpools, and to the full fury of these we found ourselves exposed. It would have been bad enough with a full complement of paddlers. Undermanned as we were, it seemed impossible to fight against the force of the waters.

Unnerved by memories of the recent tragedy in which da Silva had lost his life, I gave a shriek of despair when I saw the canoe immediately behind me upset. I thought for a moment that all was lost, but fortunately the very impetus of the waves carried the boat and its cargo and the struggling men into the calm water beyond, and before long everything and every one was rescued.

Nothing was gone, but we found that the contents of several boxes were badly damaged by water. Most of my maps, prepared at infinite trouble, were rendered useless, and many of my note-books were so soaked as to become almost illegible. This was nothing, however, considering that all the occupants of the boat were saved.

One of the minor troubles arising from the accident was the fact that several of the hammocks became wet. They would dry off, we knew, in a day or two, but for the time being we were faced with the prospect of sleeping in damp bedding. Rather than expose my party to this risk, I got out the hammocks which formed part of the ethnological collection, and in addition decided to make use of da Silva's hammock, which, with his other effects, had been carefully stored away since his tragic end. None of these things had been in the capsized boat, and consequently they were all dry.

My men made no protest against sleeping in the hammocks collected for museum purposes, but to my astonishment I found that no one was willing to make use of anything that had belonged to our dead comrade, fearing that they might be haunted by his ghost. My own bedding had suffered less damage than that of the others, but I was forced to lend this to Pequenino and sleep in da Silva's hammock myself. Even this awakened a certain apprehension in the minds of my companions, but eventually we all settled down for the night.

Suddenly we were awakened by a queer, unearthly cry that seemed like the sorrowful wailing of a soul doomed to utter desolation. The sound came from a spot only a few feet away, but we could see nothing that could have been its cause. For a moment we were all startled, and I for one felt the hair rising on my head. Then a false note told us that our spook was one of the queer Amazonian owls, known as the "mother of the moon"—an owl which gives no hoot, but emits instead an extraordinarily human sob.

The "mother of the moon" is frequently considered a bird of ill omen, but on this occasion we were so relieved at finding an animate cause for the strange sound that we thought no more about it all and were soon sound asleep again, and the next morning without further ado we set off down-stream again.

At any moment I hoped to catch sight of some European settlement, but hour after hour went by without a break of any sort in the jungle on the banks. Another day we paddled, and there were still no signs of life. At last we passed the entrance to a large lake and, shortly afterward, the mouth of an important tributary, both of them to the north of the main stream. The water of this, and of all the smaller tributaries for several days previously, was black, and under their influence the color of the Apaporis itself was gradually changing from its lovely green to a darker hue.

We judged that the tributary must be the Tara-ira, the head-waters of which we knew were not far away from one branch of the Tiquié. Mandu informed me that some of his Tukano brethren had left their homes on the Tiquié and founded *malokas* on the Tara-ira, but we dared not waste time going up this tributary in quest of the Tukano settlements. It was imperative that we get on with our journey as fast as possible.

All of us were worn out by our long continued exertions, and, to make matters worse, two of the party, Mannling and Kandi's elder son, became ill. I dosed them full of medicine and they soon improved, but it was obvious that we must get to a place where we could rest at the earliest possible opportunity.

For another whole day we rowed steadily on without knowing exactly where we were or how long it would be before we got out of our difficulties. Of a sudden dolphins became plentiful. These played about in the water around us, to the consternation of my Indians, who thought they were being bewitched. From time to time others stuck their heads above the surface of the water and peered at us full of curiosity. Scores of jungle birds flew over our heads. Seeing these, my own birds, the trompeter, the parrot, and the macaws I had secured from the Indians, flapped their clipped wings and vainly sought to get away.

Late in the afternoon, Kandi's quick eye noticed a slight break in the jungle. The line of trees along the water's edge was untouched, but as no further tree-tops could be seen towering behind this line, it seemed probable that a clearing of some sort had been made within the forest. Excited by this fact, we made a detailed examination of the neighborhood and soon found a large Indian habitation. It was unlike an ordinary *maloka*, for the floor was built upon a framework of high bamboo poles, giving the place the appearance of a two-story house.

There was not a soul in sight, but the remains of food and the embers of a fire showed that the inhabitants had not been gone for more than a few hours at the most. As I thought that they might merely have fled into the near-by forest upon hearing us approach, we yelled friendly greetings for more than half an hour but received no reply. Undeterred by this, we determined to make ourselves at home. We slung our hammocks between the pillars, and Joaquim busied himself preparing the evening meal.

Scarcely was the food ready, however, when the owners of the house returned. To our joy we found that they were Tukanos, so that we had no difficulty in making ourselves understood. Our coming had not frightened them away as we at first supposed. Their absence had been due to a visit to the Brazilian outpost.

We soon learned that this outpost was at the junction of the Apaporis and the main stream of the Japurá, only two or three miles away. More surprising still was the news that a river-steamer had that day arrived at the outpost and was to return to Manáos the next morning. As I knew that in this part of the world steamers ran only once in two or three months, I determined to go on to the outpost immediately, late as it was, so as to be sure not to lose a passage on this heaven-sent boat.

It was now long after dark, but without waiting even to eat the food which Joaquim had cooked for us, we embarked on our canoes again and set off down the river. Two of the local Tukanos we took with us to act as guides. In the afternoon we had felt ourselves nearly dead from fatigue, but now our exhaustion was completely forgotten, and we sent the boats flying through the water.

An hour and a half later we came to the mouth of the Apaporis. Passing beyond this we began to float down the broad waters of the Japurá. Shortly afterward we saw a number of lights twinkling in the distance ahead of us. At long last we were back in the land of the white man.

Our return to civilization was destined to be more exciting than I had imagined. To announce our arrival, Mannling let off a rifle-shot. To our astonishment the garrison of the outpost immediately proceeded to open fire on us. We later found that they mistook us for Indians making a night attack. Bullet after bullet whistled in the air around us, but fortunately the soldiers had been trained in the South American school of marksmanship, so that none of us were hit.

At last, by repeated shouting, we got the stanch defenders of the outpost to understand who we were. Firing then ceased, and when we landed we received a very warm and generous welcome from the Brazilian officials. We learned from them that we had long been reported missing, and that it was generally supposed we had met our death in the jungle.

As soon as the excitement caused by our arrival had died down, I inquired about passage on the returning steamer. In ordinary circumstances I should have preferred to continue my journey westward, up the Japurá and over the Andes, as this would have brought me directly to Inca land. The death of da Silva, however, had considerably altered my plans. He had left a number of effects, and it was necessary to look after these and to see that provision was made for his family before proceeding any further. This meant that we had to journey on the steamer all the way back to Manáos.

I had no difficulty in getting myself, Mannling, and the Brazilian servants accepted as passengers, but when I attempted to arrange for the transportation of my five faithful Indians I struck a snag. In accordance with government regulations, the captain refused to have any "unclothed persons" on board his ship. New clothes were unprocurable, but I eventually rescued my natives from their illegal nakedness by draping them with some discarded rags bought from the steamer's stokers.

There was now no further hindrance to our departure. We crawled aboard the river-boat at dawn and shortly afterward were under way. A trip on an Amazonian steamer is always exciting, and this voyage was no exception. Neither captain nor pilot had any sort of chart or map. Both men had only the haziest notions regarding latitude and longitude. The pilot was, as his Brazilian title implied, a *práctico*. Guided partly by instinct and partly by long experience, he was able to guess where the river was shallow and where it was deep. Occasionally, however, his guess proved wrong. Thrice while steaming down the Japurá the boat rammed itself on a sand-bank, but each time the skill of the captain got it loose again. Eventually we emerged from the Japurá upon the main Amazon River. We continued down this and a few days later found ourselves back in the metropolis of Manáos.

I am afraid that our appearance gave the good citizens of Manáos something of a shock. With our torn tattered khaki clothes and our long scraggly hair it was perhaps no wonder that every one turned to stare at us as we passed through the streets. The magnificently unkempt beards sported by Mannling and myself were the especial objects of attention and whispered witticisms. The news that my Indians were wild savages from the jungle spread like wild-fire and caused a sensation more natural in a sleepy English village than in the capital of the State of Amazonas.

These poor Indians of mine unwittingly caused me a good deal of trouble. There were all sorts of things I could not make them understand. They were surprised when I prevented them from making a fire by lopping off branches from the trees in the little public park. They were even more astounded when I told them that they could not sling their hammocks between these trees. Not knowing what mischief they might get into, I took them to a lodging-house in the native quarter and gave the landlord strict instructions not to allow them to go out un-attended.

The rest of the day I devoted to making myself half-way respectable and to paying off my Brazilian ser-vants. Because of their faithful service, I gave them considerably more than I had promised them, and they seemed more than pleased with the successful conclusion of their journey.

The next morning I was free to devote myself to the Indians. Releasing them from their bondage at the lodg-ing-house, I took them to see the sights of the city. The effect upon them of the gay imitation of Paris life was an amusing thing to watch. The hugeness of the buildings and of the ships in the harbor left them un-moved. Horses were much more interesting to them than motor-cars. The cars made only a casual impres-sion upon them until I pointed out to them the tires on one of the cars, and they at last comprehended

why the white man had such an insane desire to secure
rubber.

When I showed them such a simple thing as a
shower-bath, however, they laughed with delight. My
greatest success was when I took them into a café and
ordered for each of them a portion of ice-cream. They
put nearly all of it into their mouths at one swallow,
but then spat and spluttered for five minutes upon
finding it cold. I tried to explain the coldness by ordering a chunk of ice, with which Kandi was particularly
impressed. He wrapped the ice in a piece of paper and
put it in his pocket, saying he was going to take it home
and show it to his tribe. He was sadly disillusioned a
few moments later when he found that the ice had
disappeared.

The opinion of my Indians concerning white women
—their dress, manners, and morals—is best left un-
printed.

A day or two later I secured for the natives an interview with his Excellency the Interventor. Upon my
recommendation the interventor was kind enough to
present to the two chiefs, Kandi and Mandu, patents
recognizing their suzerainty in their respective domains,
and in addition gave each of them the title and per-
quisite of a captain in the Brazilian army. As a final
token of his esteem he ordered his secretary to provide
each of the Indians, not merely the chiefs, with a bank-
note. These the natives accepted with a great show of
gratitude, taking them no doubt for additional patents
of nobility.

After the interview with the interventor was over,
I took the Indians to one of the great stores and, in
compensation for the unfailing ardor and loyalty they
had shown me, provided them with enough fish-hooks,

beads, knives, and clothes to last them the rest of their lives. When we left the store they appeared gorged with pride.

The shopping had taken much longer than I anticipated. This fact very nearly led to an awkward predicament. I was eager to arrange for the Indians to return to their homes in the most expeditious manner. With this end in view I had secured passage for them on our old acquaintance the *Inca* as far as Santa Isabel, knowing that from this point they could make their way back to the Papuri by means of canoes.

The *Inca* was advertised to sail at five o'clock in the afternoon. Bearing in mind my previous experience about the time of departure, I was not worried by the fact that the task of shopping was not completed until 4:45, but when we at length arrived at the docks, I found that for the first time in history the boat was departing according to schedule. She had already cast off her ropes, and was rapidly getting up headway.

There was no time to be lost. There were already two or three feet between the wharf and the side of the boat, and every second the distance between them was increasing. It was necessary to give up all thoughts of a formal leave-taking. The boxes of the Indians were hurled on to the rapidly receding deck, and the Indians themselves leaped after them. Kandi, the last to jump, missed his hold and very nearly fell into the river, but he was soon hauled to safety by his two stalwart sons. This was a fittingly dramatic conclusion to my association with my well beloved Sons of the Forest.

CHAPTER XXVII

TO THE HEAD-WATERS OF THE AMAZON

MY Indians had gone back to their home in the distant jungle; my precious specimen-cases had been shipped back to England; I was free to embark on the second phase of my undertaking. That was to ascend the upper waters of the main Amazon stream, cross over the Andes, and make an effort to see something of the mysterious Inca and pre-Inca ruins on the Pacific coast.

This was destined to be a long and complicated journey. The first part of it, however—the two weeks' voyage on a huge river-steamer from Manáos, the capital of Brazilian Amazonas, to Iquitos, the capital of Peruvian Amazonas—promised to be fairly humdrum, if journeying on the Amazon River ever could be humdrum.

On this voyage we avoided all tributaries and kept to the turbid brown waters of the main stream. This continued to be of the utmost majesty and grandeur, in spite of the fact that our journey was taking us to a place more than two thousand miles from its mouth. Here, as further down-stream, however, the river was continually broken up by islands with a number of channels, no one of which seemed to be more than a mile wide.

For the first two hundred miles, as far as Teffé, the course was known to me. Consequently I could devote myself to an examination of the passengers, some fifty in all. These were as interesting as any of the zoölogical specimens I had sent back to the museum.

Here in the heart of the everlasting wilderness, where the "very name of slave and sultan" should have been forgot, there was a fierce competition for social prestige. Most of my fellow-passengers had lived for years surrounded, engulfed, by the jungle, but they knew nothing of its secrets. The birds, the beasts, and the men of the jungle formed an unregarded background; and the social ladder and cheap imitations of Paris fashions were the only things that mattered. The best dressed women on the boat were two sisters on their way back from Spain. Their parents were traveling by the same boat, but third-class—downstairs with the cattle. To the shame and mortification of the girls, the parents would occasionally come up to the first-class deck to see how their offspring were faring. It was a complicated world of fashion. I was not allowed to come to the lunch-table when I wore a silk sport shirt without putting on a necktie. But all the men appeared at breakfast every day clad only in their pajamas.

However, I was soon out of the social welter altogether. My health, which had been splendid during all the weary, trying months in the jungle, suddenly collapsed. My stomach and other portions of my anatomy suddenly went on strike and refused to function an instant longer. All the medicines I took only made matters worse. Cure and cause of the mysterious malady were alike unknown. Wise busybodies shook their heads and declared that I had been given some slow-working poison by the Indians of the forest, and that it was now beginning to take effect.

This explanation was as good as any other, and as in any case there was no known remedy or antidote, I had my hammock slung on the top deck, and after crawling up to it gave strict instructions that I was not to be disturbed until such time as either I had to be thrown into the river or was able once more to look after myself. These instructions were obeyed. For several days I lay in a deep stupor. Then gradually I found myself able to crawl around and to appreciate once more the routine of life on an Amazonian river-steamer.

Every few hours we would lay in to get fresh supplies of wood for the insistent boilers. From some wretched hut, frequently raised on piles near the river-bank, would come out a lean, haggard form, without shoes or stockings, a draggling mustache partly concealing a dreary face, marked by vacuousness and malaria. The man was invariably a *coronél* with some high-sounding name. His presence marked the spread of vaunted European civilization into the heart of the everlasting wilderness. We were on the great waterway, and all true aboriginal life had slunk far back into the hidden recesses of the jungle.

Hundreds of miles were traversed without even this sign of life, nothing but the thick intertwined boughs of the trees. At infrequent intervals we came upon larger settlements, assembling centers for rubber, for Brazil-nuts and ivory-nuts, which came from the back country; in exchange for which commodities we gave boxes of imported wares, and huge casks of *cachaça*, the fiery native rum.

The most important settlement, after we had left

Teffé behind us, was on the Javary River, up which we steamed for a couple of hours until we came to the metropolis known as Remate de Males. In this land of fond illusions, where every miserable hut bears some such name as Boa Vista, Vista Alegre, or Esperanza, it was refreshing to meet a frank acceptance of facts in the name of Remate de Males—literally, Culmination of Evils.

This city consists of a long line of rickety huts, the lower parts of which were obviously submerged each year at the time of high water. Here the chief activity was shown by the pigs, who at least were always busy looking for food, while the human inhabitants were content to loaf indoors. There were no signs of agriculture; but as the price of rubber was soaring, while the roofs of the huts remained leaky and the walls caved-in, the women put on silk stockings and frilled dresses, and the men uncorked champagne-bottles, to welcome the arrival of our boat.

The Javary River, on which Remate de Males stands, marks the boundary between Brazil and Peru. It is notable as being one of the few really recognized boundaries in the Amazon region. In this wild, unexplored expanse of jungle, each country claims the greatest amount of territory possible, and as there is no supreme court of appeal to recognize or enforce such claims, political map-makers have a merry task and can make and remake boundaries very much as they will. Particularly in the northwest there are hundreds of thousands of square miles which belong either to Ecuador or Peru or Colombia—but to which Heaven alone knows.

When the last champagne-bottle had been finished, and the last silk stocking had returned to the hovels, we steamed down the Javary to the Amazon, and on up that great river again.

A day or two later we passed the mouth of the Napo, the tributary down which Orellana came in 1536, when he discovered the mighty river and invented the myth of the Amazons. Not long afterward we steamed alongside Iquitos and once more disembarked.

Iquitos is the third largest city of the Amazon basin, Pará and Manáos alone being larger. Strategically Iquitos occupies a very important position. Although it is two thousand miles from the mouth of the Amazon, even large ocean-going steamers can come up to this point; it is in fact one of the most important of the Peruvian ports. It is a little above Iquitos that the junction occurs of the two main "source rivers" of the Amazon, which, with their numerous sub-tributaries, are navigable by smaller river-boats for many hundreds of miles.

Like all other Amazonian cities, Iquitos would be shocked at the appearance of a real live Indian on its streets, although many savage tribes live but a few miles away in the jungle. The only means of communication between the city and the jungle is supplied by the strange and wild rubber men, half-caste mostly. These men, after a few weeks of riotous living which sweep away every penny they possess, secure on credit a large supply of trade goods and go out into the distant wilds, there to fight with the unfriendly Indians and to bribe and browbeat others into securing for them the precious rubber. Many of the rubber men never come back; they either succumb to some disease, are lost in the jungle, or fall a prey to the Indians whom for so long they have pursued. Others, more lucky, return at the end of six months or a year, laden with the precious rubber. Repression of long inhibited desires means another cycle of rioting, followed again by borrowing or buying on credit. But of what these men have done or seen or learned, one hears little—only wild, strange rumors. The lore of the forest remains uncommunicated, and the average respectable citizen of Iquitos has no idea at all of the land or life that lies but a few miles outside the city.

Yet for the ethnologist and anthropologist, as well as the zoölogist, there is still a rich field in many of the tributary basins in the neighborhood of Iquitos. There are strange tribes here whose culture is quite different from that of the Indians of the northwest Amazon, on whom we had been making our observations. There are the Konibo Indians, who kill off their aged and infirm. There are the Ungoninos, who inflict strange nameless tortures upon their girls at the age of puberty. There are the Kahsibos, or Vampire Indians, who, like the loathsome bats, suck the blood of beast and of man. There are the Andokes, the most feared of all the cannibalistic tribes, who feed upon the brains of their enemies that they may acquire wisdom, upon the hearts of their enemies that they may acquire courage, and who have their women-folk feed upon the genital organs of their enemies that they may acquire fertility.

Perhaps the most noted of the tribes of this region are the Wambisas and the Jivaros. Their manhood tests are the most severe of all. Unlike the other Indians, these tribes are in the habit of mummifying their dead before burial according to a process which makes the corpses look like huge leathery dolls. It is only their fellow-tribesmen who are completely mummified, however. Should an enemy fall into their hands, he is decapitated, and his head artificially shrunk by some strange process until it is the size of an orange or a man's fist, though the features are preserved intact.

Iquitos itself was particularly interesting when I was there because it was in the process of recovering from its last revolution. Courts martial were still the order of the day, and there was a general air of unrest about the place. I heard for the first time the name of Leguía, the present strong-handed president of the republic, whose influence was felt even from far-distant Lima.

The revolution in Loreto, the Amazonian province of Peru of which Iquitos is the capital, was no ordinary South American revolution; it was unlike even the revolution in Brazilian Amazonas. An ordinary every-day South American revolution is a purely personal affair, a sort of family row between the outs, who want to get in, and the ins, who are forced to get out. A little mild fighting takes place, a number of offices change hands—and the revolution is over.

The Iquitos revolution was peculiar because it was fighting about some *thing* and not about some *person*. Iquitos and the whole of Peruvian Amazonas wanted to be free and independent, and no longer to be ruled by the bureaucrats from far-away Lima. For this attitude there was a clear and definite geographical explanation. Peru, like Gaul, is divided into three parts. There is, first, the long, narrow strip of land, bare and barren, except for occasional fertile valleys, facing the Pacific Ocean, known as La Costa. There is, secondly, the long stretch of elevated land between the East and West Cordilleras, known as La Sierra, which is also barren of trees, and chiefly valuable for pasturage and for its mines. Finally, east of the Cordilleras there is the vast rich jungle land, known as La Montaña, which includes the province of Loreto, and which is but a part of Amazonas.

A similar division could be made of Bolivia, Ecuador, and Colombia; but in Peru the Amazonas region is more populous and has been better developed, so that the question of government has come sooner to a head.

From Iquitos over the Andes to Lima is a month's journey, and this journey is so encompassed by difficulties that the only real gateway for Iquitos is the Amazon River. In every way, Loreto, and in fact the whole of La Montaña, is far more a part of the Brazilian Amazon region than it is of Peru. The revolutionaries, realizing this fact, wished to make of Loreto an independent state, though one to be affiliated in some way with the rest of the Amazon.

But they reckoned without the clever, restless, ambitious little man who at present controls Peru's destinies. Immediate and strong measures were taken by the central government at Lima. Troops were sent over the mountains. But this alone would not have sufficed. The revolutionaries held out until the news came that the central government was sending two cruisers up the Amazon River to bombard Iquitos into submission. Immediate panic followed, and overnight the revolutionary government was no more.

In Iquitos I gave myself over to a doctor, who tapped and probed and punched, and shook his head wisely but sadly, and gave me daily three or four different medicines, in the hope that one out of the lot might be good for the mysterious malady, whatever it might be, from which I had been, and was still, suffering. There was a slight improvement, but it was obvious that I must get out of the jungle and into the highlands as soon as possible, if I wished to recover my health.

There were several routes that I could have taken,

nearly all equally bad, for the means of communication between La Montaña and the other parts of Peru are still in their infancy. In the end I decided to take the Pichis trail, as likely to be the quickest and most expeditious. This was to take us up the Ucayali River in a southerly direction until we came to a place from which we could strike out more or less due west for Lima.

The first two weeks of the trip were accomplished in a tiny river-steamer owned by a Maltese Jew—all the weird creatures of the Amazon are not in the jungle. A day or two after leaving Iquitos we came to the point of convergence of the Ucayali and Marañon rivers, which together form the Amazon.

There has long been dissension among geographers as to which of the two tributaries is the main source-stream of the mightiest of rivers. Generally the palm is given to the Marañon, which flows for another two hundred miles from the west until it too makes a great bend and flows from south to north. But without question the other stream, the Ucayali, is far longer, drains a much larger area, and is commercially much more valuable. During much of its course the Marañon runs through high broken land in a groove between the East and West Cordilleras. It is only at Pongo de Maseriche that the Marañon manages to break through the great wall of the Eastern Andes and falls into the Amazon basin. For this reason only a small portion of the Marañon is navigable.

The Ucayali, on the other hand, keeps to the lowland, running parallel to the great line of the Eastern Andes, and is therefore without cataracts or waterfalls, though it too is fed by the brooks and streams which trickle through the passes from the great Peruvian highland, the ancient Empire of the Incas.

On account of the greater navigability of the Ucayali, it was up this river that we continued our voyage.
Paris fashions no longer held sway. We were a wild-
looking lot. Pajamas were no longer limited to breakfast but appeared also at lunch and at dinner. All of
us took a personal interest in the food question, as he
who wanted to eat sufficiently had to look out for himself. True to color and type, the owner of the ship provided food that was in quality fit only for pigs, and
in quantity so small that no respectable pig could have
subsisted on it. Consequently at every halting-place
while the boat was taking in wood it was necessary
for us to "scrounge."

For some extraordinary reason it was extremely
difficult to persuade any of the slatternly, weary-eyed
settlers to sell us anything. They had probably little
enough for themselves. But it seemed to be the custom in this part of the world that what you could not
buy you took. In each "port" we lightened the fruit-
trees of a part of their burden, and occasionally we
were able to "find" some eggs.

The most interesting of our fellow-passengers was
a political prisoner. He had played a prominent part
in the revolution and at the time of the final crash
had fled to the jungles of Ecuador. Recently he had
come back to Iquitos and had voluntarily given himself up. He was now being sent back, under guard, to
Lima for trial. But though a prisoner he was very
much the chief gentleman of the ship.

In this part of the world a political prisoner is a
highly respected person. He may be an "out" to-day,
but very likely he will be an "in" to-morrow, and it is
always well to be on the safe side. This prisoner was
traveling first-class, had his wife along with him—al-

though she was ostensibly his sister—and had special attention paid to him. His guards on the other hand as third-class passengers were forced to stay with the pigs on the lower deck. One of them was unfortunate enough to be caught trying to purloin some valuables from the captain's locker. Whereupon he, for the rest of the voyage, was locked up in one of the empty pens, from which it was rather difficult for him to continue to act as prisoner's guard.

For days we followed our course up the Ucayali. It is a single stream and not the maze of channels and islands which make up the Amazon itself. To the trained botanical eye there may have been a slight change in the character of the foliage of the encircling jungle, but to the average mortal it was ever the unchanging forest, trunk thick on trunk, intertwining boughs, eternally the same dull, dark green. Very occasionally, here and there, a settler had made a clearing in this virgin forest, a few hundred yards broad, but it would seem as though in fighting the jungle the settler was fighting against overwhelming odds.

The settlers for the most part have come from the chill mountains of Peru and have here lost themselves in the jungle. In the rainy season the river invariably overflows its banks and submerges their plantations, and in general they seem to lead a hand-to-mouth existence, though, with a little more head and hand work, the land would be rich in possibilities. The laborers are mostly Indians whom the settlers have captured or enticed from the forests, but, more often than not, after a few months' experience with the white man, the Indians steal back into the jungle and are never seen or heard of again—and woe to him who attempts to follow.

CHAPTER XXVIII

SCALING THE ANDES

AFTER voyaging up the Ucayali for ten days we at length came to the mouth of an important tributary, the Pachitea River, which flowed in from the southwest. We were to follow this river up its course, but first we had to change boats, as even our tiny little steamer was of too deep a draft.

Our new bark was a tiny little tug not twenty feet long. Every inch of available floor-space was occupied either by the woodpile, the engines, or the cooking-stove. But we philosophically slung our hammocks above these impedimenta, tried to forget about the heat, smell, and fumes which arose from beneath us, and went cheerfully on our way. The river-channel was so treacherous and so little known that we could only feel our way along by daylight. Each night we tied up at the bank to rest.

Every river in the Amazon basin has peculiarities of its own. On the Ucayali mosquitoes had been plentiful and stinging gnats rare, but on the Pachitea it was exactly the contrary; it was the gnats that predominated. Millions and millions of these little blood-sucking pests were continually around us, attacking every exposed inch of flesh. The air was literally black with them. They knew how to sting through the thin stockings and shirts we wore; and so, in addition to donning our head-nets and gloves, we had to wrap ourselves up in blankets, in spite of the heat, to keep a whole skin.

The Indians once more began to be more plentiful and more primitive. A canoe laden with four or five Indians would suddenly shoot out from the bank, its occupants would gaze at us for a minute or two, and they would then as quickly shoot back into the shelter of the jungle bank and be lost to view. Occasionally a more adventurous group would paddle out to us, their boats laden with fruit and yucca, which were bartered to us, either for a few beads or, more often than not, for a swig of the vile spirits the boat specially carried for barter. Of the houses and plantations of the natives we saw nothing. They were all hidden far away in the jungle. For us the Indians were but phantom figures which silently and mysteriously appeared and disappeared.

Suddenly, however, I lost all interest both in insect pests and in Indians. The mysterious malady from which I had never fully recovered came back in full force, and for some time I lay in a state of stupor hovering between this world and a world of phantoms stranger than those of the Indians of the forest.

No sooner had the illness begun to abate than it was necessary to change once more our mode of travel. The Pachitea broke up into a number of subsidiary streams, and the one we were to take, the Pichis—following as ever our southwesterly direction—though still respectably broad, was too shallow for even the lightest of launches. We had once more to trust our lives and our goods to frail native canoes, manned by denizens of the forest, though this time, because of the shallowness of the stream, we were to be punted or poled and not paddled.

My new-found friend, the prisoner, and "his party"

were to follow later in another canoe, so that Mannling and I were again thrown back exclusively on the companionship of the Indians. Consequently I had now the opportunity to study more closely the natives of this region and compare them with the denizens of my beloved Northwest.

In main racial type they were very similar, though, on the whole, the natives of the Pichis were not such magnificent physical specimens.

The magic coca-powder that we had met on the latter part of our journey through the jungle was here everywhere in evidence. This confirmed my theory that coca had spread from the old Inca culture of Peru. It is more than probable that the forest Indians here at the base of the Great Mountain, though never subject to the Inca emperors, had assimilated several of the more easily transmissible culture phases of the People of the Hills.

The clothes worn by our boatmen were an instance of this. Whereas the true dweller of the forest goes naked except for his loin-cloth of bast, the Mochigua Indians from time immemorial have known how to weave cotton cloth, which is nearly always dyed red. But the "clothes" worn by men and women alike were very simple, a form of the Peruvian poncho, which can best be described as a blanket with a hole in the middle, through which the head could be stuck.

The most curious thing about these Indians was their head-dress, a plaited band of bamboo with a projecting ridge or brim. From a short distance it looked remarkably like a saint's halo (if saints do really carry these impedimenta); but it is only another example of the saying, "everybody is not a saint who wears a halo," for on the Pichis the Indians are still a much feared group. We had been specially warned to keep our pistols and rifles ready to shoot at the first sign of treachery. Many small parties have been caught unawares and have paid for their carelessness with their lives.

Indeed I had more than a suspicion that in our case all was not as it should be, and so began ostentatiously to polish my rifle, with the result that in the end all quieted down, and eventually we reached Jessupe, our destination, in safety. From here we could see the long line of the first outlying ranges of the Andes. After months of the swamped and flooded jungle, we were face to face with the stupendous mountains that barred our way to the Pacific.

At Jessupe, a city with one house and perhaps five inhabitants, I was able to arrange for nine mules to carry my little party over the mountains, and the next day we started out on a new stage of adventure.

From the point of view of creature comfort our journey on mule-back was far from ideal. Under any conditions, riding a full-blown hard-headed 100 per cent mule is never a joy, but only a mule was capable of covering such tracks as those we now had before us. Any self-respecting horse would have slid and broken his neck the first day out. Perhaps because of his greater sureness of foot, a mule in this part of the world, as in many others, costs twice as much as a horse.

But if managing a mule is enough to make a saint cast aside his halo and take to swearing, the trail over which we went was enough to give a mule the disposition he has. At the best of times, it was an almost invisible trail, up and down hill, over tree-trunks, stones, and rocks, frequently winding along dizzy precipices. Even when scaling the Himalayas, I never experienced an equal number of hair-raising, walking-the-plank bits of road, where directly beneath us would be an open abyss of hundreds, and occasionally thousands, of feet. And the mules insisted, as mules always do insist, on walking at the extreme edge of the path so that their riders could get a full view of the nothingness below. In many cases the thick jungle undergrowth had entirely reconquered the trail that had been blazed through it, and Indians had to be sent ahead to cut out a new path for us.

Such, at best, is the highroad that connects La Montaña with the real Peru, but at the time of our journey it was rendered doubly difficult on account of the heavy and almost constant downpour of rain. The eastern slope of the Andes is always wet. The moisture-bringing clouds which sweep from the Atlantic are unable to cross the barrier of the Cordilleras, and consequently, condensed by the cold, deposit their huge burden of water on the eastern slope of the mountains. For this reason, whereas the western or Pacific side of the Andes is one of the driest and most rainless parts of the world, the eastern side is one of the wettest.

From May to November there is less rain, though there is always at least one heavy shower a day, and hence it is known as the dry season; from November to May the rains fall with full force. And here we were in the latter part of December, in the midst of the rainy season, with the result that we were not infrequently nine or ten hours in the saddle and sopped to the skin. It was worse for our mounts than for ourselves. The trail was a long line of slime and mud—mud up to the knees of our mules, concealing sharp-edged stones and slippery rocks, so that we had patiently to plow through the mud and slither over the rocks—with the chasm waiting for us at the first misstep.

Once indeed my mule lost his footing and nearly buried me in the mud, but I preferred the mud to the empty space on the other side. A pack-mule from another caravan was not so lucky. He tripped and, in trying to right himself, slid over the precipice, and he and his cargo were lost.

Considering the difficulties of the road and the bad state of my health, I had grave forebodings that I should never be able to live through the journey. For the first two or three days I had to strap myself in the saddle to keep from falling from weakness; and once I actually had to call a halt in the middle of a day's journey, as I was unable to go farther. But gradually the clear, vigorous mountain air had its effect; and the strange illness, which no doctor could diagnose, no medicine could cure, gradually disappeared as we rose higher and higher, and nearer and nearer the magic realm of the Incas.

But the gods of perversity had still another prank they wished to play on me. As my illness disappeared, a raging toothache began to develop. Neither hot water and salt nor anything else had any effect. Finally the abscessed tooth seemed the one important reality; jungle and mighty mountains sank into insignificant background. It was a devilish journey.

In the meantime my friend, the prisoner, and his party had caught up with us. He was mounted on a splendid mule, hired at government expense; while his escort and guard, two poor devils of soldiers, had to tramp it, or rather slop it, through the never ending mud. Not only in this way but in another, he proved, to use the words of my American cousin, that there were no flies on him. He had no intention of paying for his wife's mule out of his own private pocket, and had insisted, and successfully insisted, that the government, whose prisoner he was, grant him a mount to carry his baggage—and his baggage was his wife.

She, poor creature, was nearly dead from exhaustion, and swore she would never come back the same way. In nearly all cases women, and a great many men, who have to go from Iquitos to Lima, prefer to go by steamer down the Amazon, and then through the Panama Canal and down the West Coast— a voyage of from two to three months—rather than brave the journey through the jungle and over the mountains.

I was surprised to see that in spite of the increasing altitude and chilliness as we ascended, the mountains were still thickly forested, and still chiefly with the same uniform Amazonas type of foliage. Gradually, however, the palms became less frequent; their place was taken by huge ferns, many feet high. In spite of this change, the forest seemed quite as luxuriant, with its really gigantic trees, as had been the case in the low-lying Amazon basin. The real reason for this was no doubt that for the first nine days of journey we were clambering along the crest of an outer range of the Andes running north and south, instead of striking due west to the heart of the Cordilleras.

As with the vegetation, the bird and animal life remained Amazonian. More particularly were humming-birds in evidence, of a hundred varieties, and of a gorgeous brilliance nowhere else to be found. In fact the real home of the humming-bird seems to be on the eastern slope of the Andes rather than in the Amazon basin itself.

Occasionally we would meet with small groups of Indians. These, too, belonged to the true Amazon type; meeting them brought home to me the sharpness of the line of the boundary of the old Inca Empire. In spite of their high culture, the enormous size of their army, and the magnificence of their engineering achievements, the Incas were forced to stop short where the forest began. Time and again the Solar Cohorts—soldiers who had conquered mighty kingdoms in the Highlands and on the coast—penetrated into the jungle, to punish the savage tribes and to bring them under the yoke of the Sons of the Sun, but in every case they were either forced to beat a retreat or else the jungle engulfed them and they were never heard of again. And what was true of the Incas was largely true of the Spaniards, their successors. The forest land both of hill and of plain remained the *terra incognita*. In this Peruvian Amazonas there still remain huge tracts of land, unknown and unexplored.

Christmas overtook us while we were still struggling to find our way out of the jungle. Christmas day itself was marked by a very comic episode, though Mannling failed to see its humor.

There were many descents as well as ascents to make, and clattering down a steep slope on mule-back was even more uncomfortable than climbing up one. On one such occasion Mannling decided to make the descent on foot. Getting down from his saddle he whipped his mule on ahead.

The mule was not loath to go on without a rider. In fact so much did he enjoy his independence that when at last the descent had been made, and Mannling attempted to remount his steed, the mule refused to allow my camera man to come near him.

The mule showed great guile and impudence. He did not dash wildly ahead. He browsed very contentedly until Mannling came within a few feet of him. Then giving a most graceful kick he trotted on a few hundred yards further. His speed was nicely calculated, not so fast as to make the game seem hopeless, but fast enough to keep him out of Mannling's reach.

Hour after hour, and mile after mile, the pursuit kept up. Mannling plowed, slid, skated, and ran alternately along the awful trail in quest of his steed, and this steed was never more than a hundred yards away— nor less than three. Curses, coaxings, and prayers were of no avail. Mannling would, no doubt, still be running in pursuit of his mule had not one of my native followers made a short cut through the jungle and got ahead of the accursed animal.

At length we came to another important mile-post in our journey over the mountains, the little town of La Merced, which lies in a valley between the outer range, over which we had ridden, and the high peaks of the true Eastern Cordillera. Until a few years ago La Merced, too, was far in the "back of beyond," but within the last two or three years an automobile road has been built from the Highlands, the Sierra, to this point. The building of this road was due particularly to the ambitious little dictator, Leguía, who was eager to establish real authority over the lawless and lost lands of the interior. We were therefore able to dispense with our mules and trust our necks to the mercies of a mountain-climbing Dodge.

Leaving La Merced meant leaving the jungle, the Amazon, and all its associations behind us. We had now to climb through and up a steep rocky pass, a pass worn out by the ceaseless force of a small mountain stream. The trees gradually disappeared, leaving only bushes. The bushes, in turn, were replaced by the great bare, scarred rocks. The valley pass was no longer a valley but a long, deep, narrow gorge, through which we climbed ever up and up and up. The road, for the most part, was but a narrow ledge with a sheer perpendicular drop above and below. Between the rocky wall on one side and the abyss on the other, there was just room—and no more—for us to crawl along. I sometimes imagine that I am fairly cool, but as we swept along the long, narrow, curving ledge, and I saw the reckless daring of our driver—a daring largely inspired by alcohol—my curly locks began to uncurl and to stand up on end.

The sections of road carved out of rock were, however, in reality, not so perilous as the occasional sections of sand over which we had to pass. There the danger of sudden slips and land-slides was much greater. At one point a recent land-slide had in fact swept away every trace of the road for more than five hundred yards. At the time we attempted the climb, the soft fine sand continued to slide and fall down the steep slope, making repairs temporarily impossible. So here we had to get out and crawl along the side of the precipice, our hearts in our mouths the whole time. The only foothold was not three inches broad, and even this was composed of the same treacherous sand which had already hurled more than one traveler into the gorge below.

But luck was with us. Over we got in safety to the place where the road began again. Then taking a new car we whirled on and on and up and up until eventually we had passed through the outer line of the Eastern Andes and were on the Great Highlands of Peru, the Highlands that lie between the Eastern and the Western Cordilleras. The damp, heavy, hot air of the jungle was a thing of the past. We were now panting or breathless in the thin, cold, biting air of the magnificent, bald, bare mountains.

Here it was that we were exposed to the danger of the dread *soroche,* or mountain-sickness, which brings splitting, blinding headaches, ringing and drumming in the ears, agonizing nausea, and not infrequently a prolonged nose-bleeding. But *soroche* is as tricky and inconsistent as a goddess. The doctors are far from agreed as to its exact nature and cause, and it picks and chooses its victims without discoverable reason. This time I was let off lightly, as was Mannling, who had never been in the mountains before; but my friend, the prisoner, and his wife were completely prostrated, and for the next two or three days were seriously ill. The Andes had exacted their tribute of suffering.

CHAPTER XXIX

OVER THE PASSAGE TO THE CITY OF THE KINGS

THE sight of the Andes is worth any tribute, so magnificent, so awe-inspiring are they. From Tierra del Fuego, the southernmost point of South America, they sweep up the western side of the whole continent in an unbroken line. One continent alone cannot imprison them, for, jumping the isthmus, they continue their royal way under a new name as the Rocky Mountains of Mexico, of the United States, and of Canada, until they are lost in the dismal cold of the distant arctic circle.

Like most of the great mountain systems of the world—the Pyrenees, the Alps, and the Himalayas— the Andes are geologically but youngsters, as the time of their great elevation was in the Tertiary period, when the era of the great reptiles was over, and life was beginning to settle down more or less to its present form. They are insolent parvenus compared with the Highlands of the old Guiana and Brazilian continents, which rank in antiquity with the Appalachian and Allegheny mountains of the Eastern United States, and with the hills of the British Isles and of Scandinavia.

For the most part through their long course, the Andes can be divided into two parallel ranges, the Eastern and Western, of which the Eastern is somewhat older. The land between the two has risen with its mountain-barriers and forms the famous Highlands, La Sierra, the seat of the old indigenous culture of the South American Continent. Farther to the South, as we were later to learn and see, the Highland is about three hundred miles wide and consists largely of great open broad basins or table-lands. Where we now were it was narrower, one hundred miles at the most, and broken up into innumerable minor mountain systems, with intervening valleys and gorges.

But whether broad or narrow, smooth or broken, there is magic in this Andean Highland. Here are extracted vast stores of silver and copper and lead. Here on this bleak barren soil was first grown the potato, which was destined to conquer the world. Here still live in remarkable primitiveness, with their language, their customs, their dress, almost unaltered, that strange people who first developed the mines and who first planted the potato; the people who built up the great culture of the Andes, which was a marvel even to their conquerors, the Spaniards.

Their empire fell nearly four hundred years ago, and since then the white man, with his strange new ideas, has been master of the land; but the old race of the Sons of the Sun survives, and with it much of the old tradition.

Reaching far, far up the sides of the desolate hills, we could see the carefully laid out terraces, where the Quechua Indians planted and worked and reaped. Lower in the valleys stood their adobe, thatch-covered huts, some lying scattered apart, others together in little villages; many of them still ruled by a village socialism reaching far back into prehistoric times.

Working in the fields, carefully guiding the scanty, much-needed water over the terraces, or at evening gathered in the villages, we could see the Indians themselves, arrayed in wide dish-shaped hats, covering knitted, close-fitting caps—red, with various designs worked upon them, as were the ponchos, the hand-woven blanket-cloaks, wondrously and dexterously embroidered. Their legs from the knee down are bare, but they wear curiously pointed knee-breeches and woven sandals.

Even more strange and other-worldly than the people was their animal, the llama, in appearance a fantastic mixture of camel and sheep, with long, swaying, graceful neck, and human, extraordinarily human, eyes. Llamas are the beasts of burden, as well as the givers of flesh and wool to their masters. Now and again on the far-distant tops of the mountains, we saw the even more remarkable vicuña, the distant wild cousin of the llama, whose proud spirit can never be tamed, but whose wool is of a texture more silky than silk.

It is eerie and other-worldly, this world of the far-reaching heights. As if to remind one of the greater glories of the long-dead past, there are scattered, all over the Highland, ruins—ruins of temples, palaces, and castles. Mysterious ruins, many of them, known only to the natives, unmapped and unexplored; others whose vastness and beauty have called to them the traveler and the scholar, but of which, even to-day, little of real meaning and history is known.

Many ruins lay around us, but we knew that to the north and to the south lay historic remains of even greater importance. Far to the north were the wondrous carved stones of Chavin. No one knows how, when, or by whom they were erected. To the south was the wonder-city of Cuzco, the capital of the old wide-reaching Inca Empire; still further south the older and even more mysterious ruins of Tiawanako.

I had to choose between the North and the South; there was not sufficient time to visit both. In the end I chose the ruins of the South. But instead of going direct I decided to pay first of all a visit to the coast, to Lima, the City of Kings, the seat of the viceroys of the Castilian rulers of old, and the capital of the present Republic of Peru.

Consequently we made our way to the little town of Oroya, whence the railroad makes its way westward over the Highlands, subsequently to cross the Western Andes, and then descend rapidly down the western slope of the mountains to the Pacific Ocean. This railway, the highest anywhere in the world, is one of the greatest engineering achievements of the nineteenth century. It was built chiefly to allow the export of the precious ores and minerals from the Andean mines; the desolate Highlands produce nothing else in sufficient quantity to allow of export.

Oroya itself is one of the drabbest and most unattractive towns anywhere in the world, but to us it meant the outpost of civilization. By means of the railroad we were once more in touch with the outer world, and merrily enough we started on our journey Lima-ward the next day. At first our train had to pull up the long slope leading from the Central Highlands to the pass through the Western Cordilleras, through the same wild, scarred mountain scenery that had marked our journey farther to the East. At the top of the pass, 15,900 feet high, we could see on either side of us great mountain peaks whose tops were covered, even in this equatorial region, with never-melting snow. Then started the long, steep plunge, circling, winding, zigzagging down the precipitous side of the mountains.

Near where we started our downward course there sprang up a tiny stream fed by the melting glaciers of the mountains. We followed the course of the valley which this little rivulet had worn out on the side of the great mountains. It was the Rimac, "the river of babbling waters," on the banks of which far below, we knew, lay the city of Lima, which derives its name from the river.

The western slope of the Andes showed us nature in still another aspect. Compared with the luxuriant forest growth of La Montaña, the Highlands had seemed to us bleak and bare. But even in the Highlands there are occasional showers, giving rise to a shimmer of faint pale green, where mosses and wild short grasses bravely maintain their existence. Consequently the Highlands are a luxuriant garden compared with the western slope. On the Pacific coast rain is almost unknown, and the hills and plains form one vast scene of desolation, a realm of sand and dust and death, save where the mountain streams, fed by the melting snows, bring life-giving moisture to the narrow valleys through which they run. Here the earth yields richly and manifoldly, and so, while we saw in the distance only desert and silence and desolation, our train was boarded from time to time by the dwellers of the valleys, peddling huge baskets of luscious fruits and great bouquets of violets and pansies.

My friend, the prisoner, who was still with us, bought indiscriminately everything that was offered— fruits, flowers, and even tickets for the national lotteries that were everywhere on sale. It was his last day of freedom; that same evening he was to enter prison. His trial and verdict were still to come, and no one knew

when, or whether, he would emerge again; he wanted
to have a last luxurious fling at life.

In a rather unexpected way I was made to share in
his anxiety. In Oroya he had telegraphed to his family
in Lima asking them to look after his wife during his
imprisonment, but he had received no reply. He therefore begged me, in case his relations did not turn up at
the station, to take his wife to a hotel with me and look
after her until further arrangements could be made. In
romantic passionate South America, looking after a
pretty young woman, who is another man's wife, is a
rather ticklish business, and I shook in my shoes at the
thought of it. I gave up looking at the scenery and devoted my time to praying that his family would not fail
to appear.

Shortly after sunset we completed our long descent.
Eight miles before reaching the coast and the harbor city
of Callao, we steamed into Lima station. My friend
looked in vain among the teeming crowd for a familiar
face. He was just about to be marched away by his
guard, leaving his fair wife under my distracted wing,
when a new group suddenly pushed its way through the
surging mass of people. It was the family, and I was
saved!

Lima is the city par excellence of modes and fashions, of elegance and face-paint; and as there were dip-
lomats and ministers of state and their wives to visit, I
spent the whole of the next two days trying to make myself shipshape. My wild hair and beard, a sort of jungle
fungus, had to be shorn, my rough explorer's costume
exchanged for the glad rags of the city, and the book of
etiquette studied up, in order to relearn how to handle
a knife and fork; for on our long journey food had been
gulped very much on the principle of catch as catch can.

Then, dolled up for the fray, I went forth to inspect
Lima and its inhabitants. It was well worth inspection.
A century or so ago Lima was the largest and greatest
of the Spanish American cities; it was the center
of art, literature, and culture. Even to-day something of this spirit broods over the old city. The old
order has changed; new states and new capitals have
arisen which vie with, and even outshine, the splendor
of the old City of the Kings. But within the last few
years Lima has awakened from the lethargy caused by
the glamour of the past.

Large splendid buildings (it is a pity the old Spanish
style has not been followed) have arisen on every side.
Beautiful avenues have been laid out and villas built;
a constant stream of motor-cars makes the streets almost uncrossable; in short Lima is possessed of all the
dubious blessings of twentieth-century invention and
progress.

But above all things, Lima is once more the center of
fashion and of elegance. It is still very much of an aristocratic city. Although with its suburbs and its harbor
of Callao, Lima has a population of only about two
hundred and fifty thousand, a large number of its citizens are exceedingly well-to-do. The vast majority of
the owners of the mines and of the great estates in the
Highlands and in the valleys of the coast spend their
time in the capital. Huge sums of money are brought in
from the country and lavished in Lima. The office-hold-
ers and hangers-on of the government reap the benefit.
Wealth and prosperity are visible on every hand, and
prices are fixed accordingly. Lima is the most expensive
city in South America, if not in the world.

A great part of this wealth appears to be expended
in perfumes and frocks for the women. The beauty of

the Lima maidens has been sung from coast to coast, and the streets of Lima are supposed to be paved with broken hearts. By a curious coincidence my predecessor in the hotel room which I occupied had committed suicide after being jilted by some fair Limaense.

After a careful—and, let us say, scientific—study of the women-folk of Lima, I came to the conclusion that they are not really more beautiful than those of other South American cities, but that they are better and more artistically powdered and painted, and know how to dress themselves with greater effect. If in this sinful day the all-powerful Eve *must* paint and powder, it is at least to be recommended that she do so artistically. And I can give the ladies at Lima another unsolicited testimonial. They can talk more and faster than any other women; and that, I think, is saying a good deal.

More interesting even than the buildings or the women is the personality of the man who at present guides the destinies of Peru. This is Leguía, in name the president, in reality the absolute dictator of his country. In his hands worthy senators and babbling deputies are but puppets. His life has been that of a soldier of fortune. He has known ruin, exile, and defeat. More than once his life has hung by a thread, but each time he has emerged from his difficulties victorious.

From one point of view he is the typical Central and South American revolutionary despot. No one knows how to stage a revolution more neatly or more unobtrusively, or to time it more exactly. No one knows better how to insure his position by a sham election, at which the ballot-boxes are suitably salted. No one knows better how to pander in small ways to popular opinion, or in the choice and management of his officials to play

one man off against another, so that all work only for
him.

From 1908 until 1912 he served his first term as
president and learned the lights and shades of the political game. In 1913 with the secret sympathy and con-
nivance of his successor, a gentleman with the very non-
Peruvian name of Billingshurst (he was of English extraction) who feared his continued influence, a mob
stormed and destroyed Leguía's residence, and he himself came within an ace of losing his life. For this incident he was convicted by the government of "disturbing the public peace" and was forced to flee the country.
He remained for six years in England.

In 1919 he staged his final and very successful revolution; since then he has remained master of the country.
For the first two or three years of his new régime, the
plotters refused to believe that he was unshakable in his
saddle, and engineered the usual military uprising. But
the acute and scheming old brain of Leguía was too
much for them, and each attempted revolution was
nipped in the bud. One time indeed he was caught napping. A group of revolutionaries surprised him and demanded that he sign his resignation immediately under
pain of death. But the wily Leguía, knowing that one of
his servants had escaped and was seeking aid, continued
to parley, bargain, and play with his captors until reinforcements arrived and he was able to turn the tables
on his assailants.

Open revolution proving abortive, there followed a
period of "palace intrigue," during which the outs
managed to buy over a number of the palace officers to
a plot to put Leguía out of the way. Even a near and
trusted relative of the president, who was an officer in
the life-guards, was bought over. But, in the nick of

time, Leguía, who has eyes and ears everywhere, and one of whose favorite amusements was to act as unofficial censor to the post that arrived for any one at the palace, learned of the plan, and the plotters had a busy period trying to escape from the country in time. Recently there has been a distinct slump in the revolution market; for the time being the outs have given up the job as hopeless, and Leguía, though loved by none—in fact hated by most—is feared and respected by all.

I had the pleasure of being received twice by him, once in the old palace, where we walked, as we talked, through the garden laid out by Pizarro. The other time was when he invited me to a seat in the presidential box at the bull-fight. The impression I received on each occasion was the same. There was about him too much of the hard, cold, and calculating for him to be what the Spanish call *simpático*. But, at the same time, one realized that one was in the presence of a *man*, and a man not lacking in the elements of greatness.

Unlike most of the South American politicians, Leguía really has the interests of his country at heart. Under him Peru has developed enormously. Roads have been built all over the land; wireless stations have linked up the most distant parts of the republic. A discriminating use of public money in filling a number of political appointments was a custom too deep-seated in South America for Leguía to do away with it entirely, but nepotism and political jobbery have been cut down enormously, and public finance placed on a sound foundation. Above all, though Leguía jealously guards the national interests, foreigners in Peru are justified in believing that as long as he remains in power, their investments in Peru are safe.

Present-day Lima was sufficiently fascinating, but in

addition there were many things which brought to our minds the charm and the romance of the old colonial days. What purports to be the mummy of Pizarro rests in a crypt in the Lima Cathedral, the largest and most beautiful church in South America. This mummy was dug up from a forgotten corner a few years ago, but it is strange how unhonored and unsung, how little remembered, Pizarro is in Peru. The Peruvians have the statue-erecting craze. There is a statue to Columbus, and one to the Liberators, Bolivar and San Martín. There are statues of tin-pot politicians of no importance in their own day and of less in ours, but there is no statue to mark the memory of the great conqueror and adventurer to whom modern Peru, as well as the city of Lima, owes its very existence. Yet what a *man* he was!

In a time and a country where pride of birth was almost insufferable, and the barrier between the classes almost unsurmountable, Pizarro, a bastard, and in his youth a swineherd, fought and starved for years as a private soldier, but was destined in the end to glitter in ribbons and gold and silver as a marquis among the Castilian grandees, and to rule the vast Inca Empire as the viceroy of his king.

The conquest of Peru was accomplished by no young dashing soldier of fortune, full of youthful zest for life. Pizarro at the time of the conquest was a man of sixty-three, whose strength had been sapped by exposure, privation, and starvation. Twice previously the parties which he headed for the conquest of Peru had come back empty-handed after suffering untold difficulty.

Laughed to scorn by his contemporaries, he set out a third time accompanied by only a hundred and sixty soldiers. Yet even to get this handful of men together had involved months of toil and hardship, of grinding poverty and incessant fighting against obstacles. But this time he was successful. With an army of less than two hundred men he defeated and conquered an empire of ten millions, which possessed a huge and well organized army and was defended by a hundred forts.

Unlettered, cruel, tyrannical Pizarro was, to be sure, but a magnificent adventurer. He not only laid the foundation for Spanish rule in America, but he took the tiny Inca settlement of Lima and, by establishing there this capital, made of it the City of the Kings.[1]

To this city came a long line of proud and princely viceroys—princes, dukes, and marquises. In the list of their long pompous names it is refreshing to meet the name of O'Higgins, who was viceroy at the beginning of the nineteenth century. From Lima these men ruled over the greater part of the Spanish possessions in South America. At this time the viceroyalty of Peru included Ecuador, Bolivia, and Chile, as well as the country that is now known as Peru. This territory was greater in size than the whole of western Europe.

With the viceroys came the officials of their court, stiff-necked but needy cavaliers, soldiers of fortune, and devil-may-cares. Some brought with them their courtly and graceful spouses from Spain; others took unto themselves as wives maidens of Peru. Thus were founded the great families of Peru, which still exert such an enormous influence in the land. Here and there, even in the modern city of Lima, one finds some of the palatial dwellings built by these early aristocratic settlers.

Nor did Catholic Spain fail to send ship-loads of priests, priests of every order; some to convert—if need

---

[1] Actually the kings referred to are the Three Wise Men or Kings from the East, who were adopted as patron saints.

be by force—the Indians; others to act as chaplains in the splendid viceregal court. Here, as elsewhere, the Franciscan, Dominican, and Jesuit fathers were particularly active, and left behind them beautiful convents and churches, memorials of their activity.

In the Dominican church are the remains of St. Anna, the first and most important of all the saints whose native land was the New World, and who is the special patron, according to the Roman Church, of all true believers in both North and South America.

Not far away from the Plaza de Armas is the site of the old Inquisition, the Holy Office, where hundreds of men were tried by torture as to the soundness of their faith. Hundreds of men and women found guilty of heresy were led from the gloomy old building to the central square, there to pay the last penalty for their unbelief.

CHAPTER XXX

IN THE HIGHLANDS WHERE THE INCAS HELD SWAY

LIMA reaches back even further than to colonial
times. Not far distant from the city are three
magnificent ruins which date from the early
Inca days. These in their decaying splendor throw a
glamour over the whole of the surrounding country. In
order, however, to appreciate more fully the vastness
of the ancient Inca Empire and the magnificence of its
culture, we made several journeys from Lima to various
places even more noted as centers of Inca influence.

One of these journeys was to take us back to the
Highlands, but to the Highlands of the far south, the
very heart of the ancient empire, in which was situated
Cuzco, its capital. It would have been possible to do the
whole journey by land, but in this land of poor communication it was advisable to travel as far as possible
by sea. Consequently we went from Lima proper to its
seaport, Callao, and there embarked on a ship which was
to take us far down the coast to the harbor of Mollendo,
where we could once more strike inland.

The ship was so packed that we were at first unable
to secure cabin accommodation, but eventually a
thoughtful "gift" to the steward produced a special

cabin for myself and my two companions. We were in a part of the world where "gifts" play an extremely important part in life.

The ship on which we were traveling was a Peruvian one. The great majority of its passengers were paid voters who were on their way south to take part in a plebiscite which was to decide whether the province of Arica was to be Peruvian or Chilean. After the famous War of 1880, wherein Peru was so ignominiously defeated by Chile, Chile annexed permanently the southern coast-line of Peru with its valuable nitrate deposits, and furthermore occupied "temporarily" the provinces of Tacna and Arica. This temporary occupation has continued down to the present time, despite the frequent attempts Peru has made to regain her ancient provinces. In 1925, as the result of renewed agitation on the part of the Peruvians, the question of the ultimate suzerainty over the disputed area was submitted to President Coolidge for arbitration. This cautious man, not wishing to offend either party by giving over the territory to the other, ordered that a vote of its inhabitants and native sons should decide its fate. A sweet and simple solution theoretically, but one fraught with many practical difficulties. All persons born in Tacna and Arica even though resident in either Peru or Chile were to have the right to vote, providing that they returned to their native home. Consequently both governments busied themselves shipping to the two provinces as many voters as possible. Voters were to have free passage and full expenses during their stay in the territory. A surprisingly large number seemed able to prove that they were natives of the almost desert region. I could only conclude that in this desert people must have bred like rabbits.

On the Pira Parana the ladies confined their dress to a pair of garters

Beneath one of the great cataracts in which da Silva sacrificed his life

The mysterious gateway at Tiawanako—part of a pre-Inca temple

The walls of a pre-Inca palace at Cuzco.   No one knows when or by whom
it was built

Voters at the best of times are strange animals, but the present crew would have taken the prize at any voters' competition. The cows and pigs on the after deck were distinctly cleaner and sweeter. A moving picture of how these enfranchised citizens ate would have thrown Charlie Chaplin into the shade. In the evenings, under the influence of *pisco,* the strong native spirit, each man developed a yearning to deliver a patriotic speech. As everybody spoke, and nobody listened, the general effect was highly edifying. I thought seriously of becoming myself a voter but was told I was too young and inexperienced for the job.

I was not sorry when the ship stood off the stormy cliffs of Mollendo and we could say good-by to our fellow-passengers. Nearly all the ports on the West Coast are wretched affairs, no true harbors at all. The so-called port of Mollendo is one of the worst of them. Our ship anchored far out at sea, and in order to land we had to plow through the high waves in a tiny boat— owned, I soon discovered, by highway robbers. Halfway between ship and shore the boatmen suddenly demanded three times the stipulated sum. I took a look at the surrounding waves and was at first inclined to accede to their outrageous request; but after thinking devoutly of some Scotch ancestors of mine, I plucked up courage enough to tell the men that far from increasing the promised rate of pay they would have to be content with one half the sum originally agreed to, as otherwise I should swim ashore and report the matter to the police. The boatmen must have believed my absurd threat, as they at once began to row toward the docks once more.

But in Mollendo there was no beach, and the cliffs were so high, and the water so rough, that it was im-

possible to disembark directly. We had to sit on a huge
chair controlled by a dock-crane, which descended to
the water, level with our boat. There was then a wild
whirl through the air, and we were suddenly dropped
down on land.

Mollendo itself we found of no importance. It was
merely the gateway to the interior, the starting-point
of a railway leading to Arequipa and the high plateau
of the Inca Land.

We therefore made our way to the railway station
as soon as possible, and in a crowded train we slowly
puffed along an incline leading up the Andes. After
two hours of puffing we emerged on La Joya plain—
a sort of terrace on the upward climb, and the bed of
a huge lake in the long distant past. A large number
of curious half-moon-shaped sand-dunes of greenish-
white sand stood out against the dark brown-red earth
of the plain itself. Other deserts in the world produce
somewhat similar phenomena, but the dunes of La Joya
are unique in the exquisite perfection of their form—
sand-dunes where no sand seems to exist, cameo pictures fashioned by Mother Nature. But these cameos
are travelers, moving mountains, driven along by the
wind that made them, at the rate of about a hundred
feet a year.

After the plain had been passed we continued our
climb through a high, deep-cut, narrow gorge, one
worn out by the water, which exposed to view some
of the most beautiful and vividly colored rocks that I
had ever seen, rocks which in their delicate brilliancy
not even the Grand Cañon, their nearest rival, can sur-
pass. In South Peru, the Western Andes are much
broader and their crumpling more complicated than
in the North, and when in the evening we arrived at

Arequipa, some seven thousand feet above sea-level, we were still far from the crest of the range.

Arequipa, the second city of Peru, I found so charming that we stayed there several days. Arequipa, too, owes its existence to the great conquistador, Pizarro, but it has remained more faithful than Lima to the old Spanish ideal, and in coming to Arequipa one feels that one is thrown back two or three hundred years. The old, rambling courtyards, inclosing Spanish houses with their elaborately carved gateways, have held their own, and in these houses still live the proud descendants of the "first families" of Spain, several of them retaining, even in republican days, the titles of marquis or duke given to their ancestors by the kings of old.

Curiously enough, among the distinguished families of Arequipa are several with English names, descendants of English settlers of several generations ago, most of them intensely proud of their English descent —and unable to speak a word of English! It seems that it is only here in South America that the conservative Englishman in the second generation can forget his language, his customs, and his ideas. And even then the race-consciousness persists.

Arequipa, with its beautiful churches and Old World houses, is rendered even more charming by the magnificent mountains which surround it. On one side is Pichipichi, on another Chacham, whose twenty-thousand-foot summit climbers have tried in vain to ascend. More majestic than either is Mount Misti, the "guardian angel of Arequipa," whose beautiful cone is all the more beautiful because from its perpetually snow-covered top there ascends a continual spiral of smoke. Misti is one of the several South American volcanoes which are still active. It is not unnatural that Arequipa, in the near neighborhood, should suffer from frequent earthquakes. It is strange how mankind dares to live in the glow of the fires of hell.

On the sides of Misti, overlooking the city, Harvard University has erected, and still maintains, an astronomical observatory to take advantage of the brilliant starlit nights of Peru.

The manager of the Southern Railroad was kind enough to give us the use of a motor-car that ran along the railroad tracks so that we could see more of the country through which we were to pass. As we continued our climb upward after leaving Arequipa, we could see most clearly, on the bare exposed sides of the mountains, that most of the rocks were of sedimentary character—built up of sediment which had been deposited on the bed of the ocean in the long distant days when the whole of the Andes lay under water. Here and there, however, were intrusions of volcanic rock. It is no doubt due to the ancient volcanoes that the region is rich in hot mineral springs, to which all sorts of medical properties have been ascribed.

It was strange to see the steam arising from the water, for, as we rose higher and higher, the cold began to make itself more and more intensely felt. By the time we arrived at Crucero Alto, the pass that leads through the Western Andes to the broad table-land beyond, and which lies some 14,700 feet above the sea, we were, in spite of our coats and blankets, chilled to the bone. Curiously enough, the only person who was at all seriously troubled by mountain-sickness was our Indian driver, a native of the mountains, who had covered this stretch for years. It reminded me very forcibly of an old college friend of mine who served for three or four years as a ship's surgeon, but was eventually forced to give up his job and go back to land, because on every voyage he suffered terribly from seasickness.

Soon after starting the long descent we passed two most beautiful lakes, the remnants perhaps of ancient glaciers, more than equal in loveliness to any of the Alpine lakes. I am sure that in the days to come Southern Peru will be one of the great tourist centers of the world.

Gradually we descended to the table-land itself, some thirteen thousand feet above the sea. Here the country was more level and open than we had found it farther to the north. On emerging from the luxuriant vegetation of the Amazon, this highland had struck us as barren and desolate, but now in contrast with the utterly desert sands of the coast the highland appeared rich in verdure, a land flowing with milk and honey. Far, far up the sides of the hills ran the terraces where the native subjects of the Incas had planted and harvested their crops. Many of these terraces are still in use; others are deserted, for since the days of the Spanish conquest hundreds of thousands of Indians have been killed, or have succumbed to oppression, so that only about a million natives survive, out of the ten million over which the Children of the Sun are supposed to have held sway.

We slept that night in the village of Juliaca, where a large and beautiful cathedral reminded us of the Spanish occupation, but where everything else was pure Indian. We were now really in the home of the Incas. Juliaca is an important junction. To the south the road led to Lake Titicaca, the sacred lake of Peru, and to La Paz; to the north, to Cuzco, the old Inca capital. Our way lay northward, but before continuing our journey, I was eager to penetrate more deeply into the native life we saw around us.

We had come to study the Incas, and as the people of the Highlands were the direct descendants of the Incas, I believed that by observing the life and customs of the modern natives we should more readily understand the remains of the ancient cultures when we came to them.

The town of Juliaca was very primitive, but I knew that in the smaller villages of the great table-land the old Inca customs and traditions were even better preserved. I was therefore delighted to accept an invitation extended to us by one of the great landowners of the region to visit his hacienda or estate, which lay about thirty miles away. Horses were provided for us, and on these we galloped across the plains toward our destination.

On our arrival at the hacienda we were greeted in an almost feudal fashion, the *administrador* of the estate and a number of Indians rushing out to meet us. The house itself, as usual, consisted of a number of courtyards, each room opening independently into its own courtyard. One huge courtyard was surrounded by various barns and stables and by a large and imposing church. Each estate here had to maintain a church in order to impress the natives. In the courtyard itself a number of trees were growing, a great achievement in this part of the world, and only to be attained by building a circular mud wall around each tree to prevent it from freezing! At least that was the story told me, and I looked wise and accepted it; though why in a courtyard, already protected from the icy wind, an additional wall can prevent the roots from freezing, is more than I can understand.

There was a sort of gloomy grandeur about the place. The walls of course were of adobe or sun-dried brick, but the rooms were stuffed full of heavy carpets, of plush furniture, and of hideous gilt chromos which must have cost a small fortune to bring here. Nothing worked; the running water did not run, the lighting fixtures did not light, and the player-piano did not play. Of books there was no sign, but I found the old *administrador* reading a newspaper two years old. He had already read it two hundred times and was working his way through it again.

But it could hardly be otherwise. My host, like all of his kind, spent the greater part of his time in his beautiful house in far-away Lima, and stayed, at most, one month of the year here at the hacienda, in order to collect the income of the estate. Country estate life, as we know it in America and more particularly in England, is entirely lacking. In South America a man would as soon devote himself to rat-catching as to fox-hunting.

It was a marvel to me that in these conditions, with only a sleepy old *administrador* to look after affairs, and at an altitude of thirteen thousand feet above sea-level, where the cold at night was so intense that very few crops could be grown, the estate paid as well as it did. The seemingly desolate acres which surrounded the house brought in a net profit of more than twelve thousand dollars a year, virtually all of which, of course, was spent in Lima. The value of the estate was therefore estimated at one hundred and twenty thousand dollars. In this bleak, desolate country, an estate which does not bring in more than ten per cent on the capital invested in it is considered a very poor one—in contrast to the rich land of England, where four per cent is considered an excellent return.

I was particularly interested to see the life led by the Indians on the estate. True descendants of the Incas, they had changed none of their customs merely because their families had been living for centuries as tenants on a white man's estate. Their houses stood in little clusters in various parts of the hacienda. All these huts —they were no more—the Indians had built themselves in their spare time. The landlord here had neither to build houses nor to spend money on repairs for his tenants. The huts themselves were much as they were at the time of the Incas. Even in the ancient days the stone palaces were confined to the Sons of the Sun and to the priests and nobles. In Cuzco, as well as in the country, the "people" lived in tiny mud huts, such as I now saw around me. The hut usually consisted of a single room, scarcely man-high, so small that no respectable cat would allow herself to be swung in it, without windows, and with a tiny door through which one had to crawl.

The ancient Peruvians may have been sun-worshipers, but the modern Peruvians are extraordinarily careful to see that the sun never enters their huts; and they seem to regard fresh air with equal animosity. Inside the hut a pile of skins furnishes a bed for the family, and a cooking-pot or two completes the furniture inventory. In view of what the light and fresh-air faddists tell us, it is remarkable that the Sierra people are racially so vigorous and strong as they appear to be.

Each man becomes owner of a certain amount of land free of rent. When he marries he receives half as much again. With this he can do what he pleases, but in return for it three days in the week he and his wife, should he have one, must work without wages for the landlord. Three days he devotes to his own land, while Sundays are devoted to church and to booze. As it generally works out, the haciendero has the direct use of only half of his property, and the other half is given to his workers. Under this arrangement the Indians fare reasonably well; better, strangely enough, than when they have the nominal ownership of the land. Next door to our host's estate was one owned by an old native *ayllu,* or clan, with its ancient communistic organization. This clan, not wishing to become subject to a white overlord, had purchased immunity, by way of a heavy annual tax or tribute to the state, but the tax was so heavy that the members of the community were kept poorer than the mere tenants next door.

Many of the tenant Indians, in spite of their miserable huts and "simple life," are extremely well-to-do; some, in fact, are really wealthy. But in the majority of cases drink and the priests take away the greater part of their savings. The priesthood here has an enormous influence and exacts huge donations from the peasantry. More particularly do the yearly festivals exert a deleterious influence upon the Indians. Each year a master of the festival is chosen, and he has to bear the whole cost of the affair, which frequently runs into many hundreds of pounds, so that the festival master, as the result of the honor paid to him, is in debt for several years afterward.

Near one of the huts I found a number of heavy polished stones, which in ancient days had served as the heads of battle-axes and battle-clubs, souvenirs of the old days when the Indian was free and independent. These old days are gone, and the present Indians do not even know what these things were meant for; but the sullen, slow-burning hatred of the native for the white is there, and it only awaits an opportunity to burst into flame.

My host, with the boundless hospitality of the South American gentleman, put himself out to see that the table was well served, but to his astonishment I insisted upon eating the real products of the land, which were supposed to be fit only for Indians, and for whites only when nobody was looking.

It is extraordinary how difficult it is for the tourist in South America to get really native dishes. In the hotels and when he is invited to private houses he is given imitation French cooking. In Lima I tried in vain at my hotel to get maize (*choclo*) and sweet potatoes (*camote*) served. The waiter was shocked at the very idea that these common things should be served in a respectable hotel. Strange this universal prejudice against the sweet potato. Even in far-away Japan it is an insult to offer a man a sweet potato, and here in South America it is eaten only by the peasants.

On the table-land of the Andes it is too cold for the sweet potato, which belongs to the coastal valleys, and maize can be grown only with difficulty. But, to make up for this, there is every conceivable variety of the other sort of potato. Peru is of course the home of the potato, and more than two hundred different varieties are known, to say nothing of the *oca*, a tuber very similar to the potato. Even my expansive appetite could not cope with all the varieties, but I sampled as many as I could.

I was particularly interested in tasting *kinoa* and *chuño*, two dishes famous in the ancient Inca days. *Kinoa* I found to consist of tiny seeds resembling millet, which when boiled in a mash and eaten with syrup was most delicious. It is considered to be extremely nourishing, and I am surprised that some wealthy American manufacturer has not put it on the market as a breakfast cereal.

On *chuño*, of even greater fame as an Inca delicacy, I could not wax so enthusiastic. There are two kinds of *chuño*, but both are in reality only our old friend, the potato, in disguise—but very well disguised. To make what is known as black *chuño*, potatoes are exposed in winter for several days and nights on the frozen fields until they are themselves thoroughly frozen. The natives then come and, with their bare feet, trample again and again on the tubers until the water is squeezed out of them. They are then left for another three weeks on the fields to dry. By this time the potatoes have become small, hard, black balls, each about the size of a walnut. In this form they last for many years—the Indians say for centuries—without going bad. They have not the slightest similarity to the potatoes which in Europe by accident become frozen or frost-bitten, and which the good housewife throws away.

The other kind of *chuño*, called white *chuño*, is made by soaking the potatoes for a week or so in water, before placing them on the fields for the same process of trampling and drying. The potatoes so treated shrivel up into small white balls, which also last for all eternity. It is indeed strange that in order to prepare a shriveled-up, desiccated potato, one has to soak it in water.

I managed to eat a fair quantity of the *chuño* balls with no great difficulty, in spite of the fact that I knew that the Indians who had trampled them had never washed their feet during the whole course of their lives. But what does a little thing like dirt matter when one

dines upon Inca dishes? After my experience in the
Amazon with *kashiri,* even *chicha,* the native beer, was
not impossible.

Chicha, like *kashiri,* consists largely of saliva, but
unlike *kashiri,* which is prepared from chewed-up *mandioca, chicha* is made by the natural fermentation of
masticated maize grains.

CHAPTER XXXI

THE CAPITAL OF THE SONS OF THE SUN

SO hospitable was our host that it was difficult to get away. But it was necessary to continue our journey without further loss of time. We made our way back to the railroad and were soon whirling over the plains, northward in the direction of Cuzco. We could see that all these plains were drained by Titicaca (or Titikaka), the sacred lake far to the south. In fact, the whole of the table-land over which we were passing must in earlier days have formed part of the lake, which was then one of the largest in the world. On either side of us, we could see from time to time little Indian villages, and here and there herds of graceful llamas. High over our heads circled a condor, the King of Birds, but now a mere speck in the blue.

It was along this road that the legendary founders of the Inca Empire are said to have come. For tradition says that the Sun-God, having pity upon degraded mankind, sent two of his children (Manko Kapak and Mama Koya) down to earth to establish a divine rulership. They first appeared at Lake Titicaca and then gradually made their way northward until they came to Cuzco, where they established their kingdom.

In the early afternoon we came to a low pass forming

a watershed. To the south were the broad plains over
which we had come, with a little river running down to
the sacred lake; to the north a long narrow valley began. Through this valley ran a tiny, babbling, rushing
brook; one to me of enormous interest, for this little
brook was one of the two chief fountains of the great
Amazon River on which we had spent so many months.
On the same afternoon we were treated to the spectacle
of an amateur and unstaged bull-fight. The railroad
was still so new to this part of the world that the animals had not accustomed themselves to it. So it came
about that a splendid specimen of a bull, who was on
the track, disapproved strongly of the puffing of our
little engine, and decided to attack in full charge. The
result was a brief moment of angry glory, then a few
blood-spots on the track.

Late in the evening we arrived at our goal, the city
of Cuzco. Our first impressions were not very favorable. In a pouring rain we were jumbled from the station into the city by a rickety tram-car pulled by two
tiny discouraged mules, who were most of the time up
to their knees in mud. Once in the city we discovered
that Cuzco has the distinction of having the worst hostel-
ries in the world.

But in spite of the filth and the vile hotels, Cuzco
was well worth seeing. As the oldest city in South
America, a great metropolis long before Columbus
sailed for America, Cuzco had all the peculiar charm
which goes with age. As the ancient capital of the Inca
Empire, the whole city seemed haunted by shadows
telling of the vanished glories of the distant past.

But during the many days I spent in Cuzco, it was
not merely the far-distant past which claimed my attention. Carnival days arrived while we were still in the city,

and these brought me swiftly and forcibly back again to the present. Carnival is a most important institution all over South America. While it lasts, every one deliberately, and with malice aforethought, goes insane, and there is a wild competition to see who can paint the town reddest. Every one saves up all the rest of the year so that he can squander freely during these two or three days in the early part of February.

I first learned of the existence of carnival as I was leaning down examining an old Inca wall. A large bucket of water emptied with deadly aim over my back told me that the festivities had officially begun. My wavy whiskers and somnambulistic appearance (an appearance assumed whenever I pretend to be an archæologist) were thereafter the frequent and special objects of attack.

Everybody was privileged to throw things at everybody else, and in a few minutes the street was knee-deep in confetti and paper snakes. The chief weapon, however, was water—water, for the most part, perfumed and colored. The odor of the water compared with that of a first-rate skunk, and its color would have made a rainbow fade into insignificance. In addition to the wholesale bucketfuls—deadly only at short range —egg-shells were filled with the precious liquid and then thrown with remarkable aim. After a charming young lady from an upper window had thrice hit the bull's-eye, with my nose for a target, I decided that the old jokes about the throwing of girls were badly in need of revision.

During carnival time the creoles, the Spanish-American women and girls, emerge from their semi-Oriental retirement, and from their first-story balconies exchange water-eggs and compliments in as "fresh" a fashion as the most flippant of English or American flappers. I and my two companions started a battle royal and a violent flirtation with three damsels in the house opposite the hostelry in which we lived. The special object of my passion was the young lady with the deadly aim, under whose fire my face had suffered so badly. In such conditions what heart could remain cold, what pulse would not beat more rapidly? When, after considerable secret practice, I managed to throw an egg into her classic features, I felt my passion was sure to be returned.

No doubt the proper thing to do was to take a guitar and sing under her window; but as I had no guitar, and as my friends tell me I am unable to sing (though on this point I always think they are wrong), I could only buy a huge bouquet of flowers and send it up to the fair enchantress. The next day, as I passed by the house, there was dropped down, not a bucket of water, but one of my roses, around the stem of which I discovered a note giving all three of us a rendezvous.

That afternoon we therefore secretly climbed up the back staircase of the House of Romance and were entertained with tea and conversation by the three young ladies. Once I put my foot in it by addressing my flame as Queen of the Incas. She flared up and said that she was no Indian, so that I had to hasten to assure her that a Queen of the Incas was not obliged herself to be an Inca. Just as we were getting this important matter settled, a maid burst in saying that Father was coming home, and we had to flee for our lives down the back staircase. So began and ended my solitary Peruvian romance.

But we were not through with the carnival yet. That same night, the culminating night of the festivities, my little party was forcibly incorporated in a large banquet held at our hotel by the leading lights of Cuzco's male society. The banquet became more and more liquid as time went on, and though I managed to escape the worst consequences by pouring the greater part of the ever-renewed contents of my glass under the table, I could not avoid having my right-hand neighbor, an eminent professor in Cuzco University, blubber in a heartbroken way upon my shoulder, nor having my left-hand neighbor, Cuzco's leading barrister, kiss me upon both cheeks, swearing eternal brotherly friendship.

My two companions were occupied with a young officer on the other side of the table, until he reached a stage where he could neither walk nor talk. Seeing his helpless condition, they then undertook to carry him back to his barracks. But when they arrived with him at the gateway, the sentries refused to let him in without the password, and he, poor man, had no more idea than the man in the moon of the proper word.

My two companions could only prop their charge up against the wall of the barracks and leave him there, hoping that in course of time either the hearts of the sentries would be softened or the fresh air would bring the password back to the young officer's benumbed intellect.

After Cuzco had quieted down from the carnival, I got to know many of its leading citizens. They were a very kindly lot, though thoroughly immersed in the spirit of feudalism. The people who counted were the priests and a small number of Spanish families with extensive estates in the surrounding country. Indians did all the work, so that the gentry had plenty of time to devote to chivalrous and courteous methods of killing time.

The prefect (or governor) of the province of Cuzco

was kind enough to provide me with horses so that I could visit the extremely interesting ruins about Cuzco, many of which are very little known. He also provided me with a constabulary officer as an escort, to see that my dignity was maintained, and no doubt also to see that I did not find and run away with the hidden treasures of the Incas.

This escort, in addition to protecting my life against all imaginable (and imaginary) dangers, was able to interpret for me in the long conversations I had with the natives. Strangely enough, even after four centuries of conquest and forcible conversion, the descendants of the Incas have never learned to speak the language of their masters. I found that even in the city of Cuzco itself the Indians could not speak ten consecutive words of Spanish, and that a mile or two out in the country they could not understand a single word.

In addition to the ordinary run of peasants, I met three natives who were of extraordinary interest. All three of them were, or at least were considered to be, descendants of the ancient imperial family, and as such were treated with extreme reverence by their fellow-countrymen. Two of them, though they remained entirely Indian in their habits and ideas, had thrown in their lot with the government of the whites and stood high in official favor. They were in fact go-betweens between the Indians of the surrounding country and the government. When an Indian had a grievance or a complaint to make, he would lay it before these two tribunes, who would in turn take the matter up with the prefect. It was rather extraordinary that both men were content to remain completely Indian in their dress and mode of life. They even took the trouble to learn the Spanish language.

The third descendant of the Incas was very much out of official favor. A native Don Quixote de la Mancha, he still dreamed of a revival of the ancient glories of the Inca Empire, when the white usurper would be cast out from his native land. Already he had been imprisoned three times for attempts to raise an insurrection. In this connection one must not forget that as late as 1786 another such leader, Tupak Amaru, managed to raise a very formidable rebellion, which for a time promised to be successful, and which the Spaniards were years in crushing.

The poor despised native of the Highlands, though broken and dispirited, still dreams of the splendor of the past and hopes for its revival in the future.

My interviews with the "rebel" had to be few and secret, but the other two imperial descendants attached themselves to my little party, and showed us, not only much of the inner life of Cuzco, but much of the Indian life led by the Quechuas all over the surrounding country.

CHAPTER XXXII

THE PAGEANT OF HISTORY TOLD IN STONE

GUIDED by our Inca friends, we made a careful study of Cuzco's many historical remains. In this ancient city every stone had a story to tell, and told it most fascinatingly. Rich churches and monasteries, old houses with the coats of arms of the grandee families of Spain carved on their gateways, told of the colonial days, when the Spaniards had succeeded to the glories of the Incas. But the stones of these colonial buildings once formed part of far older buildings erected by the Incas at the dawn of history. Most, if not all, of the Inca palaces were of one story, but with walls so well and strongly built that the Spaniards continued to use the existing walls for the lower part of their own structures. They merely erected second stories upon these foundations.

Thus at Cuzco are seen buildings hundreds of years old, superimposed upon walls many, many centuries older. But everywhere one is struck by the fact that the Incas were far better builders than their conquerors. The Spaniards never learned the secret of Inca stone-polishing and stone-fitting. In the case of the Spaniards their stones were cemented together with mortar; their walls are crumbling and falling to pieces: while the older walls, which are fitted together without mortar of any kind, are as even and strong to-day as on the day on which they were completed.

I had heard the story of the impermeability of the Inca walls, but I was astounded to find how true it was. In spite of earthquakes and centuries of decay, I was unable to slip a safety-razor blade between the stones of the Inca walls, so neatly and closely were they placed one upon another. There was an air of magic about it. Occasionally we could see where the Spaniards in search for treasure had torn down a portion of the old wall, and later *with the same stone* had carefully tried to rebuild the wall, but it had been a miserable failure; only by the use of copious mortar and plaster were the stones made to hold together at all.

Cuzco has indeed fallen from its ancient high estate. No longer is it the capital of a vast empire, far vaster than the limits of present-day Peru. To-day it numbers only some thirty thousand souls, whereas the ancient city had more than ten times that number. Most of its ancient palaces and temples have been destroyed by the Spaniards, but the main outlines of the city as it was in the days of the Incas can still be traced.

On a high hill to the north of the city lie the remnants of the giant citadel and fortress of Saksawaiman, which dominated the city and guarded it against attack. Three huge towers, the military residence of the Incas and their soldiers, were destroyed to provide building-stones for the Spaniards, but the enormous stones of the triple ramparts still remain—stones far larger than a man's height and weighing many tons. How were they brought there, and so accurately, so delicately, put into place?

Near the fortress are several strange caverns reaching far into the earth. Here altars to the Gods of the Deep were carved out of the living rock, and the many bones scattered about tell of the sacrifices which were offered up. The end of one of these caverns, Chincana, has never been found. It is supposed to communicate by a long underground passage with the Temple of the Sun, in the heart of Cuzco. In this cavern is supposed to be hidden a large part of the golden treasure of the Inca emperors, which was stored away lest it fall into the hands of the Spaniards. But the cavern is so huge and so complicated, and so manifold are its passages, that its secret has never been uncovered.

One man indeed is said to have found his way underground to the Sun Temple and, when he emerged, to have had two golden bars in his hand. But his mind had been affected by days of blind wandering in the subterranean caves, and he died almost immediately afterward. Since that time many have gone into the cavern—never to return again. Only a month or two before my arrival the disappearance of three prominent people in this Inca cave caused the prefect of the province of Cuzco to wall in the mouth of the cavern, so that the secret and the treasures of the Incas seem likely to remain undiscovered for the present.

The fortifications must have extended far down the side of the hill and well into the city of Cuzco itself. Half-way down the hill we noticed some curious terraced walls, ornamented with the usual Inca niches. In one of the garden terraces were the ruins of a palace popularly supposed to be that of Manko Kapak, the first of the Incas. From this spot the founder of the Inca dynasty could survey the whole of the imperial city.

At the foot of the hill was the great plaza or public square, faced by the imposing cathedral and the beautiful church of the Company of Jesus, one of the architectual glories of South America. But this great square, in the middle of which the last of the Incas was put to death under the gloating eyes of the Marquis of Toledo, the viceroy of Spain, must in the still older days have been even more impressive. At one time it seems to have been a lake, but the lake was filled in by one of the Inca rulers, with earth brought from all parts of the empire to typify the universality of the Inca régime. The newly filled-in ground was then the central square where the chief important public ceremonies, both temporal and spiritual, were held.

Around this central square were erected the palaces of all the later emperors. Listening to the many stories told by the natives of the old imperial city, I learned that it was the custom of each emperor to erect a palace and a household of his own. Each emperor formed a clan (*ayllu*), which persisted even after his death. These imperial clans have indeed persisted even down to the present time. Each divine ruler after his death was carefully embalmed, and in his mummified state he continued to rule over his own clan, even though the empire fell to the lot of his living successors.

Important questions of the clan, and even of the state, were solemnly propounded to the embalmed dead, even though the answers came through the mouths of the priestly servants of the discarnate rulers. On important occasions the mummies took part in the public processions, and not infrequently the dead king paid visits and shared banquets with one another, though the skeptics may believe that the accompanying retainers enjoyed the dinners more than their ghostly rulers.

Attached to each of the palaces was a huge compound, of the size of a block or city square, with an encircling wall, containing numerous smaller buildings. This outer wall was of one story, with the usual slant reminding one of Egypt, and surmounted by a heavy roof of thatch. The wall itself was entirely without windows and had only one huge entrance door. Some of these palaces themselves have entirely disappeared, but at least the wonderful encircling walls have been preserved.

At the time of the conquest the palaces were divided up among the high officers of the Spanish army. On the north side of the square can still be seen the walls of the palace allotted to the great conquistador Pizarro himself. Next to it was that of his brother in arms, Almagro, who was later his bitterest rival and the cause of the first civil war.

On the south side of the square there are the walls of two other palaces. One of these belonged to Wainya Kapak, the last of the really great Inca rulers, who completed the conquest of Ecuador not long before the arrival of the Spaniards. The other was the Palace of the Chosen Ones, the huge convent in which were housed the "Vestal Virgins" of the old Inca régime. The long narrow street between the two walls is exactly as it was in the days of the ancient empire. It was along this lane that the great imperial processions took place from the central square to the Temple of the Sun, which lay further to the south. Along this street came the thousands of adoring devotees following the footsteps of their divine ruler, who went to offer up sacrifice to his father the Sun-God.

Curiously, and rather appropriately enough, the ancient Palace of the Chosen Ones is now a convent of Catholic nuns, the natural successors of the Vestal Virgins of old. Entrance to this nunnery is as impossible now as was entrance to the Palace of the Chosen Ones in former times. Under the strict rules of the order, no outsider, and above all no man, may under any condition enter the convent grounds. The restriction is rather unfortunate, because the interior of the old palace is said to be better preserved than any other building in Cuzco, and well worth careful study.

The old Inticancha, the Palace of Gold, the farfamed temple of the Sun-God, the supreme divinity of the Incas, is now a Dominican monastery. Most of the Sun Temple itself was destroyed in order to build upon it the monastery church, though a rounded outer wall gave us some idea of the perfection of the stonework which was lavished upon this, the most holy place in the Inca Empire—a place so sacred that no living man was allowed to enter it except the high priest of the empire and the emperor himself. A huge disk of gold was placed to catch and reflect the rays of the rising sun, and another, smaller, to reflect the rays of the setting sun.

Into this holy of holies the Spaniards on their arrival roughly pushed their way, and through the long hours of the night they threw their dice on the temple floor to see who should have possession of one of the burnished disks of gold—the other had been secreted by the Inca priests. It is said that one of the common soldiers won it, and lost it again, during the long hours of play.

To the west of the Sun Temple was the famous Garden of Gold, a curious prototype of a national museum of natural history. Here the principal plants and animals of the empire were to be found, modeled in gold. Needless to say, since the Spaniards took possession one looks for these models in vain.

But the magnificent walls of the subsidiary "chapels" of the old temple are well preserved, being incorporated in the cloisters of the monastery. On one side are the temples of the Moon and of the Stars; on the other the temples of the Rainbow and of Thunder and Lightning. The walls of each of these temples are lined with niches, and there is a curious black band that runs, high up, around the walls. The space above this line was no doubt especially dedicated to the gods, to which not even a priest might ascend, but to which, by raising the hands, sacrifices could be offered up to the ghostly divinities.

In one of the stones of the Temple of the Stars we noticed a small hole, through which could be felt and seen a bone, apparently from a human skeleton. How it was worked into the stone, and what its exact purpose there, is a mystery, but it seems likely that the Incas must have shared a primordial belief that no building could be well built unless it rested upon a blood-sacrifice. The whole idea of sacrifice, so prevalent in nearly all religions, played a very important part in the Inca creed.

We were reminded of this fact by a little chapel, between the temples of the Rainbow and of Lightning, which seems to have been especially dedicated to preparing various blood-sacrifices. Special ruts were cut in the stones of the chapel, so that the blood of the offerings could run out into the street at the side, and the people might see that the gods were being duly appeased. In spite of the protests of some of the chroniclers, we now know fairly definitely that on important occasions human beings were offered up, and that even in the course of ordinary festivals, hundreds, and in some cases thousands, of llamas were sacrificially slaughtered.

Religion was a vital thing in those early days. In the earliest period of the empire the posts of emperor and of high priest seem to have been identical; and even in later times, when the offices had been separated, the high priest was usually the brother of the temporal ruler, and himself possessed of enormous powers. The priests formed a close and highly important class, and a third portion of all the estates of the land were allotted to the service of the "church."

As we dreamily walked through the long lanes of Cuzco and gazed upon the remains of ancient days, it was easy enough for us to picture to ourselves the glories of the mighty empire that was destroyed at one blow by the hand of Pizarro. That empire appears to have been a thing of magic. According to most of the chroniclers, the empire was founded in 1140. Arising suddenly, it was destroyed in 1532, but in the four hundred years of its existence it was continually extended until it eventually embraced millions of square miles, reaching to the north as far as Colombia, and to the south far down into Chile. It has left hundreds of monuments to testify to its architectural achievements. Its highways stretched to all parts of the realm. In its capital were amassed innumerable trophies, which spoke of the might of its armies, the wealth of its people, and the artistry of its craftsmen.

The arts and crafts of the Incas seem to have spread, with the Inca arms, to many vast stretches of territory where previously only barbarism had reigned. The working of stone was brought to a state of perfection probably never surpassed either before or since. In addition to the working of gold and silver, copper and bronze were very extensively used—to such an extent that the ignorance of the use of iron was very little felt.

Communications were so good that with no horses, and of course no mechanical means of transport, messengers crossed the empire in a few days. They were able to reach Quito in eight days, a journey which to-day, with all modern facilities, is supposed to take more than a month. By railway it takes three days to go from the coast to the capital; the Inca messengers by series of relays made the journey in two, and daily brought fish from the sea to supply the emperor's table.

A Spanish chronicler, Montesinos, one of the greatest liars of history, asserts that in prehistoric days the Peruvians had some mode of writing, which was later forgotten. I am firmly convinced that this statement was only one of the many other misstatements of fact on the part of Montesinos, but what was certainly an Inca invention, the *kyipu,* was a very creditable attempt to supply the lack of a written language. The *kyipus* consisted of series of cords, of different colors and lengths, which were knotted in a number of different conventional ways. The invention was probably at first merely a tally to count the number of llamas in a herd, or of men in an army, but it was later developed so that long reports of battles and campaigns could be made by means of it, and a class of scribes or learned men, *amautas,* grew up, who were initiated into the mysteries of tying up and deciphering the curious cords.

It was in their customs and their laws that the Incas showed their greatest originality. One of the eccentricities of the Inca régime was the fact that each emperor was supposed to marry his oldest sister, who was the supreme lady of the land. His unofficial wives, selected from the Virgins of the Sun, were numberless, but the heir was supposed to be the son of the sister spouse. This custom, so at variance with the usual Indian ten-

dency toward exogamy, was prohibited to every one
else in the realm, and it is probable that it was an inno-
vation of the later years, introduced to raise the dignity
of the imperial line. No other family was divine enough
to provide a spouse worthy of the emperor. Curiously
enough, no physical degeneration seems to have resulted
from this intermixture, but it is probable that the popular conception of racial degeneration by reason of intermarriage is largely exaggerated.

The most interesting feature of the ancient régime
was the combination of rigid despotism with an equally
rigid communism. Backed by the prestige of supposed
divine origin, and by an elaborate religious system,
doubly enforced by an army of three hundred thousand
men, the Inca rulers were the absolute masters of the
land and of the people. The government controlled
every activity of the population. Elaborate censuses
were kept of all human beings, and of whatever property they were allowed to possess.

A government controller was in authority over
every ten families. Every hundred families were governed by a *kurakuna*. A *kuraka* ruled over three or four
thousand families. A province with forty thousand
families or so was commanded by a viceroy in direct
touch with the central government. The authority of
these officials was absolute, and there was no promotion
from one rank to another. Nearly all the offices were,
in ordinary circumstances, hereditary. An Inca subject,
high or low, was supposed to stay in the class in which
he was born and do the work of that class. A commoner
was not to aspire to a higher position; he was, moreover, not to be educated in the higher arts, lest he become ashamed of his parents and be dissatisfied with
his lot.

But upon this autocratic basis the state was as communistic as the most fanatical Moscow emissary could desire. Every inch of the land, all the flocks, all the mines, were the property of the state, and were periodically doled and redoled out to individual families, in accordance with the number of working hands which each family contained. No land could be bought or sold, but each youth on arriving at manhood was certain of securing a plot of land which he could cultivate.

Moreover the land was divided into three sections, one dedicated to the sun-god, from which of course the priests received the income; one to the emperor, from the revenues of which were fed the state officials and the army; and the third to the community. Each man received a plot of land from the third division, and, in lieu of paying rent, was forced to spend a certain time each week in cultivating the land of the sun-god and the emperor. Huge storehouses were erected to receive the crops of the sun-god and those of the imperial lands. Provisions to last for years were stored there, and in case of famine or drought these public coffers were opened and the population fed from them.

True to good trade-union principles, no man was allowed to work more or better than his fellows, lest he gain more than the others. Each man's life was divided into a number of periods reaching from infancy to old age. To each period a particular kind of work was allotted. On reaching the age of sixty the peasant was allowed to retire from active labor and was fed thereafter from the public coffers.

But the state, once it begins interfering, seemingly knows no limits. If by a certain age the peasants had not already chosen their life-mates, they were forcibly married off by the higher officials. State regulations decided exactly what was to be worn and what was not to be worn; the exact method of cutting and wearing the hair was laid down; also exactly what ornaments could be used. Commerce of every sort was prohibited. Each community was supposed to be self-supporting. The hereditary gilds of craftsmen provided their beautiful artistic products chiefly for the use of the imperial court.

Compulsory and very elaborate systems of irrigation were enforced. The guano birds were strictly protected, and the guano droppings carefully used as manure. From the state mines were extracted gold, silver, and copper, the use of which was limited to the imperial service. The origin of the enormous stores of Inca gold is still a mystery. Peru is rich in silver and copper, but during the centuries of Spanish rule very few gold-mines have been discovered, and the source of the Inca gold is as unknown as is that of the mines of King Solomon.

The Inca régime is usually represented as a benevolent despotism. Of the despotism there can be no doubt, but the benevolence became more obvious the higher up in the social scale one stood. The use of gold, of silver, and of the fine vicuña wool was limited to the court and the highest nobility. The pleasures of polygamy were likewise limited to the highest classes—if polygamy can be called a pleasure—the average man no doubt found it difficult enough to rule one wife. Ease and luxury could be acquired only by birth.

Pizarro and his adventurous conquistadores are generally pictured as bloodthirsty ruffians who destroyed an idyllic reproduction of paradise, and are blamed for compelling, by brute force, a sweet, peaceable people to adopt a new religion, a new language, and new customs, and for compelling them to slave for their new rulers. This picture is true, but it must not be forgotten that the Incas had done exactly these same things. The Quechua language and the official sun-worship were forced upon the peoples of the conquered provinces, many of them with highly developed languages and religious organizations of their own. Two thirds of the conquered land was devoted to the central Inca organization, and the peasants of the newly incorporated territories were forced to work the land for the benefit of their Inca masters.

No, the Incas were not very much better than the Spaniards, and could scarcely with justice complain of the treatment they received. They were only wiser than their conquerors. Where the Spaniards wasted and destroyed, the Incas conserved and built up, and because of their magnificent organizing ability they are assured of immortality in the history of human culture.

But in spite of the architectural monuments which they have left us here in Cuzco, in spite of the *kyipus* and of the records of early Spanish chroniclers, there is much concerning the Inca Empire which is still shrouded in mystery. Strangely enough, it is only within the last few years, since the various chronicles have been critically examined, that we fully realize how little we really do know about the origin and development of the Incas, or even of the building up of the city of Cuzco.

The vast majority of the Spanish conquerors who came to Peru paid little attention to the culture and history of the land that had fallen into their possession. A few of the more enlightened wrote down what they themselves saw, and incorporated in their accounts the legends and traditions of the natives as to the events of the long distant past. These chronicles are of very unequal value. Some were written by dashing young soldiers who switched from pen to sword and from sword to pen. A few were written by prosy, wordy government officials. These wrote official reports for their superiors in the same dead style in which official records are written by any bureaucracy. A large number were composed by priests.

By far the most readable of the chronicles was written by a gentleman who styled himself Garcilasso Inca de la Vega. His father was one of the Spanish conquistadores, but his mother was a daughter of one of the last of the Inca emperors, and the chronicler was born, and spent his boyhood days, in Cuzco, the capital of the old empire.

Because of the charm of his style, the romance of his ancestry, and his native background, the "Comentarios Reales" of Garcilasso remained for centuries the chief authority on early Peruvian culture and history. It was one of the principal sources from which Prescott drew for his epoch-making "History of the Conquest of Peru," but in the last few years it has been realized that Garcilasso gives us a very one-sided, and in many cases very inaccurate, account of the cultural development of his native land.

Some of the other chroniclers were as accurate as Garcilasso, but unfortunately no two of the chronicles can be made to agree.

Montesinos, the Münchhausen of Peru, states that Manko Kapak had ninety-nine successors, giving the Inca Empire a long and varied history, dating from long before the Christian era. All the other chroniclers give Manko only thirteen or fourteen successors, and would allow the Inca Empire, at the earliest, the eleventh century as a starting-point. But the discrepancies

do not end here. *All* the chroniclers flatly contradict one
another on every important detail. Events ascribed to
one monarch by Garcilasso are reported of quite another emperor by Cieza. Garcilasso, with his rosy-hued
spectacles, makes the succession of the Inca sovereigns
regular, orderly, and uneventful; Sarmiento records a
whole series of court intrigues, revolutions, and usurpa-
tions. With the chronicles, you pay your money, and you
take your choice.

minor variations, there are three absolutely different styles of building and of stone-craftsmanship. In one, which is typically Inca, the stones are perfectly smoothed down and polished, in the shape of more or less perfect cubes, each of approximately the same size and shape, as are bricks, so that when the stones were put together the "seams" form long parallel lines. The Sun Temple and the ruins of the palaces around the central square all belong to this style.

There is, secondly, a type of building, found isolated in various parts of the city, where the stones are left rough and irregular, their joining forming no regular seams, the surface unpolished, and only the sides worked down so that the various stones will fit into each other. Unlike the Inca buildings, where no mortar was used, I found by careful examination that in several of the buildings of this type a thin layer of mud had been placed between the stones, so that they might better fit together. Isolated walls of this sort exist to the east and west of Cuzco, and are evidently of great antiquity. None of these can be explained by reference to the chronicles, several of which attempt to give a geographical survey of the ancient city. Of very similar construction are the terraced walls of Kolkampata, which is popularly supposed to have surrounded the Palace of Manko Kapak, the first of the Incas.

The third style is even more distinctive. Here the stones are of enormous dimensions, many times the size of a man, placed together absolutely unsymmetrically though with consummate artistry. The interior sides of the enormous blocks are wonderfully polished and worked down, but the exterior surface is usually left in a semi-rough state. The best examples of this style are found in the northern triple ramparts of the fortress

Saksawaiman (which differ very considerably from the other extant parts of the old castle), and in a curious palace in the eastern part of Cuzco called Hatun-Rumiyok.

At first sight it would appear that the second style, with the small irregular stones, represents the earliest, most primitive type. Most primitive it may be, but there are many reasons for supposing that it was later in point of time than that of the huge massive stone blocks. In one case, in fact, one style is superimposed upon the other. A wall of Hatun-Rumiyok, perfect in every way, has its outer surface covered by a wall of the small rough stones; a fact which was only recently brought to light when, in the course of certain house repairs, part of the outer wall was torn down, revealing the masterpiece of the inner wall. Why in the world this beautiful and massive inner wall should have been covered up by the rougher stonework is still a complete and inexplicable mystery, but it shows that the rougher walls are of later construction.

In the light of the most recent discoveries in other parts of Peru, it seems almost certain that the megalithic or huge stone type even in Cuzco belongs to what may be called the pre-Inca period; one existing certainly long before the eleventh century of the Christian era, and certainly long before the establishment of the Inca Empire. The stones of Cuzco show that a period of high architectural craftsmanship represented by the pre-Inca remains was followed by a period when the ancient arts were forgotten, either because of foreign invasion or because of internal degeneration—who can say?

On the coast the change and decay and regrowth of culture can be rather accurately checked by a study of the graves of the different periods of the cultures con-

cerned. In the Highlands this procedure is more difficult, because of the scarcity of graves. Here the bodies
were hidden in natural or artificial caves, and most of
these have been ransacked and destroyed by treasure-
hunters. The seekers after the hidden gold of the Incas
have done much to destroy all traces of the really old,
which might serve as a clue toward solving the problems
of ancient history.

In the short time at my disposal in Cuzco (my leave
had long expired, and I should have returned home
before), it was impossible to do any extensive excavation there. To do this would require an expedition entirely devoted to the purpose, but in pottering about
with a pick, haphazardly, on the ground of the ancient
fortress, I was delighted to come across an old kitchen-
midden, or rubbish-heap, about three or four feet below
the surface. This showed that the rounded top of the
fortress hill had in former times been inhabited, and was
not merely a place where soldiers were occasionally
posted. Among the various bits of broken pottery which
I uncovered, it was obvious that those which were
furthest down differed very considerably in color and
design from what is usually known as Inca pottery.
From the small scattered fragments found it was impossible to trace its exact relation to other styles, but
a casual glance sufficed to show its divergence from
the style in vogue at the period of the empire.

I am strongly of the opinion that systematic excavation on the ground of the old fortress would bring to
light an enormous amount of new material, and am
only surprised that this work has not yet been attempted. But to possible future excavators I would add,
in the language of "Treasure Island," "Look out for
squalls." The native Peruvians regard every archæolo-

gist as a treasure-seeker and put every obstacle in his
way; therefore unless he is armed with every sort
of letter from the highest powers that be, he will very
likely have occasion to continue his archæological reflec-
tions inside a lousy jail.

On account of the discovery of pre-Inca remains in
various parts of Peru, various attempts have been made
in the last few years to refurbish that old "drawer of
the longbow," Montesinos—he being the chronicler
who attempts to explain the gradual development of the
various styles. According to him, Manko Kapak had
ninety-nine successors. He would place Manko Kapak
before the Christian era. In the time of the early rulers
of this dynasty the Inca Empire with its capital at Cuzco
was already as great as it was ever destined to become,
but a great invasion or rebellion destroyed the empire as
such, and for several centuries the Inca emperors ruled
over only a tiny territory, whose capital was no longer
Cuzco but Tamputokko. It was only in the eleventh century that Suchi Rokka reëstablished the seat of government in Cuzco and set about rebuilding the Inca Empire.

A very interesting hypothesis, and one which would
be worthy of consideration if it did not rest solely upon
Montesinos's mendacious word. His record is full of
obvious falsehoods, self-contradictions, and impossibili-
ties. Archæological discoveries in other parts also show
not the slightest evidence that in the old pre-Inca days
Cuzco exercised any influence over the other parts of
the country; in fact, there is much evidence exactly to
the contrary.

We must therefore conclude that in the great pre-
Inca days conditions prevailed in the Highlands similar
to those on the coast of Peru. The coast we have reason

to believe was broken up into a number of different small, but highly evolved, city kingdoms. These were of comparatively small political extent, but created a wide sphere of cultural influence. We must suppose that the Highland was equally broken up into a number of small confederations, principalities, and kingdoms, the names of which have in many cases come down to us. Conditions must have been somewhat similar to those in ancient Greece, with its numerous city states; all the more similar because, in spite of their political differences, the various principalities belonged to a vague general cultural unity, speaking for the most part different dialects of a common language, and having a number of common religious beliefs.

In this early period, there was a strange mastery of the art of working huge stones. Not far away from Cuzco is the extraordinarily interesting fortress of Ollantatampo, whose walls are built of stones even larger than those of the buildings of Cuzco, and which likewise belong to the pre-Inca period. These, however, have certain marked peculiarities of their own. In various other parts of the Highlands similar monuments exist, so that this early period is usually called the megalithic period. Following this early period there seems to have been everywhere a stage of decay, an epoch marked by the use of the small rough stones that I have referred to as belonging to the second class.

Somewhere toward the close of this period there must have taken place the foundation of what was later to become the Inca Empire. We have already heard the legend of Manko Kapak and his spouse coming from Lake Titicaca; we are also in possession of a more elaborate legend, whereby, out of certain caves, there appeared two tribes, and later out of another cave four brothers, each with a spouse, who were to be divine rulers of the tribes. These tribes slowly moved northward seeking for an ideal spot to found their kingdom. In the course of their wandering, three of the brothers were got rid of, and in the end only the youngest brother Ayar Manko, later Manko Kapak, was left. He eventually settled with his people in the fertile valley of Cuzco, gradually amalgamating with the inhabitants who were already living there.

This legend is very interesting from many points of view. In the first place, all the legends speak of the migration from the south, and yet we have overwhelming evidence to suppose that the Indian people, as a whole, came from the *north,* entering South America over the isthmus of Panama. It is quite likely, however, that the particular tribes that founded the Inca Empire came from the south, from the high, desolate table-land of Lake Titicaca, attracted by the fertility of the Cuzco valley. The legend of the four brothers is usually explained as representing the four leaders of four different tribes which were gradually amalgamated into one.

Another point of importance is that all the legends agree that Cuzco was already inhabited at the time of the Inca invasion, although the Incas seem to have met with little resistance. It has sometimes been suggested that the Inca conquerors were of another race than the ordinary Peruvian. From the few skulls we have in our possession, it would seem that the skulls of the ruling class indicate a higher intellectual capacity and that the facial angle was somewhat different from that of the modern Peruvian native, but there seems no doubt that the Inca conquerors belonged to the general South American Indian race.

More important still, it has recently been shown that the official language of the Inca Empire, usually called Quechua, and which was at one time thought to have been artificially imposed upon all the other tribes, was in reality only one of the many different dialects of a common language spoken over a large portion of the Highlands. Although in the outlying parts of the empire different languages were spoken (Aymara in the South, and Quito in the North), to a very large extent the famous law in the empire, forcing the Quechua language upon its subjects, was merely equivalent to stating that one dialect was to be considered the standard form of the language.

The fact that the Inca invaders were able to amalgamate so easily with the primitive inhabitants certainly suggests a unity of general race and language.

In the early days, the new government formed in Cuzco seems to have been content to maintain a loose system of alliance with the surrounding tribes, a system which gradually developed into a definite confederation similar to the other confederations and principalities into which Peru was divided. These principalities were frequently at war with one another, but it was due to the genius of the Inca military organization that the Cuzco confederation was able to inflict such signal defeats upon its rivals that they could be incorporated into the rapid expanding Inca dominion.

In the early days, however, there was no elaborate imperial organization (contrary to what Garcilasso and the chroniclers would have us believe). The chiefs of the conquered territory continued to rule over their tribes, as *kurakas*. They were merely vassals of the mighty Cuzco war-lords, and were forced to recognize the suzerainty of a higher power. This arrangement continued in great part down to the very latest days of the empire.

What is of importance in this connection is that the Incas were able to build up their mighty and wonderfully organized empire in such a short time, largely because the foundation for such an empire was already there. Contrary to what Garcilasso tells us, the Incas did not force an absolutely barbarous people to adopt clothing, or to adopt a new language, a new religion, a strange new social organization. Their rôle—an extremely important one—was to impose the unification and standardization of various customs and organizations already in existence.

It was only in their expeditions into the Amazonian jungles that the Incas met with absolute savages. It was only there that they were forced to fight one petty tribe after another. And it is to be noted that it was only in the jungle that the Incas were eminently unsuccessful. Even the most powerful of the Inca emperors could never civilize or really subjugate the denizens of the forest.

In the Highlands things were entirely different. When the Incas had defeated the chiefs and the army of a neighboring confederation, a large territory, with a great number of highly organized and civilized communities, possessed of an organization and civilization similar to their own, fell into their hands. It was therefore no impossible task to make the newly conquered country an integral part of the Inca Empire.

Two features in the ancient social fabric call for especial consideration. One is religion; the other the curious socialistic basis of economic life. We have good reason for supposing that the elaborate sun, moon, and star worship of the Inca Empire was a later development. It was not only alien to the other, non-Inca, tribes

of Peru, but was foreign even to the earliest period of
the Inca régime.

The earliest Incas seem to have shared the religious
views common to nearly all the peoples of the early Peruvian culture. Apart from many features reminiscent
of animism and ancestor worship, there were certain primeval Peruvian deities concerning whose nature and origin very little is known. The names of three
of these deities have come down to us. They are Illak,
Pachakamak, and Wirakocha. The three were frequently identified or confused with one another, and in
the later period all were vague, dark, creator deities, the
source of all life and activity.

Wirakocha seems to have been the particular god of
the early Incas and of their Highland neighbors. At one
period the Wirakocha cult seems to have developed into
a very high form of monotheistic belief. But Wirakocha
worship was too abstract and too indefinite for the mass
of the people. Each tribe, and each clan, had in addition
its own particular object of worship. The particular object of worship of the Inca clan was the sun, which in
the early days was regarded far more as a tribal emblem
than as the supreme deity. But gradually as the Inca
clan increased in power and prestige, their tribal emblem
became more important, and it soon began to press the
older Wirakocha worship into the background. Even
inside the Inca Empire we find traces of a conflict between the devotees of old primeval Wirakocha worship
and the official hierachy devoted to the worship of the
sun, which later expanded into the added worship of the
moon, stars, and other celestial bodies.

The common origin of the Inca and non-Inca religious concepts helped in the unification of the Inca
régime. Through Wirakocha and the earlier beliefs

there was a point of contact. The new worship of the celestial bodies struck in most cases a responsive cord, and in any case only added a few new deities to those already existing. For the Incas were wily enough politicians (like the ancient Romans) not to destroy the images or temples of the principalities they conquered. The worship of the old gods was allowed to continue. In many cases the tribal gods were brought as a "special honor" to Cuzco, to form a part in the National Pantheon, and in return the subjected tribes were expected to pay tribute to the supreme symbol of the Incas.

Even in the last days of the empire, in addition to the worship of the sun-god with his many priests, there were remnants of the worship of the older deities, as well as oracles and witch-doctors, who represented a survival of the oldest common beliefs of the Andean peoples.

To the ancient Peruvian almost anything was sacred —a river, tree, a misshapen stone, a prodigy of a potato. His credulity was elastic and comprehensive, and he found no difficulty in paying reverence to the new Inca emblem, provided he were also allowed to continue to worship the old one.

The socialism of the Incas is another point of great historical interest. During my stay in and around Cuzco, I made a point of visiting a number of the native communities in which the ancient customs have been preserved. The average historian has been too busy describing the socialism of the Inca Empire to notice the socialism the natives still possess; but a study of the organization, as it is, gives overwhelming evidence for supposing that the Incas were in no sense the originators of communism as is usually supposed. At the most, they modified the social and economic system as it had existed for hundreds and even thousands of years, so that it might better fit into the general imperial organization.

The famous communism of Peru was not *state* communism imposed on the people from above, but a family communism evolved by the people from below, which the Inca state adapted to its imperialistic purposes as best it could.

The earliest and most primitive division and grouping of the Peruvian natives, but one which has persisted to the present time, is the *ayllu,* the clan, or collection of families claiming a common lineage—the *ayllu* is the family itself in the biggest and broadest sense of the word. At the present day, as in the days of long ago, all property is owned not by the individual but by the *ayllu,* the family group. Each member of the *ayllu* has a claim to his fair share of the family property, or rather to the income from the family property; for the land can never be broken up or given finally and definitely to any individual. The chief of the *ayllu*—we might call him the patriarch of the clan—allots to each member of the group a certain portion of the land to cultivate, but this allotment is only a loan.

This economic system is by no means confined to Peru. Traces of family ownership of property are still found in Europe, and to an even greater extent in the Orient, indicating that at one time family communism must have been a more or less universal custom. Among many primitive peoples this primeval communism persists with almost unabated force. Our journey through the Amazon basin had shown us a striking instance of this. Each *maloka* had constituted an economic unit very similar to a Peruvian *ayllu,* and characterized by the same communal ownership of all the plantations.

Peruvian communism, instead of being a jump forward into the utopian future, represents a clinging to primitive conditions. A social organization through which probably all of our ancestors have passed has been made rigid in Peru, and has persisted with but slight modifications.

When these various *ayllus* were bound together into larger groups, into small states and confederations, as was evidently once the case, the chief or *kuraka* of the larger group did not disturb the internal organization of the individual *ayllus,* but simply insisted that each community as a whole pay him tribute. This tribute could only be in kind, and consequently certain lands were set aside which had to be cultivated, for the central authority, by the various members of the community.

Even in the earliest days the members of each community set aside, of their own free will, a further contribution as an offering to the local gods for sacrificial purposes. It is highly probable that the early confederations likewise demanded tribute from each of the communities to support the central temples.

The Incas therefore, far from originating the communistic system, found it already waiting for them. They had only to decree that each community pay tribute to the central government, instead of to the already existing petty chiefs, for the system to be more or less complete, though it seems likely that under their organizing genius the old spontaneous communism was placed on a mere definite and less elastic basis.

I was interested to find that after the downfall of the Inca Empire many of the minor improvements which the Incas had brought about in the primeval communism (such as organization of the families into tens and hundreds, in place of the old *ayllu*) disappeared, but the ancient communism as a system continued. The land was indeed divided up between various Spanish nobles and the churches, but, as we had seen on our visit to the hacienda shortly after coming to the Peruvian Highlands, the nominal change in the ownership of the land had brought about very little real change in the economic life of the peasants.

In reality the system whereby each Indian is granted a certain amount of land free of rent, provided that he cultivates his landlord's estate as well as his own property, is only a continuance of the economic policy of the ancient Inca. This fact became particularly evident to me when I discovered that it was the custom on many of the estates in the neighborhood of Cuzco for the landowner to make his agreements with the natives, not individually, but with a whole *ayllu,* represented by its chief or patriarch.

In such cases the land lent to the Indians was considered communal property and was doled out in equal amounts by the chief of each *ayllu* to the various members of his community.

CHAPTER XXXIV

THE CITY OF OUR LADY OF PEACE

DURING our stay in Cuzco I became so much interested in the problem of the pre-Inca civilization that I determined to make a journey southward into Bolivia, in order to examine some of the ruins there which are known to date from pre-Inca times.

On the day before our departure our two Inca guides came to bid us good-by, but during the preceding night they had made such good use of the money I had given them as a parting present that they were scarcely able to walk or to talk, and eventually we had to push them outside on to the street. The proud descendants of the Inca emperors had drowned the sorrows of their race and of destiny very effectually in drink.

After leaving Cuzco behind us, we retraced our steps as far as Juliaca, and from there continued on our way due south, across the broad open plain, until we came to the little town of Puno on the shores of the sacred lake of Titicaca. There we boarded a little steamer which was to take us in twelve hours to the other side of the lake and land us in Bolivia.

A journey across Lake Titicaca is something never

to be forgotten. The highest navigable body of water in the world, Titicaca lies more than twelve thousand feet above the sea, and through the hundred miles of its extent, there is scarcely a spot which is not of surpassing beauty. The scenery to the west is particularly magnificent. On this side there is a long series of mountain peaks, covered with perpetual snow, rendered all the more beautiful by being mirrored in the clear crystal water of the mountain lake.

Here and there during the course of our voyage the surface of the water was broken by charming little islands, islands even more sacred, if possible, to the native mind than was the lake itself. These were covered with some of the oldest and most interesting ruins in the country. Particularly famed were the islands of the Sun and of the Moon, where the Incas erected magnificent temples to their deities.

At many other points along the shores of the lake we saw even stranger remains, dating from pre-Inca times, and built, tradition says, by a people which has long since completely disappeared. There is good reason to suppose that the plains around Lake Titicaca were the cradle of the higher Andean culture.

When we eventually arrived in Guaqui (Waki) we had several hours to wait before our train started for La Paz, and I had a chance to see something of our new surroundings. Most striking was the change in Indian life. We had left the land of the Quechuas behind us, and were now in the land of the Aymaras, the second great racial group of the Highlands, whose distinct racial individuality neither the Incas of old nor the Spaniards of the present have been able to suppress.

The Aymaras constitute a racial puzzle. No one knows who or what they are or where they come from.

Even their true name is in doubt. Physically it is certain that like the Quechuas they belong to the same general South American Indian race, and to the same Andean branch of this race. There is a general similarity in the grammatical structure of the two languages, but when a comparison is made of words, about one third of the vocabulary is similar, and the other two thirds are utterly unlike. It is probable therefore that the two groups developed at different times and places, and that the common words are due to inter-borrowing. But scholars are still at variance as to whether the Aymaras borrowed from the Quechuas or the Quechuas from the Aymaras.

The Aymaras are a people without a history. It is known that they formed part of the Inca Empire, but it is very strange that they were the only people who managed to maintain their individuality out of all the other tribes which the Incas subjugated and standardized after the Cuzco pattern.

There are many reasons indeed for supposing that the Aymaras extended at one time all over Peru—were, in fact, at one period the dominant race. Many places all over the country, now inhabited solely by the Quechuas, have names purely Aymara in origin. The *chull-pa,* a round tower made of stone probably for burial purposes, and a typical feature of Aymara architecture, is found in many parts of the North where the Aymaras are not known to have penetrated.

The same social and economic life is found among the Quechuas and the Aymaras, the same communistic basis, the same division and grouping of the people into *ayllus,* or clans; the very word *ayllu,* though used by the Quechuas, seems to be of Aymara origin. Are we then to suppose that the Aymaras are the original inhabitants of the Andean Highlands, and the founders of its culture? Our ignorance, in spite of the myriad of chroniclers and their theories, is as yet too great to make it possible to suggest an answer.

Even to the layman there is an enormous difference between the Quechuas and the Aymaras. The Aymaras go in for more vivid and striking colors, and for color contrasts—certainly as far as the dress of the women is concerned. The Quechua women wear one skirt of dark colored stuff, usually of black or blue plaid. The Aymara women wear as many skirts as they can carry. There are usually from fifteen to twenty of these skirts, each of a different but uniform and startling color. The outermost layer is usually either yellow, green, purple, or scarlet; and the color of the shawl-like scarf each woman wears around her shoulders is chosen so as to present as glaring a contrast as possible. To cap it all, in place of the picturesque Quechua hats, the Aymaras, both men and women, wear a hat shaped like a European derby-hat, made either of hard native felt, or of fine straw (similar to a so-called Panama hat), but glazed so hard that a cannon-ball might be expected to rebound from it.

If the natives of Bolivia presented a problem to us, it seemed that they regarded *us* as something of a mystery. In Guaqui I noticed a placard announcing, in true Barnum & Bailey style, the "special appearance" of some professional humorist, and in large letters it was especially stated that the man was so comic that he would make even an Englishman smile. In this far out-of-the-way place, where an Englishman is still a rarity and a curiosity, it seems that a man humorous enough to make an Englishman smile must make a poor dreamy melancholic Bolivian native roar with laughter.

Eventually we sped on our way across the rolling

plain. Obviously there was a time when this plain was covered by Lake Titicaca. For three hours we journeyed southward, and then westward toward the majestic mountains, as if our train were determined to mount their peaks. We were supposed to be very near La Paz, but not a sign of life could be seen on the level plain before us. Suddenly without warning the plain gave way —a long cañon ravine had been eaten away by a mountain stream, and far below, at the bottom of the chasm, lay the capital city of Bolivia.

This first vision of La Paz is one of the most beautiful sights in the world. The sides of the ravine had been eaten away in all sorts of fantastic gargoylesque shapes. Beyond, on the other side of the ravine, the great Andean peaks reared up their snowy heads. A little apart from the others lay Illimani, the Queen of Mountains, shrouded in an eerie glory all her own.

The ravine was so steep that our locomotive had to be unhitched, and an electric engine with specially powerful brakes attached, before we could attempt the descent.

My first act in La Paz was to make an arrant fool of myself. Scarcely had I alighted from the train than an American stepped up to me and, after gazing dubiously at me for a moment, asked if I were McGovern. On my pleading guilty, he said that he would be pleased to aid me in any way. I wondered who and what he was —his name told me nothing—and why in the world he had come to meet me.

Thinking, however, that as an old resident he could give me a bit of advice on local matters, I told him that my chief worry was to get my various cameras through the customs (customs examination was held here in La Paz and not on the frontier), and asked him if it would not be advisable to give one of the customs officials some "cigars" in order to save time and trouble. To which he responded, "You had better not do that as long as I am around, for you see I am the director of customs."

Then I learned that the Americans through their Financial Commission had a large control over the national finance, including the customs service. As my cameras really were not dutiable, I soon had my baggage disposed of, but I could not help wishing that all customs people, however high up, would wear a badge whereby they could be recognized on all occasions.

So weak and petty is human nature, moreover, that as my august new-found friend decided to come to the hotel with me, to see that I was comfortably settled, I decided not to go to the cheap place I had originally planned upon, but wandered instead into the chief (and most expensive) hostelry in the city. This brought me vividly to the realization that La Paz competes very competently with Lima for the honor of being the most expensive city in the world.

But in spite of this and other drawbacks, La Paz, or more formally La Ciudad de Nuestra Señora de la Paz, the City of Our Lady of Peace, is well worth a visit. It is, above all things, a city of contradictions. The chief city of the Highlands, it lies thirteen thousand feet above sea-level, yet it is built in a narrow ravine. It is the headquarters of the Bolivian government, without in the legal sense being the capital. Officially Sucre, far to the southwest, is the capital, but as the residence of the president, the Senate, and the Lower House are all in La Paz, and permanently so, I was puzzled to find out in what sense La Paz is *not* the capital. I suggested, to a prominent Bolivian statesman, that it would be better to say that Sucre *had been* the capital but is so no longer; but he was immediately offended by my remark and insisted that Sucre is the capital because the government declared it to be so, although the government continues to have its seat in La Paz.

Finally, there is the enormous contrast between the present and the past. As in the case of Peru, with its capital, Lima, all of the wealth of the country is centered here in La Paz. Private and public incomes gathered all over the land are squandered here, with the result that La Paz has a number of very pretty, ultra-modern buildings, but in its social organization it belongs still far back in the Middle Ages. Its most modern parallel is the old American South, before the Civil War.

Either you are "white," and a gentleman, or a mere Indian, and lead a life of perpetual drudgery. Bolivia is still far more Indian than any other South American state; and the enormous proportion of its population, whatever that may be (the government has no idea, but it is either two or three million), retains the aboriginal language, customs, and dress. But all of the property, the wealth, the political offices, and influence are in the hands of the small number of "whites"—descendants of the old Spaniards, though many of these so-called whites are strongly intermixed with Indian blood.

Politics here is a small "family affair"—a thing "fixed up" between gentlemen, even though, in the excitement of the game, most of the politicians forget their gentlemanly ways, and there are the usual intrigues and revolutions between the "ins" and the "outs."

I noticed in Bolivia one curious and un-South American similarity to the party machinery of the United

States. Real authority and control seemed to be in the hands of one or two "bosses," who for the most part preferred not to take office. The official positions were occupied by men appointed by the "bosses," and supposed to act as mere puppets. But sometimes the puppets became restive and refused to obey orders; this was more or less the case when I was there.

A few months previously an election had taken place, whereby a certain gentleman was chosen president. But he made the mistake of talking too much before he took office, and of letting it be known that he intended to rule in his own way, and not as he was told. The chief boss, therefore, found that a technical error had taken place—that the president elect had forgotten to resign his previous post before running for office, and so the election was declared void.

The new president had been much more crafty. He kept his mouth well shut until he was safely and securely installed in office, but then promptly appointed as ministers a number of men who were directly opposed to the boss, so that there was now a good healthy rivalry between the two, with the public anxiously awaiting interesting further developments.

It was refreshing to escape from official lunches and receptions, from the whispering of intrigues, and to slip away to see how the "other half" lived—to go to the market-place and watch the native life in full swing. This was far, far more vivid and colorful in La Paz than in Lima; more so even than in Cuzco. One must travel to distant India to see its equal, for in South America it is only the Aymaras who dare to wear vigorous and clashing colors.

The market-place was indeed a splendid rival to an Oriental bazaar. Only a few of the elect had booths in-

side the market building; the others squatted on the
floor of the corridors, or outside on the ground of the
steep slanting streets. There was a homeliness about the
whole thing—women suckling their infants, while vigorously bargaining with a customer. In moments when
business was slack these women would gather together
and with obvious relish pick the lice from one another's
hair.

And what a gorgeous selection of things they had
to sell! Strange, graceful llamas had brought the products of the high cold table-land; stubborn, stupid, pro-
testing donkeys had made their way up the mountain
valley from the low-lying tropical plantations far to the
east. The fruits of the cold, the temperate, and the tropical regions were all assembled together. There were
pineapples, oranges, coffee, and sugar-cane next to ap-
ples, barley, and wheat. In addition there was many a
fruit and many a cereal of which we had never heard,
with strange colors and odors and tastes.

In true Oriental style, everything, however small
or valueless, had to be bargained for. A customer next
to me wrangled for half an hour as to whether she should
pay six cents or ten cents for a cabbage. It was a pleasant and entertaining way of killing time. When her
ladyship was tired of the game, she picked up the cabbage, paid exactly what she saw fit—irrespective of the
protests of the Indian market-woman—and marched
serenely away. It was the custom! If a customer were in
a hurry, he took what he liked, flung down whatever
small coins he had in his pockets, and the matter was
settled. The Indians dared not raise their voices, much
less their hands, against one of the gentry.

And yet how difficult it was to be a gentleman! I
was silly enough after buying a tiny package of fruit

to carry it back to the hotel with me. Thereafter I could no longer call myself a gentleman, for a gentleman would not dream of carrying anything as large as a collar-button. There must always be an Indian youth along to relieve him of any burden.

CHAPTER XXXV

A CENTER OF PRE-INCA CIVILIZATION

A FEW days after our arrival in La Paz, I
made, in the company of several gentlemen
from the British and American legations, a
special trip to the famous ruins of Tiawanako (Tia-
huanaco or Tiaguanaco), which lay not far away from
Lake Titicaca. I had undertaken to guide the party,
though I had never, of course, been there before. But
your guide is not held back by a small obstacle like that.
A true guide to these wonderful ruins does not exist,
as no one has the slightest idea of the history or meaning of the remarkable place. It is the super-problem
of South American archæology.

As we approached the ruins, we were first of all
struck by a curious pyramidal mound or hill which
arose from the plain. This hill seemed to be the work
of human hands and not placed there by nature. In various parts of this mound we observed huge worked
stones, the purpose of which was entirely incomprehensi-
ble to us.

What most attracted our attention was three stone
inclosures which stood at the foot of the artificial hill.
One of them was far larger than the others, and was
obviously a center of an ancient unknown culture. This
inclosure was a huge quadrangle surrounded by a series
of enormous polished sandstone blocks. There was a

curious irregularity about these stones: all were huge, but some were larger than others; some were beautifully smoothed, others somewhat irregular. Careful study seemed to show that the spaces in between the monoliths were originally filled in by smaller stones, although these smaller stones have now disappeared. They were probably taken away by the Spaniards to aid in the building in of their colonial houses and churches.

This ancient wall probably inclosed a temple, or rather a temple city, as numerous subdivisions could be noticed inside the great square. On the eastern end could be seen the ruins of a huge entrance gateway, the steps of which were also formed of enormous single stones.

At the other or western end were two other very curious remains. One was a huge monolith statue, rudely carved. The extraordinarily thick lips, bulging eyes, and flat nose of the statue did not in the least correspond with the facial characteristics of the Highland Indian of to-day, and we were set wondering how this type of face came to be portrayed. This monolith stood alone; but as several similar statues have been found in the vicinity—two have been placed at the entrance to a near-by church—it seemed as if there must have been at one time a special holy of holies here, filled with fearsome images of the gods.

Even more curious than the monolith was a huge stone portal near the northwest corner of the great inclosure. This portal has been said to be the most remarkable ruin in South America. Although ten feet high and over twelve feet long, it too was obviously cut from a single stone. Over the center of the gateway was carved in high relief a curious figure, probably representing the chief deity of the ancient pantheon. On either side of the central carving were three rows of

weird figures cut in profile; underneath it a frieze of
human faces, carved full-face.

For years scholars have racked their brains trying
to find an explanation for this gateway, and for the
figures carved upon it. But no adequate explanation
has ever been found. In the first place, it is a profound
mystery why this gateway should be tucked away in a
corner—in a place where it could scarcely have been
used as a gateway at all, unless to a tiny holy of holies
between it and the outer wall, but of this no trace can
be found.

For this reason it has been suggested that the portal
has been moved here from another place, but in view of
its enormous weight this seems almost incredible. Again
it seems strange that the doorway and the main figure
above it should not be in the true center, but considerably to one side, so that there are eight figures on one
side and seven and a half on the other.

For a long time it was supposed that the central
figure represented the sun-god. One native scholar, in
the exuberance of his imagination, not only assured me
of the truth of this theory but added that the other figures represented the calendar or the months of the year.
Obviously he had never taken the trouble to count the
figures, for he blandly informed me there were twelve in
each row, whereas in reality there were fifteen and a
half! It is well known that the ancient Peruvian calendar had twelve months, as has our own.

No, this frieze was probably made long before the
rise of the sun-god worship, and in all probability represented the ancient creator-god, Wirakocha—the soul
and the maker of all things. In later days Wirakocha
may have been identified with the sky-god—the "tear-
lines" on the figure fit in with this idea, for in many

CHAPTER XXXVI

IN addition to Tiawanako we visited several places of
note in the neighborhood of Lake Titicaca and of
La Paz. To many of these we had to go on horse- or
mule-back. To others we could go part of the way in
any case by rail.

But the fact that a certain place lay near the railroad track did not mean that we could journey there by
train, but we found that in this part of the world there
was a regular service only once or at the most twice a
week. Consequently on several occasions, in the absence
of a locomotive to pull us. I hired from the railroad company a rickety old push-car—which, however, instead
of being pushed along the line was drawn by a mule.
We soon found that railroading behind a mule was one
of the most exciting of all possible amusements.

After one of our excursions even this failed us, and
as the next passenger train was not to leave for several
days, I thought we should have to walk the whole of
the seventy miles which separated us from La Paz. But
just as we were starting I learned that a special freight-
train was due to pass along our section of the line.

By standing on the line in spite of reiterated whistling from the engine, we eventually succeeded in bringing the train to a halt. After this, the breaking open of one of the locked carriages was a comparatively easy matter, despite the threats and imprecations of the guard. At last the train started on its way again, and after many hours of slow bumping we eventually found ourselves once more in the Bolivian capital.

It was now high time to consider getting back to Lima, but instead of returning by the route over which we had come, I determined to take a boat from Antofagasta on the Chilean coast. This would allow me to see still another aspect of South American life.

As the journey through Chile necessitated a Chilean visé, I went down the day of our departure to the Chilean consulate to attend this formality. (When, I wonder, is this accursed passport nuisance to be done away with?) I found the place packed with people. The consulate hours were supposedly from 8 to 11:30. It was already eleven, but as the consul had been on a spree the preceding night he had not yet got up, and none of the waiting queue had had courage enough to have him wakened.

Even the consular servants dared not perform this task; so I myself was forced to storm the consul's bedroom. Poking my watch in his face, I informed the Sleeping Beauty that my train left at two o'clock, and consequently I had no time to wait. Needless to say this action awakened no love for me in the consular heart, and I thought for a moment that my visé was going to be refused. But after I had explained what a great man I was (I neglected to state that my greatness was recognized only by myself) I not only got my visé, but got it free of charge, with some letters of introduction as well.

That same afternoon, therefore, I was able to bid a regretful farewell to La Paz and start on the long journey south, over the bare, bleak plains of the Bolivian table-land. We were riding, as it were, on the backbone of the Andes. On either side in the far distance rose the majestic walls of the mountain ranges.

A few hours after leaving La Paz we came to a point remarkable on account of the enormous number of fossils found there. Little boys came to the train carrying huge loads of these curious trophies. After much haggling, I secured a whole bucketful for about fifteen cents. It was a cheap way of conducting paleontological research. Most of the trophies were fossilized marine shells which showed very vividly how in ages past the whole of this huge table-land, now thousands of feet high, had lain deep under the ocean.

Both in the bleak table-land, and in the desert sands of the coast, are found other, later, but even more interesting remains; viz., the bones of the megatherium, a now extinct species of jungle-loving ant-eater. These remains show that in the not very distant past, geologically speaking, the now desert wastes of both regions must have been covered with forest.

Two even more recent types of remains are equally mysterious. Among the ruins of the most ancient human cultures are found in large numbers bones of two different types of dogs. Yet the Spaniards of the time of the Conquest tell us nothing about the existence in South America of these useful animals. Why is it that they died out? Quite as curious is the disappearance of the horse. We know that at the time of the Conquest neither in North nor South America was any kind of horse known; yet there is very strong fossil evidence to show that the horse had his origin somewhere in the New World and that he certainly existed for centuries both in North and South America. He seems to have disappeared very shortly before the advent of man. Some even hold that he was killed off by the early hunters, who thus deprived themselves of an invaluable ally in their struggle toward civilization.

Most of the table-land we found very sparsely inhabited, so desolate was it. On two occasions, however, we came to junctions where branch lines led far away to the east through gaps in the Eastern Cordillera, to the prosperous slopes on the other side. These branch lines brought very vividly to mind an important difference between Peru and Bolivia. In Peru we had found the main centers of life to lie in the Highlands between the east and west ranges; the eastern slopes, leading down to the Amazon, were scarcely known or explored. In Bolivia the table-land was too bleak for comfortable habitation, and the cities had consequently been founded on the hills and slopes which lay to the east of the main eastern range.

One of these railway lines led, we were told, to the pleasant Old-World Spanish town of Cochabamba, the fruit garden of Bolivia; and the other to the even more famous town of Potosí. Potosí has become almost a legend because of the fabulous wealth extracted from its silver-mines. For centuries it was the world's chief source of this precious metal. The Potosí Mountain, situated near the city to which it has given its name, is almost a solid mass of silver. It has been estimated that more than five hundred million dollars' worth of metal has been extracted from this mountain alone. This hidden wealth was first discovered by accident by an Indian peasant; but, needless to say, it was a Spaniard who, in 1546, wrung the secret from the unfortunate

Indian, and secured a charter to exploit the mines for his own benefit.

The mountains of Bolivia are still enormously rich in mineral resources. Not only silver, but copper, lead, and tin as well, continue to be found in large quantities. It is rather remarkable that Bolivia should be one of the chief sources of the world's supply of tin when one remembers that in Peru, with a very similar geological formation, this metal has never been found.

Beyond Potosí lay Sucre, the old-time, and, as we have seen, still the legal, capital of the country. Sucre is noted as a center of Old World culture.

It was impossible for us to stray into by-paths, fascinating though these promised to be. We kept, therefore, to the main line, which continued to make its way across the arid plateau. But even this brought us into contact with many interesting problems. For some time we skirted the famous Lake Poopo, which—through the Desaguadero River—receives the surplus water of Lake Titicaca, but no one has the slightest idea what Poopo does with all the water it receives. More than two hundred thousand cubic feet of water pour into the lake every minute, and by the only known outlet only some two thousand cubic feet per minute flow out; yet the lake does not appreciably increase in size. In the ordinary way evaporation might account for the discrepancy, but in that case Lake Poopo would become salt, and the water is beautifully fresh. There must be some subterranean outlet, though where this is and whither it leads is unknown.

Really "dead" or "dying" lakes, however, were next on the program for us. A large portion of the table-land consisted of *salars,* huge stretches of sand and salt, the beds of what were formerly great seas, which had gradually evaporated, leaving a beautiful carpet of salt, or rather salts, behind. Many of these deposits, such as borax, were of great commercial value. In many cases we could see considerable rivers flowing into the *salares,* but their waters soon disappeared, leaving no permanent trace.

After twenty-four hours of traveling we eventually came to a pass leading through the Western Andes down to the Pacific Ocean. This pass marked the boundary between Bolivia and Chile. The whole of Chile is in fact only a long stretch of coast on the western slopes of the Cordillera.

At this point we were destined to have a little further excitement. Up to the frontier I had been given a free pass by the railway officials in La Paz, but it was understood that I was to pay for the journey through Chile, as this portion of the line, though belonging to the same company, was under different management.

So far so good! But by an error I had been given to understand that the amount required was less than was actually the case. Consequently I did not have sufficient Chilean money to pay the fare from the frontier to Antofagasta. The fact that I had about me more than sufficient English, American, and Peruvian money did not ease the situation. All these currencies were termed worthless by the guard who came to collect the tickets. Even the almighty dollar failed to be almighty.

I had in fact to fight like a hero of old to prevent my little party, with bag and baggage, from being thrown out upon the tracks in the midst of the desert. Eventually, after three good rounds, I proved victorious in the contest, and it was agreed that we were to be allowed to proceed to Antofagasta and pay at the other end. But we had fallen from our high estate as privileged guests of the company; and thereafter, as suspicious characters, we were closely watched to see that we should not escape at some wayside station.

This was my first but by no means my last experience of Chilean impoliteness. Only a short time after my own fight had been concluded a glorious one broke out between two groups of Chileans as to the right to certain seats. To my great regret only two of the five contestants were placed *hors de combat*. The Chileans have often been called the "English of South America," but this can hardly be considered a compliment to English manners. The Chileans are more active, more enterprising, more aggressive, than the Peruvians or Bolivians, by whom they are hated and feared, but they have none of the old Spanish chivalry or courtesy.

The excitement of the two fights only heightened my enjoyment of the beautiful country through which we passed on the long winding journey to the coast. Utterly desolate it was, of course, but of a wildness and grandeur hardly to be described. We were once more in the region of volcanoes. On the frontier itself was Mount Ollaque, where subterranean fires had blown half the mountain-side away, and where fire and smoke still arose to the sky.

Not long afterward we passed by a wonderful borax lake, some twenty-four miles long. The glistening surface of the lake, with occasional stretches of vivid green water, was all the more beautiful because of the background of snow-capped mountains, their lower slopes bright with metallic hues.

When at San Pedro we had gone through a huge lava-bed lying at the foot of another volcano, and had come in sight of a great water reservoir blasted out of the solid rock, I realized more than ever the desert-like character of the whole of the vast territory we were traversing. It was a death desert teeming with mineral riches—riches which without these water-lines, extending in parts nearly two hundred miles, would be forever unattainable.

It was only because of this water that the huge mining camp of Chuquicamata, handling some thirty thousand tons of copper ore a day, and one of the chief copper mines of the world, was able to keep alive its thousands of workers.

It is strange that the most modern of mining engineers so often find that the best mining sites were picked out by primitive peoples thousands of years ago. It is so in Asia. We found it so in South America. Quite near Chuquicamata was the town of Calama, a center of copper mining far back in the days of the Inca Empire. What an enormous undertaking it must have been in those days to bring the precious bars of metal from this arid desert to Cuzco, then the center of arts and crafts.

As if Nature had been anxious to heap riches upon riches in this desolation of sand, not long after leaving Calama we passed through a series of nitrate fields. For many centuries after the Spanish Conquest these fields remained untouched, being regarded as utterly valueless. But when toward the middle of the nineteenth century it was discovered that nitrate was the one thing needed to renew the fertility of the farming lands of Europe, exhausted by centuries of use, these arid lifeless plains of South America became "a pearl of great price" in the eyes of the whole world.

But, as in the case of many historical jewels, the possession of this new-found treasure was destined to be a curse to its owners. At that time the land at this point belonged to Bolivia; the nitrate fields further north, to Peru. Dish-water governments and their hangers-on led a champagne-and-silk-stocking existence, and corruption knew no limit. Envious of this easily acquired wealth, the Chileans, the barbarians of the South, began in 1880 a marauding expedition, called the War of the Pacific, which in the end deprived Bolivia of the whole of her seacoast, and Peru of her southern provinces. Chile thereby secured for herself the whole of the nitrate fields, and since then has lived largely on a tax levied on all nitrates exported from the country. With the change in ownership, bribery and corruption likewise shifted from Lima and La Paz to Santiago.

As the sun rose the next morning after we had passed the nitrate fields, we caught a glimpse of the ocean and of the city of Antofagasta, the sea-outlet for the riches through which we had been passing. By a curious coincidence, as we wound our way down the last incline, the ship on which we were to take passage steamed slowly into the harbor. We had timed our arrival to the minute!

The city of Antofagasta offered few attractions, so that after we had spent an hour or two wandering around the streets, we went on board the ship. We found, however, that the boat had a great deal of cargo to load and unload, so that it was another three days before we could leave the harbor.

During this period of waiting we were kept in good spirits by one or two rather interesting events. The first was the arrival of a huge flock of birds—birds of a type peculiar to the West Coast of South America, blackish in color, and in shape and size not unlike a snipe. I had never before seen such a large number of birds at one time. There must have been more than twenty thousand in the air and water around us. When settled in the water, they formed such a compact mass that they looked like a floating island, and when they arose from the water and circled around us it seemed as though the horizon had been blotted out.

Even the work of loading and unloading was not without incident. Although Antofagasta was rather better than most of the other harbors on the West Coast, it was impossible for our boat to lie along the docks, and all cargo had to be carried from the shore to the ship, and vice versa, in large barges. The ship's cranes transferred the loads from the barges to the hold. On one occasion, however, the chain holding many tons of copper bars slipped in mid-air, and the bars dropped to the bottom of the bay.

Not long after this a sharp wind caused large waves to rise, with the result that a launch bringing some barges from the docks was driven with terrific impact against the side of our ship. Fortunately the ship received little damage, but it was obvious that the launch was doomed. Water rushed in at several places, and the little craft soon began to sink. Ropes were thrown from our ship, and the launch's crew rapidly clambered up to safety—with one exception.

The engineer of the launch had rushed upon deck to see what had gone wrong, but before climbing to safety with the others he shot down to his cabin to retrieve the little hoard of savings which he kept there. His cupidity very nearly cost him his life. Just as he reappeared on deck, the launch gave a final lurch and sank beneath the waves. The poor engineer did indeed manage to catch hold of a rope, but the pull of the waters engulfing his craft was so great that it seemed for a moment that the rope would be torn from his grasp. Seeing his danger, however, the sailors on our ship gave a tremendous pull on the cable and succeeded in hoisting him above the level of the water. When the man at last clambered over the ship's railing, I went down to question him, so interested had I been in the whole proceeding. I soon found that the engineer, though indeed born in Chile, had had a Scotchman for a father and an Armenian for a mother, which no doubt went a long way toward explaining his heroic effort to rescue his cash.

In spite of these contretemps, the work of unloading and loading was at last completed, and we set out on our voyage toward the north, which was to bring us back to Lima. To our left lay the Pacific Ocean; to our right, the changeless, desolate, lifeless, but magnificent scenery which we had come to recognize as characteristic of the greater part of the West Coast of South America. A narrow strip of low-lying desert sand. Behind that a series of mountain ranges running for the most part parallel to the coast. The range nearest to us was the lowest; the other ranges behind it rose higher and higher above the level of the sea. At the uttermost horizon could occasionally be seen some of the great peaks which formed part of the main ridge of the Western Andes.

From time to time we cast anchor off some insignificant harbor. The most interesting port at which we stopped was Arica, where preparations were going on for the plebiscite which was to decide whether Peru or Chile should have the rulership over the surrounding district. An American cruiser was stationed in the bay, a sign of the part which the United States had been called upon to play in settling this long disputed problem.

A number of the officers of this cruiser obviously had little faith in the Volstead Act or in the quality of Chilean beer, for scarcely had our ship dropped anchor when a launch set out from the American boat and came at double speed in our direction. The steward of our ship obviously knew what to expect, for even before the launch arrived he placed a case of his strongest brew in the smoking-room. Needless to say he proved an excellent prophet. Before long the first case had to be replenished by a second.

As the only English-speaking person on board, I was delegated to act as host to the visiting officers. I found my task most delightful, and before long we all considered ourselves boon companions. I was particularly interested to hear what the visitors had to say about the progress of preparations for the plebiscite.

Needless to say, as representatives of a power called upon to act as arbitrator, they were all, in spite of the action of the beer, exceedingly diplomatic in their remarks. Even apart from diplomacy it was obvious that the American members of the Plebiscite Commission were strictly neutral and declined to give favor either to Peru or to Chile. But it was also obvious, even at this time, that the attempt to hold a fair vote on the subject was doomed to failure. There were almost daily fights between the partizans of the two countries, and it was not an unusual thing for these fights to result in the death or serious injury of several persons.

Unfortunately, out of consideration for Chilean feeling, and fearing lest she be considered to have imperialistic designs, the United States had not arranged to take over the government of the disputed area during the course of the plebiscite. The control of the whole area, and the duty of maintaining order there, remained

in the hands of the Chileans, with the not unexpected
result that all Peruvians and Peruvian sympathizers
were subjected to all manner of "third degree" treatment. In the rioting between the Chilean and Peruvian
mobs it was always the Chileans who were officially in
the right. The additional fact that in any case one
Chilean was and always is worth three Peruvians with
respect to physical strength and courage meant that
to show leanings toward the restoration of Peruvian
ownership was almost invariably attended by exciting
consequences.

In these circumstances the plebiscite seemed certain to degenerate into a mere farce, and I was not surprised to hear a few months later that this method of
deciding the suzerainty of Tacna and Arica had been
abandoned. In view of the high feeling both in Peru
and in Chile, the idea of giving the provinces to neither
of the two countries, but of ceding them to Bolivia in return for a monetary consideration to be paid to both
of the present claimants (an idea talked of by numerous persons in South America, and subsequently
formally propounded by Mr. Kellogg, the American secretary of state) would appear to be the best
solution. Unfortunately the Peruvian president, in
spite of his astuteness on most points, has refused to
entertain this plan, so that the Tacna-Arica affair
seems likely to continue a source of trouble for some
time to come.

We could only stay in Arica a couple of days.
Thereafter we continued our way up the coast. The
never ending barrenness of the whole region made it
seem extraordinary that there should be any serious
dispute as to the ownership of any part of it. Even
Arica lay north of the nitrate fields and the coastal

copper mines, so that the desolation had no redeeming feature in the way of mineral resources.

We were told that far to the north, from Ecuador onward, the West Coast enjoyed abundant rainfall and was consequently covered with dense vegetation, and that this held true, though to a lesser degree, of the southernmost part of the coast. But throughout the whole of our voyage to Lima, the land along which we passed was one "abomination of desolation," save where an occasional rivulet running down from the distant snow-covered mountains had cut a way through the intervening hills and brought life-giving moisture to the valleys of its own creation. And yet the old, curious combination of desolation and civilization on the one hand, as opposed to abundance and barbarism on the other, was exemplified in this as well as in other parts of the world.

We knew from the early chronicles that the forest-covered regions to the far north and south were inhabited, before the Spanish conquest, by tribes of a very low order of culture, while valleys of the intervening expanse of desert had been the centers of civilization even before the period of the Incas. Even from the ship we could occasionally see huge pyramidal mounds indicating great architectural skill which had been erected at the very dawn of history.

At last we reached Callao, and shortly afterward we were back in the Peruvian capital again. Here I found a very unpleasant surprise awaiting me. Not wishing to be encumbered with a superfluity of luggage during our journey to the Highlands, I had left a number of boxes, and the greater part of our paraphernalia, in Lima in charge of a young American business man called William Gregory.

On my return from the long journey to the south I found that in the meantime the esteemed Mr. Gregory, having got into serious financial trouble, had sold out his employer's goods, lock, stock, and barrel, and had then absconded with the money. As my first investigations failed to show any trace of my own boxes containing a good part of the material which had been collected during our long sojourn in the jungle, I began to fear that the work of many months had been accomplished in vain.

My delight was unbounded therefore when I eventually discovered that the young runaway had left most of my belongings with the editor of the local Anglo-American newspaper. One important item, however, was missing, a cage containing the parrot, and the two macaws or *araras,* which I had secured on the far-away Pira Parana.

For sentimental reasons, quite apart from the question of value, I was very loath to lose these birds forever, so I instituted a careful search for them all over Lima. My first clue to their whereabouts I got at the pension where Gregory had been living. The proprietor, a very obese and windy Austrian, declared that he had strong reason for supposing that the birds had been presented to one of the denizens of a house of ill fame in another part of the city.

Further inquiry failed to elicit either the name of the lady who had secured my pets or her exact address. I could only discover that she lived on one of the last houses on the Avenida Victoria. I was somewhat scandalized to find that pretty ladies were permitted to reside on a street with the name of Victoria, but nothing daunted I determined to follow the quest to the bitter end.

Access to the houses of pretty ladies is a comparatively simple matter in South America, even to persons filled with the most innocuous intentions. Such institutions, in fact, play an important part in the semi-social life on that continent. Because of the great seclusion of the women and girls of better family, ordinary social intercourse between the sexes is extremely restricted. To make up for this hiatus in their life, the young men are in the habit of spending many of their evenings in establishments of a looser kind, solely for the purpose of dancing, and conversing with members of the opposite sex. The high prices charged for refreshments more than recompenses such establishments for the absence of more serious intentions. The drawing-rooms of some of the more noted institutions are the social centers of the younger set of fashionable males.

It might have been advisable for me therefore to have waited until evening, when by attending the usual salon I could have ascertained whether my birds really were being kept in the house in question, but I thought it might prove difficult to retrieve my pets in such circumstances even when and if found. Accordingly about ten o'clock in the morning I went to the nearest police station and secured the services of a policeman, a miserable tubercular youth, to aid me in my search.

A taxi soon brought us to the end of Avenida Victoria, but thereafter the trail was made difficult by the fact that this section was found to contain, not one house, but eight houses, inhabited by pretty ladies. Not to be baffled by this, we proceeded to pound on each of the houses in turn. At five places we interviewed sleepy-eyed "mother superiors" in vain. No one would admit having seen or heard of the parrot and macaws. I did not put much confidence in their protestations, and as I knew that the macaws were in the habit of giving a loud squawk at least once a minute, I kept up a long conversation at the doorway of each establishment, hoping that a telltale squawk would tell me of the presence of my birds within.

At last my perseverance was rewarded. At one house at which we sought admittance, the "mother superior" was particularly rude and particularly vociferous in her denial of all knowledge of the objects of our quest. In the midst of my inquiries she attempted to slam the door in our faces, but I succeeded in interposing my foot just in time to prevent her doing so. Almost immediately afterward I heard a screech from upstairs, and I knew that we had come to the right place.

The little policeman squirmed through the door and tried to get up the stairway which started immediately beyond—I following in his wake. But we had reckoned without our hostess. She was a great brawny woman weighing well over two hundred pounds. Taking me by one hand and the policeman by the other, she literally flung us out on the street. Quite a crowd had collected on the street by this time, and this crowd greeted our sudden and forcible exit with loud cheers.

This was too much for the dignity of my companion. He blew his whistle repeatedly, with the result that three other policemen soon ran up to join him. With this reinforcement we returned to the fray. The door was soon battered down, but when we attempted to ascend the stairway we again came to an impasse. The good lady was so broad that she blocked up all the space, and so strong that we could not force her to retreat.

When we resorted to diplomacy, the outraged lady demanded if we were in possession of a search-warrant, and finding that we were not, she shrieked that our at-

tempt at forcible entrance was entirely illegal, a statement which unfortunately was only too true. When at
last we secured the promise of the fair dame to let us
in should we come armed with the proper warrant,
I and my police escort departed to the nearest police
station, leaving the other guardians of the peace on
watch to see that my birds were not spirited away.

On our arrival at the police station we found that
the *capitán,* the only person who could issue the warrant, had gone out to lunch, and that we should have
to await his return. My escort then said he would go
around the corner for his lunch, but would be back in
a quarter of an hour. A half an hour I waited alone
in the inner sanctum, and as no one appeared I
thought that I too would go out in search of refreshments. But unfortunately the sentries at the gate had
not been informed of my true status. They had seen me
come in under escort, imagined that I was under some
sort of arrest, and consequently refused to let me out,
until at last my friend returned and vouched for my
innocence. Into such scrapes can birds—and women—
lead one.

An hour later the *capitán* returned, but just as he
was making out the warrant, the "mother superior" herself appeared at the police station attended by one of
her houris. A guilty conscience had no doubt brought
her to the bar of justice. By this time, however, my
little policeman had almost forgotten about the birds.
His dignity had been so ruffled by the man-handling
—or shall we say woman-handling?—that he wished to
bring in a charge of assault and battery.

The situation grew livelier and livelier, and I began to fear that the original purpose of my quest was
being lost sight of. So that with the permission of the

capitán, I got the "mother superior" into the corridor, and told her that if she would only return me my birds I would see that no further trouble befell her. She burst into tears of relief and then, swearing that she was only too pleased to accept my terms, flung her arms around me, and gave me a very forcible kiss.

Disentangling myself from her embrace, but with the kiss still burning upon my cheeks, I made my way back to the *capitán.* After a short private talk with him, the matter was eventually settled to every one's satisfaction, and before long I had my pets back again.

Fortunately the macaws had never learned to speak, but the vocabulary which my parrot had picked up during his sojourn in the house of beauty gave me a new insight into the capabilities and range of the Spanish language.

CHAPTER XXXVII

GRAVE-SNATCHING AMID INCA AND PRE-INCA RUINS

DURING my stay in Lima I became deeply interested in the remains of the ancient cultures which have been discovered in recent years all along the coast of Peru. Most of the chronicles would have us believe that these coastal civilizations were the result of the Inca conquest, and were therefore established only some two or at the most three centuries before the coming of the Spaniards. Modern excavation has shown how erroneous the chronicles are on this point. It was the obvious antiquity of many of the ruins of the coastal valleys which first led the scientific world to suspect the existence of the pre-Inca cultures. Further examination of these remains has shown that the early city states of the coast, far from having received their civilization from the Incas, had reached a remarkably high stage of culture long before the Incas were dreamed of. Not only do many of the coastal ruins belong to the pre-Inca period, but it seems moreover that it was on the coast that the pre-Inca civilization reached its culminating point.

The coast of Peru seems to have been to the Inca Empire of the Highlands what Greece was to Rome. The various valleys of the coast constituted little city states possessed of an exceedingly high civilization but incapable of political union. After a long period of cultural splendor these little states fell into decay and were eventually incorporated into the powerful new military empire established by the organizing genius of the Inca rulers, though the Incas seem to have been influenced by the coastal art and culture.

I have already spoken of the ruins found near Trujillo to the north of Lima, and in the valley of Nasca far to the south. These seem to have been the chief centers of the coastal culture in the old pre-Inca days. A certain amount of digging has been done in both places; and some of the "finds," particularly the pottery, are among the most prized treasures of various museums.

Many of the best specimens, however, are only to be found in some of the private collections in Lima, and I was delighted to find that I was eventually able to inspect these. The pottery from the north, the so-called Trujillo type, was found under the ruins of an ancient city usually called Chan-Chan, the capital of the pre-Inca kingdom of the Great Chimu. Nearly all of these pieces were extraordinarily realistic in modeling. Among them were jars in the shape of human heads, of birds, of animals, and of plants, which were of really remarkable artistic skill and naturalness. This was the more surprising because many of the things portrayed, such as parrots, *araras,* toucans, and monkeys, belong strictly to the Amazon region and, so far as is known, have never appeared either on the Coast or the Sierra. The pottery from the southern valley of Nasca was of a quite different order. Here the form and size were more conventional, and instead of being modeled, the chief objects were painted, but painted with a dashing element of style and a vividness and freshness of color which filled me with astounded admiration.

The date of the Trujillo and Nasca cultures is still very uncertain. Underneath the true Inca remains found at both places are found specimens of pottery which seem to indicate Tiawanako influence, but the finest examples were found even further beneath the sand, which shows that they were made at a still earlier period, many centuries before even the Tiawanako culture spread to the coast. Much, very much, is unknown, and even more is uncertain regarding all of the coastal ruins. Archæological research in this part of the world is still in its infancy. Trujillo and Nasca were not the only centers of culture, and much work has to be done among the other ruins before a valid account of the cultural history of any portion of the coast can be written.

It was therefore with great pleasure that I accepted an invitation to join a commission appointed by the University of San Marco to carry out some research work in the peninsula of Paracas, a little more than a hundred miles south of Lima. Here Dr. J. C. Tello, the chief anthropologist and archæologist of the university, had started excavation; it was one of the chief purposes of the commission to investigate and evaluate the ruins which were gradually being brought to light.

It was arranged that our little party was to be transported by two motor-cars, while an additional truck was to carry the camp equipment. After a long delay in starting we eventually set out on the road winding southward along the coast. Coastal communication is very bad in Peru. There is no railway connection between the various valleys, and the road is for the most part an invisible trail over the drifting sands. Every few hours we would strike a river valley with cultivated

fields and a little village or town. But in the long spaces
between there was only the grandeur of utter desolation.

The general formation of the country was similar
to most other parts of the coast. Parallel with the ocean,
and, at the most, only two or three miles distant, ran the
low outer ranges of the Cordilleras. Behind these, the
peaks of the second and third ranges could occasionally
be seen rearing up their splendid heads. Here and there
the hills would narrow down to the water's edge, and
then we would clamber for hours over the low, long,
uneven cliffs.

It is in the occasional valleys of the long narrow desert stretch of the coast that Peru secures her chief agricultural products. La Montaña is virgin jungle; La
Sierra lies too high up to allow of great agricultural development; therefore it is on this seemingly insignificant strip of coast that Peru produces the sugar
and cotton which form such a large portion of her national wealth. It is only in the last few years that cotton has formed an important item in the list of exports;
yet it was one of the oldest products of this region. The
very oldest graves contain beautifully woven cotton
cloth, made apparently from cotton of first-rate quality.
But whereas the valleys are great producers of agricultural wealth, towns situated in the valleys presented
to us a poor bedraggled appearance. As the owners of
all the important haciendas or estates lived and spent
their money in Lima, it was only natural that their
country houses were badly neglected. Chincha presented an exception, and a slight improvement. Here
the valley was broken up into a number of small hold-
ings, so that each man was fairly well-to-do, and yet
none wealthy enough to follow the fashionable flight
to the capital.

We found the people of the coast different, as regards character, appearance, and race, from the folk of the Highlands. The Highlanders were dour, melancholy, hard-living, whereas the *costeños* (as they were called) lived more merrily. They were certainly more mercurial and temperamental. Even in the earliest times there seems to have been this distinction between the two peoples, due probably to climatic difference. But in the last century or two it has been accentuated by reason of racial intermixture. The Highland is still essentially Indian. Its inhabitants wear the costume and speak the language of the ancient Inca Empire, but on the coast the Indian element is less vigorous; waves of foreign immigration have left their impression. The Indian is still an important element in the coastal cocktail of races, but other elements are equally prominent. The Spaniard, of course, gives a gloss to all, but the negro strain is equally in evidence. To this curious conglomeration of races has been added in the last few years a strong admixture of Oriental blood, furnished by settlers from Japan and China.

The peoples and problems of the coast, as it is today, were exceedingly interesting, but naturally it was the past which especially claimed our attention. Striking memorials of this past were to be seen at many places at which we stopped during the course of our journey. The first valley, after Lima, brought us to the magnificent ruins of the temple city of Pachakamak. Long, long before the days of the Incas, the temple and the oracle of Pachakamak—the fish-god or the water-god, symbolizing the creative principle—were famous all over Peru, and pilgrims flocked there from every part of the country. When eventually the Incas conquered the coast, crafty statesmen that they were they did not prohibit the old cult, but on the higher and overshadowing hill they erected a magnificent pyramid temple to their own god, the God of the Sun, and, to one side of the temple, a huge convent where were housed the virgins dedicated to the worship of that deity. Below, on two smaller hills, could be seen the remains of the old city, with rest-houses for pilgrims and palaces for its priests and rulers. All these buildings were made out of sun-dried brick—adobe—as were the buildings everywhere on the coast. It was only in the Sierra, and then only for the principal buildings, that stone was used. The extreme dryness of the coastal climate has to some extent preserved these adobe buildings down through the long ages to the present time.

Shortly after leaving Pachakamak we were told to keep a sharp lookout for bandits. Ten years ago the road was infested by highwaymen, and even to-day small parties are not infrequently robbed and even murdered. We were to see a pathetic reminder of a tragedy that had taken place only four or five months previously. In one of the lonely stretches of desert a peasant woman, returning home from the next valley and accompanied only by her dog, had been set upon by the ruffians. In spite of a vigorous defense, she was killed, though the brigands were put to flight, before they could loot the body, by the arrival of a group of villagers. The woman was buried where she lay, far in the desert, with only a small wooden cross to mark her grave. Here the faithful dog had remained. We saw him as we passed. In this barren waste he would soon have starved to death had he not been fed by the occasional travelers who knew of the romantic tale.

The next landmark on our journey southward was a curious Inca graveyard. By the side of the desert trail, with no sign of habitation in the past or present, lay buried, close to the surface of the ground, thousands and thousands of bodies. Treasure-hunters had found the place by accident, but taking advantage of the accident we halted for an hour or two, in order to continue the digging which they had begun. The bodies lay in shallow trenches covered over by tree-branches, which the dryness of the climate had preserved. Over these were heaped up masses of sea-shells, and above all was the drifting sand, which had leveled and evened everything. Grave-snatching under such conditions was extremely interesting work. As far as we could ascertain, no artificial method of mummification had been used; yet the bodies were perfectly and marvelously preserved, and were as fresh as the Egyptian mummies. This, too, no doubt was due to the dry sand of the desert.

The great object in opening up strange graves is to ascertain the type of race and culture to which the long-buried belonged. In this case—as in others—a casual glance was enough to give an approximate answer. First of all, the smallish bodies, the roundish heads and faces, and the texture of the hair told us that the people we dug up belonged to the general South American Indian race, and were not invaders or intruders from the outside. Further, we knew from our museum visits that the earlier inhabitants of the coast, of the so-called Nasca period, practised a curious type of skull deformation. These skulls were not deformed; therefore they must belong to a people of later period.

Finally, the texture and patterns of the cloths in which the bodies were wrapped, and the ornamentation and shape of the vases and pots which were buried with them—these had meaningless geometrical designs, and many of the pots had curved point-bottoms, so that they could not stand up unsupported—were utterly out of keeping with those of the oldest remains, and likewise out of keeping with the styles prevalent after the Spanish Conquest. They corresponded so closely with the well known Inca remains that we concluded definitely the bodies were either those of colonists from the far-away center of the Inca Empire, or at least those of a folk long subject to Inca influence.

The indiscriminate way in which the innumerable bodies lay together, and the extreme shallowness of the graves, also suggested the Inca mode of burial, at least as practised on the coast. In the oldest period the bodies were much more elaborately prepared for burial and were put much deeper into Mother Earth. The large number of llama heads found in the graves told us that the people buried here came from the Highlands, or had close relationship with that region, because this curious animal was never acclimatized on the coast.

The further south we went, the more invisible the road, the more strenuous and nerve-racking the driving. The long desert cliffs between the valleys became more uneven, more treacherous. But our Peruvian driver thought little of these matters. He, like most other native chauffeurs, was about as reliable as a college student driving with three sheets in the wind. He kept his foot on the gas, irrespective of gradients or the state of the road, and we whirled on, uncertain whether we were headed for our goal or for annihilation. We were fortunate. A continuous succession of bumps and jolts constituted our chief suffering. But we could see that many of our predecessors on the road had not been so lucky. Every few miles we came in sight of a little wooden cross which told us a story of reckless adventure now at

an end, for it was the custom to bury the victims of accidents where they lay in the desert sand, with only a cross
to mark the grave. We heard that in one of the most
recent accidents a car had turned a threefold somersault.
All its passengers had, of course, been killed, but the
chauffeur himself, by some miracle, had escaped. I began to understand why our driver had in front of him a
gaudy placard bearing the inscription, "Holy Mary,
pray for us."

In many parts, in the more level section of the long
desert sand, there were wonderful clear mirages to be
seen, beautiful lakes, in the midst of the sands of death.
Death-traps are these shimmers of unreality. By the
whitening bones we could see how cattle had wandered
far out into the desert, in search of the cooling water
always receding before their eyes, to die in the end of
thirst and exhaustion.

And everywhere ruins, many of them quite as interesting as the Inca "graveyard." To mention only a few,
and without regard to chronological order, there were,
in the valley of Chincha, the well preserved remains of
an Inca city. Erected on three or four low, partially artificial hills, or mounds, the dwellings or chambers, arranged terrace-fashion along the sides, bore a striking
similarity in form to the pyramids of Egypt. Particularly was this so in the case of the chief mound, which
had been the Temple of the Sun and the residence of
the priests. Here there was a long slanting path which
led to the top to a place which had been the holy of holies. Next to this was a room, beautifully adorned with
a geometrically designed bas-relief, and near this we
saw, by peering down, a huge dungeon-chamber which
reached down to the very bottom of the mound, some
hundred feet or so. Its exact purpose we could not

fathom, but it was most probably used in connection with the sacrifices offered to the sun-god.

A neighboring mound gave us a good idea of how the average man lived in the days of old. Some twenty or thirty houses were grouped together to form a compact "block," separated from other groups by a high wall and a long narrow street. Each group had been the residence of an *ayllu* or clan, the huge family group which was the social unit of the old Peruvian civilization.

Most of the rooms were very small; not a few were without doors and had to be entered by means of ladders from the roof. Windows were virtually non-existent. What light was necessary came through the apertures in the roof, but many rooms contained half-way up the side of the walls the curious "Egyptian-shaped" niches which played such an important part in Inca architecture. In a number of houses there were mysterious little alcoves which seem to have served some religious and sacrificial purpose. In one room, particularly well preserved, we could see how the men of old carried out their mural decoration. All of the walls were whitewashed; and around the room, a foot or two above the floor, ran a band or border with a brilliant design in red, green, and black.

These ruins belonged to the distant past. They had been deserted for hundreds of years. Their very existence was long forgotten; yet a careful study showed that all we had seen belonged to the Inca times or to a period not long before the Inca conquest. Tradition tells us that when the Children of the Sun conquered the coast they found Chincha a thriving and powerful little principality; though we must conclude it was much later than Nasca. After the conquest it became an important center on the coast.

It was from Chincha that we saw, a few miles away
in the ocean, the famous Guano Islands. For thousands
of years the guano birds—millions of which we could
see hovering over the water—have used these islands as
a resting-place, and their droppings have formed, in the
course of centuries, deposits hundreds of feet deep. This
has produced a valuable fertilizer, a fact discovered by
men of the oldest of the Peruvian cultures. The Incas
greatly developed the exploitation of guano. In Inca
days it was an imperial monopoly, and during the last
century these desolate barren islands have again brought
in untold gold into the national coffers. It is to their very
bleakness and desolation that Peru owes this wealth, for
rainfall sufficient to permit cultivation would ruin this
curious deposit.

In the valley of Cañete we saw an interesting mixture of Inca and pre-Inca styles. A large double-
crowned sandy hill rose up in the middle of the valley.
On the higher crown or peak stood a huge, well constructed fortress; on the other, the remains of an extensive city. But the adobe bricks of the fortress were of
the long quadrangular form, obviously molded in
wooden presses. This represented the more "modern"
style and corresponded to the Inca period. The bricks
of the city were smaller and rougher, and obviously were
molded by hand, the finger-marks in many cases being
clearly recognizable. This sort of brick belongs to a far
older period and is frequently spoken of as the "Nasca
style." Brickmaking was one of the few points in which
the Inca culture was superior to that of the older civilizations. The adobe brick made even to-day on the coast
are virtually duplicates of the old Inca models.

It was obvious therefore that Cañete was the seat of
a very ancient culture, and that it was subsequently con-

quered by the Incas, who continued to dominate the city from their fortress built on the highest point. The bodies we found buried along the slope of the hill (there must be thousands there) told the same story. The majority of the skulls were of the round, even, undeformed Inca type; the Incas must have sent huge numbers of colonists to all of the conquered regions. But here and there were the curious artificially deformed skulls which marked the much earlier type. In the few hours we were there we were able only to scratch the surface. I am, however, of the firm opinion that the site presents one of the richest and most promising fields for future detailed research and excavation.

It was interesting to observe the great cleavage on the coast between the cultures of the past and of the present; a cleavage much more marked on the coast than in the Highlands. The cities of the past, whether Inca or pre-Inca, were built on high hills overlooking the valleys, the modern towns are all built on the lowlands, in the valleys; a very useful fact for the archæologist, as subsequent building and rebuilding have not disturbed the ancient sites. In many cases one can see where, in the old Inca and pre-Inca days, the area under cultivation was much greater than is the case at the present day, because of the old elaborate aqudeuct systems, which allowed of irrigation of the higher ground. The improvident Spaniards permitted this system to fall into decay, with, of course, disastrous results; and it is only within the last few years that irrigation has been reintroduced.

CHAPTER XXXVIII

WHEREIN A BURIED CITY COMES TO LIGHT

AFTER several days of journeying we arrived at Pisco, which was to serve as our base of supplies during the course of the work which the commission had undertaken. The town of Pisco is famous throughout Peru, because of its namesake, the spirit of grapes, distilled here in great quantities, which is the cause of half the national crime, but also of half the national poetry, to say nothing of the service it renders in fostering perennial revolutions. *Pisco* is as colorless and as uninteresting-looking as water, but it tastes like liquid fire and works like the devil unchained. It was near the home of this enchanting nectar that we were to delve into the fathomless past.

Still another twenty miles to the south we had to make our way across the sands of an ancient bay. No longer could we whirl; most of the time we were up to our axles in sand, and many a time we had to get out and push. It was only late at night that we arrived at our goal, the peninsula of Paracas, which throws itself far out into the sea.

Paracas, which in the old Quechua language means "The Windy," is worthy of its name. Day and night there howls a gale, with neither tree nor bush to offer protection. A weird eerie place is Paracas, for the wind howls like the cries of souls who had been cast into outer darkness. In the teeth of the wind it took us hours to erect our tents, in the soft powdery sand, and frequently, in the days that followed, they were blown down and had to be reërected.

The day after our arrival we set about our work. Dr. Bravo busied himself making a detailed geological survey of the peninsula. To the geologist Paracas presents a very interesting problem. Whereas nearly all the coastal hills, and most of the Andean peaks, consist of land formed in the Secondary period and elevated in the Tertiary, the hills of the Paracas peninsula are far older and, in fact, represent one of the most ancient bits of sedimentary land anywhere in the South American continent. In these hills lie layer upon layer of coal, but the coal begins and ends here. None is found anywhere for hundreds of miles around. It is an isolated deposit.

The unique geological formation of the site of Paracas—this finger of South America pointing into the sea —is one of the principal reasons for supposing, as many geologists do, that Paracas is the last remnant of a former vast Pacific continent, one which existed before the upheaval of the Andes. The one-time Pacific continent is supposed to have begun at about this point, and to have stretched far into the sea; perhaps, as some think, as far as the islands of the East and Australia: this would explain why certain animals, such as the marsupials, are common to both parts of the world.

At present, however, Paracas is but a wreck, a pitiful and desolate remnant of what once may have been a vast continent. It is deserted and lifeless except for the screaming of the albatross, the seagull, and the guano-bird. When we were there even this screaming was subdued, for the sea-shore was lined with the corpses of thousands of the birds, and many others were sickly and dying.

This was the result of a trick which Mother Nature had within the last year played on the Peruvian coast. The high gods of destiny were napping apparently, and a poor innocent ocean current lost its way and went hopelessly wrong. The West Coast owes its extreme dryness, and its consequent desolation, to a cold current, the Humboldt Stream, which sweeps up the coast from the antarctic. The dryness has made of the coast a desert; but because it is a desert, the rich guano and nitrate fields have been preserved.

The cold Humboldt Stream has a timid rival coming from the north, which produces the hot moisture and the luxuriant jungles of the coast of Colombia. Usually the Humboldt Stream checks this little braggart north stream off Ecuador, but suddenly in 1925 the Humboldt Stream ceased to function properly. The hot northern current came further and further south. Heat and torrential rains followed, rains that washed away railways and bridges and caused untold damage to property. Moisture, the very thing the barren coast is supposed to need, proved a curse—because it was unexpected. Under the new climatic conditions the old bird life could not flourish, and millions of birds along the coast sickened and died.

Strangely enough, no one understands what had really happened. What became of the antarctic stream? Did it suddenly disappear, or did it shift its course to some new direction, and if so why? Some think it went further to the west; some, and I with them, hold that the Humboldt Current continued to function *under-neath* the surface of the water, and that the warm current from the north was merely a layer which flowed in the opposite direction on the top. Who knows? And an even more important question: Is this new condition to be permanent? Or is it merely a temporary freak? It is a vital matter, as it means a radical change in the climate and in the whole life of the coast. Should the change prove permanent, jungle would grow up where now there is desert land. It is a question which only time can solve. In 1926 there was a recurrence of conditions similar to those of the previous year, but in lesser degree. The Humboldt Current was again on the job, but only half-heartedly. Heavy rains again fell, and the birds once more died off in great numbers.

Only the seals continued to sport with full vigor on the sands of Paracas; and it was to secure their precious skins that a few fishermen had come to this silent, deserted peninsula. One of these men, while digging a place for a camp, had come across a "mummy." News of this find gradually spread north and eventually reached the ears of Dr. Tello, who ordered systematic digging operations begun.

The native diggers had been at work for some time before our arrival, so that there was already much for us to see, and day after day thereafter some fresh discovery would be made, or some interesting development occur.

Unlike many of the ruins we had seen, which were still more or less exposed to the light of day, in Paracas everything was covered over with a thick layer of sand. At first sight there was absolutely nothing that would lead one to suppose that this lonely peninsula was formerly inhabited. There was not a drop of fresh water anywhere for miles around. All our own water had to be brought from Pisco by motor; and when on one occasion the car broke down, we were left for hours in agonizing distress from thirst. Because of the physical position of the peninsula, a subterranean stream anywhere within well-digging distance of the surface was out of the question. It seemed incredible that such a forlorn stretch of sand could ever have been a center of human culture.

And yet, from the excavations, it was obvious that at three different periods Paracas had been the seat of a considerable population. The remains of the three periods lay not, as is frequently the case, in layers one on top of the other, but well separated, and each with marked characteristics of its own.

The latest, poorest, and smallest of the three settlements dated from the time of the Incas. It seemed clear that at that period Paracas had already assumed much of its present desert character. After carefully establishing the Inca nature of these remains, little further work was done here. The other finds were more interesting and more exciting.

The second settlement, obviously much older than the first, was found some distance away, on a low sloping hill which ran down to the sea. On the flanks of this hill, called by the commission Cabeza Larga, a large number of stones were uncovered. It was soon recognized that they were part of numerous foundation walls marking the sites of ancient houses, palaces, and temples. The stones were of red porphyry and were loosely cemented together with sand and clay. It was obvious that this was no simple collection of huts in a fishing-village, as I had been at first inclined to think, but represented the remains of a city of splendor which had existed in days long gone by. The buildings—such vestiges as remained—and the mummies buried near them, spoke of pomp and wealth and luxury.

The mummies were even more interesting than the remains of the ancient buildings. They lay much deeper than the Inca bodies found on the coast, being covered over by five or six feet of sand. They were also much more carefully wrapped up than were the common folk of the Inca period. The mummies with their wrappings measured between three and four feet in diameter, because of the enormous number of clothes which had been draped around each body. The outermost draperies were of coarse uncolored cloth, but then came layer after layer of the most beautifully woven and embroidered fabric I have ever seen. Although these robes were falling to pieces from age, their magnificent colors were wonderfully well preserved. All the cloth was of cotton, and we were set wondering where the huge cotton-fields which produced such mountains of cloth could have stood. Certainly not in barren desert land.

With each mummy, between two layers of embroidered cloth, was a handful of brilliantly colored feathers plucked from birds at present found nowhere on the coast. Whence could these have come? Stranger still was the fact that many of the more important mummies had in the folds of their wrappings a curious spiral ring made apparently of human tendon. What were they—mascots—fetishes—and how were they made?

The bodies inside the wrappings, like other Peruvian mummies, were buried in a sitting position, the knees brought up to the level of the shoulders, the head bowed between the knees. The heads of these mummies were especially interesting. Whereas in Inca times it was very unusual to deform the heads of the children artificially, in the older periods of the coastal culture this custom was almost universal. Here, judging from the mummies, the custom had been carried to an extreme degree.

From early infancy onward light bands were bound

around the heads of the children. These bands, aided no
doubt by boards, caused the skulls of the people, as they
grew up, to assume a most extraordinary shape, not unlike that of a bishop's miter. The back of each skull was
almost perpendicular; the whole front resembled a long
sloping forehead and slanted back at an astonishing
angle. The high culture evinced by the remains showed
that even this amazing deformation of the skulls had
no deleterious effect upon the intelligence of the people.

Such extreme deformation has been found nowhere
else on the coast. This showed not only that the remains here were of Inca influence, but also that Paracas must have been at one time the center of a culture
distinct from that of all other pre-Inca civilizations.

The most extraordinary and unique thing about
these mummies was the fact that the wrappings of all
of them were to a certain extent *charred*. They could
not have been subjected to a subsequent accidental
fire, because the *outer* layers of cloth showed no trace
of fire or carbonization, but as one worked inward the
vestments gradually became brown, and then black, and
were finally a huge tissue of ashes, but ashes so perfectly preserved that even the fabric and the design on
the cloths remained perfectly intact. More wonderful
still, the bodies themselves were not burned, and the
bones showed no sign of carbonization.

This was indeed a mystery. Nothing similar has ever
been found in Peru, nor, as far as I know, in any other
part of the world. It seems inconceivable that the inner
wrappings of these mummies *could* be charred, when
neither the bodies themselves nor the outer wrappings
had been. But so it was. In my own opinion this fact can
only be accounted for by supposing that the ancient
Peruvians smeared the bodies of their dead with some

kind of preservative, perhaps some weak solution of
nitric acid, which gradually burned out all the surrounding textiles.

If this be so, it is the first time that an artificial
preservative for the dead has been found in Peru, for
whereas the Egyptians invented elaborate embalming-
fluids, the Peruvians seem to have relied only on the
extraordinary dryness of their climate for the preserva-
tion of the bodies of their ancestors. Either this, or else
their embalming-fluids were of such a delicate kind that
modern chemical analyses have not been able to trace
them.

We were particularly interested in trying to fix a
date for the remains found at Cabeza Larga. A careful
examination of the pottery, the weaving, and the mummies convinced us all that we had stumbled upon the
site of a city which was not merely pre-Inca but older
even than the civilizations of Trujillo and Nasca.

Ancient as these remains were, however, they were
not the most ancient which our little party had the good
fortune to see. In various likely places all over the
peninsula, long thin iron rods were thrust deep into the
ground. According to the resistance to pressure, we
were enabled to tell with a fair degree of certainty
whether the earth was virgin and undisturbed, or
whether some foreign substance had been buried underneath it.

A great deal of this work led, of course, to no result. But on the top of another hill, called Cerro Colorado, which lay about a mile away from Cabeza Larga,
it was found that the rods could be thrust down to their
hilts. Encouraged by this fact, the native workmen under Dr. Tello's able direction immediately began serious
excavation.

This turned out to be a long and arduous task. At first nothing whatever was found. But when three or four feet of sand had been cleared away, we came to what had originally been the surface level. Here the ground consisted of a very hard rock-like clay. Further examination showed that several long deep perpendicular shafts had once been cut through the clay; although they had long since been covered in again. Digging out the refilled earth, the excavators followed the course of one of these shafts for ten or twelve feet without finding anything. Only the fact that the walls of the shafts were lined with rough-cut porphyry stones encouraged them to go on with their task.

Finally some fifteen feet below the old surface of the ground, and nearly twenty feet underneath the drifting sand, the diggers came upon a layer of desiccated cane-stalks, and immediately below this a number of ancient dried boughs. Breaking through the cane and old tree-boughs—preserved by the dryness of the climate—the workers found themselves looking down into a large, hollow, artificial cavern, along the sides of which were seated a number of mummies!

The discovery of the first cavern led to opening up many others. Later it was found better to trace the other caverns by sending out horizontal tunnels from those already discovered rather than by following the courses of the ancient perpendicular shafts.

It gave me a weird, uncanny feeling to crawl through one of these tunnels and suddenly find myself in a cavern filled with the fingers of men dead many, many centuries ago. I had in fact the startling impression of having dropped into a secret tribal council carried on in the deep recesses of the earth. I must confess I gave a cry when I saw—or thought I saw—one of the figures move. I breathed again—only when I found that the moving figure was one of the workmen who had been resting in one of the dark burial-caves built no doubt by some of his distant ancestors.

The mummies discovered in the caverns, when removed to the light of day, revealed to us a number of interesting facts. It became clear that these people had lived in a cultural period some centuries earlier than that of Cabeza Larga, though the cultures of the two settlements must have been closely affiliated. The head deformation on Cerro Colorado was simpler, giving the skull a wedge shape. There was no trace of the charring such as had been found in the remains at Cabeza Larga. The pottery was more primitive; the embroidered cloth, though equally beautiful, was less plentiful. We were here at the very threshold of the high civilization which Peru was later destined to evolve.

Unfortunately, during the short time I was able to stay at Paracas, no trace could be found of the buildings erected by the men of this older culture, but the contents of the caverns gave us a good idea of the life they must have led. The ancient inhabitants of Cerro Colorado were representatives of the oldest culture which had been found anywhere on the coast of Peru up to the present time, yet it was obvious that they even then had already reached a high level of civilization. Agriculture was certainly well developed, for, in addition to cotton, the desiccated remains of maize, potatoes, and several other plants were found in large quantities.

The Cerro Colorado culture must have arisen when the Peruvians were gradually emerging from the stone to the metal age. The weapons found in the caverns had been hewn out of stone or flint, but the discovery of a number of long thin gold plates, used evidently as headbands, showed that the working of metals had already begun. Of silver or copper I could find no trace, although both these substances were extensively employed in the later Inca times. As the Peruvians never learned the use of iron, the absence of this metal was not surprising.

What to me was most interesting was the fact that both the weaving and the embroidery were far superior to the pottery. In the evolution of most of the primitive cultures, pot-making seems to have come first, and weaving later. In the Amazon I had met with many tribes where ceramics had reached a comparatively high stage of development, but where weaving was still entirely unknown. Here, however, the pots were coarse and crude, mostly uncolored, and without pictorial design, although the shapes and forms characteristic of the later Nasca culture were clearly foreshadowed.

It is probable that these early inhabitants lived far more upon fish than upon flesh. But in the entrance to several of the shafts, huge whale-ribs were found, and it seems likely that even in these primitive times the men had found means of hunting the mightiest of ocean dwellers.

From the position and arrangement of some of the bodies it appeared probable that these ancient Peruvians followed the interesting custom of burying with the chief his retainers and women-folk, who were either killed or committed suicide, that they might continue to serve their master in the other world. The other world —that strange lodestone of human sentiment from the dawn of human existence down to the present-day table-rapping and spook-gazing.

The skulls both here and in Cabeza Larga showed moreover that even in the distant past represented by these cultures the delicate and difficult operation of trepanning was known and carefully carried out. It was extraordinary what a large percentage of skulls had huge holes cut in them, and yet from the well healed edges it was obvious that in most cases the victims of the operation had lived for years afterward.

What was the cause of all these operations? Probably in warfare the stalwart soldiers got their skulls broken by a stone ax or club, inflammation set in, and it was necessary to cut out the whole of the infected area. But without antiseptics or anesthetics the victim must have had a gay time, sitting still while his head was being bored open.

Everybody was on tiptoe with interest in the things which were being brought to light. Even Mannling, the photographer, whose interest was usually confined to beer and skittles, sat up and gazed. The native workmen were as enthusiastic as the most highbrow archæologist. Their attitude was very interesting. "Are not the things *we* did and made more beautiful than anything made by the Spaniards?" one of them asked me. I was startled by the question. In spite of the four centuries that have elapsed since Pizarro, the old racial pride and feeling had not disappeared.

I should have liked to stay for months to follow the course of excavations, but it was necessary for all of our party to return to Lima; so, regretfully enough, we started on the return journey. The workmen, however, were left behind to continue the digging, and it was arranged that Dr. Tello was to return to the scene of excavation in a few weeks' time, to see what had been done.

The ruins at Paracas, and the other ruins which we visited in Peru, in Bolivia, and in northern Chile, gave

clear evidence that the history of human culture in
South America is far more ancient and far more complicated than is usually supposed. Hundreds and even
thousands of years ago dwellers of the Andean regions
built up not one but a series of high civilizations. The history of these civilizations is still largely a closed book.
For the student, epoch-making work remains to be done,
and I longed for the opportunity to peer more deeply
into this ancient and mysterious past. My leave, however,
had long expired, and it was necessary without further
delay to embark on the ship that was to bring me home.

I was left with a wealth of memories, memories of
the strange primeval life of the jungle, and memories of
the grandeur of the ancient cultures of the Andes.
Whether or not time ever allows me to return to this
fascinating land, the recollection of the journey, in spite
of its difficulties and hardships, is one which I love to
recall, and one over which I love to dream.

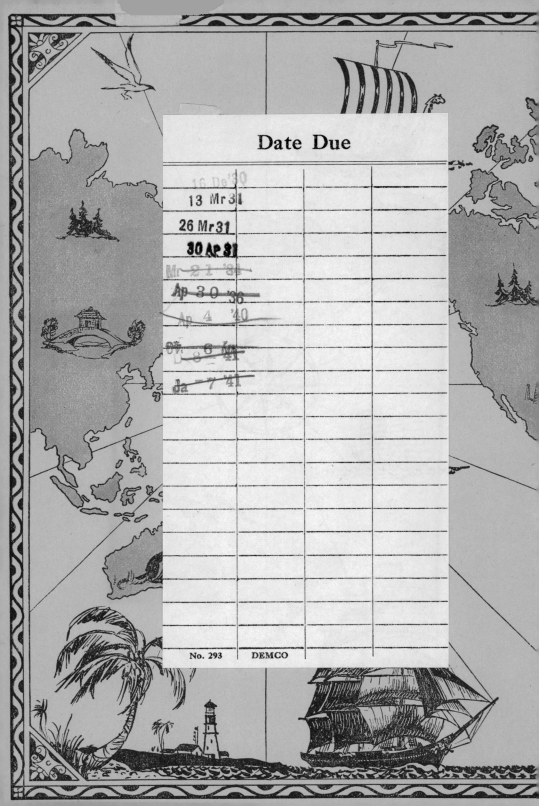

Date Due

16 De'30
13 Mr 31
26 Mr 31
30 Ap 31
Mr 21 '31
Ap 30 '36
Ap 4 '40
40 6 My 40
Ja 7 41

No. 293   DEMCO